Advance Praise for *Testing Women, Testing the Fetus*

"This book marks a watershed in our anthropological understanding of how people in diverse walks of life are weaving genetic knowledge together with their concepts of parenthood, childhood, family, and work. Meticulously and thoroughly researched in multiple sites from genetics labs and genetics counselors' offices to the homes of families raising children with genetic anomalies, Rapp's work opens new horizons of understanding: she shows how distinctions along lines of class, religion, gender, sexuality, age, language, and ethnicity differently refract scientific genetic knowledge into social and cultural knowledge. Beautifully written and engrossing to read, this book is essential for teachers, researchers, and participants in the culture and politics of reproduction."
 —Emily Martin, author of
  The Woman in the Body: A Cultural Analysis of Reproduction

"*Testing Women, Testing the Fetus* is a compelling ethnography of the lived experience of geneticization of American society. It is a deeply human account of the embeddedness of reproductive technologies in fundamental social processes involving gender, class, political economy, and moral contestation. From family homes through clinics and hospitals to laboratories and disability settings, this incisive study takes the reader across a huge landscape of people and power participating in technological transformation in America. A richly rewarding read!"
 —Arthur Kleinman, M.D.,
  Presley Professor of Medial Anthropology, Harvard University

"This is a complicated late twentieth-century tale in which we never lose sight of the human minds and persons behind it—an account shot through with quite dazzling perceptions of particular, located, dilemmas which epitomize the intersections of genetic knowledge, prejudice, and diagnosis. With remarkable skill, the author brings each dilemma back to its moment of human impact. A rare book in the field, it documents in vivid detail the complexity of the social circumstances surrounding genetic testing, quite as much as the cultural and technological. This brilliant study has been long awaited—it will exceed expectations."
 —Marilyn Strathern, author of *The Gender of the Gift*

"Methodology bleeds into daily life for Rapp in this ethnographically innovative book in more than metaphorical ways. *Testing Women, Testing the Fetus* chronicles the struggle, hope, confusion, exhilaration, and, above all, the thoughtfulness of pregnant women—as Rapp calls them, 'moral pioneers'—as they come to fraught decisions about which children will or will not be born.... Rapp provides an incisive account of the realities of stratified reproduction in this book; her unrelenting attention to the fleshy, thoughtful, living people who shared their stories, their work, and their thinking with this anthropologist-at-home is remarkable."
 —Donna Haraway, author of *Primate Visions*

This book is the first in a new series from Routledge:
The Anthropology of Everyday Life
Brackette F. Williams, Editor

Testing Women, Testing the Fetus

The Social Impact of Amniocentesis in America

Rayna Rapp

Routledge
New York and London

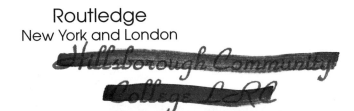

Published in 1999 by
Routledge
29 West 35th Street
New York, NY 10001

Published in Great Britain by
Routledge
11 New Fetter Lane
London EC4P 4EE

10 9 8 7 6 5 4 3 2 1

Library of Congress Cataloging-in-Publication Data

Rapp, Rayna.
   Testing women, testing the fetus: the social impact of amniocentesis in America /
   Rayna Rapp.
      p. cm.
   Includes bibliographical references and index.
   ISBN 0-415-91644-5 (hardbound).
    1. Amniocentesis — Social aspects — United States. I. Title.
  RG628.3.A48R37 1999
  618.3'204275—dc21
                                                   98-45968
                                                    CIP

To the memory of XYLO and the futures of Mira and Teo,
all already and always children of a brave new world.

Contents

Acknowledgments

WHEN A BOOK HAS TAKEN AS LONG to develop as this one has, it accumulates many significant debts. There is thus a story-within-a-story acknowledging all the help I have received over my fifteen years' journey from my personal experiences with amniocentesis through research to writing.

My own first encounter with amniocentesis in 1983 is described in the chapter that follows. In its aftermath, I set out to map the terrain of a then emerging technology, beginning by interviewing twenty-five patients of Dr. William Rashbaum, a New York physician who has provided innovative and humane late abortions to women whose fetuses had serious health problems. I thank him and his staff for their immediate belief in the importance of my then very tentative study, and his insistence that he and other medical practitioners had everything to gain from letting an anthropologist poke around their practices. I especially thank the patients to whom he sent letters on my behalf requesting participation in my study, the women who first shared their painful stories with me. Even now, their search for words remains vivid in my memory: It impressed upon me the need to collectively construct new ways of talking appropriate to new ways of diagnosing.

In 1984, my proposal to undertake fieldwork was approved by the Medical and Health Research Association Inc., which has responsibility for Health Department research in New York City, and I was warmly welcomed by the staff of the Prenatal Diagnosis Laboratory (PDL) of New York City. As the largest cytogenetics laboratory attached to a public health department in the United States, the PDL stood as a national model for what the design and delivery of mass prenatal diagnostic services were and might become. It had a sliding scale for fees in order to offer prenatal genetic testing to medically appropriate candidates, regardless of ability to pay, and it accepted not only whatever any private insurance plan deemed appropriate payment, and Medicaid, but "forgave" debts incurred by the uninsured. No collection service was used to track bills by the lab. In the spring of 1998, the PDL was disbanded, its services contracted out to metropolitan-area hospitals after a series of federal cutbacks in health spending were passed along to the city and state. New York City's Health Department has always led the nation in its outreach to low-income, poor and/or immigrant residents, and it was the first venue in the country where well-publicized and accessible prenatal genetic services were offered to women across income scales. But the PDL fell victim to the complexities of health care restructuring, cutbacks, and privatization now affecting our city, state, and country, despite the protests of many health service professionals and their allies. The PDL's work informs much of this book and is especially central to chapters 3, 4, and 5. Drs. Lillian Hsu and Sarah Kaffee, its geneticists during the years I conducted research there, tolerated with grace and understanding my long hours in their lab and the time I stole from their busy counselors and technicians. Often, they thoughtfully volunteered to discuss experiences and opinions of their own.

To Hody Tennenbaum, PDL's first head genetic counselor, and Eva Kahn, who later replaced her, I owe a great debt of gratitude: They invited me into their working lives, allowing me to shadow them as they moved from one city hospital to another, counseling patients from a wide variety of cultural and linguistic backgrounds. Both became deeply involved in my research, providing many important insights and observations, and suggesting that I speak with specific patients whose stories they thought I needed to hear.

In 1984, June Eichbaum, a founding member of the Down Syndrome Parent Support Group of Manhattan and the Bronx contacted me after reading an article I published in *Ms. Magazine.* Her philosophical challenges and practical help transformed my thinking and deepened this study. I thank her and all the parents I came to know, interview, and occasionally work with through support groups in the New York area, and through two early-intervention programs where directors suggested I anonymize their patient populations. My education in the largely segregated and too often stigmatized world of family and professional knowledge surrounding children with disabilities was profoundly enriched through encounters with these many parents and service providers.

In 1989, Diana Punales-Morejon, head genetic counselor at Beth Israel Medical Center, called me back to working life after a particularly traumatic period. I was recently widowed, and focused on making a life for my small daughter, to the exclusion of any energy for research or writing. Diana's gentle but firm suggestions that I resume practicing anthropology because it would benefit counselors to know more about the cultural practices and aspirations of their patients also benefited me in many consequential ways. Invited into her professional world, I spent many days at Beth Israel, where I was welcomed into the cytogenetics lab by Dr. Arvind Babu and had my first lessons in PCR/DNA analysis from Dr. Gabriel Kupcheck. Dr. Victor Penchaszadeh, director of the Division of Medical Genetics at Beth Israel, has been more helpful than he can possibly ever know, incorporating me into his genetics team with humor and insight. There have been moments in which I have imagined that he might well have written this book for me, based on his own experiences and curiosity as a permanent and professional inhabitant of a multicultural world.

At Beth Israel, Diana Punales-Morejon recruited me to countless projects, papers, and poster presentations as "her" resident anthropologist; we truly became friends as well as colleagues, sharing maternity clothes, baptisms, and weddings, as well as coauthoring publications. During the time I have worked through the Beth Israel Division of Medical Genetics, Lauren LaKosta, Susan Hina-Levine, Gayna Fletcher Havens, and a rotating crew of student interns have also taken me into their counseling process, answered my questions with patience and sympathy, and helped me to understand both the technical and social aspects of medical genetics.

The intersection of disability rights and reproductive rights is a busy crossroads. Here, an extraordinary group of feminist activists within the disability rights movement, including Adrienne Asch, Michelle Fine, Anne Finger, Deborah Kaplan, and Marsha Saxton, argued with me and supported me. Their work, both activist and scholarly, has inspired me to explore an emergent political terrain with far more focus and openness than I ever could have mustered on my own. I thank them all for recognizing long before I did that I was educable.

The scores of women (and a smaller number of men) who agreed to spend a few hours answering my questions may not remember me, but I remember them all quite vividly, having pored over their tapes and stories for hundreds of hours. Without their collective generosity, honesty, and wisdom, I would never have learned enough to write this book. My gratitude remains unending, if anonymous, to those accepting amniocentesis, and those rejecting the test; to those who shared "positive diagnosis" stories with me, and those whose children have some of the same conditions that prenatal testing can now diagnose.

At the New School for Social Research, so many generations of graduate students have "grown up" with this book project that I fear I've lost track of their many contributions, both formally as research assistants and informally as sharers of extensive conversations and purveyors of media clippings and insights. I am especially indebted to those who tracked references and institutional connections for this project, including Liz Fitting, Kim Fountain, Garth Green, Yvonne Groseil, Marlene Hidalgo, Lauren Martin, Arline Mathieu, Sarah Orndorff, Ruth Shou-Leopold, Carol Watson, Sherrill Wilson, and Gayatri Patnaik, who recently became my expert editor at Routledge. When this book was in its penultimate draft, it was read by members of a course in "the anthropology of science" that I offered in the spring term of 1997: Athena Athanasiou, Amanda Barnhart, Liz Fitting, Kim Fountain, Hélène Guay, Erin Koch, Yolande Pelchat, and Alison Stratton all contributed wise suggestions and posed important questions that helped me to finish writing. The "Alien Writers Group" of the New School also commented astutely on this manuscript. I thank its members—Elaine Abelson, Steve Caton, Vicky Hattam, Amit Rai, and Don Scott—for their support. Rachel Roiceman, who wrote an honors thesis on prenatal diagnosis and sex selection in India at Dartmouth College in 1996 for which I served as outside reader, led me to many comparative sources, for which I thank her. I also served as an outside reader for Alexis Feldman's master's thesis on feminism and genetic counseling in conjunction with her training at Sarah Lawrence College's graduate program in genetic counseling; I thank her for the professional references she sent in my direction. I have presented aspects of this work at so many academic institutions and conferences that they cannot all be named here, but collectively, the discussions generated by students and faculty around the country have influenced this book.

In the realm of friendship, I have been particularly fortunate. For the last decade, Faye Ginsburg and I have collaborated on projects so dense and numerous I can no longer separate them in my mind's eye. She was the first person who read this manuscript in its entirety, and she applied her usual and quite extraordinary editorial skills to its improvement, insisting that I identify the "national character" of the phenomena I was discussing. Her friendship has sustained me through many aspects of my life. Donna Haraway has lived inside my arguments for such a long time that I can no long tell where her generous and imaginative influences are located. Her reading of the manuscript deeply influenced this revision; chapter 8 was refashioned after she took it apart and suggested how it might be reconstructed. Donna's belief in the importance of this study sometimes exceeded my own, convincing me to plough on. Deborah Heath also applied her deep knowledge of laboratory life and her respectful engagement with bioscientific researchers to chapter 8, insisting correctly that I animate and nuance each and every description. While I cannot be said to have followed her advice to its exact letter, its spirit improved my endeavors. Sarah Franklin and Marilyn Strathern sent important encouragements to this project; it is surely Marilyn's fault that chapter 11 was constructed in its current brief and indexical style. Karen Sue Taussig also provided enthusiastic and astute suggestions that helped me to clarify some of my arguments. Martin Olsson constantly clipped articles drawn from his copious reading on genetics, gender, bioethics, and many other realms, faxing them from the global invisible college as it docked in Sweden. I deeply appreciate his enthusiastic support for my work as a mother as well as my work as a researcher.

I have been fortunate to receive generous and substantial material support from institutions and foundations that gave me the time to work apart from teaching. At various stages in its development, this project benefited from grants from the National Science Foundation, the National Endowment for the Humanities, the Rockefeller Foundation's "Program in Changing Gender Roles," the Institute for Advanced Study, and the Spencer Foundation. A sabbatical semester from the New School early on in this project came at just the right time. I thank them all for their support and absolve them of any shortcomings in what I have chosen to make of it.

This book is dedicated to my children; I hope someday they will understand why.

1

How Methodology Bleeds into Daily Life

Why am I having amniocentesis? I'm 42. I think at my age I'd be foolish, anyone would be foolish, not to have this test. (Brenda Kelly, white lawyer)

What is the purpose to this test? The purpose is to know what God has in store for you, so you can wonder at the marvels of his ways. (Lynthia Cato, 37, Trinidad-born factory worker)

You ask me why I am crying? I am crying because no one told me that I could have such a problem as sickle cell, that I carry this in my blood, and that it is now too late to test the baby. That is the reason I am crying. (Janis Winter, 32, African-American teacher's aide)

I don't smoke, I don't drink, I don't take drugs, I eat good food, I take good care of myself. What do I need this test for? (Dominique Laurent, 39, Haitian garment worker)

THIS BOOK EXPLORES the social impact and cultural meaning of prenatal diagnosis, one of the most routinized of the new reproductive technologies. In the United States, as in most late industrialized countries, amniocentesis and related prenatal diagnostic technologies are used to screen fetuses for chromosomal anomalies and neural tube problems during the second trimester of pregnancy, when women and their supporters may choose to continue or end the pregnancy should a positive diagnosis of a serious fetal problem be made. How and why has this reproductive technology devel-

oped? How has it become part of routine pregnancy care for some segments
of the population? Who uses, refuses, and might desire to use it, and under
what conditions is it offered? How do health care providers understand their
own role, and how do they communicate the benefits and burdens of the test
to their patients from diverse social backgrounds? How do women and their
supporters describe and evaluate their experiences with this test? Is this test
"revolutionizing pregnancy," as is often claimed, and if so, for whom? How
are we to discuss the simultaneously eugenic and liberating agendas of prenatal testing, and how are they enacted for and by different individuals and
communities? How are popular understandings of genetics and inheritance
shaped in contemporary America? What does scientific literacy mean in a
culture as deeply stratified as our own?

    I have worked on these problems as an anthropologist and as a feminist
activist for more than a decade. In learning about the social impact and cultural meaning of prenatal diagnosis, I have used standard anthropological
methods of participant observation. That professional umbrella is a catchall
label for hands-on research that is open-ended, and locates the researcher as
far into the experiences of the people whose lives are touched by the topic as
she can figure out how to go. My methods have been as conventional as sitting through medical school lectures or interviewing candidates for prenatal
diagnosis in English, Spanish, and sometimes French; as arcane as learning
to recognize and cut up laboratory photographs of chromosomes so they
could be assembled into karyotypes; as familial as taking my toddler to a
charity performance of the circus to benefit the National Down Syndrome
Society at which she appeared to be the only nondisabled child. The use of
standardized interview topics has provided broad comparability across
many constituencies with whom I have spoken. But the basic benefit of participant observation is its open-endedness: I set out with one set of research
questions, and was forced to enlarge and transform them as people educated
me on the complexity of the issues as they perceived them.

    This book is divided into eleven chapters. These chapters are organized
neither chronologically nor ecologically, the two dominant genres of classical anthropological presentation. Rather, I begin with a chapter discussing
the history of prenatal diagnosis and its related technologies, sketching the
complex social, legal, and political transformations that supported its development. I then follow the technology through its trajectory, as pregnant
women encounter it. Each chapter takes up a communicative and practical
problem posed by the development of this new technology: communication
and miscommunication between providers and patients; pregnant women's
anxiety and interpretation of what sonograms and chromosomes mean to

them; the role of the fetal imaginary in thinking about disabling conditions; refusing the test; culturing chromosomes; getting bad news; living with children who have diagnosable conditions; and more. My goal in intersecting and juxtaposing many diverse perspectives on this topic is to create a Venn diagram, overlapping the social spaces in which amniocentesis and related technologies have developed. In making a map of both the obvious and the more interstitial places within which the simultaneously liberating and eugenic aspects of this technology develop, I attempt to describe and interpret the range of practices and problems associated with it. It is my contention that the construction and routinization of this technology is turning the women to whom it is offered into moral pioneers: Situated on a research frontier of the expanding capactity for prenatal genetic diagnosis, they are forced to judge the quality of their own fetuses, making concrete and embodied decisions about the standards for entry into the human community.

In overlapping many perspectives on amniocentesis, I hope to make a contribution to at least three discussions. The first concerns the technological transformation of pregnancy, a discussion which usually focuses on what have come to be called the new reproductive technologies: How "new" or "revolutionary" are the cluster of fertility-controlling practices like amniocentesis, when we examine their concrete social matrix, and not just their abstract potential as pieces of technology? The second examines the practical intersection of disability rights and reproductive rights, where issues of abortion on the one hand, and inclusion on the other, are now aspects of a national political discourse in the contemporary United States. The third examines the role of scientific literacy in late-twentieth-century American culture, with an emphasis on both practical knowledge and the very American nature of how we use it. The idea that science and technology provide positive resources for improving or even perfecting life is deep-seated in the history of the United States. So, too, is unequal access to those resources, and a consequent range of perceptions and responses to the burdens as well as the benefits that their stratified presence may impose. These concerns all take the diversity of gender, power, and culture as the starting point for analysis.

The Need for Women-Centered Analysis

When I began to study the impact and meaning of a new reproductive technology, my initial goal was to wrest understandings from the discourse of experts, and to relocate them in popular practices and perceptions. I came to this formulation the hard way: As a 36-year-old feminist health activist, I had chosen, with some ambivalence, to undergo prenatal diagnosis in my first pregnancy in 1983. When my fetus was diagnosed as having Down syndrome, the shock, grief, and confusion were enormous. Mike Hooper and I had ardently desired this pregnancy; together, we now chose to end it. In trying to recover from a devastating experience, I turned to the mundane tools of intellectuals: A medical library search quickly convinced me that the voices of experts (bioethicists, lawyers, doctors, and health economists, most of them male, all of them highly educated, and overwhelmingly white) dominated the discourse on prenatal diagnosis. Absent from the published literature were the concerns of the women of different class, racial, ethnic, and religious backgrounds who use, or might use, or might refuse to use the new technology. I also turned to the tools of feminism, constructing a network through other health activists to locate a few women who had sustained similar experiences. Together, we amassed huge phone bills, supporting one another as we tried to make sense of the painful decision to end the life of a fetus we had first desired and carried. Increasingly convinced that the complex topic of prenatal testing and abortion begged for a woman-centered analysis, I sought the help of sympathetic health care providers to gain access to other women, and began interviewing in late 1983. In 1984, I published an account of my own experiences in *Ms. Magazine,* hoping to provoke popular feminist discussion and awareness of this topic (Rapp 1984). I also gave birth to a healthy baby; the small, ordinary miracle of her existence served to increase my interest in what happened to other women whose pregnancies, like my own earlier one, did not lead to happy endings. By the mid-1980s, other feminist scholars and activists also began writing on what were loosely coming to be called the "new reproductive technologies." I read their work with enormous appreciation and relief; surely, the ambiguous problems posed by technologies that offer more control over pregnancy outcomes while enforcing more medical surveillance deserved extensive feminist commentary. Those early works spoke with passion and courage about what women lost in having their pregnancies increasingly medicalized. But they also often spoke as if women's interests in reproductive technologies were both clear-cut and unified: Feminists usually described pregnancy as a natural process and its technologization as a male power play to contain Mother Nature. In many early analyses, male pharmacrats (to borrow Gena Corea's felicitous phrase) had controlling interests in the biotechnology companies, the experimental research, and the private medical practices within which women submitted to the new reproductive technologies. While enormously sympathetic to the critique of economic, social, and gendered power at the heart of such analyses, I was also skeptical on the basis of the complexity of my own experiences and those of the women I had begun to interview. We were both grateful for and critical of the technology, and we knew that "nature" was too simple a label for our pregnancy problems and possibilities. Who speaks for the diversity of women in such a circumstance? We will return to the problems of expert discourse—whether biomedical, feminist, or other—in chapters 2 and 3.

Recognition of the power of expert discourse reinforced my predilections to use anthropological tools in the service of telling another story: The discourses and practices of biomedicine and technology are played out on a complex cultural ground at the end of the twentieth century in the United States. Indeed, recent developments in science studies remind us that biomedical technology is itself a highly contested cultural object, porous in its diverse social constructions, uses, and exclusions. The transformations of pregnancy, experiences with disabling conditions, and family life on which prenatal diagnostic technology touches are deeply gendered; they are also powerfully influenced by class position, ethnic and cultural community background, and the resources and orientations provided by religions. Moreover, the institutional resources, constraints, and possibilities within which pregnancy is now monitored are highly contested in our current political-economic system: Access to comprehensive health care and abortion stands at the heart of contemporary political transformations and struggles. There can thus be no simple evaluation of this, or any other, new intervention into reproduction. I hope this book makes a case for the complexity, diversity, and contradictory nature of the impact of reproductive technology.

Attempting to set my own amniocentesis experiences against a larger social background, I set out to map the terrain of an emerging technology in 1983. My prior research projects had always engaged what I took to be social problems or circumstances requiring a structural understanding; now, the dilemmas I was confronting were simultaneously political-economic, epistemological, and ethical; I had become a guinea pig in my own research. Working through a sympathetic private physician, I began by interviewing twenty-five women who had chosen abortions after receiving what is so antiseptically labeled a positive diagnosis. In the face of a confusing and traumatic experience, they often described themselves as at a loss for words. These women were working in a communicative system whose vocabulary is exclusively medical, whose grammar is technological, and whose syntax has yet to be negotiated. It was not always easy for them to frame alternative descriptions with which to more accurately represent the impact of amniocentesis in their own lives.

Inventing a Methodology

In 1984, my proposal to undertake fieldwork was approved by the Medical and Health Research Association Inc., which oversees all Health Department research in New York City, and I was warmly welcomed by the staff of the Prenatal Diagnosis Laboratory (PDL) of New York City. The PDL stood as a model for what mass prenatal diagnostic services are, and might become, and it was the largest cytogenetics laboratory attached to a public health department in the United States. Its work informs much of this book, especially as presented in chapters 3, 4, and 5. Over the next four years, I spent from one to four days each week in the company of the genetic counselors who worked for PDL, following them on their rounds through city hospitals. I observed them and their PDL colleagues counseling more than 230 patients and often turned to them for help compiling historical and statistical information on PDL's services. Over the years, I was welcomed into sessions by the three full-time and two part-time genetic counselors who also worked at the PDL, and by the numerous graduate students who interned there. All consented to be observed and interviewed; all also provided much informal and valuable information for my study. The laboratory staff was more than tolerant during the two months that I imposed a maverick internship upon them, learning to spin and culture fluids, focus a microscope, and cut chromosomes into karyotypes. They must often have wondered why I thought science was exotic, when I could have gone to more traditional anthropological locations.

Through observations of PDL intake patient interviews, I also began to recruit a sample of women who were having amniocentesis and were willing to be interviewed at home (ideally, during the long weeks of waiting for test results).[1] I initially attempted to conduct interviews with the partners and other close supporters of this patient population, but this proved a difficult task; I was able to interview only fifteen men (or FOFs, fathers of fetuses, as I came to think of them), compared to more than eighty women. I describe what I learned in all of these interviews in chapters 5 and 6, and I speculate on why men became an endangered species in this study in chapters 6 and 7. I have included whatever I know both from men directly, and about men less directly, from their partners, throughout the book, but the quality and quantity of my information concerning the exotic male sex and prenatal testing remains spotty.

PDL counselors and staff also helped me to recruit a sample of women who had received the news that a serious problem has been diagnosed in their fetus, and that a decision to continue or end the pregnancy had to be consciously made. These immeasurably enriched the understandings I had developed in the first pilot study. Later, I added interviews with ten more women with positive diagnoses through another medical center, bringing the total to forty-two.

Just as I began working through the PDL genetics team, my *Ms. Magazine* article appeared (Rapp 1984). It elicited more than one hundred letters in response, and I entered into correspondence with scores of women about their own amniocentesis stories. The outpouring was very moving. Often, their authors and I remained in correspondence through many rounds of missives, and in some cases I asked for and received permission to quote from the letters.

Through my observations at the PDL, I also began to interview women who chose not to take the test, to understand how a routinizing technology does not necessarily stay en route for everyone. Informally, I spoke with scores of women who opted during routine intake interviews not to use the test; eighteen women and two men granted me more formal interviews, sometimes through home visits, more often over the telephone. Their reasoning is discussed in chapter 7. Through my work with PDL counselors, I became interested in counseling as a new women's profession, and I set off to interview thirty-five counselors, at least one from each medical center in New York City where prenatal diagnostic services are offered. Later, with my colleague Diana Punales-Morejon, I conducted a survey of the (then) fifteen North American programs that offer master's degree programs in genetic counseling (Punales-Morejon and Rapp 1993; Rapp 1993a). While we focused on the problem of training counselors to understand ethno-cultural diversity among the urban populations they would soon serve, we also learned a great deal about how the profession has developed, and how curriculum and certification procedures change. Most recently, I interviewed ten geneticists to understand their perceptions of both the development of their field, and its social and ethical impact.

In 1984, right after the *Ms. Magazine* article was published, I also received a phone call that changed the course of my research dramatically. One of the founding members of a Down Syndrome Parents Support Group (Manhattan and the Bronx), the mother of a child with Down syndrome, challenged some of my descriptions of disabled children and the social services available to them. I quickly joined the support group, and with her philosophical and practical guidance began learning my way around the world of disability rights and educational services for children with special needs. I eventually interviewed thirty-eight families in which a child had Down syndrome, first through meeting activists in two parent support groups, later through the work I did on the education committee of one of those groups, and then through a family-court-funded early-intervention program for developmentally delayed children. On a more haphazard basis, I spoke with a dozen grown siblings of children with Down syndrome, and interviewed a handful of parents whose offspring had other chromosomal or genetic disabilities. Over the years of this study, I learned a great deal about two related and tension-fraught issues. The first is the need to champion the reproductive rights of women to carry or refuse to carry to term a pregnancy that would result in a baby with a serious disability. The second is the need to support adequate, nonstigmatizing, integrative services for all the children, including disabled children, that women bear. The intersection of disability rights and reproductive rights as paradoxically linked feminist issues has emerged as central to my political and intellectual work.

In 1989, I added another piece to my research puzzle. Because the patient population served by the PDL was highly polarized, I was learning a lot about middle-class professional families (disproportionately white) and working-poor families (disproportionately African-American and Latino). In order to avoid conflating race and class in both my data collection and its interpretation, I sought and received permission to work in the Division of Medical Genetics, Beth Israel Medical Center, which held the contract to perform amniocentesis for several Hospital Insurance Plan (HIP) groups in the metropolitan area. As the oldest health maintenance organization in New York City, HIP has always served a solidly working-class, often unionized, and quite racially diverse population. More recently, HIP has added middle-class constituencies as the crisis in U.S. health insurance dictates cheaper employer-provided plans. Beth Israel provided what I hoped would be the "missing middle" to my data set. The Beth Israel genetics team had also developed an innovative outreach program in New York's Chinatown, whose hardworking and linguistically isolated population was not always easy to reach. And the genetics staff included several native Spanish speakers with professional commitments to serving new immigrant communities. For an anthropologist, it provided another excellent research site. Using protocols developed at the PDL, I observed one hundred intake interviews, conducted another twenty-five home interviews with women awaiting amniocentesis results, and met with ten women who had received positive diagnoses. I also visited the neonatal intensive care unit, observed weekly rounds, hung out in the laboratory, and learned about DNA diagnosis as the genetics team graciously incorporated me into their working life.

Decomposing Method

Through the PDL, Beth Israel, and the genetic counselors that I interviewed, I spent more than 130 days observing hospital-based counseling sessions. Initially, I intended to contrast observations and interviews with patients from white, Hispanic, and African-American backgrounds, distinguishing middle-class, working-class, and working-poor groups. With some effort, I managed to collect my comparative sample, primarily at Beth Israel, Harlem, Roosevelt, and Woodhull hospitals, with a few additional observational days and follow-up interviews at hospitals in Staten Island, the Bronx, and Queens. But the diversity I encountered quickly underlined how static such sociological classifications can become. Ethnic identity is, of course, far more complex than such census categories indicate; and while occupation and payment plan yield good approximations of socioeconomic status, they barely touch the experiential meanings of social class. Moreover, variation across New York's hospital catchment areas is profound: "Hispanic" on Manhattan's West Side virtually stands for Puerto Rican and Dominican. Many who use this label for themselves are second- or even third-generation members of long-standing urban communities. But in the parts of Brooklyn where I worked, "Hispanic" was also likely to cover people from Honduras, Nicaragua, Guatemala, or Panama, many of whom had only recently arrived, and substantial numbers of whom were from rural backgrounds. And in Queens, Ecuadorian, Colombian, Peruvian, and Argentinean women and their families fell under this label. Sometimes socioeconomic standing varied throughout an individual's lifetime, as was true of many Colombians, Argentineans, and Ecuadorians who had middle-class educations by the standards of their home country but found themselves in working-class jobs after migrating to New York. Thus the Venn diagram I had hoped to construct, in which class differences could be distinguished from, and overlapped with ethnic and cultural resources, was muddied by variations in micro experiences as well as macro economics. This is a subject I discuss in chapters 5 and 6, where I speculate about the ethnic and cultural contributions to responses to prenatal diagnosis.

Yet over the course of several years of research, I came to pick out patterns that *did* reflect the resources and boundaries of the class and ethnic identities to which people were assigned or assigned themselves. There is thus an analytic tension throughout this text between the abstract and categorical labels I occasionally use ("white, middle-class professional"; "Hispanic service worker") and the descriptive particularity of individual stories I attempt to tell ("Ileana Mendez, Ecuadorian baby-sitter"; "Linda Scott,

U.S.-born theater set designer"). I intend these labels to signal the routes and life trajectories within which an individual's consciousness is forged, without creating pigeonholes into which people are too easily slotted. Individual consciousness is always complex and cannot be reduced to the analytic categories within which empirically minded social investigators are most comfortable working. Yet we cannot do away with such categories, even as we interrogate them, for they provide not only sorting devices, but signposts on the way to understanding socially significant differences. And throughout this research, different differences took on salience according to context. Matters of class, for example, figure large in problems of scientific literacy, confidence, and agency in medical settings. But religion and community background are more likely to shape attitudes toward disability and abortion. Children with disabilities may, paradoxically, have more stimulating environments when they come from larger families; such families are, on average, less likely to be middle-class than the more privileged homes in which a child with a disability is more likely to be a first or only child. Tracking these differences became a central concern of this project. Although the biomedical technology I was tracking produces universal and uniform claims about the advantages of prenatal testing, my research increasingly revealed alternative and sometimes competing rationales through which members of different communities made sense of its burdens and benefits. And these other forms of articulation were at once deeply individual and highly social; I needed to read them through the grid of differentiating collective categories as well as individual narratives. The problems and possibilities offered by access to a specific biomedical technology fall upon social ground which is always already crosscut by prior resources and hierarchies. The specificity and accuracy of our descriptive tools are thus always incomplete; such categories can permeate the problems we attempt to understand, helping to clarify them, but their effects are quite partial. And the form of their partiality is never impartial, for they bring with them the possibility of (re)creating stereotypes as well as illuminating generalizations.

My awareness of this tension evolved as I moved from hospital to hospital, discovering similarities and differences among the people from whom I was learning. My initial observations took place in a hospital with a robust mix of private and clinic patients, and I eventually conducted fieldwork at seven hospitals which ran the gamut of services and populations that characterize health care in New York City's hospitals. Each hospital staff and patient population had its own characteristics, but I have chosen to agglomerate them into three hospital types in the interests of protecting anonymity: Elite, Middle, and City. Implied in those names is an obvious comparison.

Elite Hospitals serve predominantly private, middle- and upper-middle-class clients; in Manhattan, these are most likely to be white, a census category I learned to challenge as I encountered its internal diversity. Middle Hospitals serve a more balanced mix of private and clinic patients, and those sent by their HMOs, and the racial-ethnic mix varies dramatically, depending on the shifting nature of immigration and housing in the particular borough. At Middle Hospitals, I realized again and again that New York's population receiving prenatal care is a rainbow of Hawaiians married to Lebanese, Mormons married to Buddhists, Iranians married to Poles, Colombians married to Egyptians, Filipinos, Greeks, Haitians, and Mexicans, and single mothers with and without partners whose roots lie all over the globe, as well as the more predictable ethnic varieties. City Hospitals serve an almost exclusively working-poor clinic population, overwhelmingly funded by Medicaid. Depending on locale, such populations tend to be African-American, Afro-Caribbean, and/or new or old immigrants who are Spanish-speaking. A great deal of diversity is thus loosely categorized into these three service types, and the neat census categories around which I had initially designed my sample kept decomposing themselves in front of my eyes. Thus, as the methods and locales of this study kept expanding, so did my comprehension of the challenges that large and diverse urban populations pose for accurate description. Moreover, "accurate" description implies many things: an historical understanding of the lack of closure to almost any population, especially an urban population in the United States at the end of the twentieth century; a commitment to interrogate how categories are constructed and used by bureaucrats and the people who "choose" to inhabit them, and the consequences of those uses; and a willingness to locate myself and what I am studying in the relations of knowledge and power which are in part shaped by the deployment of such categories.

Interrogating Methods

I have provided a narrative of how my understandings of the topography of amniocentesis developed for four reasons. The first, methodological accuracy, dictates that I describe the sample, and its limits, from which my understandings emerged. Though I have spent thousands of days as a participant-observer of this issue in its social context, there are inevitable gaps in my knowledge. Silences in my understandings as well as the clamorous conversations between myself and the many constituencies with whom I worked must be judged by readers. To do so, they need to know how, where, and under what conditions I came to know what I now claim to know.

Closely linked to this is the second, more theoretical problem of how to study a social phenomenon that differs considerably from the usual objects of anthropological investigation: in this case, a new reproductive technology. New medical technologies surely fall under the domain of medical anthropological analysis (e.g., Berg and Casper 1995; Koenig and Casper 1996; Lindenbaum and Lock 1993). They also benefit from the methodological debates available in science and technology studies (e.g., Feenberg and Hannay 1995; Hess 1995; Jasanoff, Markle et al. 1995; Pickering 1992, 1995). We are here far removed from the study of "ethnic groups," "neighborhoods," "women's reproductive histories," or even "cultural beliefs about pregnancy," all of which appear as minor themes in this study; all have provided fodder for rich anthropological analyses of gender, childbearing, health, and illness (Ginsburg and Rapp 1991). I hope that tracing the intersection of the multiple constituencies, contexts, and conflicts in which a cultural analysis of a developing reproductive technology is constituted will provide materials for a collective rethinking of technology at the end of the twentieth century.

Third, and more abstractly, this problem of a new object and ever-expanding pools of research subjects marks an empirical terrain that is by its very nature open-ended and unbounded. Many anthropologists studying "complex societies" have noted the problem of a lack of boundaries to their units of analysis: Our ethnographic work is continuously relocated in practice, as we incorporate an appreciation of lack of holism, nonclosure, and self-positioning into the representations of the phenomena we study. This study is also a contribution to a discussion of what some have called "multi-sited ethnography" (Marcus 1995), as many anthropologists endeavor to break the connection of space, place, and culture (Appadurai 1996; Gupta and Ferguson 1997a, 1997b), studying "multiply inflected cultural objects" (Harding 1994). Such studies are premised on a lack of clear boundaries to our unit or object of analysis. No matter how many Haitian women accepting or refusing "the needle test" I interview, however many medical journals I read as cultural texts, nor how many professional genetics congresses I attend, there will always be another mother of a child with Down syndrome in East Harlem from whom I might learn a slightly different story, another geneticist who has thought deeply about the ethical implications of piloting cystic fibrosis carrier screening, another educational TV program on the Human Genome Project, or a sitcom featuring an "older" pregnant woman as trickster-heroine. Engagement with all would enrich my cultural understandings of a new technology. This study thus has no obvious theoretical or situational limits.

Which leads to my fourth reason: In choosing an open-ended "complex cultural object" which is a piece of reproductive technology, I am also engaging a cascade of issues that travel under the sign of science studies. Here, I join a growing corps of anthropologists who work in and around various sciences, attempting to understand their sociocultural infrastructures (Franklin 1995; Heath 1998; Hess 1995, 1998; Layne 1998a, 1998b; Martin 1998; Nader 1996; Traweek 1992, 1993). Most obviously, the science of biomedicine makes universal claims to investigate, describe, and intervene in embodied processes which are deemed precultural or acultural. But as an anthropologist studying both the claims of biomedicine and its interventions in the realm of prenatal diagnosis, I am arguing that the very objects of its knowledge—chromosomes, health risks, fetuses—and its technologies of intervention—sonography, chromosome studies, maternal and fetal health statistics—are culturally constituted. I hope to show that constitution on multiple levels. For example, the practices which make up amniocentesis are simultaneously globalized and localized: Though the history of contemporary genetics includes a growing international consensus about how chromosomes and genes should be described, there is far less agreement about what these entities specifically do, and even less about how their abnormalities should be treated. When investigating prenatal diagnosis in New York City, I came to understand its practices as at once broadly international in scope and highly national. U.S. national ideologies of transparency and perfectibility figure large in its expanding use, and local public health policies regulate not only the laboratories and clinics within which these services are offered, but the very populations who are likely to become its practitioners and patients. Thus, "science as culture" is constructed inside clinical laboratories, consulting rooms, and technical services; it is also a site of cultural intersection. The "different differences" through which local communities understand fetuses, heredity, disabilities, and abortions constitute both the terrain on which biomedical science makes its powerful universalizing claims, and a continuous source of challenges to those claims. In the contemporary United States, and especially in a multicultural city like New York, not all populations or individuals accept the rationality of prenatal screening for disabilities as self-evident; learning about a rich and diverse range of culturally organized gender relations, kinship connections, and interpretations of what counts as illness and health allows us to examine the acultural discourse of scientific benefits and burdens through an empirical cultural grid. As I learned my way around the clinic, the laboratory, and the homes of pregnant women and their supporters, and families with disabled children, I was continually challenged to rethink biomedical science as a cultural object with enormous discursive and practical powers to define what it is to be normatively human, and to resist alternative versions and challenges to that normativity.

Of course, the quality of the data I collected, and the consequent density of my understandings of these open-ended, intersecting, and highly charged terrains on which amniocentesis is constructed, are quite variable. Much of what I know I learned from routinized, repetitive observation over many years. In citing or paraphrasing individual stories, I have relied heavily on standard interview techniques whose results were almost always taped and transcribed. But some interviews took place on the telephone and lasted only twenty minutes, while other women called me back as frequently as I called them, pursuing their own agendas through many encounters, often using me as a sounding board for thinking through tough decisions and situations. Sometimes, a projected two-hour home interview expanded into multiple visits, and some "informant" families became friends. With them, the tape ran only episodically, but I learned a lot at family outings to the beach, business lunches with mothers and occasionally fathers, and our mutual agonizing over nursery schools and kindergarten experiences, and about how to convey respect for women's work in the home and the rights of disabled children to our own offspring. The open-endedness of prenatal testing as it intersects issues of disability, abortion, and family life affected me, as it affected my respondents, enriching our lives with hard choices, contradictions, and situated knowledge (Haraway 1988b). In social science parlance, I am describing the benefits, as well as the burdens, of reflexivity: I am necessarily (and partly) positioned within the phenomena I seek to understand, and my knowledge depends, in large measure, on the work of social connection as well as on scholarly questions and resources I developed with many others in the course of this study.

Indeed, the boundaries between self and other, or, more properly, several selves—researcher, pregnant woman, teacher, mother, activist, and many others—are inherently blurry. Beyond the rich research materials generated under the conditions outlined above lies another round of informant collection that Michael Agar would describe as "opportunistic" (Agar 1980) and that I would describe as "serendipitous" or "karmic." When old friends and neighbors have amniocentesis or chorionic villus sampling, I call them up. When their friends and neighbors have a question about amniocentesis or a prenatal diagnosis problem, I am likely to receive a phone call in return. Such contacts provide an escalating whirlwind of data that blows through my daily life, and the daily lives of my friends and family members. In the summer of 1991, for example, a friend of a friend of a friend kept me on the phone for a solid hour, obsessing about the lack of statistical data concerning the potential threat to eggs, sperm, and embryos of air-travel-induced radiation. She and her husband were planning a vacation overseas, during which she hoped to get pregnant. She had already called the EPA, the FAA, and the FDA for information, and no one had a clue; could I help her? Information-seeking calls are not infrequent, and in them, I am doubly positioned, trying simultaneously to share what I have gleaned from years of research, and to incorporate the call as research data. My right brain counseled calmly, reminding her of how the heightened concern about low-level radiation had developed, and how little information she could possibly ever collect on the subject for epidemiological reasons: Given the numbers, we can barely say anything about the effects of continual air-travel radiation on the pregnancy outcomes of airline staff, let alone episodic passengers. My left brain made notes on the controlling preoccupations of white, middle-class, scientifically savvy professional women: How could anyone devote this much time and energy to reinventing an old existential question framed in new and unanswerable terms? Only after I hung up the phone did I remember that I had recently crossed the Atlantic twice with a first-trimester fetus in my womb, without thinking to obsess about this particular issue.

A more prolonged connection to the intersection of research and personal life occurred when one of my closest friends became pregnant. As her husband was out of town, I happily attended her amniocentesis "in civilian disguise." She joked about not wanting to bond with the screen fetus while I cracked comments about medico-genetic language and the measurement of pregnancies. "Who are you girls?" the doctor queried in disbelief and annoyance. When the test results were negative, my friend said in scientific resignation and existential consternation, "Well, now I know enough to know that my fetus doesn't have three things. That doesn't tell me very much." I probably shrugged in knowing agreement, both of us amused by her guinea pig status in my study. Using dear friends as informants would have been funnier, however, if their adored new baby had not fallen mysteriously ill in infancy. At the age of six months she was diagnosed as having a rare autosomal recessive genetic condition[2] (Ginsburg and Rapp 1999). To say that I have followed every step of the family's process in coming to terms with a genetic condition with passionate concern might be a bit of an understatement. Their child is a "sister" to my daughter and son. I speak with her on the phone frequently, I posed as the aunt when we teamed up to check out the early-intervention nursery schools funded by the family court for disabled children. Much of what I now believe, and what is most unreportable, I have learned with and from them. My friend once said, for example, to another anthropologist whose analysis of prenatal testing smacked of medical conspiracy theory, implying that the government would support it for eugenic reasons, "Now listen carefully: I give a tenth of my salary to the foundation which funds scientific research on my daughter's condition so they can find the gene that causes this thing. The whole foundation is supported by the families of kids with this condition—it isn't a fancy research outfit bankrolled by the state. And if they found it tomorrow, I don't know if I'd use the prenatal test they'd develop. I don't know if I could do that to my kid, make that statement about the value of her life. It's very complicated."

And complicated data are potentially everywhere. I began to write this introduction on the day that the Development Office at the New School (where I teach) sent a new employee to do a story on my grant research. In preparation for the interview, I sent her some of my recent articles. The young reporter has a sister who is mentally retarded; writing university publicity on my research led her to interview her own mother on the impact the sister's life had had on the rest of her family. In such a situation, we agreed that it is unclear who is interviewing whom, and I incorporated her story into my own. And so it goes. Working "at home" has methodological, ethical, and interpretive consequences that would have been hard to foresee from the places I was initially trained to explore as an anthropologist.

When conducting fieldwork at home, the "outer reaches" of the sample bleed into daily reality. This constitutes both a great advantage for enforced wisdom, and a confusion for sampling parameters. We no longer can picture DNA, genes, or bodies as bounded units; nor are scientific, medical, or political interventions into the people bearing them any less open-ended. This study thus focuses on the constant intersections and boundary crossings that an emergent social phenomena like prenatal testing reveals. It suggests an empirical methodology for studying science in context: The powerful universal explanatory claims and attendant technological interventions of science are continually constructed, crosscut, and sometimes undercut by the social hierarchies, identities, and economies through which "science as culture" is shaped, and its resources distributed and contested. Thus, it is the unbounded nature of science and technology as a powerful congeries of practices that are broadly cultural as well as more narrowly biomedical that has beckoned me toward this open-ended methodology.

Concretizing Ethics

This methodology also constitutes ethical problems that bear some discussion. Ethical dilemmas in anthropological fieldwork, in feminist research, and in medically based social science investigations which have at least an implicit (and sometimes a quite explicit) applied and policy edge have been well discussed (Agar 1980; Association 1996; Gluck and Patai 1991; Lather 1999; Stacey 1988, 1990). In recent years, much of the anthropological discussion of ethics has blurred into the postmodernist preoccupation with the politics of text construction: Who is represented, who does the representing, what symbolic violences are associated with citation and silence? (Behar 1993; Clifford 1988; Fox 1991; Visweswaran 1994; Wolf 1992). While I take these questions seriously, as I hope to demonstrate throughout this book, they are not the only important concerns which I believe are appropriate to "writing culture," nor do I believe that the scope of power-laden questions anthropologists confront are only text-driven. I have retained a more old-fashioned focus on ethics because I want to emphasize that field-based research in anthropology is much broader than the process of "writing ethnography." The daily problems and choices with which the field worker is confronted have practical consequences for the people whose lives she touches, as well as for her own data collection and interpretation. They include such mundane problems as the protection of confidentiality; language translation and power; the contamination of data through continuous intervention; and paradoxes of feedback and consulting. Each deserves a few words now and will surface again throughout the pages of this text.

The problem of confidentiality is something of an obsession among anthropologists. But styles, of course, change. Whereas once it was considered de rigueur to disguise "my village" but claim "my people," many of us now think that the claims of historical accuracy and the delineation of power relations (theirs and ours) override the conventions of both masking and owning subjects (cf. Association 1996). The topic on which I am working is a highly charged one. It lies at the intersection of personal pain and national political struggles concerning health care, abortion rights, and disability rights; of "the right to informed consent" and the meanings of sexuality, pregnancy, and parenting; of the role that biomedical science plays in a society with no commitment to equal access to health care for all of its members; of the uncertain links between new knowledge generated in genetics research and applications in clinical medicine. Because I was asking people to tell me stories which often felt like crucibles of tough decision-making, I promised and have delivered confidentiality via pseudonyms for any pregnant woman or mother or child or their supporters I have interviewed. Occasionally, I have found it necessary to change or at least generalize some bit of descriptive information (e.g., a highly specialized profession that might have identified someone, or the name of a small town where someone opted for an abortion after receiving a prenatal diagnosis, but told everyone she'd had a miscarriage to avoid stigma) as well. It has been harder to provide anonymity for genetic counselors and other medical service providers, many of whom have discussed hard ethical situations and personal values with me, both on and off the record. Some have been named in the acknowledgments to this book in grateful appreciation of what they contributed to my methodology and sample. Others appear in their professional capacities throughout this text. While general readers of this book won't know or need to know Who's Who in the World of New York Prenatal Diagnosis, it is a small professional world, and speculations, if not positive identifications, may easily abound. I apologize in advance for any discomfort my chosen quotations and generalizations may cause; while I have checked the text with several trusted "insider" colleagues, it is never possible to assure both a consensus on accuracy and fairness, and real confidentiality, in a study conducted in one's own highly literate culture.

A second ethical problem concerns the subject of language. In writing this book, I have constructed a story using medical vocabulary, the words of people I interviewed, and a political language intended to intervene in policy debates and practical pregnancy and child-rearing services available to women and their supporters. Sometimes, I use the language of "polymerase chain reaction," "proband," and "balanced translocation" as aspects of native text construction in the field of genetics, explaining what I have learned of their meanings as I do so. At other times, I have gone to some length to write out the vernacular cadences of West Indian women's anxiety over "choosing" amniocentesis, or the subtle distinctions that Spanish-speaking women use to describe their pregnancies and abortions as "older" women. Social movements for both reproductive rights and disability rights have so influenced my thinking that I cannot use phrases like "birth defect," "fetal defect," "positive diagnosis," "termination," or "therapeutic abortion" without putting them in quotation marks, insisting on the alternative understandings such words muffle, and the biases they project.

The power of language is a theme that runs throughout this book; it is especially relevant to chapters 3 and 4. Attention to this issue immediately raises unsettling questions that range from the practical to the abstract. Practically, can there be "informed consent" without funds for interpreters for low-income patients whose first language is not English? How can resistance to building second-language training into the curriculum of genetic counselor training programs be overcome, given the overwhelming and ever-expanding amount of scientific expertise students truly need to acquire? More abstract issues are also embedded in an analysis of the politics of language. For example, can the specialized vocabularies of science, especially genetics, ever be popularized and democratized, or is this discourse overde-termined to remain highly specialized, hence secret and professionally hege-monic? When should we interpret a pregnancy story self-consciously told in the language of the streets as "resistant" to medicine or social control, and when is it reproducing the relative institutional powerlessness of its teller? The power of speech and silence, technical and popular vocabularies, Eng-lish and its translations all enter into the ethics of the research and its inter-pretation reported here.

The ethics of language choice became immediately clear to me when I began observing at Woodhull Hospital in Brooklyn, which serves a predomi-nantly Afro-Caribbean patient population. There, I sometimes found myself translating the genetic counselor's explanations and questions into Spanish or French for recent migrants from the islands. In translating, I was perform-ing a payback service for the pregnant women and counselors who were allowing me to observe their interaction; I was also contaminating my own data collection process, for my translation choices were exquisitely baroque, and often paralyzing, and had to be made in a split second. Was my agenda to make sure the counselor's technical information had been passed on as perfectly as possible? Or was I translating "a woman's right to choose" to use or refuse the test, based on whatever I could glean from the patient herself? Might my goal be to evoke an active, articulated response to the complex issues raised by prenatal testing, so that I might pursue them as part of my own research agenda, despite how unsettling they might well prove to be for the patient? There was no neutral space from which translation could occur.

Later, I realized that this lack of neutrality ran through my interactions at every level. It was hard to listen to myself on the early, taped interviews: I talked too much, identified too much of my own experience, reiterated too much of the technical information in what I took to be its most practical for-mat each time I spent a few hours with a woman awaiting amniocentesis results. For many months, I practiced silencing myself in the interviews, thinking I might lessen the contamination of the stories I was collecting. But I was also learning an obvious and painful lesson. I had located myself at the intersection of all the discourses I was studying, and was overcommitted to two contradictory goals. The first, more scholarly and distanced, was wit-nessing and interpreting the clash of scientific thinking, maternalism, and social analysis inherent in how women recounted their amniocentesis stories. This task was easiest to perform when working with women "like me": well-educated, secular, most likely middle-class, white, and relatively empowered, even in the world of medical services of which they might have significant criticisms. With them, I had at least the illusion that their understandings of biomedical discourse and its complex resources were consonant with both those of health care providers and my own.

The second goal was more activist and engaged, and was often brought into play in interactions with women I perceived to hold less power in the world than I do: Women who were poorer, often lacking in privileged education, and coming from ethnic, national, religious, and racial communities that were as likely to have been the guinea pigs as the beneficiaries of scientific and medical research. Under these circumstances, I was laboring to put medical and scientific resources into a social perspective, and to ensure that the women I was interviewing fully understood the benefits and burdens of the services they were being offered, and the choices they were being forced to make. My role as a teacher was overdetermined. Identifying the contradictions and conflicts in my own role was, of course, one of the hardest lessons I had to learn; college professors don't abandon their lecterns without great effort, and activists always need an audience. While I painfully learned when to hold myself back and when to intervene to give information or suggest how a woman might gain access to needed resources, I also came to accept the inevitable contamination of data that serious interactive feedback entails. The issue was not simply "establishing rapport" with informants. The issue was how might I contribute, in whatever small ways possible, to their empowerment in a world where scientific and medical services are inequitably distributed. Similar ethical problems lie at the heart of many anthropologists' fieldwork experiences. They are necessarily heightened when one (this one) works at home in a culture as fraught with discrimination and inequality as our own.

Contamination of my data also occurred less dramatically (and perhaps more productively) in my interactions with health care providers. It is a truism of fieldwork that if you hang out long enough, the majority of the population on whom you are imposing your research agenda eventually comes to accept and trust you. I remember with both pain and appreciation the afternoon when a genetic counselor whom I'd been observing said, "I'm learning a lot from having you watch me. I respect you as a social scientist and a mother. It makes me more conscientious, having to respond to your questions, knowing you're thinking about what the patient is getting out of all of this." Her compliments signaled the palpable presence of the Heisenberg uncertainty principle—that observation contaminates the very processes it seeks to observe—inside my research terrain.

Over years of participant observation, I have become something of a trusted insider on various genetics teams. Team members have felt free to ask for feedback, and sometimes, quite a bit more. I have therefore occasionally been called in to speak with crisis-racked patients who were in shock and in grief; to advise counselors on how to improve their services; and to provide criticisms of the lack of cultural sensitivity built into some kinds of provider-patient interactions. While, in principle, I might have demurred, insisting that I would provide feedback "once the study is over," in a case like this, the study seemed unending. And the practical needs of service providers and patients are immediate. I know that my interventions have sometimes been incorporated into counseling protocols, influencing things said or unsaid to patients. Such interventions have real effects on both my interactions with health care providers, and on the services whose impact I am observing. I hope they have been modestly effective, as well as effectively contaminating. The ethics of giving feedback in a "real world" situation where access to resources and the conditions of choice are everywhere at stake had to be resolved in a way that was biased toward what I considered responsible application of my accumulating knowledge.

The problems of ethical feedback easily escalate when working in one's home society, accumulating knowledge that bridges the powerful world of highly literate science workers and their frequently less literate and almost always less powerful clients. Soon after my publications on amniocentesis began appearing in medical anthropology and gender studies journals, they were abstracted by the genetics community. I have been privileged to be asked to report on aspects of this study at medically oriented conferences, workshops, and policy meetings of such institutions as the National Society of Genetic Counselors, the Federal Bureau of Maternal and Child Health, and the National Institutes of Health. At first, I was a bit overwhelmed to find myself on the genetics speaking circuit, and always tried to coauthor whatever I presented with colleagues in genetic counseling, both to ensure its scientific accuracy, and so that I would not be perceived solely as a critical outsider. Gradually, I have learned to stand up for my own interpretations, asking health professionals to examine the scientific assumptions that form a part of their own cultural backgrounds. I am honored that my work has seemed valuable, if only to raise controversies and debates, within the world of genetic health services and policy.

But I have also come to be wary of the available slots into which anthropological analyses can be placed in the world of biomedical science. When I began observing counseling intake interviews, for example, I was immediately struck by the neo-Freudian working assumptions many counselors use. When a patient from a radically different linguistic, social, and cultural background than their own was silent, or refused the test, or wouldn't engage in probabilistic thinking, some counselors would say, "She's denying," "She's passive," "She's regressive," rather than looking for the chasms that were separating their own communicative concerns from those of their client. Over time, as I unearthed some of the complex meanings behind silences or refusals, especially as articulated by women whose cultural backgrounds were very different from those of their counselors, some counselors came to rely on the new interpretations I was providing them. But what does it mean to have a counselor now say, when discussing a noncompliant patient, "She's Haitian" or "She's Chinese," rather than "She's fatalistic," as an explanation of behavior she does not quite understand? Has my hard work only served to re-create what Michel-Rolph Trouillot called "the savage slot" (Trouillot 1991), a role impatiently awaiting a cultural occupant, as the new, poor, ethnic immigrants of America's cities become anthropological stand-ins for the tribal peoples my profession once studied? Medical anthropology has always had an applied edge; this is especially true of medical anthropology practiced at home. The ethics of fieldwork must include a constant assessment of the limited benefits and possible harm researchers can do, in situations where racial, ethnic, national, and religious stereotypes are built into communicative and social service interactions across class differences.

In speaking about the ethical tensions that shadowed this study, I have, of course, been speaking about power. Power is inscribed in all aspects of this study: It resides in the increasingly well-funded and metaphor-producing world of molecular genetics (Bishop and Waldholz 1990; Fleising and Smart 1993; Heath and Rabinow 1993; Martin 1992, 1994; Rabinow 1992, 1996; Suzuki and Knudtson 1989). Power is shot through the world of biomedicine, where the cutting edges of genetic research converge with social policy and its translation into inequitably distributed health services. It blasts communicative chasms between health care providers, already stratified by differences attached to gender, education, and often racial-ethnic or national background, and their multicultural, multiclass patient populations. Powerful discrimination segregates the hard-earned knowledge of families raising disabled children with stigmatized differences from much of civil society. And power exquisitely stratifies public, media representations of the complex issues surrounding prenatal diagnosis, abortion rights, prejudice against disabled people, and access to scientific literacy and medical services. Power differences are everywhere represented and enacted in the anthropological methods, data, interpretations, and ethics whose limits I have tried to suggest in this chapter. It is to the discursive and practical consequences of an examination of these power differences in the construction and uses of prenatal diagnosis that we now turn.

2
Accounting for Amniocentesis

We are in a fast-moving train, and we manage to learn how to eat in the train, even sleep in the train. But I don't think we think very much about where the train is going. Or, at the least, we are very simplistic. . . . Of course, geneticists are the ones creating the technology. But it is being created without too much thought. Of course, if you really want to get to the social issue, you'd better get to whoever is driving the train. . . . When I began, this work belonged in academic medicine; now it is rapidly commercializing. Pretty soon, it will just be profit-making labs offering kits. They'll have a roving genetic counselor to pay lip service to malpractice insurance. This is not what geneticists wanted when we insisted on genetic counseling. (Avram Terguvnick, medical geneticist, in a conversation with the author)

Technoscience is made in relatively new, rare, expensive, and fragile places that garner disproportionate amounts of resources; these places may come to occupy strategic positions and be related with one another. Thus, technoscience may be described simultaneously as a demiurgic enterprise that multiplies the number of allies and as a rare and fragile achievement that we hear about only when all the other allies are present. (Latour 1987, 179–180)

THE TECHNOLOGIES OF PRENATAL DIAGNOSIS which pregnant women encounter appear reassuringly routinized: When a pregnant woman is assigned an appointment for amniocentesis, a professional team of medical secretaries, genetic counselors, radiologists, and obstetricians guides her through the multiple appointments, paperwork, counseling, and procedure itself, and then provides the results. Increasingly, patients with private obstetrical care may even obtain the test in their physicians' offices. As I hope to show in subsequent chapters, pregnant women and their supporters express heterogeneous and complex responses to these routinized services based, in large measure, on the individual and social experiences that frame each pregnancy.

Here, I parse the technological routine whose action the rest of this book follows in order to offer an account of its historical development. At the center of this account lies my conviction that the technologies of prenatal diagnosis, like all technologies, are produced at multiple intersections where the work of particular scientists, research clinicians, and health service providers engages social relations far beyond the purview of their laboratories, clinics, and consulting rooms. What come to count as the technologies of prenatal diagnosis, now and in the past, are shaped by large-scale transformations of biomedical knowledge, our legal structure, widely shared and sometimes contested cultural values, and the social identities within which service providers and patients encounter one another. In other words, I will argue that an understanding of the history and ongoing evolution of this biomedical technology requires us to see how its developers, because of and despite their individual expertise and achievements, became enrolled in larger social projects to which their scientific accomplishments were conscripted.[3] These technoscientific enrollments are produced by international research collaborations and medico-legal reforms; the evolution of nationally diverse health services; and highly localized aspirations for what constitutes a viable and healthy pregnancy. They depend on forces as diverse as transnational trade agreements, revisions of national medical school training protocols, the falling birthrate throughout the developed world, and the opposition to abortion of the Catholic Church. It is within this heterogeneous social web that amniocentesis and its related technologies have been produced.

Historical Detours

Of course, Jerome Lejeune was not thinking about his enrollment in large-scale social transformations on that April day in 1958 when he peered through an aged microscope discarded by the bacteriology department at the Hopital Saint-Louis in Paris at a sample of smooth muscle tissue taken from three patients with Down syndrome. Lejeune, a French geneticist, and his cardiologist colleague Marthe Gauthier had used the innovative techniques of tissue culture to treat the sample. The full complement of human chromosomes had only been confirmed as forty-six in 1955–56. Lejeune was trying to assess whether his patients with Down syndrome lacked one human chromosome (as, by analogy, some abnormal fruit flies lacked one fruit fly chromosome). Instead, he (or, perhaps more accurately, he and Gauthier) discovered that they had a surfeit. Then, and in subsequent studies, tissue samples taken from people with Down syndrome yielded a chromosome count of forty-seven. With great hesitation, he published his results in 1959. At the same time, a research group at the University of Edinburgh independently arrived at the same findings, confirming the Paris research. As a provost at University College wrote to pioneering English geneticist Lionel Penrose upon hearing of these discoveries, "It must be one of the most important things that have happened in genetical studies for a long time" (Kevles 1985, 248).

Such "genetical studies" should be placed in a long philosophical and scientific genealogy that extends back to at least the Ancient Greeks. There, philosophers and healers speculated about the causes of generation, and the capacity of organisms to reproduce themselves. Influenced by the rediscovery of Hippocrates's materialism and Aristotle's concern with the fusion of form and matter, Early Modern natural philosophers attempted to resolve the debate between "epigenicists" and "preformationists": Did organisms develop progressively, from formless matter to fully formed entity, or were they present at Creation and at each of its iterations like little homunculi, already fully shaped? Long before the modern science of genetics took disciplinary shape, eighteenth- and nineteenth-century concepts of inheritance were deeply rooted in the idea of estate or property transmission. As biology emerged as a field of study, "inheritance" was already freighted with a double meaning: it indexed both the structural properties of the organism and debates about that which constitutes it. A focus on both development and transmission comprised "genetic" thinking. This tension between developmental and iterative reproduction characterizes the history of biology and its daughter disciplines. Embryology, biochemistry, and physics all influenced the field of genetics, carrying a dualistic heritage of both linear or fixed replication and holistic, relational development with them (Olby 1990; see also Keller 1995, 1996, 1999).

Early scientific interest in developmental and transmissible inheritance had, of course, practical significance: Many of its most ardent students hailed from animal husbandry and agronomy, where experiments in hybridization were discussed under the rubric of "transmutation of species." The classic work of the Swede Carl Linnaeus had posited plant sexuality as the route to the production of new species via hybridity in the middle of the eighteenth century. He was followed by a long line of botanists who sought to prove experimentally that desirable characteristics could be successfully hybridized and retained across many generations. Opponents countered with theories of "reversion," observing that older, less desirable traits also reappeared across generations. Thus reversion and hybridization stood for a complex debate concerning the relative roles of nature and nurture, heredity and environment. The resolution of this problem would in part await the work of the Moravian monk Gregor Mendel, whose elegant mathematical ratios of pea traits across hybrid generations were published starting in 1865, but not "rediscovered" until the turn of the present century (Bowler 1989; Sandler and Sandler 1985).

This long-standing scientific and agronomical interest in retention, reversion, and improvement of organic characteristics over the generations resonated through thinking about humans, as well as plants and animals. By the nineteenth century, a focus on the effects of the mother's imagination on the fetus gave way to a concern with consanguinity as a possible site of perfectibility and degeneration. Rapid urbanization in England and parts of the European continent also provided an anxious context for the study of degeneracy: It was widely presumed that civilization was both meliorable and degradable, and that properties such as propertylessness (pauperism, vagrancy, and associated ills like alcoholism and mental degeneracy) were transmissible across generations. Using methods from the evolving mathematical field of statistics in the later nineteenth century, Francis Galton reconceptualized inheritance as a statistical relation between human populations of successive generations. In his hands, "inheritance" became "heredity" and was measured by "biometry," the statistical description of variable population characteristics ranging from height to intelligence, from "nomadism" to alcoholism. Galton's foundational influence on the international eugenics movement is anchored in this work, a point to which I will return below.

These scientific, practical, and sociological interests in inheritance resonated in the search for the actual entities through which intergenerational transmission might occur. Mendel's presentations of pea plant attributes across many generations of breeding were developed in his search for "factors" to explain plant traits; he made a strong case for the existence of a limited number of constant or "unit" characteristics that were carried by heritable material. By 1906, the English biologist William Bateson had coined the term "genetics" in his ardent attempts to substantiate both Darwin's and Mendel's work; in 1909, the Danish botanist Wilhelm Johannsen distinguished phenotype (external characteristics) from genotype (underlying hereditary units) carried by "genes." And the work of the American biologist T. H. Morgan brought together emergent techniques of cytologic microscopy and Mendelism in the study of fruit fly genetics in papers he published between 1911 and 1913. The material substances Morgan actually studied were not "genes" but "chromosomes," those threadlike structures which are visible with the use of a microscope. By enrolling drosophila and their conveniently short generations to the project of scientific inquiry, chromosomal variation could be bred and manipulated under laboratory conditions. Morgan, along with the English zoologist Lyell Darlington, established that unit characteristics visible in the organism were passed on together or separately at different rates, depending on their location on chromosomes. This work also directed researchers to the study of sex-limited (now called X-linked) characteristics as a prime locus of genetic investigation. For Morgan, Darlington, and their followers, the study of chromosomes in germ-cell nuclei was the key to genetic discoveries. And, according to Morgan, "In the same sense in which the chemist posits invisible atoms and the physicist electrons, the student of heredity appeals to invisible elements called genes" (Morgan 1926, as cited in Hubbard 1990, 71).

Across the Atlantic, the German zoologists August Weismann and Oscar Hertwig also used cytology to study germ-line cells, but they rejected "nuclear monopolies" in favor of a more interactive theory of the cytoplasm (extranuclear cellular material): Once again, the debate between fixed entities carrying the instructions for reproduction and a more relational theory of organelle, organ, and organismic development preoccupied many scientists.

By the time of World War I, the international European and American collaborative effort to study genetics had come of age. Its focus was on sexual reproduction via reduction division involving chromosomes; its objects of study were chromosomes on which still invisible but posited genes were "known" to be lodged; its methods were at once microbiological, biochemical, and statistical (Hubbard 1990; Kevles 1985, 1992; Levins and Lewontin 1985; Lewontin 1991; Olby 1990; Spanier 1995). While the highly visible chromosome quickly became an international consensus object of scientific investigation, genes have had a more checkered history: To this day, scientific debates about the relation of genetic information and organismic development remain intense, replaying earlier scientific controversies in a molecular register (Keller 1995, 1996, 1999; see also Kitcher 1992; Olby 1990a, 1990b; Portin 1993). It is within this international collaborative scholarly network and its debates that Lejeune's discovery should be situated.

A few years later, in 1967, American researchers reported the first detection of a fetal chromosome problem in a sample of fluid drawn from the amniotic sac inside the womb of a pregnant woman. Amniocentesis—the technique of extracting amniotic fluid transabdominally through a hollow catheter—was first performed and described in Germany in 1882 by a doctor attempting to relieve harmful pressure on the fetus of a pregnant woman.[4] It became an experimental treatment for polyhydramnios (excess fetal fluid which threatened fetal development), but was not widely used until the 1950s, when researchers in Great Britain and the United States discovered they could deploy the same technique to test for maternal-fetal blood group incompatibility and to assess the severity of Rh disease. In critical cases, amniocentesis led to intrauterine transfusion. It also led to the assessment of fetal lung maturity, so that fetuses with serious disease could be delivered as early, and as safely, as possible.

The treatment of polyhydramnios and Rh disease established familiarity with amniocentesis as an invasive technique. Advances in prenatal diagnosis awaited the development of technologies that isolated, cultured, and characterized chromosomes in amniotic fluid. That story begins with the discovery of sex chromatin—the inactivated somatic cell X chromosome, or barr body, distinguishing females from males in humans—which was characterized in the late 1940s and early '50s. Its discovery paved the way for experiments in Minneapolis, New York, Copenhagen, and Haifa to predict fetal sex via amniocentesis. Some of the earliest experimental "fishing expeditions" inside women's wombs were undertaken on mothers who already had a son with hemophilia and wanted to know the sex of the fetus. If it was determined to be chromosomally male, then they ran a 50 percent risk of having another son affected by the disease. In 1960, an obstetrical team in Copenhagen reported the first abortion after the determination of male fetal sex in a carrier of hemophilia. By the time that researchers in Sweden, Denmark, Great Britain, and the United States began experimenting more widely with amniotic prenatal diagnosis for Down syndrome and other chromosomal conditions, the technology to invade the uterus, extract its liquids, and characterize fetal chromosomes was an international project (Cowan 1992, 1993; Davis 1993; Kaback 1979). It had enrolled not only researcher-clinicians from several continents but mothers of "blue babies" and hemophiliac sons in its experimental development.

The evolution of amniocentesis was accompanied by closely related international developments. In the same year that Lejeune observed the chromosomes of his Down syndrome patients in France, midwifery professor Ian Donald and his colleagues in Glasgow published an article called the "Investigation of Abdominal Masses by Pulsed Ultrasound." In it, they described the adaptation of sonar technology—originally developed during World War I for detecting enemy submarines—to the detection of fetuses inside their mother's wombs (Oakley 1993, ch.14). Though the idea of sound navigation and ranging (SONAR) had been patented in England directly after the Titanic disaster for the detection of icebergs at sea, it was the French who developed it for naval military uses. In the decades after the Great War, commercial engineers and physicists investigated the technology's potential for revealing metallurgical flaws in the Soviet Union, and later, in the United States. Initial medical experimental uses focused on the energy generated by sound waves as a rehabilitative therapy. Only after decades of clinical experimentation were the image-producing capacities of the technology fully recognized, and methods to harness it developed (Yoxen 1989, 281–296).

Diagnosis of pregnancy was thus neither the first nor most obvious use claimed for sonography, which was initially thought (wrongly) to be beneficial in scanning for brain tumors and, later, for kidney masses. While the technology has certainly proved to have many medical uses (especially in cardiology), its most routinized successes developed in obstetrics. Pulse-echo sonography (ultrasound) works by bouncing sound waves against the fetus, creating an image as the waves return to a cathode. After decades of perfecting transduction (the ability to attach the machine to the exterior of a patient's body so as to image interior soft tissue) and sectoral scanning (the capacity to render a three-dimensional object into two dimensions in regularized segments), it became clear to Donald and his colleagues that sonograms offered the possibility of normalizing representations of the fetus throughout its gestation. After their reports, sonography's diffusion in obstetrics was rapid and dramatic, and physicians hailed it as "totally safe" long before any actual safety studies were conducted (Oakley 1984, 1993, ch.14).

Toward a Technological History of the Present

As many feminists have pointed out, the technology intervened in the doctor-patient relationship dramatically, allowing the physician to bypass pregnant women's self-reports in favor of a "window" on the developing fetus (Mitchell 1993; Oakley 1984, 1993; Petchesky 1987). Additionally, radiologists and obstetricians working together could use sonograms in the developing technology of amniocentesis. It enabled them to picture where the fetus wasn't, and the fluid was, rather than groping blindly for a pocket of liquid into which to insert the amnio-bound catheter. As "real time" sonography became available, the technology allowed doctors to observe a moving image of the fetus while sampling its environment. When used in conjunction with sonography, experimental invasive techniques of the womb became safer, and the miscarriage rates attributable to these procedures dropped dramatically.[5]

The technology of prenatal diagnosis continues to evolve at a rapid pace.

During the more than a decade in which I have been investigating its social and cultural geography, another intrauterine technology has waxed and waned. Initially hailed as a "revolutionary" replacement for amniocentesis, chorionic villus sampling (CVS) works on preplacental tissue, allowing diagnoses to be completed within the first trimester. Like amniocentesis, CVS developed from an international collaboration: First tested in Copenhagen in the late 1960s, biopsy of the chorion using a fiber-optic device for its direct visualization was surely influenced by doctors' experiences with women at high risk for passing on genetic disorders who wanted information as early in their pregnancies as possible. In the '70s, researchers in both Denmark and Sweden abandoned CVS efforts because of what they deemed unacceptably elevated miscarriage rates following the test. But Chinese researchers reported high success rates in diagnosing fetal sex using a variation of CVS at the same time, and by the 1980s, doctors in the Soviet Union, Great Britain, France, and Italy all described successful prenatal diagnoses of specific conditions using this technique. Miscarriage rates declined as doctors' experience with CVS expanded, although they remain close to 1 percent, which compares unfavorably with the less than one-half percent attributable to amniocentesis. In the late 1980s, CVS appeared to be the wave of the prenatal diagnostic future, as its miscarriage rate declined (Cowan 1993, 13–15). But despite the attraction of earlier diagnosis, serious safety objections have been raised: A relatively high percentage of babies born after CVS have malformations of fingers and toes attributable to its use (Firth 1991). More recently, experiments in early (twelve-week) amniocentesis are moving from the anecdotal to the clinical, although controlled national trials have yet to be established (Sundberg, Bang et al. 1997).

Additionally, another prenatal diagnostic technology became routinized throughout the United States in the 1980s and '90s, based on research conducted in Edinburgh in the 1970s. Maternal serum alpha-fetoprotein screening (MSAFP) identifies a chemical in the blood of pregnant women that is produced by the fetus. Elevated levels of alpha-fetoprotein may indicate a neural tube problem such as spina bifida or anencephaly, which is relatively common throughout the United Kingdom and in some other parts of the world. Alpha-fetoprotein is routinely sampled whenever amniocentesis is done. Additionally, the development of an inexpensive blood screen in the 1980s made it possible, in principle, to test all pregnant women receiving prenatal medical services. But the blood test conducted on pregnant women is itself a screen, and not a direct diagnostic: It identifies only a population at relatively elevated risk for neural tube defects, who are then offered additional testing. Ninety-five percent of positive test results turn out to be false positives, but this can be ascertained only by pursuing other tests, of which the most likely are ultrasound and amniocentesis. MSAFP testing thus increases the expanded use of ultrasound and amniocentesis, enrolling women who would otherwise have had no age-related or familial history indicating their candidacy for these tests. In the United States, California was the first state to mandate its offering to all pregnant women, with psychosocial results that are fundamentally unknown (Press and Browner 1993, 1994, 1995). Increasing knowledge about the relation of insufficient folic acid and elevated risks for spina bifida is also leading to public health dietary regulation, with B vitamins being added to cereal supplies (Corcoran 1998; Koren 1993; Morrow 1988; Pietrzik 1997; Seller 1987; Steegers-Theurrissen 1995). Meanwhile, MSAFP is also being used in conjunction with multiple biochemical markers (estriol, human chorion gonadotrophin, and increasingly, inhibin-A) to develop new, non-age-related screens for Down syndrome. These biochemical triangulations screen for populations who are then offered level II (high resolution) ultrasonography and possibly amniocentesis if markers are positive. Currently, experiments in maternal-fetal blood centrifuges and cell sorters, especially, PCR-assisted FISH (fluorescent in-situ hybridization) are under way.[6] Ideally, researchers aim to separate the very small number of fetal cells circulating in maternal blood within days or weeks of the onset of pregnancy, so that a prenatal diagnosis can be made ever earlier. All the technologies which I have just described depend on transnational enrollments of scientists (or their research reports) in one another's projects. Collectively, they point toward a medical future in which the maternal body may be invaded less deeply, while tracking the fetus through more intersecting biochemical values and organ systems.

As clinical reports of successes, anomalies, and failures with these new technologies accumulated in medical journals, several national health authorities authorized their investigation. Large-scale collaborative empirical studies of these emerging reproductive technologies focused on diagnostic capabilities of the procedures and their relative safety. It quickly became apparent that chromosomal analysis, for example, was virtually 100 percent accurate; alpha-fetoprotein determination in amniotic fluid is now considered 98 percent effective for open neural tube defects (Davis 1993). Accuracy of diagnosis, however, doesn't predict the severity of a condition's consequences, a problem that deserves a more extensive discussion; we will return to this topic in chapter 9. And while the North American collaborative studies led to a National Institutes of Health consensus conference indicating that amniocentesis was a very safe technology, adding less than one-half of a percent (.5 percent) to the miscarriage rate (Development 1976; Kaback et al. 1979), British studies reported a doubled miscarriage rate among amniocentesis users as compared to nonusers (Amniocentesis 1978).[7] Commentators on both sides of the Atlantic criticized one another's studies on methodological grounds (e.g., Chalmers 1987), and the issue has remained unresolved (McDonough 1990). As feminist commentators have consistently pointed out, the focus on technological capability and safety all but eclipsed psychological and social evaluations of the emergent technology, especially evaluations of women's experiences, aspirations, and criticisms (Black 1993; Farrant 1985; Kolker and Burke 1994; McDonough 1990), a point to which I return below.

National and International Contexts

Yet when we step back from the intersecting enrollments of international biomedical progress, clinical reports in medical journals, and government-sponsored safety evaluations, it is apparent that larger, more complex social transformations are also at work in the development of this (or any other) medical technology. Throughout this brief historic overview, I have stressed the past and present transnational enrollment of scientific communities. The network of dense debates, collaborative studies, competitive races to publication, and shared techniques is a powerful force in increasing the velocity with which basic scientific research is translated into practical technology, and the consensus with which protocols for its viable use are developed (Cowan 1992, 1993; Crane 1972; Ubell 1997a, 1997b). Such scientific communication, however, is played out against a background of national and intranational differences which affect many aspects of an emergent technology, such as governmental investments in research and design costs, funding and prestige of research centers, consumer subsidization, and exposure to both a technology's benefits and burdens.

These national differences are particularly easy to spot when we compare the experience of prenatal diagnosis in Great Britain and some continental European countries with that of the United States. Though specific policies and fiscal strategies have varied considerably from country to country, virtually all of the Western developed nations except the United States have a commitment to a national health policy and its funding. This has affected aspects of prenatal testing as overt as recommended age and cost efficiency, as covert as the directiveness or neutrality of the counseling that accompanies testing, including the issue of whether and how directly women are pressured to continue or end a pregnancy in which a diagnosis of serious fetal disability has been made. Most European countries, for example, initially recommended amniocentesis for pregnant women who would be 40 or older at the time of delivery; in the United States, 35 was quickly established as the recommended age for the test, and the "age barrier" has dropped into the lower thirties in a free market economy in health care, in contrast to nations with commitments to population-wide cost-benefit analyses. In America, the commitment to a "value-free" counseling process is, in theory, absolute: The decision to have or reject the test, and to continue or end a pregnancy should a serious fetal disability be diagnosed are, in principle, sacrosanct (a problematic ideal to which we return in chapters 3 and 4). In England, by contrast, three-quarters of the obstetricians surveyed in one study replied that they required women to agree in principle to terminate an affected pregnancy before they perform an amniocentesis. In the Federal Republic of Germany and in Hungary, geneticists see no problems with directive counseling. While a woman may change her mind, the medical-administrative rationale behind such requirements assumes that any response to a "positive diagnosis" besides abortion is a waste of scarce national medical resources (Farrant 1985, 113; Wertz and Fletcher 1987, 1989a, 1989b). In light of this international variation, it is not surprising that feminist and women's health movement responses to the routinization and regulation of prenatal diagnosis have also varied widely. This, too, is a problem to which we shall return.

The developing technologies of prenatal diagnosis were also enrolled in other large-scale international and national social transformations without which successful diffusion would have made no sense. I refer here to the remarkable speed with which abortion laws were reformed internationally in the developed world; although the struggle for such reforms continues apace, especially in countries where Catholic or Islamic religion plays a key role in governance, it is important to note that the widespread deployment of prenatal diagnosis only became conceivable and possible when enrolled by and through legal access to abortion. Abortion laws were liberalized throughout most of the Western democracies in the 1960s and 1970s, and earlier in Japan (Glendon 1987). The movement of laws reflecting more liberal attitudes toward the control of fertility, including abortion, has a checkered and uneven history. Nor is this trend absolute, as Americans caught up in the current struggles to protect or dismantle Roe v. Wade surely know. Abortion law itself is connected in both direct and indirect ways to the rise of women's movements, consumer health movements, and their intersection in women's health movements, as well as to broader demographic trends which have influenced the decline of fertility rates throughout the West, and indeed throughout much of the world. These surely include such international trends (with significant national variations) as an increase in full-time participation of women in the paid labor force throughout much of their lives; the extension of "childhood," including the high costs of educating children, making them "luxury consumer goods" for many sectors of the population; the rise of divorce rates and concomitant dependence of some groups of mothers and small children on government-provided welfare benefits increasingly under attack; and various versions of "sexual revolutions" in which women's aspirations for sexual pleasure and autonomy have depended, in large measure, on their ability to control their own fertility (Cowan 1992).

In the United States, a massive transformation in the attitudes of health care providers, especially physicians, also assured support rather than suppression of legal abortion in the 1960s, in contrast to official professional positions taken even a decade earlier (Joffe 1995; Solinger 1993). Churches and religious communities also played a role in the struggle over legal and social aspects of fertility control, including abortion rights. While the role of the Catholic Church (and more recently, fundamentalist Protestant groups) in antiabortion activism is well-known (cf. Ginsburg 1989a, 1993; Solinger 1998), the role of liberal churches in forming coalitions, networks, and lobbying efforts on behalf of liberalization of laws affecting reproduction has evoked less popular scrutiny (cf. Garrow 1994). Complex coalitions and inadvertent imbrications thus frame the social conditions under which prenatal diagnosis became conceivable.

Women's Agency?

Such macro-historical transformations are inscribed in the lives of individual women in complex ways. As historian Ruth Cowan points out, it is often hard to spot the agency of women in the development of a technology for which they become consumers, but some clues are available and should be followed. The desperation of some carriers of X-linked diseases, for example, was a clear factor in early experiments with amniocentesis, and the desires of "Pakistani women living in London; African women, many of them Muslims, living in France; Chinese women in Anshan, and Russian and Hungarian women" all stand behind the national medical research teams reporting on CVS (Cowan 1993, 15). For these women, carriers of serious, often life-threatening diseases, early abortion was a more acceptable solution than late abortion or no abortion at all; they therefore enrolled their bodies and their fetuses in the experimental search for prenatal diagnosis. Indeed, women's participation in abortion liberalization movements is a topic which has recently begun to receive increased popular and scholarly attention (Bonavoglia 1991; Garrow 1994; Joffe 1995; Kaplan 1996; McCorvey 1994; Solinger 1993, 1998). Often, women have sought abortions at great cost to themselves and their families. In the 1960s, journalists reported that nearly five thousand women die each year from illegal abortions (cited in Garrow 1994, 284), and in 1962, both *Time* and *Newsweek* covered the trips of American women able to afford a plane ticket to Japan, where abortion was already legal, following a German measles epidemic. Scores of women also pursued court cases in the epidemic seeking legal abortions performed in hospitals, rather than in back alley offices (Solinger 1993). Sherri Finkbine's struggle to receive a legal abortion after she realized that the thalidomide her doctor had prescribed was likely to severely compromise the fetus she was carrying, for example, was well publicized in 1962 throughout the United States. As the hostess of Phoenix television's *Romper Room* program for children and the mother of four, she had impeccable credentials when she and her husband reluctantly chose to go public after her petition for a legal therapeutic abortion lay snarled between the hospital and the courts. Rather than risk an illegal abortion, the Finkbines eventually flew to Stockholm; they were condemned by Vatican Radio and received hundreds of hostile letters. Their public ordeal was reported on the front pages of many American newspapers for several weeks, prompting debate on the grounds for legal abortion in many state legislatures and medical associations. In this case, a pharmaceutically damaged fetus called the question of whether there might be grounds for legal abortion other than saving the life of the mother (Garrow 1994, 285–289). These cases contributed to national consciousness about the problematic nature of abortion laws. They also set the stage for the idea that "a severely deformed fetus" is a justifiable reason for an abortion, a position which was debated in national Gallup polls of the era. The "deformed fetus" argument became one of the few grounds on which constituencies who are otherwise totally deadlocked in oppositional positions over the ethics of abortion have concurred (Goldberg and Elder 1998). To say that abortion reform or prenatal diagnosis were "consumer driven" would distort the complex history of medical and legal coalitions, religious splits and oppositions, and single-issue lobbying efforts in many state legislatures that also entered into these legal and medical metamorphoses (Garrow 1994; Joffe 1995; Solinger 1998). Nonetheless, many individual women, some publicly visible, most anonymous, enrolled themselves in the struggles for access to abortion.

Eugenics and Geneticization

Into this potent and heterogeneous social mix, the histories of various national and international eugenics movements must also be added, for they, too, have influenced the cultural climate concerning normative reproduction. Coined as a label in 1883 by Francis Galton, "eugenics" indexed the study of the improvement of the "race of man." While Galton's success was tied to the development of contemporary statistical tools for the measure of human variation, it rested on older traditions of popular and scientific thought that attempted to "know" internal human characteristics through their external variation, including phrenology. In its heyday, during the first third of the current century, eugenics became a popular political movement, providing counsel to governments on questions ranging from immigration and abortion to penal reform and psychiatric asylum (Proctor 1992). Attacks on pauperism in England, sterilization legislation in the United States, and racial hygiene programs in Germany were, of course, all outcomes of eugenics movements as they influenced social policy (Kevles 1985; Nelkin and Lindee 1995).

But as many recent historians have noted, it is no longer tenable to simply label eugenics "bad science"; it had (and one might argue, still has) a complex relationship to "pure" science. The rise of a Darwinian-Mendelian genetics that focused on discrete unit traits, rather than biometry's blended population inheritance, posed a scientific challenge to early eugenics. In its place, there arose a Mendelian eugenics movement, primarily spearheaded in the United States by Charles Davenport of the Eugenic Records Office at Cold Spring Harbor, New York. The Race Betterment Foundation in Battle Creek, Michigan, and the Galton Society of the American Museum of Natural History were also sites of eugenics organizations. Many scientists of renown were eugenicists, and their political commitments ran the entire gamut from left to right (Allen 1989; Kevles 1985; Lubinsky 1993; Nelkin and Lindee 1995; Paul, 1984, 1995; Resta 1992). There was a contradictory amalgam between Mendelian eugenicism, which focused on the inheritance of traits that could be clearly tracked, like color blindness or albinism, and social characteristics alleged to run at high rates among "Aryans," like intelligence or sobriety (Kevles 1992). Under the combined and contradictory shadow of Nazi eugenics and the accomplishments of laboratory genetics, there arose a generation which Daniel Kevles labels "reform eugenicists." A gifted cohort including Ronald Fisher, J. B. S. Haldane, Lancelot Hogben, and Julian Huxley in England, and Hermann J. Muller in the United States, they were often "men of the left," dedicated to the development of a genetics which would be allied with medicine and freed of racial and class biases. Under their influence, for example, great strides were made in the classification of human blood groups, which they saw as universal genetic markers. Hogben even suggested that such markers might be used to catalogue the human genome—an idea which prefigured contemporary genomics (Kevles 1992, 11–13; Paul 1984, 1986).

As many authors have noted (and as the great majority of geneticists and genetics counselors among whom I have worked believe), the atrocities of World War II disparaged eugenic thinking in its older, popular forms. Most professionals with whom I have spoken code the current context as one that promotes individual reproductive choice, stressing its difference from state-mandated reproductive limitations. In that sense, there may be "positive eugenic" aspects of prenatal diagnosis, for screening promotes the reproduction of healthy offspring; but there are no "negative eugenic" factors, for no central powers are limiting who may or may not reproduce. But recent scholarship concerning the impact of genomic research on eugenic consciousness suggests a somewhat different story, on at least three grounds. First and most important, recent analysts caution us "not to fight today's battles with yesterday's tactics." They do not expect a eugenic resurgence to assume the forms it took earlier in the present century. Second, and as a direct response to this posited difference of social location, there is a growing consciousness that current eugenic dilemmas will be rooted more thoroughly in the free-market economy of contemporary capitalism, rather than in legislation aimed directly at controlling reproduction. Threats of eugenic exclusions now involve insurance coverage or its lack, employer discrimination, and struggles around extending coverage of disability legislation to those with genetic susceptibilities. They also include the highly stratified access Americans in all their diversity have to both health services and confidentiality in a context in which "health care reform" is being provided by the insurance industry, with its policies excluding those with "preexisting conditions," rather than by a single-payer unit like a national government, or a government-medical profession coalition, as is the case in many other developed nations. Third, the "individual choice" model of reproduction as noneugenic requires some interrogation. Because "choice" is market-driven in contemporary North American culture, it appears to be based on expanding possibilities. But at the same time, available options are shaped by complex forces that travel as the "invisible hand" of the market, in this case the market in genetic research. When "everything" from well-characterized single-chromosome conditions like Down syndrome to polygenic syndromes like manic depression or alcoholism to alleged syndromes like a propensity for antisocial behavior or obesity can be popularly attributed to genetics and prenatally diagnosed, we may soon be standing on a "slippery slope" of a "eugenic boutique" (Keller 1992a; Marks 1996a, 1996b, 1997; Muller-Hill 1994; Resta 1992; cf. Proctor 1992). Whose individual choices will these be? More subtly, who will frame the values within which those individuals making reproductive choices come of age? That is, attributing safety to an individual-choice model foregrounds personal liberty while backgrounding the social matrix of a technoscientific marketplace to whose requisites individual choices are increasingly enrolled.

One way to think about the current cultural fascination with genetic determinism is suggested by Evelyn Fox Keller, who asks us to revisit the decline of eugenics after Nazi atrocities made its universalizing and murderous messages intolerable. She convincingly describes the creation of "a more general demarcation between biology and culture; the force of genetics was confined to purely physiological attributes, while behavior came increasingly to be seen as belonging to the domain of culture" (Keller 1992a, 285). Human behavior became a "free zone" in which nature/nurture debates could be played out, a scenario quite familiar to students of American anthropology, if we recall the late-Boasian "culture and personality" school, and the reform of post–World War II physical anthropology away from the study of "race" in favor of ecological adaptation (Haraway 1988a). Precisely by assuming a distinct nature/culture divide, this modern worldview left its advocates unprepared for the imperial expansion of a new determinism linked to the development of molecular biology: The realm of "nature" is dramatically unfolding while "culture" now seems a weak explanation for behaviors increasingly characterized as biologically programmed. Yet as popular consciousness evolves in the shadow of the expanding molecular biological revolution, the issue becomes more complicated than any reference to old-style positive-and-negative eugenics might suggest. For its first decade and more, the most extraordinary successes of early molecular biology were in the manipulation of viruses which appeared to many observers to be far removed from humanity. But at the same time, the age-old dream of perfectibility permitted an expanding structure of sentiment in favor of what Robert Sinsheimer as early as 1969 called "a new eugenics." In his view, an emergent biomedical eugenics would be implemented on the individual level in favor of normalcy (Sinsheimer quoted in Keller 1992a, 289). This idea of "the right to normalcy" as a new eugenics is "an ideological expansion of molecular biology into both popular culture and medicine" (Keller 1992a, 291). To advocate a "right to normalcy" presumes that we know what that means. To characterize normalcy in the language of biomedical "rights" is also to individualize it. It is this trust that "the normal" can be well characterized and individually "selected," which lies at the heart of the new eugenics. This new eugenics will be individually choice-driven. "It entails the responsibility for arbitrating normality," in Keller's terms (299).

This idea that "normal" is unambiguously understood, individual in characterization, biomedical in nosology, and genetic in origin, segues into what Abby Lippman has described as "geneticization": The extreme reduction of all problematic differences to an individual and genetic basis (Lippman 1991, 1993). Though many geneticists and their allied technologists do not subscribe to geneticization as a worldview, it is, ironically, a widespread and prevalent modernization of a much older version of biological determinism over whose popularity they have scant control. Like earlier ideologies of religious predestination or social Darwinism, geneticization fits comfortably with the prejudices of its age, coloring the popular imagination with causal explanations that seem at once magically, scientifically arcane, and intimately reassuring: You are the product of what your (genetic) lineage has made you, and problematic social differences can hardly be alleviated by social policy because our diseases, disabilities, distresses, and troublesome demeanors lie locked in our genes (Beckwith 1993; Hubbard 1990; Hubbard and Lewontin 1996; Levins and Lewontin 1985; Nelkin 1995; Nelkin and Lindee 1995; Nelkin and Tancredi 1989). Within such a powerful worldview, the enrollment of prenatal genetic diagnosis in the service of individual, perfectible choice "makes sense."

Genetic Services and the Law

So far, I have argued that the development and routinization of prenatal diagnosis depended on complex intersections in biomedical scientific research, social policy affecting abortion, and social movements influencing cultural climates. In all, individual accomplishments by researchers, crusading lawyers, eugenic activists, and women struggling for reproductive control require expanding contextualization. In the United States (in contrast, once again, to most European countries), the routinization of prenatal diagnosis needs to be framed within the expansion of medical services in the post–World War II period, which was deeply influenced by the lack of a national commitment to universal health care. It was only in the 1960s and '70s that most Americans switched from a fee-for-service to a third-party payment system. And it was at this same time that a series of legal cases began to challenge prevailing standards of care in obstetrics and pediatrics, leading to an uneven, indeed, contradictory record of statutory, regulatory, and case laws concerning the provision of prenatal genetic testing services. Under the threat of lawsuit, the prevailing standard of care concerning informed consent and informing women and their partners who are considered to be at risk of having children with genetic and chromosomal problems has dramatically changed. Prenatal diagnostic technologies were thus enrolled in case law that varies, of course, from state to state; it is often fraught with inconsistencies.

Across a large terrain of somewhat contradictory case law, two kinds of suits concerning babies born with prenatally diagnosable conditions have emerged: The wrongful-birth and the wrongful-life suits. The first is brought by parents against obstetricians and other health care providers, alleging that they would have avoided a specific pregnancy, or aborted it, had they been properly informed of its risks (or specific diagnosis) in an appropriate and timely fashion. In one of the first successful wrongful-birth cases, a 37-year-old woman was awarded her child's medical costs for life after suing over not being given information about amniocentesis. Her case influenced the American College of Obstetricians and Gynecologists and the American Academy of Pediatrics to advise their member doctors that the offer of pre-natal diagnosis to medically appropriate candidates was now constituted as the standard of care, at risk of a lawsuit (Cowan 1993, 13). Since that time, most jurisdictions have accepted the legitimacy of this type of suit, awarding settlements which range from the recovery of costs involved in raising a child with special needs to compensation for emotional damages.

More controversial have been wrongful-life cases. In such cases, children born with disabilities that could have been prenatally diagnosed, or for which their parents should have been informed that they were at substantial risk, sue medical providers for negligence. These suits have usually been rejected, on the philosophical grounds that a child cannot allege that it would rather never have been born.[8] Wrongful-birth and especially wrongful-life suits also raise powerful, stigmatizing problems for disabled children and their families: In order to recover financial resources that may well make family life with a disabled child less stressful, parents and children themselves are placed in the untenable position of rejecting the value of those very lives the suits aim to compensate. Strictly speaking, those who sue for wrongful birth are saying they would rather not have had a specific child, no matter what they actually feel about that child whose life they hope to improve through a court settlement (Asch 1989, 93–95).

From a sociological point of view, two aspects of this evolving body of case law seem to be particular precipitates of American culture. The first is that individual suits are a powerful, indeed, we might argue, *the* powerful route used by consumers to pressure health care providers to improve their standards of care. On the basis of such suits, for example, the American College of Obstetricians and Gynecologists revised its recommendations for

standards of care (Pediatrics and Gynecologists 1983). The "power of consumers" (or at least those consumers who have the resources to mount lawsuits) is indeed remarkable, when compared with most Western European
countries. But the flip side of this scenario is also peculiarly North American:
Without a commitment to national health insurance or equitable access to
health care, the families of children born with disabilities are unevenly, or
often insufficiently, covered for the costs of the special medical services their
offspring's optimal development may well require. Europeans do not live in
comparably litigious societies; nor are they as vulnerable to the lack of
"safety nets" when a child with a serious disability is born.

Most Americans, of course, do not mount lawsuits in order to get better
prenatal diagnostic services. Access to those services is determined by a complex mix of factors: Local and regional availability of service providers,
including laboratories and their state and federal regulation; service costs
and their coverage by a range of third-party payment plans, including private insurance and Medicaid, which vary dramatically from state to state;
and state-based regulatory and statutory law mandating services.

In the United States, the regulation of health care has traditionally been
construed as the responsibility of the individual states. But in the 1970s,
Congress passed a variety of laws providing monies for the screening of various genetic diseases as dramatic advances in their diagnosis and treatment
became well-known. Often, such laws were a response to consumer lobby
groups representing families in which specific conditions were prevalent;
these groups enrolled congressional support for the amelioration of genetic
conditions of which they had intimate, familial knowledge. Advocates for
federal support for screening and/or treatment for Tay-Sachs disease, galactosemia, and sickle-cell anemia were quite successful in Washington during
the early 1970s (see Duster 1990; Reilly 1977). In 1976, such single-disease
legislation was collected together in the National Genetic Diseases Act,
which provided grants to the states to establish genetic services. By the early
1980s, many of the laws covering screening for specific diseases were
repealed in favor of this omnibus legislation. Under the National Genetic
Diseases Act, the secretary of Health and Human Services is still technically
empowered to give grants for research and education surrounding genetic
diseases, and to develop programs for their diagnosis, control, and treatment.
But the funds for such programs were slashed in the early years of the Rea-
gan administration and must now come out of the Maternal and Child
Health block grants, which have been cut to the bone, and are highly competitive: A cutback in the political economy of governance here disenrolled

services for genetic diseases, which have a very low priority when compared to more pressing maternal/child health needs.

Additionally, federal guidelines prohibit the use of funds to pay for abortions unless a pregnancy threatens the life of the mother or resulted from a promptly reported instance of rape or incest. These conditions are extremely unlikely to be met in general, and especially in the case of a woman choosing to abort a pregnancy in which a serious fetal disability has been diagnosed (Clayton 1993). The confluence of these factors—the Reaganizing of block grants and hostility to funding virtually any abortion with federal monies— has left individual states remarkably unfettered and unfunded in their decisions to provide or not provide genetic services, and to define (or not define) what such services might include.

By the early nineties, thirty-three states provided some sort of genetic services, ranging from newborn screening programs to comprehensive education, prenatal diagnosis, and payment plans that covered abortions. Five states explicitly covered selective abortions for fetuses diagnosed as having grave (usually, life-threatening) medical problems under their state Medicaid guidelines. Thirty-six states in principle covered some of the costs of amniocentesis under their Medicaid regulations, but very few also covered subsequent abortions should a "positive diagnosis" be made, and only six states conducted aggressive outreach activities informing poor women that prenatal health care would be covered by Medicaid. It is thus not uncommon for women who might be eligible for Medicaid-funded prenatal care, including amniocentesis if medically indicated and personally desired, not to know of their eligibility (Clayton 1993; Institute 1987). Some states have antidiscrimination statutes designed to protect those with genetic diseases and their families. Others make no provisions for protection of patient confidentiality. And very few state health departments have actually allotted funds to keep comprehensive statistics on prenatal diagnosis or genetic services.

This lack of attention to describing and evaluating genetic services at the state level is an artifact of both Reaganomic philosophy (which enjoined the states from using federal monies to keep statistics on expenditures made with health block grants), and the penurious position into which it placed them. Among its many consequences is the extreme difficulty American health planners and evaluators have in predicting the need for prenatal diagnostic services or in describing their efficacy. Once again, the contrast with European countries, which usually keep excellent national health statistics, including those covering prenatal diagnostic services, is striking. Some states have established programs (by either statute, state law, or regulation—usually through the state health department), but have imposed substantial restrictions on the use of prenatal diagnosis. Minnesota and Missouri, for example, will provide testing in many instances but abortion rarely if at all. Tennessee, which otherwise has a quite expansive program, provides that prenatal diagnosis will not be funded unless it would lead to treatment for either the pregnant woman or the child, stating that "the use of this program to abort unborn children is against the public policy of the state of Tennessee." (Clayton 1993, 41)

Thus genetic services are available in an uneven and often contradictory patchwork; in this patchwork, New York stands out as arguably one of the best-served states in the nation in terms of genetic services mandated and funded by statute, a claim to which I will return in chapter 9. Yet in general, such services depend upon state legislators' attitudes toward genetic diseases, eugenics, abortion rights, and finances, a complex and voluble mix in which prenatal diagnosis plays a small part. Legislators' enrollment in support of genetic services, in turn, depends on factors as idiosyncratic as personal experiences with disability and as political as the strength of the Right-to-Life movement in local electoral districts and campaigns.

Bioethical Commentary

These contradictory, mutually coproducing, and highly complex transformations associated with prenatal diagnosis in American life did not go unnoticed among various intellectuals, academics, social commentators, and policy analysts. Among the first voices to be raised in the discussion of prenatal diagnosis were those of bioethicists. Bioethicists are a relatively new academic hybrid, philosophers specializing in the study of ethical, legal, and social issues growing out of advances in modern medicine. Since the late 1960s, this emergent field has grown from three think tanks located in Hastings, New York, Washington, D.C., and Philadelphia, into a full-fledged national and international academic discipline, enlisting and placing trained adherents in many medical schools, philosophy departments, and interdisciplinary academic programs. It has also influenced the development of two federally funded public commissions: the National Commission for the Protection of Human Subjects of Biomedical and Behavioral Research, and the President's Commission for the Study of Ethical Problems in Medicine and Biomedical and Behavioral Research (cf. Fox 1990, 204). In 1996, after a political hiatus of Republican opposition, President Clinton named a new Bioethics Commission, which immediately tackled many complex questions that abut on genetics, including, of course, the vexed problem of cloning. Bioethics perspectives and personnel are woven into the "ethical, legal, and social issues" committee structure and funding apparatus attached to the Human Genome Project.[9] Bioethicists are often recruited by the media, make television appearances, and write news editorials concerning compelling cases in medical ethics which fascinate the public (cf. Dreifus 1996). The field has become something of a darling of the media. As a profession and a social movement, the field of bioethics has had a remarkable amount of success in shaping public awareness and debates surrounding such issues as the meaning of informed consent; problems of dependency and decision-making at both ends of the life cycle; and, most recently, the need for equitable systems of cost containment and the possibility of rationing health services as scarce goods.

Mobilizing experts from the disciplines of philosophy, theology, law, medicine, and biology, these new specialists have produced a field of discourse that is quite consonant with its American cultural roots, and self-confidently unaware of its own sociocultural context. Growing out of the American version of analytic philosophy, the perspective through which bioethicists tend to work focuses on "the value-complex of individualism, . . . the notion of contract . . . [the importance of] veracity and truth-telling . . . and 'the principle of beneficence'" (Fox 1990, 206). The field of bioethics has had less use for the social sciences, whose work they tend to reduce to numbers crunching (Fox 1990, 212–215). There has also been relatively little concern with the kind of qualitative, empirically grounded work in medical sociology or anthropology which might challenge the presumptive universality of these more abstract, analytic percepts (Fox 1990; Marshall 1992). The basic corpus of bioethical work currently exhibits a magisterial definition of American "society" as a unified field and a presumption that the impact of advances in medicine and its technologies might be universally assessed.

This stance has concrete significance for the public understanding of genetic screening and prenatal diagnosis, for the voices of bioethicists were among the first to be publicly raised on these subjects. In conferences, newsletters, and academic publications dating from the early 1970s forward, bioethicists debated such important topics as the implications for family life of choosing one's children's genes; the eugenic consequences and values of making prenatal diagnosis widely available; and the effect on society of believing that we can make perfect children (e.g., Hilton, Callahan et al. 1973; Kessler 1979; Lipkin and Rowley 1974; Lubs and de la Cruz 1977). Much of this early work culminated in a Hastings Center Genetics Research Group Report which promulgated "Guidelines for the Ethical, Social and

Legal Issues in Prenatal Diagnosis" (Powledge and Fletcher 1979). First published in the prestigious *New England Journal of Medicine* and reaffirmed in a report from the President's Commission for the Study of Ethical Problems in Medicine and Biomedical and Behavioral Research in 1983, the guidelines suggested eighteen conditions affecting the use (or potential abuse) of prenatal diagnosis to which attention should be paid. These ranged from quality control of laboratory results to parents' right to not know as well as to know the chromosomal and/or genetic makeup of fetuses at risk of diagnosable problems, to the need to protect both privacy and autonomy of testing and abortion decisions, to third-party payment coverage of these expensive services. The guidelines have been widely influential in both public discussion of prenatal diagnosis and the training of physicians and counselors involved in its practice. They have themselves become a kind of "new reproductive technology."[10]

The guidelines have provided an admirable caution against acceptance of prenatal testing as a wholly unambiguous good. They have clearly fostered increased awareness among health care professionals of the complex issues raised by this new piece of reproductive technology. But because they are couched as general "ethical, legal, and social issues," the guidelines have also been consistent with the assumptions that experts can judge what an abstract, unified social good would be. They do not, for example, call for empirical impact studies that would invite women and their supporters to discuss their experiences with this technology, or the monitoring of problem cases, or suggest that observations of the actual practices of health care providers and patients might feed back into the evolution of future guidelines. This lack of interest in the empirical, variegated reality of practices surrounding prenatal diagnosis is deeply linked to the assumptions of the fields from which bioethics experts are enlisted, on the one hand, and the tendency to dismiss grounded social studies of biomedicine as irrelevant to philosophical concerns, on the other.

It is hard to break into such a hermetic and self-confident narrative of what constitutes cutting-edge issues in the study of evolving technologies in medicine. As a marginal participant-observer at various conferences and working groups of one bioethics center on several occasions when my anthropological perspective and data were actively solicited, I have been struck by both the respectful curiosity and philosophical dismissal that met my insistence on recognizing the diversity of problems that prenatal diagnosis poses for different sociocultural groups. Despite a commendable commitment to abstract notions of distributive justice, the definition of "expert" is weighted toward representatives of powerful academic and humanist fields like philosophy, jurisprudence, and medicine. It is rare to find a social worker, nurse, or genetic counselor invited as an expert to the conferences I have attended. This means that the guests around the bioethics table tend to be disproportionately male and white, despite the fact that many practical health care workers and their patients are neither.

My point is not to abstractly criticize the traditional expertise which lies at the heart of bioethics, but rather to point to the range of practical expertise and new questions that would necessarily evolve if other, more capacious definitions were developed of who belongs "inside" an evaluation of scientific progress and problems (cf. Harding 1991). A Chinese-American medical social worker with years of grounded experience in New York's Chinatown, for example, might add rich reflection to any abstract discussion of whether prenatal diagnosis will necessarily lead to imbalances of sex ratios; a Spanish-speaking genetics counselor with long-term experience in counseling non-privileged populations might speak to the real conditions which make informed consent more or less possible in a busy clinic serving Medicaid patients. Not uncoincidentally, such experts are less likely to be exclusively drawn from the same classes, gender, or ethnic communities as the overwhelming majority of currently practicing bioethicists. Yet current commitment to universalizing abstract definitions of what constitutes a relevant bioethical problem make the inclusion of such voices relatively rare. This problem of who counts as an expert, and who gets to represent varied constituencies with practical stakes in evolving medical technologies will confront us throughout this study.

Social Movements

By the mid-1980s, other voices laid claim to some of the same terrain initially mapped by the emergent field of bioethics, articulating concerns and criticisms of the ways in which prenatal diagnosis was being routinized. Among them, two social movement constituencies stand out: Feminists concerned with the increasing medical control of women's childbirth experiences, and disability rights activists concerned about eugenic judgments and practices affecting the stigma of physical and mental difference. Both social movements are deeply involved in debates on prenatal diagnosis; both are also far from unified in the positions taken about this topic. A brief discussion of each may help us to better understand the multiple interests, claims, and enrollments staked in a routinizing technology.

For feminist activists and writers, a healthy skepticism about the burdens, as well as the benefits, of medical interventions into childbirth is long-standing (e.g., Arms 1975; Collective 1978; Ehrenreich and English 1978). Among the more negative interventions are the suppression of the female profession of midwifery in favor of the mounting prestige and power of predominantly male doctors; the removal of childbirth from home to hospital; and the increasing fragmentation of all aspects of sexuality and reproduction accompanying medical specialization (Kobrin 1966; Oakley 1984; Rothman 1982; Shaw 1974; Wertz and Wertz 1977). More recently, feminist writing has focused on the new reproductive technologies, including amniocentesis, stressing their harmful recruitment of women as guinea pigs, the profit motive which drives their advances, and a seemingly boundless male obsession to take over and control the mysteries of the female womb (Arditti, Duelli-Klein et al. 1984; Corea 1985; Corea, Duelli-Klein et al. 1987; Rothman 1989; Spallone and Steinberg 1987). The experience of having a "tentative pregnancy" (Rothman 1986) while anxiously awaiting the results of amniocentesis has been the subject of feminist criticism. Much commentary on the new reproductive technologies is available in popular women's magazines and in *Reproductive and Genetic Engineering: A Journal of International Feminist Analysis,* which provided a platform for the Feminist International Network of Resistance to Reproductive and Genetic Engineering. Founded in 1983, the group had branches in more than twenty countries until 1998, when it officially disbanded. At the risk of reducing its complex history, including a history of many political differences and splits within the organization, FINRRAGE represented an opposition to the continued spread of the new reproductive technologies on the grounds of a feminist-ecological critique. Neither women as mothers, nor Mother Earth, will benefit, in the long run, from hypertechnology in reproduction. FINRRAGE and its fellow travelers tended to regard biomedical scientists as "pharmacrats" (Corea 1985) intent on testing their ever-escalating interventions on women's bodies, and making money in the process. In FINRRAGE'S narration, a universal and victimized Earth Mother who also represents Mother Earth has the potential to resist masculinist technological rape and plunder. She is, of course, constructed as a foil against biomedicine's/bioethics' Universal Man. Passionately oppositional and fearless in calling the question(s), Universal Woman is no less a problematic epistemological, social, or political figure than Universal Man, as feminists of color have been pointing out since the beginning of second wave feminism (Beale 1970; Davis 1981; hooks 1982; Hull, Scott et al. 1982).

More recently, other voices have joined the feminist debates on the new reproductive technologies. While also skeptical about profit motives and masculine privilege in medicine and, indeed, in reproductive relations, some recent authors have assumed that science might be, or be made to be, more user-friendly to women's interests, and that those interests might themselves be fraught with tensions and contradictions. Women may, for example, desire high-tech treatment for infertility while bemoaning its risks and distortions; they may eagerly seek the "reassurance" of prenatal testing while recognizing its high psychological and social costs (e.g., Birke, Himmelweit et al. 1990; McNeil, Varcoe et al. 1990; Stanworth 1987). Another international organization founded on these insights, and dedicated to exploring differences as well as similarities in women's health care interests, has attempted to unite women struggling for reproductive rights across national boundaries. The Global Network for Reproductive Rights, which was founded in 1984 and has branches in ninety countries, tries to speak to the national and class complexity of women's experiences with technology as only one aspect of their need to win and retain reproductive autonomy. More recently, international networks for reproductive rights forged during the U.N.'s decades for women, for children, for ecology, for population, and for human rights, have led to extraordinary collaborative research, resource sharing, and policy advocacy (Correa 1994; Correa and Petchesky 1994). The substantive intellectual, political, and practical differences among these authors and activists should not obscure the audacious and creative critiques of "man's control over human reproduction" that they share.

As a participant-observer, sometimes activist, and marginal author in such debates, I find their political evolution essential and heartening. To speak, as bioethicists so often do, as if there were unproblematic unified interests in society—which allow women to be represented by men; or ordinary health consumers to rely on scientifically and humanistically trained experts to articulate their needs and protect their rights; or the aspirations of poor people around the globe for health and justice to be articulated by Western middle-class experts—glosses the lived social reality of prenatal diagnosis (or anything else). This problem is built into the way bioethical discourse has been constructed, as I have tried to indicate above. But I am also aware of a tendency among some feminists (no less than other committed experts and activists) to speak as if both women and the scientific institutions upon which we depend, which we confront, and in which we are increasingly located as researchers, technicians, and service providers, were far more unified than they actually are. Perhaps because our experiences in the women's health movement have been so closely allied with the critique of scientific assumptions and medical practices, we tend to see all health care providers as potential adversaries, despite changes at both the individual and social levels that feminism (among other forces) has helped to bring about. Perhaps because our experiences as women have been so closely elided with our status as mothers (or nonmothers), we tend to see the defense of biological naturalism as isomorphic with women's reproductive rights, despite our own criticisms of this reductive way of picturing women. Yet recent science studies scholarship describes science as an enormously heterogeneous domain, in which biology, bodies, and gendered representations and practices uneasily coconstruct one another (Clarke 1998; Haraway 1988b, 1989a,1989b, 1991, 1997; Oudshoorn 1994; Strathern 1992).

In other words, the discourses of both feminism and bioscience are fraught with polarized reductions in which scientists are too frequently represented as either heroes or villains, and women are represented as their victims or resisters. Images of pregnancy "as if" it were located exclusively in the domain of either technical medicine or timeless maternal identity both exhibit similar rhetorical errors. The seeming universality of pregnancy is continuously undermined by its concrete historical and local embeddedness. A more powerful description of the complex social conditions through which biomedicine both serves and constrains women's diverse interests, of course, lies somewhere outside of this discourse, as I hope to show throughout this book.

Feminists concerned with health care have not been the only critics of the routinization of prenatal diagnosis. Since the mid-1970s, the movement for disability rights in the United States and internationally has grown tremendously. This movement has multiple roots. The successes of medicine—especially the development and widespread use of antibiotics, and later the development of infant and then neonatal surgery—made longer lives possible for newborns, children, and young adults with disabilities, even while it often kept them defined as chronic patients. Voluntary associations, especially those organized around the interests of veterans, provided a model for health advocacy and legislative intervention. And the powerful inspiration provided by the civil rights movement's insistence upon social justice for excluded Americans also contributed to the birth of various grass-roots disability rights movements (Gliedman and Roth 1980; Miringoff 1991; Shapiro 1993).

Many disability rights advocates and groups have raised questions as feminists and for feminists concerning prenatal diagnosis, as well (e.g., Asch 1989; Finger 1984, 1990; Kaplan 1993; Saxton 1984). These constituencies contest the powerful medical definitions of disabilities that predominate in contemporary American society. The disability rights movement points out that socially constructed attitudes of stigma and prejudice, not absolute biological capacities, lie behind the segregation of disabled children and adults.

Disability rights activists frequently focus on legal and policy solutions to their constituencies' problems, and the rhetoric and strategies of the civil rights movement have influenced successful lobbying for a series of federal laws since the mid-1970s. These include Section 504 of the National Rehabilitation Act of 1973, the Education for All Handicapped Act of 1975, and the Americans with Disabilities Act of 1990. These laws explicitly deployed models developed in the battles against racial discrimination to mandate access to education, housing, employment, and public facilities for disabled citizens (Miringoff 1991, 45–46; Scotch 1984; Shapiro 1993). The movement contains many divided allies and is continually debating such questions as the relation of mental to physical disabilities, and the ethics of prenatal diagnosis for any or all disability. But virtually all members of and advocates for disabled groups insist on a wider social, rather than a narrower medical, definition of the problems they confront.

This position is enormously persuasive on moral and social grounds. But it also has a certain irony, for it is based on a truth that medicine itself helped to produce. Prior to antibiotics, infant surgery, and deinstitutionalization, children with Down syndrome had a mortality rate of more than 50 percent in their first years. "Spina bifida" is a relatively new label that agglomerates diverse open neural tube defects (encephalocele, hydrocephalus, myelomeningocele, anencephaly), most of which led to stillbirth or newborn death until the 1950s, when neonatal surgery, especially shunting for hydrocephalus, was developed. The medical practices that saved such newborns also constructed them as permanent and incurable patients, trapped in a discourse of medical management. It has taken competing voices—from the disability rights movement, the family support networks, the professional "special education" sector—to contest the powerful medical definition of disability (e.g., Featherstone 1980; Gliedman and Roth 1980; Hahn 1988; Scotch 1984; Seligman and Darling 1989; Shapiro 1993). We will return to these perspectives on the social and medical construction of disabilities in chapter 10. For now, it is sufficient to note that new actors and a new social terrain have emerged in large measure under the influence of new technoscientific practices, sometimes enrolling themselves to contest the very conditions that in part gave birth to them.

At the intersection of the disability rights movement and the feminist movement for reproductive rights lies a thorny problem: How is it possible to contest the eugenic and stigmatizing definition of disabilities which seems to underlie prenatal diagnosis, while still upholding the rights of individual women to determine what kind of medical care, and what sorts of pregnancy decisions, are in their own best interests? Can there be both legitimate public criticisms of some of the assumptions which drive prenatal diagnosis, and support for the abortion decisions women who have chosen the test then make? Can public policy encompass a position of support for disabled children and their families at the same time that it supports women who use prenatal diagnosis and abortion to avoid giving birth to children with some disabilities? If we are to support both a woman's right to use prenatal diagnosis as well as the rights of disabled people, how do we then protect ourselves against insurance companies and employers practicing genetic discrimination? Such questions increasingly influence the language of health care legislation at both the state and federal levels, and the guidelines promulgated under the Americans with Disabilities Act of 1990 (Billings, Kohn et al. 1992; Greely 1992; Holtzman 1989; Natowicz and Alper 1992; Nelkin and Tancredi 1989).

Divided interests in all their heterogeneous diversity lie at the heart of this newly emergent issue; without the social movements, medical advances, and legal struggles whose coproduced histories I have attempted to sketch in this chapter, the intersection where prenatal diagnosis is located would not have been constructed. The very existence of a public conversation concerning eugenics, disability rights, and pro-choice feminism presumes that differences among women—as mothers and potential mothers of children with disabilities, and as disabled women with adequate health insurance and social services, and those without—are built into the permanent nature of both the stigma and the empowerment to which prenatal diagnosis speaks. Ironically, in the United States, this same conversation also presumes that these problems are contradictory; we lack viable narratives to encapsulate this complexity both collectively and individually.[11] These conflicts can be described philosophically, politically, sociologically and personally (e.g., Annas and Elias 1992; Asch and Fine 1984, 1988; Finger 1984, 1990; Kitcher 1996; Saxton 1984). A wider social recognition of their complexity is just emerging (cf. Berube 1996). Public awareness is undoubtedly shaped by media representations of the aspirations, rights, and struggles of disabled Americans like those that occurred in the popular TV family drama series, *Life Goes On*, which featured a teenager with Down syndrome in the late 1980s and early 1990s. What did American viewers make of the episode, for example, in which the very loving and sensible mother of that teenager chose to have amniocentesis in a subsequent pregnancy? What was she saying about her values and the value of her son when she explained to him, and to millions of TV viewers, that she would never have chosen for him to have so many extra struggles in his life? How and why are we led to see the actor's double role as mother and pregnant woman as in conflict, rather than "simply" expressing the complexities of contemporary reproductive and family life? These intertwined issues and their representations—in media, in law, in medicine, and above all, in the lives of pregnant women and their supporters—thread their way through many of the subsequent chapters.

Of course, the technological history, legal contexts, and expert and political debates that I have been describing are inscribed inside the routinized practices through which prenatal diagnosis now operates. To understand the social impact of this new reproductive technology, we need to do more than sketch its history and the complex social and political stakes in its dissemination. We need to focus on its effects in play. How was the lay public enrolled to an appreciation of both the technical aspects and shifting implications of prenatal diagnosis? What did pregnant women need to know before they could "choose" (or refuse) amniocentesis? How are the eugenic and liberating aspects of prenatal testing both presented and suppressed in routine medical discussions? To answer these questions, we need to explore the production and labors of genetic counselors, members of a new allied health profession who translate technical aspects of genetic testing for the lay public. The history and practice of this interpretive work as it enrolls pregnant women for prenatal diagnosis are the subject of chapter 3.

3
The Communication of Risk

Once I counseled an Orthodox couple. They'd had three miscarriages; they came in to find out if there was a genetic problem for all
that loss. Maybe there was a translocation,[12] or some other reason for
the miscarriages. But they told me right away that they wouldn't con-
tracept or abort if there was a problem, so I asked them, "Why do you
want this information?" The wife said, "I'm sure there's something
wrong with me, and I want you to tell me what." The husband said,
"I'm sure there's something wrong with me, but I don't want to know
about it." Both said, "We don't want to involve our families, they don't
need to know. We just need to know as a couple.". . . Genetic counselors, we're in the business of searching for bad news and giving it to
whoever needs it, whoever can tolerate it. (E.R., genetic counselor)

IN 1969, PROGRAM DEVELOPERS at Sarah Lawrence College in Bronxville,
New York, planned a new master's-level science degree, and ten "returning"
women were its first students. Two years later, the first formally trained
genetic counselor was born. "Genetic counseling," a label coined in 1947,
initially stood for a position of ethical neutrality, favoring personal choice in
the century-old eugenics debate about society's responsibility to encourage
or discourage reproduction in certain individuals and families. While geneticist Sheldon Reed, who coined the phrase, undoubtedly believed in the
moral superiority of the position he was trying to map, older scientific practices assumed that experts should give directive advice in order to promote
racial improvement (Paul 1986, 1995; Paul and Spencer 1995).

   Eugenics was defined by its founder, Francis Galton, as "the science of
improvement of the human germ plasm through better breeding" (cited in
Paul 1986, 27). As a worldview, it fascinated adherents of both the left and

right, enrolling many nineteenth-century feminists and socialists among its members. Its followers considered that "imbeciles" and "mental defectives" were the products of recessive matings, and responsible for a goodly portion of society's ills. Eugenicists focused on mental traits like "feeblemindedness" because they believed that problems like low intelligence, poverty, crime, and alcoholism were directly passed down through family lineage. Inbreeding and the general reproduction of inferior stock were threatening to swamp society with inherited social ills. By the turn of the century, when the Mendelian rules of genetic transmission had been rediscovered and were highly influential if controversial, complex forms of mental "deviancy" were considered by most eugenicists to be "unit traits"—that is, they were thought to be inherited as a single package. Thus the problem of "mental defectives" was viewed as potentially enormous; after all, known "imbeciles" represented only the tip of the iceberg of conditions that many believed were endemic to the lower classes and to immigrants (Paul 1995, 1998).

In light of contemporary eugenic theory, two seemingly normal carriers of a submerged trait could mate to produce a degenerate or recessive offspring. In this case, the "recessive" individual might well express characteristics thought to belong to an older or lower stage of racial development. Not only were "races" immutably ranked; throwbacks within higher races reflected the lower orders. It is not accidental, then, that the condition we now call "Down syndrome" was initially labeled "mongolism." According to Gould, Down's description of "Caucasian idiots," as akin to African, Malay, American Indian, and Oriental peoples, reflected his belief that they represented an atavism toward a more "primitive" type of individual. Down believed that these individuals "had arrests of development" and that their mental deficiency was due to a "retention of traits and abilities that would be judged normal in adults of lower races" (Gould 1980, 164, cited in Lippman and Brunger 1991).

Eradicating the reproduction of such individuals through suasion (especially in England) and sterilization legislation (especially in the United States) was one of the movement's chief goals. The other was to encourage those of "good stock" to reproduce more copiously and self-consciously, to combat the "takeover" of the population by the "submerged tenth" who produced its social problems (Paul 1986). Triumphalist eugenics of the later nineteenth and early twentieth centuries had envisioned a world in which "high-quality" individuals were encouraged to reproduce ("positive" eugenics), and "low-quality" stock was discouraged, or even actively prevented, from bearing additional children ("negative" eugenics). While the scientific and applied aspects of the eugenics movement were fraught with debates and differences, its basic practical orientation lent itself to extreme biological reductionism through a focus on stocks or races: Disadvantaged or stigmatized groups were easily described as immutably responsible for their own problems due to their heredity (Beckwith 1993; Kevles 1985; Paul 1995). Eugenicists focused on what they took to be the most obvious sign of racial inferiority: low intelligence.

Despite the many differences between turn-of-the-century eugenics and contemporary genetic counseling, the focus on mental retardation persists, constituting an icon in which both the history of the field and the cultural meaning of "bad" heredity are condensed. And the elision of putative "low intelligence" with "race" runs through public discourse and policy debates that replay themselves across many generations, as recent controversies surrounding *The Bell Curve* should remind us. Down syndrome is a contemporary scientific label which barely hides a prior racial nomenclature—"mongolism"—and its racial assumptions. "Mongolism" continues to index mental retardation, thus conflating a history of Eurocentric racial hierarchy with a stigmatized disabling condition. This is a problem to which we return in chapter 10.

The heyday of direct, flagrant assumptions and institutions promoting social Darwinist "positive" and "negative" group eugenics was, of course, eclipsed by reactions to Nazism throughout the world. More subtle versions of eugenic ideologies continue to proliferate in ways that will be discussed later in this study. But the more blatant forms of this problematic ideology were gradually dispersed into other areas of evolutionary thinking, both scientific (e.g., aspects of sociobiology and evolutionary psychology) and popular (e.g., the widespread belief in "criminal" genes). As genetics developed as a science, eugenics was replaced by an applied individual and familial counseling model: "Reform eugenics . . . encourage[d] the use of genetics for medical purposes and to improve the biological quality of human populations . . . [by] the establishment of facilities devoted explicitly to genetic advisory services" (Kevles 1985, 71–72, 1992; Reed 1974). At pioneering clinics at the Universities of Michigan and Minnesota in the 1940s, geneticists set up counseling bureaux using basic Mendelian methods and family pedigrees to predict recurrences of hereditary diseases for affected families concerned about their chances. While a condition as dramatic and devastating as Tay-Sachs disease followed Mendelian rules of autosomal recessive transmission, and its risk of recurrence could therefore be accurately predicted as one in four for each pregnancy, most conditions that brought concerned family members to the clinics had more complex modes of transmission and expression. By using extensive pedigrees collected from families in which several members suffered from the same disease or syndrome, geneticists made predictions, but their counseling was "certainly a very imperfect art even in the hands of the very best of us," as one geneticist put it as late as 1958 (Kevles 1985, 75). Early medical genetic counseling thus focused on individuals and families, rather than on outmoded notions of "race" or "stock."

The Invention of the Genetic Counselor

In the post–World War II period, just before the invention of the modern genetic counselor at Sarah Lawrence, research pediatricians, geneticists, immune biologists—that is, medical doctors and researchers, the majority of whom were men—would counsel families with genetically disabled members about recurrence risks and disease management. Most had M.D. or combined M.D./Ph.D. degrees, and envisioned counseling as an adjunct service to other research and disease management. Once amniocentesis developed as a clinical service, the need for an "interface" also developed—someone to convey the risks and benefits of the test, to translate scientific possibilities into personal calculations for potential patients. That gatekeeper between science and social work, between epidemiology and empathy, became a woman. Women students seemed especially suited to a field that was designed to counsel pregnant women. And counseling was a field in which "female qualities" like empathic listening seemed particularly appropriate. Not uncoincidentally, an emergent women's field backed by a two-year professional training degree slotted its occupants into the medical hierarchy with far less prestige and pay than the male researchers and physicians whose episodic counseling they replaced (Rothman and Detlefs 1988). In the early years of the development of genetic counseling degree programs, there was extensive discussion of whether an advanced medical or research degree was desirable or necessary to the process (e.g., Lustig and Poskanzer 1976; Powledge 1979; Reilly 1979), and plans for mounting Ph.D. programs in genetic counseling and administration continue to attract attention among the current generation of counselors and administrators (Doyle 1996; Scott, Walker et al. 1987; Walker, Scott et al. 1990). But over the last twenty years, as amniocentesis has proliferated and become a routine medical service, the role of the M.S.-holding genetic counselor has also become routinized. The first wave of genetic counselors, reflecting the wealthy, white suburban community around Sarah Lawrence, were mostly well-educated homemakers living near the college, often wives of doctors, lawyers, and businessmen. Many had raised their children and were ready to go back to school. They brought with them enormous resourcefulness and a specific set of upper-middle-class family values. The program promised an amalgam of hard science and counseling skills, while also holding out the possibility of part-time work.

Genetic counseling quickly became a profession in formation (Dicker and Dicker 1978; Kenen 1984, 1986; Rollnick 1984). While Sarah Lawrence remains the largest and perhaps the most respected program in the country, there are now twenty-seven other training programs in North America, twenty-four in the United States, and three in Canada. Most programs require two years' study. While the curriculum varies somewhat, all provide training in human genetics, medical genetics, counseling skills, and supervised clinical internships. Some programs include seminars on bioethics or ethical issues in genetic counseling, with a strong orientation toward individual choice. According to the counselors I have interviewed, however, there was not much discussion of the cultural constraints and resources within which different pregnant women and their families (or counselors themselves) may be operating in their training. Indeed, a shift toward "group thinking" may be resisted by counselors who have been taught to distance themselves and their profession from an earlier, problematic history that assigned inferior heredity to specific races and stocks. Those who responded to my questions were trained between twenty-five and five years ago. More recently, two programs—one at Brandeis University, the other at the University of California at Berkeley—have made special efforts to incorporate sensitivity to disability rights and ethnocultural differences into counselor training. They serve as models to the expanding numbers of counselor training programs which have recently opened, or are about to open, in this growing field.[13]

It is hard to build a more cultural and social perspective into the training of counselors. In a survey that focused on training counselors to serve an increasingly multicultural urban client population (Punales-Morejon and Rapp 1991, 1993), questionnaires were sent to the heads of the fifteen genetic counselor training programs that existed then and to fifty of their graduates running services who were particularly committed to reaching underserved, predominantly minority and immigrant populations. Our survey results suggest that perceptions of what is both necessary and possible may be hard to reconcile. Most program directors and all frontline counselors agree that materials on patients' cultural backgrounds, especially reproductive beliefs, aspirations, and practices as they vary among ethnocultural groups, should be incorporated into the curriculum, preferably in the first year. But the problem of "teaching the teachers" is substantial: Instructors, many of whom hold part-time appointments in the counseling programs, do not necessarily have the time or resources to learn a subject matter which abuts on medical anthropology or cross-cultural counseling. Moreover, the need for language training (especially, but not exclusively, in Spanish) is also profound. Program heads confront a difficult situation in instituting curriculum reform: In the midst of the DNA revolution, the amount of basic science their graduates must master is enormous and rapidly growing. They cannot easily envision adequate space to add more sociocultural training. Many counselors, on the other hand, feel that they can keep up with the science, but were never given the tools to keep up with the cultural differences they now encounter (see also Weil and Mittman 1993; Smith, Warren et al. 1993).

This problem reflects more than a difference of opinion: The counseling protocol developed from the early 1970s onward assumes the stability of "the individual" or "the couple" as a universal decision-making unit. The assumptions of the counseling protocol are, as one program head pointed out, highly reactive against the directive nature of earlier, eugenic-influenced advising. Current models tend to be based on neo-Freudian and Rogerian psychology, framed as a crisis intervention. Counselors explore patients' reactions to difficult situations, helping them to clarify values presumed to underlie the feelings they express. Counseling orientation is determinedly value-neutral: A counselor should, as a matter of principle, support whatever decisions regarding testing and pregnancy outcome that a woman or a couple makes. Implicitly, the pregnant woman is counseled as if her choices were individual, unconstrained by larger constellations of kinship and community, and as if her male partner were most likely to be appropriately available and supportive of communication concerning pregnancy. Thus the woman herself, or the couple into which she is easily elided, are pictured as an autonomous decision-making unit. The assumptions of individual or coupled free choice and value neutrality closely mirror dominant American values and deserve examination.

Feminist psychologists, ethicists, and political theorists have long argued about the importance and limitations of an ethic of free-choice individualism as a normative goal for women's lives. There is a tension between the pursuit of individual liberties for women (especially when such liberties have long been assigned to men) and the recognition that a "male" view of individual rights may be more socially disconnected than is ideally or practically desirable. The critique of individualism as male has particular problems, for it often ignores or minimizes differences among women based on their racial, ethnic, religious, and class backgrounds. Women from some communities may have struggled for precisely those individual rights that other women now criticize as "male." Others may value their connection to men (and people of many generations) as the core of the identity from which their values and decision-making take their shape. Some feminists might reply that what is needed is both respect for the different experiences among women, and a thorough investigation of the patriarchal aspects of many communities' control over women's reproductive decision-making (Correa and Petchesky 1994; Petchesky 1995; Purdy 1996; Williams 1991). Inherent in this philosophical debate is a very practical problem of forging alliances across differences, when the defense or extension of both individual rights and community resources is on the political agenda, for example, in mobilizing to defend abortion rights, or access for disabled children to educational resources, or designing and extending relatively low-cost, high-quality health care and child care. Understanding these community-based differences might well augment counselors' abilities to communicate with women from backgrounds different than their own.

The counselor's goal of value neutrality is a thorny one. It is hard to argue for the neutrality of a technology explicitly developed to identify and hence eliminate fetuses with problem-causing chromosomes (and, increasingly, genes): The biomedical and public health interests behind the development and routinization of the technology itself evaluate such fetuses as expendable. Ethicists and counselors are surely right to respond that parents of such potentially atypical fetuses have a right to know as well as to not know about the chromosomal status of their fetus, and to use the information however they may wish, whether that means preparing for the birth of a child with special needs or ending the pregnancy. But the very existence and routinization of the technology implies anything but neutrality. It assumes that scientific and medical resources should be placed in the service of prenatal diagnosis and potential elimination of fetuses bearing chromosome problems. In principle, then, counselors are trained to offer a value-charged technology in a value-neutral manner.

The practical problems of value neutrality are even more complex when the cross-cultural nature of genetic counseling is taken into account. Some individuals and populations may not want what they perceive to be the burden of individual choice: To them, the doctor (or "his" stand-in, the counselor) is shirking responsibility by not directing the patient toward the appropriate choice. Several Haitian women for whom I translated at counseling sessions, for example, were adamant in commenting, "'suis pas medecin" ("I'm not the doctor") when asked how they evaluated information on prenatal testing. Others may find the assumption that the individual woman (alone, or with her spouse) is responsible for decision-making unreasonable; in their communities, elder kin have an important, often determining, role to play in reproductive life. This is surely the case for some Chinese women sent for counseling, most dramatically if they are recent immigrants and/or speak little or no English.[14] Recent immigrants from the former Soviet Union and East European countries, too, sometimes express discomfort with the burdens of individual "choice": In their experience, medical experts attached to the national health system are expected to interpret complex facts and recommend appropriate treatment strategies. Urban counselors have, of course, encountered clients for whom the model of value-neutral decision-making does not work very well. Their experiences are reflected later in this chapter. Some have expressed the need to build awareness of this problem into their training.

But adding courses in ethnic or cultural diversity is made difficult in counselor training programs because professional demands profoundly influence the limits of curriculum. The escalating amount of scientific expertise for which counselors are responsible is obviously a direct requirement for employment. Graduates of the twenty-four programs must be "board eligible," which means that they are, in principle, qualified to sit for boards, including sections on human genetics, medical genetics, statistics, embryology, and biochemistry. The board examination is conducted by the National Society for Genetic Counceling. Before taking the exam, they must have passed master's-level course work in a certified program and completed at least fifty supervised counseling cases.

The National Society of Genetic Counselors (NSGC) estimates that there are currently about one thousand practicing genetic counselors, including those who have completed a two-year M.S. program and served supervised internships, as well as those "grandfathered" (in this case, "grandmothered") into the profession through prior genetics experience in nursing, social work, and related fields (Doyle 1996). While the number of trained counselors is growing annually, the expanding availability of prenatal diagnostic technology in the context of escalating efforts to map the entire human genome makes clear that there will be a shortage of counselors over the coming decades.

As professional development has evolved, so has the student body. Current students and recent graduates are less likely to have attended elite women's colleges, are more likely to have considered a pre-med track and rejected it, and are slightly more diverse in class, ethnic, and racial background than the first wave of graduates. While consciousness of minority issues in counseling is growing, the numbers of NSGC counselors from African-American, Hispanic, or Asian-American backgrounds remains small—not more than 6 percent. The first NSGC workshop on "counseling

the culturally different" was conducted by a team of minority genetic counselors at the annual meetings in 1985 (Biesecker, Magyari et al. 1987). At that
time, members of that team estimated that no more than thirty minority
counselors were trained and practicing nationally, although the situation
may now be changing (Doyle 1996; Smith, Warren et al. 1993). Both the definition of "minority" and of "practicing" are open to interpretation, however. Latin Americans from privileged backgrounds, for example, become
minorities when they enter the American system of racial and ethnic stratifi-
cation. And several "minority" counselors have successfully moved into medical schools or health care administration for reasons they describe as both
political and financial.

But some aspects of genetic counselor recruitment remain unchanged.
Genetic counseling is still very much a "woman's field." And many younger
counselors express frustration that the first generation of counselors were not
only females, but relatively well-to-do homemakers who they believe were
willing to work for "pin money." Had men been included among the counseling pioneers, they reason, pay scales would now be much higher. Men are
scarce in the world of genetic counseling: About 5 percent of the graduates
of genetic counseling programs are men, and many of those are employed in
administration. As the female director of counseling services in one program
put it, "Men just use genetic counseling to jump into administration. If a
man got hired here, he'd want my job." Several seasoned counselors
expressed great ambivalence about the capacities and limits of men in the
profession. "Men aren't sensitive to counseling issues, to the anxiety of pregnancy," one said. "Science, that's just information; the skilled part of this job
is in the female psyche. Oh, it might work here at Middle Hospital, they're
[hospital staff] well organized. But imagine him at City, where we work in an
examining room, and women run around half-dressed. What would we do
with a man?" Despite their consciousness of male-dominant biases affecting
their own professional standing and pay, counselors are hardly immune to
gender stereotypes. But the questions this counselor is raising—whether men
are by nature or training less empathic than women, whether identification
with similar bodies is necessary to provide the best pregnancy counseling; in
other words, "Why can't a man be more like a woman?"—reverberate inside
all counseling skills. There is some evidence that women patients feel their
questions are more directly and deeply addressed when the counselor is also
a woman (Zare, Sorenson et al. 1984). But the vast literature on communication between counselors and clients suggests profound chasms separating
their various agendas and accomplishments that are not dependent on the
sex of the service provider (Kessler 1989; Lippman 1989; Wertz and Fletcher

1987; Wertz and Sorenson 1986; Wertz, Sorenson et al. 1986). What makes counselor-client communication so problematic? To explore possible answers to that question, I will first describe both the structure and content of counseling sessions.

The Counseling Session

In the state of New York, a genetic counseling session almost always precedes the use (or refusal) of amniocentesis.[15] Counselors meet with their pregnant patients (and any supporters the woman brings with her) in the hospital where the test is offered. Some genetic counselors work only individually, while others present background information to a group, and then collect personal health histories from each group participant privately. In very busy City Hospitals, the individual intake may be done before or after the group session, with many people in the same room, as there is no time or space for privacy. In the course of an hour's visit, counselors convey a great deal of medico-scientific information, ask and answer questions, and prepare women to take the test. The interaction is conversational: In a session, meanings are actively and interactively produced by patients and counselors together.

But the discourse of genetic counseling is resolutely medico-scientific, revealing and creating some meanings, which mask or silence others. Medical language commands great authority in the interview. While many counselors modulate their discussion of genetics according to their assessment of an individual client's scientific background as I describe below, there is still a profound potential gap built into much of their communication process. Genetic counselors are inherently bilinguals, raised in one language community, but having acquired science as a second language. While this is undoubtedly true for many health care providers, not all speak a dialect of science as resolutely specialized, statistical, and rapidly evolving as do members of the genetics community. Genetic counselors learn to speak about risk figures and DNA probes with fluency, and their specialized vocabulary is always expanding. As one workshop leader at a counseling conference pointed out, "We all speak in anagrams [acronyms]. Can you remember when you learned to talk about LMP, AMA, TOP, FISH, PCRs, RFLPs? And when you learned to stop talking about RFLPs [a gene-splicing technology that quickly became obsolete]?" Not only do counselors science-speak; they also lay claim to words which appear to have commonsense meanings, reassigning them specialized ones. Thus, a "positive family history," an "uneventful pregnancy," or "unremarkable family background," even the concept of "reassurance" or the notion of "ethnic background" hold specific meanings in counseling discourse. Often, these invert commonsense understandings: A "positive family history," for example, is anything but, as it refers to the presence of a serious, genetically transmissible condition. It is rare that a woman codes her own pregnancy as "uneventful," although this label marks the counselor's assessment that no further testing is indicated. "Ethnic background" for a genetic counselor has nothing to do with community traditions or tastes. Rather, it marks certain populations as "at elevated risk" for specific diseases.

Moreover, the terminology of genetics comes attached to a scientific worldview which suggests that adjusting the material world to human aspirations is a positive goal. This positive evaluation of intervention into the biological conditions of human life is shared by many, but certainly not all, of the pregnant women and their supporters sent for genetic counseling. Miscommunication as well as communication, silence as well as conversation may thus characterize a genetic counseling appointment, as patients and professionals negotiate arcane idioms as well as core cultural issues.

These communicative scripts are played out in routine interactions. Every counselor develops an opening statement with pregnant patients with three goals in mind. The first is to convey significant information about the risks of birth defects and the availability and nature of amniocentesis: Here, the counselor's fund of knowledge dominates the interaction. The second is to take an individual and family health history: Here, the patient's knowledge is central, but it is normatively organized by the counselor's medical protocols. The third is to communicate with the patient well enough that her questions and concerns can be addressed, and this problem shapes all aspects of the counseling interaction, especially the code-switching to which I repeatedly refer in the examples below. By "code-switching," I mean to foreground the ability and perceived necessity of counselors (or anyone else) to move from one language framework—statistical, biomedical, familial, colloquial—to another, adjusting the message to the speaker's perceptions of who the listener might be.[16]

In laying out their first goal, that is, conveying significant information about the risks of birth defects and the availability of prenatal testing, genetic counselors must become science educators, for the information they want to present is unfamiliar, or only partially familiar, to most of their clients. In order to effectively present the background to prenatal testing, most counselors adjust their standard speeches to the audiences they are accustomed to serving.

To a group of clinic patients at City Hospital:

Each time a woman gets pregnant, there is a 2 to 3 percent chance of a birth defect. Now nobody likes to talk about birth defects, but we're here today talking about them because there's something you can do to prevent some of them.

Have you heard of genes? Genes are the hereditary units. We all inherit many things from each of our parents: The way we look,the way we act, the way our bodies function.

But every woman has to make up her own mind if she wants to take this test. Today, we just talk, no needles. That's what counseling means.

At Middle Hospital, both the seriousness and reassuring nature of the test are stressed:

This procedure is designed to pick up birth defects. Mostly, we give out good news and reassurance, but occasionally, we pick up something that will make you confront a very hard decision. . . . But remember, no matter what her age, a woman's chances are always in favor of producing a healthy baby.

At Middle, the counselor is likely to present the group with richer technical descriptions and metaphorical elaborations:

Chromosomes are the basic units of heredity, carrying all the information on physical and mental makeup of their individuals. Genes are contained within chromosomes, and genes are made up of DNA. If your heredity is a library, then chromosomes are the volumes, and the pages and chapters are genes. There are forty-six volumes to the set. This is a karyotype. It's a picture of chromosomes enlarged eight thousand times and put into order. To be normal, you need to have forty-six chromosomes in all the cells of your body. To an untrained eye, chromosomes look like sticks or caterpillars in the microscope.

Chromosomes are like a string of pearls. The genes are on that string. Our genes determine everything about us—our hair, our eyes, how tall we grow. They're even starting to say that our personality is genetic. So you can see how important chromosomes are. Look at the number on your chart: That number, forty-six, is very important. Any wrong number causes serious problems mentally, neurologically, physically, from having too much or too little genetic information.

Inside these descriptions, many kinds of work are being done. Metaphors are being used to move a potentially distant object closer, supplying known images to substitute for unknown (or incompletely known) objects of discussion: Books, pearls, and caterpillars are easier to envision than the squiggly lines on the karyotype, which shows chromosomes paired and size-ordered. In such "user-friendly" descriptions, the authority of science is also being conveyed. Some scientific information quickly becomes more technical, but counselors are convinced that its importance merits detailed elaboration:

The first part of the test consists of a sonogram. Now, how many of you have already had a sonogram? We use the sonogram for three reasons: To date the pregnancy is the first one. If you measure the long bones of the fetus and its head circumference, you get a date which is accurate to within three days of how old the pregnancy is. Second, we look at the fetus to rule out any serious anatomical problems in the extremities, the spinal chord, the abdominal wall, head and brain. Third, we can locate a pocket of fluid with the sonogram, so we know where to insert the needle.

Technical information flows rapidly: The rare reasons that a test might need to be repeated are mentioned, and potential complications are described in some detail. These include the small but real risk of a test-induced miscarriage.[17] At Elite, this information is often handed out in printed form for patients to carry away and study. At Middle, it is given orally, and counselors stress its seriousness. At City, counselors certainly describe potential problems, but they are not likely to stress them. As one counselor said, "Why frighten them more than necessary? They're already a little overwhelmed by all this new information. The bottom line is just knowing that a miscarriage is a slight but real possibility with this test. Nothing else is going to help them to make up their minds."

One interpretation of the Middle and Elite counselors' stress on repeat tests and complications as well as potential miscarriages is that their patients begin the sessions better informed in scientific terms and are therefore ready to hear the complexity. Less charitable explanations might focus on the fact that Elite clients are more likely to be lawyers or to come from other litigation-prone professional backgrounds, or that the pregnancies of the poor are not as highly valued by medical service providers as those of the rich. But as one counselor pointed out, when describing the risk of miscarriage to her City patients, "This risk is very small; in fact, scientists might say it's statistically insignificant. But we know that no one's pregnancy is insignificant, and you're concerned about *any* problems this test might cause."

There is a fine line upon which any interpretation of the meaning of counselors' code-switching among audiences rests. It is appropriate and effective to simplify a complex message for nonscience speakers, assuring that central information is accessible. But such a strategy also diminishes the base of information upon which decision-making rests: Nonscience speakers get less scientific information than their more privileged pregnant peers, and this is a small piece of what reproduces their disadvantaged position. Counselors are thus caught between being effective and being thorough, between giving too little or too much. While counselors must assess and solve this problem individually in each case, its structural antecedents are not amenable to individual solution, for they lie in the complex intersections of class background and education resources within which openness to scientific literacy is forged.

Interpreting Risk

Much of the scientific information that counselors want to convey is technical and invisible. Most counselors therefore work with visual aids, especially with less educated patients, attempting to map with charts, graphs, and karyotypes what patients cannot see for themselves. When highly enlarged, paired, and ordered, the forty-six human chromosomes on didactic display can easily be identified by number and size as normal or abnormal. When a problem is detected, its description can be keyed to such visual images. Many counselors also show pictures of children with Down syndrome, and almost all discuss the sonogram accompanying amniocentesis, in which "you can see the baby moving around."

Developed to present the mysteries of the womb, the workings of heredity, and the universe of epidemiology graphically, such icons of professional knowledge are not, to be sure, self-evident. They require interpretation during which health professionals not only reveal some of their arcane wisdom but also shape the perceptions of the client. Sonograms are constructed on a terrain which is shot through with power differences in both personal and institutional terms (cf. Petchesky 1987; Rapp 1998; Stabile 1992).

> I saw the sonogram of the twins, and I was thrilled. But I really couldn't read it, I didn't know what it meant. They had to interpret it

for you, to say, "Here's a heart, these are arms." Afterwards, it made me queasy—they made the babies real for me by telling me what was there. If they hadn't interpreted, it would have just been gray blobs, and now I'm more frightened to get the results of the amnio back. (Daphne McCarle, 41, Irish-American college professor)

It was nothing, really, it looked like nothing. Then they showed it to me, and made it something. (Ileana Mendez, 37, Ecuador-born baby-sitter)

That baby was so active, jumping around, I swear it was mugging for the camera. But I couldn't tell what was what. I know somebody's in there, but I don't know who. (Lauren Smith, 39, Anglo-American lawyer)

As a counselor, I consider it my job to accompany my patients to everything. The sonographer here at City is a right-to-lifer. When he knows someone has a positive diagnosis, that they are going to abort, he hands them a photo of the fetus. Imagine being forced to take it, to take that picture, when you know the pregnancy is Down's, you know you're going to abort! (Felicia Arcana, 50, South American–born genetic counselor)

While sonograms and their interpretations provide dramatic evidence of the power of visualization in prenatal testing, the language of genetic counseling is, above all, resolutely statistical. And statistics, like medical terminology, is a genre of communication, not simply a neutral vocabulary. It is an axiom of good counseling that a patient must be told her risks before she can decide to take or refuse the test. Yet statistics implies an abstract mathematical universe that may not be shared by clients who have little formal schooling. The majority of genetic counselors confront this problem by simplifying the numbers and adding information if it is requested:

To someone perceived as unable to handle numbers, often at City Hospital: "At your age, the risk of having a baby with mongolism is about one in a hundred."

To someone perceived as not scientifically educated, but attentive, at City or Middle Hospitals: "Pregnant ladies your age have a one in 106 chance of having a baby with this condition. That means that of every

106 pregnant ladies your age, 105 will have no problems, and one will have a child with the problem."

To someone perceived as scientifically sophisticated, at Middle or Elite Hospitals: "At 35, a woman's risk of bearing a live born child with Down syndrome is one in 385; at 40, it increases to one in 106; at 45, it is one in thirty."

Likewise, miscarriage rates following amniocentesis must be shared by using probabilities.

This is a very safe test, but there's always *some* risk to any test in medicine. The risk of losing the baby after amnio is very small, but it isn't zero.

Amnio adds three miscarriages per one thousand to those having the test. Of one thousand women your age sixteen weeks pregnant who don't have amniocentesis, thirty-two will not have a live born child at the end of the pregnancy, through miscarriage or stillbirth. Of one thousand women who have the test, thirty-five will lose the pregnancy.

One extremely experienced counselor at City Hospital often added, "Remember, one in a bigger group is a smaller chance." I observed other context-sensitive counselors searching for usable metaphors for low-income Spanish speakers. To a Dominican couple, both carriers for sickle-cell anemia, and therefore at 25 percent risk of producing a child with sickle-cell disease in each pregnancy, the counselor said: "This is like flipping coins. Each flip of the coin is independent, but if you flip enough times, half will be heads, and half tails. Here, it's one in four tails. Not one-half, but one in four."

Another counselor said of advanced maternal age:

It's like crossing a street with each pregnancy, and when you are older, it's a little easier to be hit by a car. But suppose there is a traffic light. Then, you want to cross on the green. This test puts you back to the green light. Oh, you might still get hit by a crazy hit-and-run driver, but it's not too likely. At the red light [without the test], your age makes you a more likely target for an accident.

The use of lively and familiar metaphors, code switching, and simplification of numbers are examples of health education. They mark the counselors' attempts to convey objective information. But the seeming objectivity of numbers is continually undermined by their subjective interpretation. From the patient's point of view, any risk may feel like either 100 percent or zero, depending on prior experience (Lippman-Hand and Fraser 1979a, 1979b). Statistics may offer a comfortable framework for information-seeking, medically compliant patients, especially those with some advanced education (read: middle-class), but they often gloss over the lived reality of less privileged women. As one savvy genetic counselor queried,

> How do we convey a chromosome risk when a low-income pregnant Afro–Puerto Rican woman experiences a 100 percent chance of running out of food stamps this month, a 25 percent risk of having one son or brother die in street violence, and an 80 percent chance of getting evicted by the end of the year? A one-in-180 chance of having a child with a chromosome abnormality at age 35 is probably the best odds she's facing.

What looms large for the counselor may seem quite small to the pregnant patient. Low-income African-American women, for example, often expressed a sense of statistics based on personal experience that varied radically from the perspective of middle-class couples. When a woman has given birth to four other children, comes from a family of eight, and all her sisters and neighbors have had similar histories, she has seen scores of babies born without recognizable birth defects. This homegrown sense of statistics can be quite powerful. As a mother of three at City Hospital put it, "It's almost like gambling—you aren't likely to hit the jackpot." And as one 40-year-old Dominican commented, when rejecting the test,

> My sister just had a baby in the Dominican Republic three weeks ago. She's 43, and the baby's fine. In my family, there are ten boys and eleven girls. Us sisters, so far we got ten babies, and everyone is fine. If I took drugs, if I smoked, then I'd need a test. But my baby is fine.

Many experienced mothers have great confidence in their bodies' abilities to produce healthy babies. Their articulation of a popular epidemiology is, of course, also quite accurate, and hence compatible with a more general statistical picture of chromosomal and genetic abnormalities diagnosable before or at birth: The vast majority of births do not involve these problems. It requires a leap of faith in abstract reasoning to contrast these experiences with a number produced by a woman you have never met before in a white coat proclaiming that the risk of having a baby with a birth defect is steadily rising with each pregnancy, which is also true. Among middle-class professional families, where childbearing is likely to be delayed, the counselor is discussing a first or, at most, a second pregnancy. Children are likely to be scarce throughout the network of the professional couple. They therefore have less childbearing experience from which to draw statistical understandings. To them, one in three hundred sounds like a large and present risk, while for the low-income mother of four, the same number may appear very distant and small. And first-time parents (who are more likely to be middle-class, undertaking a first, consciously delayed pregnancy) are less confident about their abilities to control the situation. One African-American computer specialist, the husband of a first-time pregnant woman, commented, "This is the first time that one in two hundred looks like bad odds to me. I think we'll have the test." Another husband, also in computers, said, "I'd be happier if there were one more digit down below." The risk of a chromosome problem is always assessed from a specific, experiential location.

Indeed, the idea of "risk" as both a quantitative and qualitative concept is central to the information that genetic counselors seek to convey. The technology of prenatal diagnosis was developed explicitly to allow the selective abortion of fetuses facing serious disabilities because of atypical chromosomes and genes (Cowan 1992, 1993; McDonough 1990). The language of genetic counseling is intended to enhance awareness of the age-related risk of chromosomal problems, but counselors rarely speak directly about disability or abortion decisions unless a problem is detected. Counselors describe their goals quite differently: to give reassurance. That consists of returning clients to the "general population," which has a background risk of 2 percent to 3 percent of giving birth to a child with a disability, rather than undertaking the larger risk entailed by forgoing amniocentesis, which adds one's age-related risk to that generic background risk. This language of "added risk," "background risk," and "reassurance" is consistently deployed by all the genetic counselors I have observed at work. It thus foregrounds a statistical, medical, age-related, universal, and wholly individual model of risk.

In the process, what Lippman (1991, 31) labels "iatrogenic anxiety" is also constructed: Though older women have long known they were more likely than younger ones to give birth to babies with Down syndrome, it is only the present generation of statistically graded pregnant women who have been given specific risk figures, and thus been led to identify generic pregnancy anxieties with their exact age and statistic. We might even suggest that the generic is becoming focused through the genetic. Genetics and its associated prenatal diagnostic technologies provide one powerful and unified discourse for organizing fears concerning fetal normality and prenatal damage which have long been multiple. The same worldview which measures risk of abnormality in chromosomal terms and constructs its iatrogenic anxiety also offers relief by providing a new piece of medical technology to assess and assuage the problem. But such powerful and totalizing models of risk silence many other background factors—like low birth weight, which is highly associated with maternal poverty—whose risks to the fetus and newborn are empirically much higher, as I hope to show below. Dominant medical frameworks thus lay claim to the conceptual space in which many alternative ideas of risk can and do flourish, as the women and families whose ideas are quoted in the next chapter illustrate.

The overwhelming majority of clients for amniocentesis are sent to see a genetic counselor because of advanced maternal age. All pregnancies carry a small risk of "birth defects" ("hereditary disabilities" would provide a more socially accurate and neutral description). But chromosomal problems are the only screenable prenatal conditions that systematically increase with age. For example, a 20-year-old woman has a one-in-1,500 chance of giving birth to a baby with Down syndrome; a 35-year-old's risk is one in 360. At 40, women have babies with Down's once in every 106 births (see Hook 1978; Hook, Cross et al. 1983). Here, the relationship is numerical and straightforward: Using age charts, graphs, or birth ratios (that is, numerical graphics), counselors explain a general risk pattern, then derive a specific risk ratio based on the particular mother's age at estimated date of delivery. Increasing age is considered a "risk factor"; having an amniocentesis and receiving negative results (i.e., that the fetal chromosomes are normal) removes the "added risk" that accompanies age, and returns the pregnant woman to the "general patient population." These numbers (and thus the "risk" and "reassurance" discourse that accompanies the technology) appear as universal, uninfluenced by the general health or nutritional status of the parents, or their country of origin. Because chromosome analysis is the only test routinely performed on genetic material in an amniocentesis, and Down syndrome accounts for about 50 percent of the chromosome problems detected, Down's looms large in the discourse of genetic counseling. There are, however, about eight hundred much rarer, arcane genetic disabilities which can now be diagnosed prenatally.

Sometimes in a counseling session, a middle-class professional will inquire about additional testing for some of these disabilities. Often, middle-class patients are appalled to learn that a routine amniocentesis is used only to diagnose chromosome problems and neural tube defects. Often, such clients have read about dramatic advances in prenatal detection of rare but serious diseases, and request the latest, most comprehensive tests. But a pregnant woman's amniotic fluid would be tested for one of these (at great expense) only if her family history provides a medical indication. Nonetheless, middle-class knowledge of the escalating availability of tests is perceived by many counselors as a pressure. They are thus more likely to accept or elicit a detailed family health history from such clients, in case it provides an indication for further testing. This worldview of the benefits of escalating technology is coconstructed by many middle-class patients and their counselors, and it contributes to the routinization of prenatal diagnosis in subtle ways.

But most childhood disabilities are not, of course, either chromosomal or genetic, but are caused by low birth weight, which accompanies poverty and insufficient prenatal nutrition or care, or by accidents and infant illnesses. The routinization of amniocentesis and its limits describe the universe in which Down syndrome has become iconic. But the expressed concerns of many women from low-income backgrounds are as likely to focus on prematurity or crib death as on chromosomal problems, for these are conditions with which they and their communities have a great deal of experience. Counselors who are sensitive to their clients' concerns are likely to find themselves talking about issues like nutrition, smoking, and preventative care, not only about their own, much more specialized services. But not all counselors can shift focus adroitly, and many do not have the luxury of time with which to address both their own professional topics and more general health issues articulated by many women from low-income backgrounds. Despite the best of intentions, there is thus ample room for the focus in a counseling session to blur; what the counselor and patient find most relevant may well not be the same thing.

Advanced maternal age is not the only "risk" that genetic discourse can describe, and whose consequences can be diagnosed. Increasingly, autosomal recessive conditions, many of which run at heightened frequencies in specific ethnic groups, can also be picked up. Thus, sickle-cell anemia (among people of African descent), Tay-Sachs disease (most prevalent among those of Ashkenazi Jewish background), and the thalessemias (blood diseases that are most common among Mediterranean and Asian populations) can now all be diagnosed. Prenatal screening for cystic fibrosis, the most common autosomal recessively transmitted "ethnic" disease encountered among those of white European descent, is now being piloted, although both its variable accuracy and lack of national funding make it a controversial test. While some of the available screens are close to 100 percent accurate (e.g., those for sickle-cell anemia and Tay-Sachs disease), others are probing for conditions caused by a series of functionally related genetic mutations which vary between families and among ethnic groups; (presently available cystic fibrosis screens, for example, are most effective for Scandinavians, less effective for Italians and Ashkenazi Jews). Screening for the more common CF mutations will identify 80 percent to 90 percent of "white" carriers, and lower percentages of other racial-ethnic groups (Tatsugawa, Fox, Fang et al. 1994). Carrier and fetal testing may therefore net more statistical probabilities, rather than yes/no diagnoses. And even when the diagnosis is unambiguous, its potential severity requires interpretation. Some conditions are dramatically and tragically consistent in their trajectories: Tay-Sachs disease, for example, causes degeneration of most body functions and death at a very early age. But a much more common occurrence is that the positive diagnosis of a given condition cannot predict the severity of any individual case. Even a 100 percent accurate diagnosis of sickle-cell anemia does not indicate how mildly or severely affected a particular fetus will be, nor can a diagnosis of cystic fibrosis or the late-blooming Huntington's disease predict age of onset of symptoms, itself a powerful indicator of life span and "quality of life" (cf. Bluebond-Langner 1991). Thus, testing often leads to additional cascades of statistically expressed possibilities which the pregnant woman and her supporters must assess. Conditions are described in terms of "degree of penetrance" (whether those with the gene manifest its symptoms) and "degree of expressivity" (the range of severity or mildness with which a transmitted genetic condition occurs), both of which are usually variable.

In sketching the proliferation of mathematically modeled ambiguities which often accompany prenatal testing, I do not mean to underestimate either the seriousness or the consequences of carrying and transmitting a genetic condition, for which increasingly sophisticated clinical interventions as well as genetic screens are rapidly being developed. I do, however, want to underline that the powerful language of risk attached to age, ethnic background, or family genetic history requires family members to focus their thinking through the sieve of statistics, muffling other positions and social interpretations from which they might respond to disease. There is little room for cultural variation in the individually grounded, genetically causative model of risk that counselors must convey if standard scientific information concerning birth defects and their prenatal testing is to be communicated. Yet counselors encounter a deluge of variation, both individual and social, in their daily work.

The Cultural Construction of Health Histories

The second goal of a counseling session is to take an individual and familial health history, in order to discover whether a pregnant woman should be offered additional testing or other services due to her particular, heightened risks. Here, too, extreme cultural differences in patients' knowledge and resources are displayed each time a genetic counselor elicits a health history, using a standard questionnaire. From a counselor's point of view recent immigrants, especially those from very poor countries, are likely to exhibit shallow knowledge of their own heredity. The cause of a father's death or the medical name of an uncle's form of mental retardation may be unknown, especially if births and deaths occurred after the immigrant left home. "I left home when I was real young," a Haitian woman told me, "and my mother, then my father, they just got sick. And then they died. That's all I know." Another says, "In Haiti, maybe it's the poverty that kills people. In Haiti, you can't always know why someone dies." And while immigrants may vividly recall some health experiences—high fevers, exposure to X rays—others seem irrelevant, or are named in a language they do not speak. Many Haitians, for example, routinely answer "no" to all questions concerning family histories of heart and kidney disease, diabetes, and venereal diseases. Their negative answers may well be ambiguous: Serious conditions may be unreported or unnamed, since they are virtually untreated for all but the most privileged elite. A community health outreach worker from Jamaica, now working in Brooklyn, told me: "Sickle-cell, do I counsel sickle-cell? Sure I do now. But then, I didn't know what it was. My brother, he died of it back then. We didn't know, no one told us. What's the difference? No transfusions back there, anyhow."

Silence or "no" in response to familial health questions from a counselor may result in one of a number of misinterpretations, for example, an absence of health problems in the family or a lack of interest or intelligence on the part of the patient. These interpretations are overdetermined by the individual nature of a medical health history, in the absence of an epidemiological and cultural context with which the counselor is conversant. But a middle-class, U.S.-born pregnant woman may say of her husband's family, "I'm sorry, I don't know that. They're not the kind of family that talks about illness, they like to keep it to themselves." Her answer will not be interpreted as deficient, for she speaks through an etiquette in a cultural context that is quite recognizable to other U.S.-born professionals. The codes, genres, and assumptions of science speakers thus contribute to the limits of the conversations that genetic counselors may have with their patients.

Medical etiquette is not confined to the areas in which patients are asked to display what they know or do not know about the health histories of their relatives. It is inscribed subtly throughout the intake interview. A specific logic orders the categories of questions counselors ask patients. To be asked, for example, about their history with gonorrhea, high fevers, and street drugs in one sentence, as patients regularly are, may be daunting. From a medical perspective, all may affect early fetal development, and are thus linked. But in the world outside the hospital, these three ailments bear no relation to one another, and to many people, all but fevers are stigmatized. Other questions counselors regularly pose concern cats and consanguinity. The handling of cat litter may spread toxoplasmosis to a first-trimester fetus, but many pregnant women do not know this, and consider pets an odd topic for a health care provider to be discussing. Consanguineous matings, of course, express a higher incidence of autosomal recessive conditions than do random matches. But the standard question, "Could you and your partner be related?" is likely to be met by a stare of disbelief, or embarrassed laughter, especially among Spanish speakers. Notions of incest are highly charged in all cultures, and this one evokes unsettling embarrassment. Pets and pedigrees, gonorrhea and ganja may be rational topics of investigation in constituting a reproductive health history, but they are not among the items most people, especially those without scientific education, comfortably group together and discuss in an intake interview.

When a counselor requests information that a patient does not have, or cannot comfortably code as relevant, something beyond negative answers occurs. Most obviously and positively, dominant notions of health education and medical entitlement are being enacted. Good counselors are also skilled teachers, for the information they convey is inherently interesting and complex. It often incites questions and discussions. For example, a low-income Puerto Rican husband interrupted a group counseling session which I was observing at City Hospital to summarize and extend the counselor's message: "So if all that's in the amniotic fluid, what is the relation of all this to the baby? I think the baby is wrapped with something that separates it from the fluid, heh?" "No," the counselor quickly corrected, "the baby swims in that fluid, it's inside what's called the sac, and outside, the placenta. On one side is the baby, on the other side is the mother. Every month, the woman begins to make a new placenta, but if she isn't pregnant, it goes away, and that's her period."

Exchanges between counselors and patients may also push the boundaries of medical entitlement, steering people toward services of which they had little or no prior knowledge. When one counselor learned, for example, that her client's older child was suffering seizures, she made a referral to a pediatric neurologist. When another counselor discovered in taking a pedigree that many of her pregnant client's relatives died young, from "heart problems," she sent the woman and her children for screening for familial hypercholesterolemia. Such information gathering is at once the gateway to better health care and an instance of medicalization: Information about the grandfather's heart is now entered in the child's medical record. What was once familiar is now frightening, and the mother's consciousness of vulnerability is transformed. Learning to think through medicine entails the recoding of the body: Its ills, systemic connections, and intergenerational history all take on new and specialized meanings.

Not all of the recoding which accompanies the questions that counselors ask has such obvious potential benefits. When a Puerto Rican low-income teenager was sent for genetic counseling at City Hospital, for example, she brought her grandmother along. The older woman answered all health history questions on behalf of her grandchild, her daughter (the younger woman's mother), and herself, producing a very rich and detailed three-generation reproductive history. But the counselor interrupted her, saying, "I'm concerned about miscarriages, stillbirths, and infant deaths at this point, not abortions. I'll write down the abortions later." This response may have made medical sense: Abortions are voluntary while miscarriage may well have a genetic basis. But it effectively split the grandmother's matrilineal reproductive story into alien and fragmented categories.

In responding to intake questions, nonscience speakers, especially immigrants, are taught to model appropriate patient behavior. Poor people, especially recent immigrants, lead very complex lives. Their need for services to which they have little or no access may be profound. When a genetic counselor asks, "Do you have any questions for me?" a middle-class family is likely to respond, "What's the rate of risk if we undertake another pregnancy in two years?" But underserved, underprivileged patients are likely to ask, "Where's the Medicaid office?" "My husband's hitting me, and I'm afraid it will hurt the baby—will it?" or "I've got a terrible infection down there." Middle-class families also have problems with bills, family violence, and sexually transmitted infections. But they usually have both the financial resources and long-standing experience with medical specialization that enable them to compartmentalize these problems. Learning to compartmentalize is built into visiting a genetic counselor, for her services are, by definition, highly specialized. In the process, behavior appropriate to middle-class life proves to be effective and is often rewarded.

Learning to compartmentalize and to accept narrow definitions of specialized problems and their solutions is built into the worldview of science speakers. The language of genetics offers powerful descriptions of the human life force itself, presented in terms of statistics, risk analysis, and arcane, rapidly expanding technologies. This language is more than lexical, for it entails codes of medical etiquette and embodied practices whose pragmatic consequences for pregnant women and their families are potentially quite complex. As I have tried to indicate throughout this chapter, this language can be adjusted through code switching on the part of counselors, but the efficacy of their discourse has limits. Each pregnant woman brings the light and shadow of her personal biography, family history, and community resources with her to the consulting room, and she hears about new, or partly new interventions into her aspirations for her own and her child's futures through these filters. Thus a deluge of difference and a mosaic of meanings await a counselor each time she meets a new client.

4

Contested Conceptions
and Misconceptions

We were furious about the session they required us to attend before
being allowed to do the amnio. These silly people made us pay $140
for a two-hour session, and it took us over forty-five minutes to get
there and the same to get back. They explained, in the most ele-
mentary language, as if we were total idiots, a few basic things
about amnio—information that we could easily have digested from
a short pamphlet in ten minutes. . . . It was the clearest case of a
for-profit bilking in the American medical system! . . . They could
devise . . . a short test to be taken at home to prove that we understood. Then they'd have no excuse to spend so much of our time on
so little information. (middle-class academic couple)

MOST COUNSELORS ARE QUITE AWARE that their clients come from diverse
backgrounds: Some bring much knowledge of genetics and prenatal testing
to the counseling session, others, almost none. Highly educated pregnant
women and their supporters may find that the counseling session and prenatal testing offer only the most rudimentary of controls over hereditary health
problems when compared to their fantasies of surveillance, while those with
little access to education may be overwhelmed by both its content and
assumptions. In this chapter, I describe the tension between the scientific
meaning of heredity and a model for its control which counselors expound,
and the range of popular conceptions of the same domain women and their
supporters from diverse backgrounds express. That tension is multilayered,
for it rests upon the difference between scientific language and worldview,
and broader, more capacious culturally specific notions of causality. The

tension also rests on the differences between genetic and socially gendered contributions to a pregnancy's health and well-being, and between medical and experiential understandings of what specific disabilities entail. Here, I will argue that the hegemony of the scientific model can never be absolute: Not only are the communicative resources on which it is based always expanding just below or beyond the reach of many clients; practical conceptions of heredity, maternal responsibility, and disability are also layered with many meanings other than those that genetic counselors can describe.

Many counselors attempt to address what they understand to be the problem of diversity in patients' knowledge of heredity by beginning the individual (intake) portions of their interactions conversationally. Often, they pose a variant of the question, "Do you know why you are here talking to me?" From the beginning, interactions are context-sensitive to the responses and resources that patients bring to the interaction. Middle-class, scientifically educated pregnant patients may respond, "We're planning to have amniocentesis," thus pushing the counseling script into high gear. Implicit in that answer is not only knowledge of appropriate medical indications for the test but also the existence of "the couple" as a decision-making unit. One white, highly educated husband (who turned out to be a biostatistician!) replied that he had come to get a decision-making tree in order to ascertain whether his pregnant wife needed amniocentesis, and what to do with the information, should the results be positive. His response effectively squelched any exploration of those counseling issues that could not be mathematically modeled.

A patient's answer may be much less formal than that of the biostatistician, but highly persuasive, convincing the counselor that the patient knows what she wants to do. As one white working-class clinic patient put it, "I know a little, my friend told it to me. It's quick, it doesn't hurt, no one said anything bad. There's no reason not to have this test." But a Dominican mother of three may answer, "Por culpa de mi edad" (literally, "For the fault of my age"), thus presenting the counselor with several options. She can assume that the woman "knows," since "age" is the factor that sends her here. Or she can confront the "culpa" head-on, explaining that older women having babies present no shame, just medical risks. Families from India may interpret such a direct and leading opening question as impolite; some African-Americans, especially if they come from rural Southern backgrounds, may remain silent, in deference to medical professionals. Wherever she begins her routine explanation, the counselor is likely to have to adjust her language to the language and assumptions of her pregnant patient (and sometimes the patient's mate).

Native Languages

In adjusting (or not adjusting) to a patient's language, genetic counselors are bound by the limits of their own communicative resources. Although many languages are spoken by the pregnant women whom counselors see, most counseling sessions are conducted in English. Availability of fluent translation is a significant problem: Depending on their catchment areas, the hospitals in which I observed served patients who were close to 100 percent bilingual Spanish speaking, 50 percent French/Creole speaking, or about 25 percent monolingual Spanish speaking. Among the thirty-five counselors that I interviewed, there are at least five in New York hospitals who are native Spanish speakers, and another five who are comfortable counseling in Spanish. Many others have learned a bit of medical Spanish and work through translators, ranging from trusted assistants who understand their agendas (a secretary in the office or a clinic nurse) to catch-as-catch-can interpreters. The problem of interpretation is not minor: An 8-year-old bilingual girl kept out of school to help her monolingual mother negotiate the prenatal clinic may have trouble translating the mysteries of LMP (last menstrual period) by which pregnancies are medically dated; male kin and neighbors may be too embarrassed to accurately call forth the information a genetic counselor needs when querying prior miscarriages and abortions. One white, middle-class counselor from a Jewish background described her baptism into the world of translation. Her first pediatric case was a Colombian mother whose newborn had just been diagnosed as having multiple congenital anomalies, an inherently serious and ambiguous situation. Unable to speak directly with the mother, the counselor worked through a Spanish-speaking visitor. Although the counselor chose her words very carefully, she could tell by the body language of the mother that her meanings were not getting through. The visitor wanted to spare the mother the pain of hearing the entire diagnosis and was dramatically editing the bad news. Distraught but determined, the new counselor spent her summer vacation in Spain at an intensive language school.

"Native language" only approximates the variety of communicative differences that genetic counselors confront. "Hispanic" glosses a range of Spanish-speaking cultures, especially in New York City. Many counselors, of course, know this. As one middle-class South American counselor told me, "I'm Spanish speaking, but I'm not Hispanic!" Another native Spanish speaker, also from a professional family, confessed that she found it tiresome to be asked to explain the hot-cold folk medicine beliefs of Central American patients. "I don't know anything about that, why should I?" she said. "Sometimes," she continued, "speaking Spanish gives you more problems, not less. People think you're from the same culture, but you really aren't." In both of these instances, the counselors were contesting a too-easy elision of language and culture. On the one hand, they were asserting that the class-based nature of their privileged education removed them from any automatic knowledge of, or identity with less educated, more "traditional" Spanish-speaking clients. On the other, they were pointing out that important national and regional differences separated clients from counselors.

The diversity of Spanish-speaking cultures at the present time in New York City (and most metropolitan areas in the United States) is quite profound. Some genetic counselors distinguished "Hispanic" (which often meant Puerto Rican and Dominican, the "old" migrants) from new migrants who might be "middle-class" Colombians and Argentineans or the "field mice" of Central America (by which the speaker meant "the poor, rural, and humble"). Although exact cultural differences among Spanish-speaking groups may be unknown, most counselors recognize something of the diversity in educational levels, familiarity with medical terminology, and religious observance that different nationalities may represent.

Nominal or deep fluency in another tongue does not ensure direct communication for science speakers. Language differences may signal communicative ambiguities far beyond the question of literal translation. Local metaphors of pregnancy, of birth, and of female and male contributions to parenthood do not necessarily translate easily into the realm of medical discourse. Two native Spanish-speaking counselors pointed out the far-reaching impact of their conversations with pregnant Spanish-speaking patients:

> This knowledge is more than genetic. They learn about things that were completely hidden—where the eggs are, what sperm does, how children get to look like their parents. They have ideas, but this is female physiology, it is knowledge, not just information. For this, they come back.

> When I see confusion, I go to work, I tell them in language they will understand, language of the streets. They are comfortable here, it is a good place to visit. They come back to see me whenever they come to the hospital.

Of course, not everyone is equally open to the complex relation between native tongue, knowledge, and communicative power. Two counselors, one of whom conducts group sessions for patients in Spanish, expressed irritation that so few of their clients "bothered to learn English": "They're here ten, maybe fifteen years. They learn enough English to pick up their welfare checks. Why don't they just learn the language? My grandparents did."

And if Spanish is a contested domain, French and Haitian Creole are virtually terrae incognitae. At the time of these interviews, only one genetic counselor felt comfortable counseling in French; none knew any Creole. The lack is significant: In at least one City Hospital, Haitians make up about 50 percent of the patients referred for counseling. In translating for counseling sessions, I discovered that there is no recognition of Down syndrome or "mongolism" among recent immigrants from the Haitian countryside. No word exists in Creole for the condition. In principle, the incidence of Down syndrome is invariant worldwide. But in a country with the worst infant mortality statistics in the Western Hemisphere, babies may die from many causes, and this one may go unrecognized as a "syndrome." Nonrecognition of the label may also reflect other cultural and political experiences. Haitians living in New York City have already confronted alternative definitions of their children's vulnerabilities. As one Haitian evangelical Christian father told me, while firmly rejecting amniocentesis on his wife's behalf, "What is this *retarded*? They always say that Haitian children are retarded in the public schools. But when we put them in the Haitian Academy [a community-based private school], they do just fine. I do not know what this *retarded* is." In his experience, "chromosomes" seemed a weak and abstract explanation for the problems a Haitian child may face. Thus a "language barrier" may eclipse a complex imbrication through which transnational migration, racial prejudice, religious beliefs, gender practices and assumptions, and scientific worldviews may all be uneasily stitched together.

Indeed, commonsense, experiential explanations and scientific, abstract ones are often in tension, a point to which I return below. This is constantly reflected in a tug-of-war of words pitting the formal vocabulary of biomedicine against the informal lexicon of most women's lives. Both codes uneasily cohabit in a forty-five-minute intake interview. Code switching occurs rapidly as counselors feel out their clients: "Babies" vie with "fetuses" for space in "wombs," "tummies," or "uteruses"; "waters" or "liquid" or "fluids" may be "taken out with a needle" or "withdrawn through an insertion"; the "test" or "procedure" may involve "looking at the inherited material" or "examining chromosomes." And, in the worst-case scenario, women must decide to "terminate" or "abort" an "affected" or "sick" pregnancy in which "Down syndrome" or "mongolism" has been diagnosed. In the standoff between medical and popular language, the more distant idiom may provide reassurance by suggesting to some pregnant women that their experiences are part of medical routine (Brewster 1984). But for others, medical terminology may muffle anxiety-provoking choices until they are expressed through dramatic disruption:

> So I was sitting and listening, listening and sitting and all the time getting more and more preoccupied. The counselor kept on talking but she never did say it, so finally I had to just say it, right while she was still talking, "You can't take the baby out *then* [i.e., so late in pregnancy], can you now?" I finally asked. (Veronica Landry, 36, Trinidad-born factory worker)

The tension between a distanced medical language and a more affective language of maternal-fetal connection may also be intertwined with often inaccurate pictures of prenatal testing. Most obviously and consistently, many Spanish speakers fear that the needle goes into the mother's navel or hits the fetal navel cord. The mother's navel, of course, is not the baby's lifeline, for it does not connect the pregnant woman to her baby, but is the severed cord of connection to her own mother, to her own babyhood. Yet both cords were intertwined as the object of concern when women told me they pictured the needle as damaging the *umbligo*. Puerto Rican and Dominican women were also the only ones who consistently brought their mothers as supporters to counseling or testing. And I often heard, of an unplanned pregnancy among women from these backgrounds, a statement like, "I'm 41. My daughter, she's 21 and pregnant. I didn't think I could get pregnant at my age if she's already started" (Feliciana Dominguez, Dominican factory worker).

Intergenerational closeness, or even fusion, appears to run deep through Puerto Rican and Dominican maternal social relations and cultural imagery. This sense of mother-child fusion reappears in chapter 9, as well. But I hazard this interpretation with some uncertainty; it is hard to know why fear of needles, or fear of striking the navel, or beliefs that the daughter's fertility affects the mother's are so pervasive among some Spanish speakers, especially Dominicans and Puerto Ricans. Only far greater familiarity with their cultural backgrounds and aspirations than I hold might reveal or repeal the validity of this explication.

And misinformation about the locus of the test and its relation to pregnancy is not confined to any one group. One 39-year-old African-American was sent to counseling, but came too late for amniocentesis. She had had the test in her prior pregnancy, and announced that she expected it to cover all her pregnancies. At first, there was barely concealed amusement on the part of counselors (and observers!). Later, we realized the logic of her position: She thought that the amniocentesis had probed her own health, rather than the health of the fetus, to ensure that she had no problem that might be passed on to any of her fetuses.

Some misconceptions are easily corrected: Many Philippinas, Dominicanas, and Puerto Ricans expressed their belief that Down syndrome occurs only in a first, late pregnancy. Some asked whether they needed the test, since their prior children had been born without chromosomal problems. "Is this the test for women having their first baby over 35 or is it for women who've had other children?" (Luisa Alvarez, 36, Puerto Rican social worker).

This idea is easily displaced by a counselor's scientific explanation about nondisjunction of chromosomes potentially occurring in any pregnancy, and becoming more likely with age. But some ideas are deeply embedded within other domains of knowledge and belief, and are less likely to be dislodged by a strictly scientific explanation. Juana Martes, a 37-year-old mother of three from the Dominican Republic, initially refused the test because members of her charismatic Catholic prayer group had already healed two cases of Down syndrome. When I asked for descriptions of the mothers and children involved, she said that praying over the pregnancy had entirely saved one baby from "a little mongolism," while the second child was cured by God, although she was still unable to speak at the age of 3. A Puerto Rican unemployed father told me that his conversion to Pentecostalism had enabled him to dream the image of his as-yet-unborn daughter. In the dream, the child was at first blind and suffered from a hole in her heart, but both infirmities were healed through prayer. These two infirmities exist simultaneously as problems amenable to biomedical and religious intervention, since Jesus is believed to cure a hole in the heart, and to bestow clear vision. The power of religious imagery and beliefs to infiltrate and transform biomedical practices is profound, as I hope to illustrate below.

Some patients invoke a causality of their own to explain the existence of a disability. A U.S.-born Irish-American school administrator said of her Irish aunt with ten children, one autistic: "I think it was her life, that's what I think caused the autism. She was a farmer's wife, she had a very hard life; one of the twins was normal, and one just was not. It was the circumstances, just the hard lot of her life as a mother that caused it." An African-American secretary who came for genetic testing during her second pregnancy related a troubled family medical history. Her first child had tuberous sclerosis, a genetic disease transmitted from her father's side. One of the pregnant mother's sisters had severe asthma, and another was born with short, uneven limbs. The specific risks of recurrence of these family-related conditions were all explained to her, and she was asked about her anxieties and concerns. She replied:

> I don't think about it, if I do, I'm going to make myself crazy. My father's brother has a son that's very, very retarded. My mother always say she didn't like that boy and she saw a lot of him while she was carrying Laney [the sister with limb problems]. That's what marked the baby, that's what she believes.

The counselor said, "I told you what we know about how problems pass down in families, and it isn't by marking. Do you believe what your mother believes?" To which the woman replied, "Yes, I grew up in the country, and it's part of me."

Puerto Rican women (like some others from Latin backgrounds) also held theories about parental-fetal transmission in which rage is substantiated:

> On my husband's side, the mother suffered a lot. The father ran around, he had thirty-nine children, eleven with that mother. But those children, they suffered her rage: Two died as babies, two are retarded. It seems the suffering descended [motions to her womb] to her pregnancies. Do you understand me? (Merced Blanco, 37, homemaker)

A Puerto Rican postal worker was even more pointed in her discussion of life's stresses and their hereditary transmission:

> My husband, he's schizophrenic. It was the pressure of going from a tranquil country to a strong one. It was just too much pressure, he cracked from the pressure. No, I don't worry about it in the kids. We got five kids, they all come up normal. They don't have schizophrenia because they were born here, they're used to a strong country.

Here, a social psychological theory about the stress of migration displaces contemporary biomedical research on schizophrenia, in which genetic propensities are asserted and debated.

Some misconceptions about genetic transmission are also widespread. African-American clients, for example, held many beliefs about sickle-cell anemia, including the idea that the youngest child always gets the trait. "So me," one woman said, "I'm the youngest, and I got it." Many spoke of the trait as something one can have in degrees. For example, "I've got a trace of it, so does my uncle. My mother says it's on her side, there's a trace of it on my mother's side."

Such beliefs can cohabit comfortably with scientific explanations. That is, a socially inflected analysis of why any particular baby was born with a disability, can be engaged with the practical technologies biomedicine offers. One working-poor Dominicana, 37, described the rage that she said damaged family members this way:

> They don't say he had a sister. They don't tell you, the sister was full of rage at him, they fought about the inheritance, then her rage made a baby that's crazy. They don't say she's having another baby, but they did that test. They don't tell you why for the test, but I'm sure it's because of the crazy baby. Now he's in a special school, they don't want to believe it. The crazy baby, he can't learn anything. The Spanish people, they just say, "loco, loco," caused by her rage at that brother. Now she's having another baby. With the test. I think it's ok.

Female Accountability

Thus the familial theories some women express about hereditary disabilities are disconnected from the age-related chromosomal problems that are the focus of amniocentesis. They index social relations and responsibilities within families—migration or birth order, for example, or the inability to control rage and fear—rather than the genetic materials on which counselors dwell. Such social relations can, in principle, be affected by human agency, allowing participants a sense of their role in cause and prevention. And an obvious, widely shared common theory of agency affecting a pregnancy's outcome focuses on maternal responsibility. Across divides of class privilege, racial-ethnic or national background, and religious affiliation, many individuals hold mothers responsible for fetal quality and health, despite the insistence of genetic counselors that the production of chromosomal and genetic anomalies are not under human control.

This gendered standoff between biomedicine and popular ideas about heredity, the causes of hereditary problems, and what can be done about them, is built on two quite significant sets of foundational ideas that can run into conflict. Most obviously, scientific knowledge assigns each parent a 50 percent contribution to the hereditary materials of a fetus at the moment of conception. The "drama of the egg and sperm" (Martin 1991) is mirrored technically in the discourse of genetic counseling, where haploid and diploid germ cells, meiosis and mitosis, and mitotic reduction division are all narrated to explain how the life force enters each new conception already equally indebted to both its maternal and paternal sides. This discourse corresponds to a popular understanding in American culture that "blood" is passed on equally from both the father's and mother's sides (Schneider 1980 [1968]). But the egalitarian nature of genetic (or "blood") contributions is held in tension with a second popular, pervasive and nonegalitarian idea, the highly gendered notion of maternal responsibility. Here the discipline of biomedicine concerns female compliance with guidelines for health pregnancy behavior, but it does not include an assignment of responsibility for genetic or chromosomal normality. Yet women and their supporters from many backgrounds believe that the behavior they define as healthy or unhealthy is responsible for a pregnancy's outcome, and they do not distinguish genetic health from any other cause or manifestation.

The widespread, popular accountability of women for the "quality control" of fetuses and children contrasts with notions of male responsibility. While there are circumstances in which male nurturance is considered essential to the developing fetus (Battaglia 1985; Hewlett 1991), men in many cultures are pictured as providing the creative spark or seed which "causes" the pregnancy, without assuming any behavioral obligations that influence its outcome. Women carry the burden of nurturance in such popular models (Delaney 1986; Stolcke 1986).

Of course, the idea that women are responsible for the outcome of pregnancies, including the production of anomalous or ambiguous births, has a long history in Western theology, natural philosophy, and medicine. Pregnancy, for example, figures in the tensions and agreements between medieval theology and natural philosophy. In that period, women's "fleshiness" was associated with the body in body/soul dualities, her fetus a cause for speculation about maternal and paternal contributions to God's purpose and perfection. Women's reproductive capacities invoked reflection on divine regulation and causes of oddity. Medieval texts and artifacts evinced enormous curiosity about pregnancy, monstrous births, and the relation of blood to milk, couched as problems of permeability and stability (Bynum 1992). This intellectual interest also flourished in the eighteenth century, when the representational arts, medical practice, and emergent scientific research all converged on grotesques, on anomalous embryos, and on "unnatural" births, using them to index debates on causality and regularity in nature. In both religious and secular discourse, women's role in purveying or perverting the life force generated by semen was a central concern (cf. Bynum 1989; Jordanova 1989; Stafford 1991). In its present incarnation, notions of women's embodied responsibility are played out inside an imaginary and bounded female-centered domain, drafting women as the nearly exclusive guardians of fetal and child health.

This engendered and entwined foundation—equal scientific material donations, unequal social practical burdens—corresponds to the scientific difference between genetic and gestational contributions. Not uncoincidentally, it also symbolically aligns women with all the labors of making a nurturant home for the pregnancy and for children while assigning men a proprietary interest, but not a practical responsibility, in a pregnancy's outcome. The consequences of such a widespread belief system have been the subject of much contemporary feminist scholarship.

This stance of holding a woman accountable for a pregnancy's outcome is undoubtedly helpful in linking some health problems like smoking or alcohol consumption to low birth weight or some congenital problems, for it suggests behavioral guides that many women can accommodate. But it doesn't aid in understanding chromosomes, whose patterns and pathologies are unaffected by maternal behavior.[18] Yet many Puerto Rican, Dominican, and Haitian women rejected the test with a variant of this statement:

> I don't smoke, I don't drink, I don't take drugs. I eat good food, I take good care of myself. What do I need this test for? (Dominique Laurent, 39, Haitian garment worker)

> Me and my husband, we saw this program on Channel 13 [PBS]. This only happens if you take drugs, that's when it happens. Nothing to do with me. (Maria Dominguez, 38, Dominican day-care worker)

Often, an assessment of age-related risks is personalized and folded into an interpretation of family history:

> My family's all healthy, they're all professionals, they're active, they take good care. Me, I cut out smoking, I've been off birth control pills for ages, and two of my cousins had babies when they were in their forties. I'm not at risk. (Angela Storrman, 41, African-American public school teacher)

Female accountability also extends inappropriately to mysterious events over which individuals have no control. Mothers often blame themselves, or are blamed by family members, for problems with which their children are born:

I fell down during my pregnancy with her two times, and then this happened. (Dominican mother describing the birth of her daughter with cleft lip and palate)

My mother-in-law says the cleft [in the first son] was caused by me using scissors during the pregnancy. This time, I've come for your counseling, but I won't use scissors during the pregnancy. (Chinese garment worker, 32)

My mom don't want me near his [boyfriend's] retarded brother now, when I come up pregnant. She's worrying in case my baby catch it. (African-American student, 17, sickle-cell trait carrier)

Embedding Disabilities

But the problems about which counselors speak are independent of maternal agency, kinship problems, or other social interventions, for they depend on statistical models of risk, not gendered or familial preventative behavior. The complex nature of chromosome problems is condensed into counselors' discussions of the forty-seventh chromosome clinically expressed in Down syndrome, and its accompanying mental retardation. As I noted in chapter 3, the eugenics movement and contemporary genetic counseling practices both focused on mental retardation, indeed, on Down's, as an index of a range of individual and social problems. While this condition is almost universally recognized, the content of that recognition varies considerably, and may well stand orthagonally to the conventional scientific description of Down's. Many families share the counselor's concerns about the limitations on independence which mental retardation represents in our culture. Yet in families who have had direct experience with children with Down's, consciousness of disabilities is more finely honed: Children with Down syndrome may be mildly, moderately, or profoundly retarded, and most fall into the middle range; they run heightened risks of heart and esophageal problems, hearing loss, and increased risk for leukemia. "Mental retardation" provides an iconic description which blurs differences among children with Down syndrome, even as it categorizes them.

Counselors refer to the burdens of raising a child with Down's in a variety of ways:

A heart defect, we can operate, pneumonia we can cure. But mental retardation, that we can't do anything about. Think about it: No baby-sitters, it's a twenty-four-hour-a-day job. Sometimes, it causes problems between the parents, some men can't handle it, and sometimes the other children feel neglected.

We're only looking for fetuses whose inherited materials don't give them a chance of a good life, who will have *severe* handicaps, where life will become very hard for the family. I'm sure you know that in this society, the responsibility for a handicapped child rests on the mother's shoulders.

Embedded in such descriptions are images of mentally retarded children that are hardly value-neutral, a topic to which I will return in chapter 10, where the differences between the medical diagnosis and management of a child with Down syndrome, and that child's location in its complex social map, are analyzed. But first it is important to point out that clients can and do contest these images:

I take in foster children, I had some that were mentally retarded. I saw a movie on Channel 13 about this. When the women saw the kids' pictures, they didn't want any abortions. Me neither. I don't want this, but I've thought about it in every pregnancy, and if it happens, I can handle it. I wouldn't want no abortion for this because it would be my child. If I make it, it's my responsibility, I wouldn't give it up or nothing. (Chloris Lewis, 38, Trinidadian foster mother)

Disabling conditions have specific local meanings that are not shared by all. Mental retardation may stand as an icon for some groups—especially, but not exclusively, middle-class professionals:

I'm sorry to say that I just couldn't accept that. I mean, I've worked hard to get where I am, I worked hard at Cornell. And I want the same for my child. I want to teach my child, and to have him learn. Maybe it's unfortunate, maybe I should be more accepting. But I don't want a child with retardation. (John Freeman, 32, African-American computer technologist)

There's a certain relationship I want to have with a child, a way of growing and being in the world. A retarded child, well, I imagine it would just be too dependent. (Cheryl Spencer, 35, white interior decorator)

The bottom line is what my neighbor said to me: "Having a 'tard,' that's a bummer for life." (Shelley Osteroff, 36, white real estate agent)

Having a retarded baby, well, we both feel life is difficult enough without putting this on a baby itself. We are practical people. . . . Having a retarded child, I suppose it becomes part of you. I know people with a retarded child, they learned a lot. But it is very hard. My husband and me, we haven't actually said this to one another, but we'll end it if it's like that. That's how we feel, I know it is. The biggest problem is, what would we tell our 5-year-old daughter? (Coralina Ramirez, 36, Colombian hairdresser)

But for some, different conditions evoke more fear. Among many of the Spanish speakers I interviewed, physical vulnerability, especially if it was highly visible, seemed a much more urgent problem for family life. Many Puerto Ricans and Dominicans expressed great anxiety about conditions that were visibly crippling. They seemed less concerned with functional disabilities, provided the child appeared "normal." At counseling sessions, questions were often raised about the appearance of children with the conditions the tests probed. A Dominican couple who were both sickle-cell anemia trait carriers, for example, queried whether a child born with that condition would ever walk; if not, they would seek abortion. When told by the counselor that the child would walk but suffer a painful blood disease, they were much reassured. Low-income Puerto Rican parents interviewed through an infant stimulation program generally expressed acceptance and confidence in their Down syndrome children being "normal," for example: "She's growing really well. We were only concerned that she wouldn't grow, that she'd be really small. But now that she can walk, and she's growing, she seems like a normal child to us." Thus, the "choice" any pregnant woman makes to take or reject the test, and to keep or end any specific pregnancy, flows from the way that both pregnancy and disability are embedded in personal and collective values and judgments within which her own life has developed.

One aspect of that totality is prior experience with specific disabilities. Migdalia Ramirez, for example, was sent for genetic counseling because her sister had spina bifida. Both she and her mother were devout Catholics, generally opposed to abortion, but determined to end Migdalia's pregnancy if the fetus had the sister's condition. Amniocentesis found no neural tube defects, but it picked up 47XXY, Klinefelter's syndrome. This sex chromosome anomaly is linked to hormonal and growth problems, sterility, and risks of learning disabilities and mild retardation. Migdalia kept the pregnancy. She explained:

> I was only concerned if my baby could walk and see. This other stuff, it didn't concern me. They said he'd be normal, he might be slow-minded, but that's ok, as long as he looks normal. I'll be there for him. If my first kid was having what my sister's got, I'd need a lot of help. But he's growing up normal: He looks ok, he acts ok, he's a really nice kid. I could never abort for *that*; he's developing each day, I can handle this, as long as the baby looks normal. (Migdalia Ramirez, 19, Puerto Rican waitress)

Lucia Morez's 5-year-old daughter has Goldenhar's syndrome, a condition involving heart defects and facial asymmetries. In talking about her daughter, she said, "Sometimes when we're out on the street, people look at her, they say, 'What happened?' She cries, she know she looks bad. That's the thing: She really looks bad." Although the child has serious heart problems that must be consistently monitored, they did not enter the mother's discussion spontaneously, but only after being prodded by many questions. She refused amniocentesis in her second pregnancy because it could not monitor and detect the problem from which her first child suffered, and she was not overly concerned about chromosomal risks that could lead to mental retardation.

Family history also carves limits into the choices women make. Carol Seeger, a white Jewish museum curator, had prenatal diagnosis at 42, determined to abort if the fetus had neural tube defects, but not for Down syndrome. Having helped to raise a younger sister with Down's, she felt committed to living with that condition. Twig Hansen, a white Protestant homemaker, expressed reverse reasons when seeking amniocentesis: Her firstborn son had spina bifida, and her family was clear that they would meet that challenge again if the need arose, but they did not want to raise a child with Down syndrome.

Even the same diagnosis may evoke different interpretations and paths to decision-making. One genetic counselor encountered two patients, each of whom chose to abort a fetus, but for strikingly different reasons, after learning that its status included XXY sex chromosomes (Klinefelter's syndrome). One white professional couple told her, "If he can't grow up to have a shot at becoming the president, we don't want him." A low-income family said of the same condition, "A baby will have to face so many problems in this world, it isn't fair to add this one to his burdens."

And the interpretation of diagnoses may be deeply distorted, despite a counselor's best efforts. During my many years of participant observation, I was told similar stories three times about couples who chose to abort after a diagnosis of sex chromosome anomalies in their fetuses because they believed those anomalies would lead to homosexuality. In each case, counselors were unable to disabuse them of this wrongful interpretation; the fear of a homosexual orientation was so profound that sex chromosome problems and sexual "problems" were irrevocably conflated.

Such conflations are more likely to occur when diagnoses involve conditions about which a pregnant woman and her supporters have very little prior knowledge. When such shadowy diagnoses involve sex chromosomes, they often index anxieties about the limits of the natural bases of sexuality. A Colombian manicurist, for example, married to a Dominican factory worker, received a fetal diagnosis of Klinefelter's. They did not express much concern about the 10–20 percent risk of learning disabilities or mental retardation which accompanies this syndrome, and they listened to discussions of gynecomastia (male breast enlargement) and micro penises without intense distress. But the husband asked, "Is this going to make him homosexual? I don't want that." And the wife said, "He won't be able to have children; I wonder if he'll blame us." Both expressed concern about knowing something hidden that the son won't know about himself until he was older.

The cultural logic of equating sex chromosome anomalies and homosexuality was enunciated in a group session at Middle Hospital in which a counselor was explaining these conditions. One father interrupted to say, "This question is not related, but does science know, if you believe homosexuality is from birth, how chromosomes are related? It's logical that if you have more Xs or more Ys, you should have more sex in that one direction" (Mort Lansberger, white accountant). Here, sex chromosomes, sexual drives, sexual orientation, and normative gender are streamlined into the mirage of a single, quantifiable trajectory.

Relative Truths?

This melding of phobias and fantasies with scientific logic presents the counselor with a conundrum: She is dedicated to disabusing incorrect interpretations of scientific information, but once she has done her absolute best to accomplish that task, she must maintain value neutrality in her counseling practices. No counselor I ever interviewed, for example, believed that conflation of homosexuality and sex chromosome anomalies was a scientifically grounded or ethically acceptable reason to choose abortion. But none could argue forcefully enough to dissuade a client from seeking an abortion, once that interpretation had been mutually explored. Along the same lines, every counselor deplored abortion of a healthy fetus for reasons of sex selection, but all could tell vivid stories of the once or twice in their careers when someone had chosen termination because their healthy fetus was the "wrong sex." And usually, the wrong sex is the female sex. Such fetal "femicide" makes feminist theorists and activists justifiably very angry and pessimistic (e.g., Corea, Duelli-Klein et al. 1987; Hanmer 1981; cf. Pre-Selection 1994). Counselors are very troubled by their collusion with such drastic actions, but also express the discipline imposed by their nondirective stance. After all, most reason, a "woman's right to choose" extends to deciding to abort for whatever cause she finds meaningful, and this one denotes profound problems in her life should she produce an extra daughter instead of a much-desired son. Counselors perceive this problem to be particularly burdensome for Chinese and Indian women, who come from groups in which sons are more highly valued. In these communities, there have been public discussions of the uses of sex selection to produce them. Every counselor can tell stories of women whose social security, marriage, and happiness depend upon producing a son. In rare cases, women threaten suicide when confronted with a lack of male offspring. In such cases, standing with the woman places the counselor in an antagonistic relation to the fetus. Despite their own ethical beliefs, most counselors provide counseling services even when they know that a diagnosis is being sought for sex selection reasons. The few who refused to counsel under such conditions would refer potential clients to other services. And all agreed that the case of sex selection challenged the limits of their nondirective training.[19]

Such noninterventionism is, of course, something of a myth. All counselors are trained to be nondirective and to support a woman whether she chooses to use or not use prenatal diagnosis, and to pursue the consequences of the information it provides to her. But almost all acknowledge that "staying in neutral" is often a difficult task. And all have encountered circumstances under which they felt justified in attempting to influence a patient's decision. Many counselors, for example, will accept religious or cultural grounds for refusing the test without much probing, but will contest fear of needles when it seems the only reason for not using amniocentesis. Women from many ethnic backgrounds expressed fear of needles, Spanish speakers especially. It is hard to get women to articulate the content of such fears. When observing, I often asked for an elaboration. Beyond the short-lived minor pain of being stuck, what did the needle connote? One Haitian patient who refused the test said, for example, "It's not just the feeling, it's what's going in and coming out. I'm used to a blood test, I know what they're taking. But not this. They are taking something else." Her aversion to the removal of amniotic fluid may condense many concerns, for example, fear of the new, or uncertainty about the status of a liminal bodily fluid connecting her and her fetus. This fluid has none of the obvious life-and-death valences associated with blood. In contrasting amniotic fluid to blood, this woman invoked a substance that is simultaneously symbolic and material in its importance. As a conduit for both mortality and immortality, blood is deeply embedded not only in the domain of medicine, but in kinship and religion as well.

But amniotic fluid is harder to place: Composed of fetal urine and sloughed-off skin cells that can be made to grow under laboratory conditions, it is the medium in which the developing fetus lives and excretes. A medical text would speak of its electrolytic isomorphism with maternal blood, with which it shares most of its contents, excepting blood cells themselves. Pregnant women, however, often describe amniotic fluid in terms of the child, substantialized, acorn to oak, in the fluid itself:

> It will be ok. The fluid came out right, light. The doctor told me the fluid looked good, so I know the baby looks good. If the fluid comes dark, then you got problems, then they take action right away. (Luz Perez, 37, Puerto Rican home-care attendant)

> "Beautiful"—the doctor said "beautiful," when he saw what was in the test tube. The baby will be beautiful. (Martha Freeman, 39, African-American schoolteacher)

Many women expressed astonishment, awe, or disbelief in the diagnostic possibilities of this substance:

> I never knew such a small amount of liquid could show so many important things. (JoAnna Lytel, white real estate sales agent)

> I don't think I really believe in chromosomes, I mean, I could see the pictures, but I can't believe everything is in the chromosomes, and the chromosomes are really just floated in that stuff. Isn't it mainly baby's pee? (Aleta Mitchell, 36, white administrative secretary)

And they may feel quite proprietary: "It's very surprising what they can find out from a little of my fluid," said Carol Jameson, 40, an African-American bus driver.

But the counselor, of course, cannot respond to these shadow concerns about the symbolic valence of amniotic fluid. In response to the wary Haitian woman whose fear of needles is cited above, she said, "The test lasts one minute. The child with Down syndrome lives with mental retardation all of his life." While this is true and very important, it elides a missing middle in the decision-making process. There is a synoptic silence when it is assumed that testing ends the problem of carrying a fetus with Down syndrome. That silence covers a discussion of selective abortion, a topic fraught with emotion, to which we return in chapter 9.

Many counselors will also challenge the assumptions women hold about their own ability to control fetal health, when those assumptions get in the way of accepting the test. For example, when a Dominican Spanish speaker refused the test at City Hospital, saying she was healthy, felt fine, and lived right, the counselor said to her interpreter, "Tell her it doesn't depend on how she feels, or how she lives. The only way to know is to have the test."

Practicing Value Neutrality

But in principle, counselors are trained to probe a woman's (or a couple's) desires about testing, rather than imposing their own values. Indeed, they specialize in putting the question "What should I do?" back on the patient. When someone asks, "What would you do if you were in my shoes?" Most counselors respond with a stock answer:

I'm not pregnant, you are. Remember that.

I don't know, and I can't tell you what to do, how to use this information. You're not going to know me in one year, you're not going to know your OB in ten years. You're going to know your kids forever. So the decision has to be yours, not his or mine.

Sometimes a patient will ask what others have done, for example: "Do most people want to know the sex [of the fetus]?" Most counselors will respond, "That's a very personal decision every couple has to make for themselves," rather than providing any social grounding. Counselors might say, for example, that about half the women who have amniocentesis want to know the fetal sex, or that some couples don't want to know right away but may seek out the information later in the pregnancy. Such statements might make the patient more comfortable with the burden of having to decide without providing specific advice. But I have never heard a counselor offer such generalized pictures. Their commitment to the personal and individual nature of decision-making is highly consonant with basic American values. But in supporting the woman (or her shadow social unit, the couple) in personal decision-making, Rogerian reflexivity, which echoes back the expressive content of the client—"I hear you saying you could/couldn't handle a child like that" or "How do *you* feel about those numbers? Are you comfortable with them?"—also reinforces the sense of isolation that some people experience in the face of new choices. The anxiety attendant upon amniocentesis may be linked not only to the content of the information it yields, but to the very process of choosing to know some "facts of life" that are not conventionally revealed.

Nondirectiveness is easiest to practice when patients direct themselves. Many middle-class women and couples will announce, for example, that they are planning to have prenatal testing before the counselor even poses the question. For them, the discourse of science fits like a second skin:

I'm 42. I think at my age I'd be foolish, anyone would be foolish, not to have this test. (Brenda Kelly, white lawyer)

I'm planning to have the test. I'm not one for mysteries. (Althea Jenkins, 37, African-American special-education teacher)

But the limits on nondirective counseling are also deeply intertwined with the counselor's assessment of a patient's ability to garner support in a stressful time. This assessment is itself related to ethnic and class factors in indirect ways. When low-income Dominican and Puerto Rican patients refused testing, for example, because they feared their partners would disapprove and abandon them, one counselor who was herself from a working-class, Spanish-speaking background would routinely query, "What if he leaves you, anyway?" At the hospital where she worked, the vast majority of pregnant women were, or would soon be, single mothers. Another, whose clients were mainly new immigrants, emphasized that having a chronically ill child would affect the family's project of successful migration and mobility. In such cases, counselors probe a bit harder because they have already relativized the limits of individualism in the life of a specific woman and family. One counselor also relativized her own background in response to my questions about nondirectiveness with patients who had little scientific literacy: "I'm not Protestant. If I were Protestant, perhaps I'd believe more in nondirective counseling. But I'm not, and I don't."

And some clients are clear that they want direction. Haitian women, for example, would often ask me what I thought they ought to do, when I was translating into French for them. I would, of course, throw the question back to them, but many spoke some variant of "I'm not the doctor. If I were, no need to be here, I'd know what to do" (Marie-Rose Charles, 35, Haitian domestic worker).

In such instances, it is hard to disentangle the generic problems of a nondirective counseling model from the specific limits that experienced counselors know their low-income, foreign-born clients confront. Here, the lack of prior scientific literacy melds with the exigencies of highly stressful, often unstable lives. Indeed, some counselors have informally questioned whether their commitment to nondirection should be tempered by their commitment to understanding what a woman is saying about how the current pregnancy fits into her life. Counseling across cultural differences sometimes creates the space for counselors to become more self-conscious of the limits of their own resources.

Many counselors, of course, are quite aware of the communicative chasms separating them from their clients. A counselor who had worked at two very different hospitals said,

> I find it lots easier to be unbiased with this population than I did at Elite. Here at City, I can't even pretend to know what's going on in their minds, I really have to just listen and work from where they are. At Elite, I could fall into the mistake of thinking they were me. Or I'm them. I sometimes found myself saying, "Oh, you couldn't accept that . . . " because I thought they were like me. And that's a dangerous situation. If I had to spend even one whole day inside the life of some of my patients here, I probably wouldn't believe what I'd see. I can't make a lot of assumptions about them, the way I do with people who look and talk like me.[20]

All counselors are aware that women from low-income and/or minority backgrounds are more likely to reject the test than are women from more mainstream backgrounds. Although many counselors will declare some version of "I'm not here to sell amnios" or "I don't think I'm a success or failure depending on whether she takes the test," each refusal underlines where the differences between a biomedical worldview and the specific objections that individual pregnant women articulate might lie. Women's reasons for refusal range from religious beliefs to fear of miscarriage, from mistrust in the accuracy of statistics and testing to discomfort with unbalancing the imagined forces sustaining this pregnancy. Among the most common reasons given for refusing the test is some variant of "My husband wouldn't let me." Just what does this mean?

When women identified their husbands as the authority on whose behalf they were refusing the test, I often wondered whether I was witnessing male dominance or female invocation of a classic manly privilege in the service of their own, polite resistance. Sometimes, I felt confident in making an interpretation. Hsia Chiu, for example, had been in this country for only three years when her husband decided she should have amniocentesis in her first pregnancy. While he was out of the consulting room, I asked what lay behind her silence at the counseling session, and whether she wanted to have the test. She replied,

> My mother, my grandmother, they all had babies in China, and nobody did this. They wouldn't do it now, if they were here. Now is modern times, everyone wants to know everything, to know as soon as possible, in advance, about everything. What kind of information is this? I don't know, but I will soon have it, faster than I can understand it.

Ecuador-born Coralina Bollo felt pressured into having the test by her U.S.-born husband. Flora Blanca from Peru had to keep her decision to have it secret from her disapproving *companero*. "He'll kill me for this, but I'm gonna do it," commented Puerto Rico–born Nilda Cintron. In such cases, I was persuaded that male dominance was driving a woman's "right to choose."

But gender scripts also revealed healthy doses of female manipulation: Many women told me they brought their partners to see the sonogram to further their own ends: "Frank just isn't as committed to this pregnancy as he should be," commented white psychologist Marcia Lang, "but once he sees the baby moving, I know he'll get excited." Juana Martes, a Dominican home-care attendant, also thought fathers should see the sonogram that accompanies the test: "When the little creature moves, they begin to know what women feel, how they suffer for it to be born, and then they respect their wives."

Sometimes, conflicts between partners surfaced in the counseling sessions, revealing the different interests women and men had constructed. When one low-income Colombian couple I observed, for example, were being counseled because both were carriers for sickle-cell trait, the man appeared uninterested, staring into space as amniocentesis was explained. But when the moment of decision-making arrived, he sat up straight and firmly enunciated: "If it's normal, I want it: I want it for the rest of my life. From my position I say, Out, out if the baby is no good, if it comes out no normal." The pregnant woman turned toward him and said quite firmly, "Who's carrying this baby?" The counselor tried to defuse conflict, saying, "That's a decision you'll make together," working from the scientific and middle-class model of egalitarian genetic and social contributions to kinship. But in her intake notes she had written that this couple had been together for only three months. There is thus a potential conflict between the gendered relations the counselor would like to see at work and the ones being enunciated in her presence.

Laura Escobar's Egyptian Muslim husband, Ibrim, reluctantly agreed to the test, stressing that he didn't believe in abortion: He *knew* God would protect his unborn child. Laura turned to me, and said in Spanish (which her husband does not understand, but I do), "When God provides a problem, he also provides the cure."

On the basis of scores of stories like these, I do not believe that a woman's decision to use or refuse prenatal testing is simply driven by the power of her partner's wishes. Rather, the very fact of decision-making in a couple involved in amniocentesis reveals the existing gender negotiations within which a specific pregnancy is undertaken. There is a complex choreography of domination, manipulation, negotiation, and, sometimes, resistance in the gender tales women tell about their decisions to use or reject this piece of reproductive technology.

Expanding the Context

"My husband doesn't want me to have this test" thus opens up a space for the interpretation of concrete gender relations as they are played out in each specific pregnancy. But such interpretations are inherently undecidable, in light of the information at hand. To understand each negotiation, we would need a different, fuller context within which to situate the meaning of this particular pregnancy in light of community values, reproductive histories, and the trajectory of each particular woman and her partner. Such a grounding would provide more ample space for examining the contradictory social relations and limits each pregnant woman faces, and the constrained agency she exercises in her reproductive choices.

This need for a fuller context emerged frequently throughout my observations of intake interviews, and inflected my understandings not only of gender relations, but of racial-ethnic stereotypes and class-based resources. Often, a chance comment by a client or counselor reminded me of how little one could understand from one single, simple observation. What is foregrounded in a genetic counseling session often requires rich backgrounding before its meaning can be understood.

For example, one 42-year-old white travel agent remained silent throughout her intake counseling session at Middle Hospital, and seemed unenthusiastic in her pro forma acceptance of the test. In my observation notes, she appears "medically compliant" but not curious. Leaving the room, I ran into her at the elevator by chance. Out of the counseling room, she launched into a highly informed, dense discussion of chorionic villus sampling (the first-trimester test performed on preplacental tissue, then considered experimental), and told me she was going to Philadelphia to speak with one of the leading researchers in the field. Only after that meeting did she intend to decide which of the two prenatal tests she would have. Her "passive medical compliance" in the counseling room was informed by considerable research which went beyond the topics discussed in the room, and which was not available to me as I observed her session.

At City, one African-American male partner dressed in gorgeous and dramatic African nationalist attire refused to answer any medical or economic questions concerning his own background, exhibiting a clear "attitude." I observed the counselor backing off, mentally labeling him as hostile and uncooperative, not only in his response to her questions, but also in his lack of visible interest in his partner's decisions concerning the test. But as the session was drawing to an end, he looked the counselor in the eye for the first time and addressed her directly, saying, "You mean there's no paternal incidence to Down syndrome? How do we know this condition is only linked to the mother's age, and not the father's?" In articulating a critical question in scientific language, he shattered the genetic counselor's stereotype, simultaneously revealing and concealing other resources, interests, and insecurities he might hold.

A pregnant Indian woman came to counseling at Elite to discuss the slow learning of her 2-year-old daughter, and the advisability of having an amniocentesis in her present pregnancy despite her young age of 31. The counselor listened hard to her concerns and arranged the test. Later, she told me she suspected the woman wanted it for sex selection, even though the sex of the fetus was not discussed. I was nonplussed: Was the counselor applying ethnocentric assumptions about South Asians? Was the pregnant woman directly asking for help in deciding whether testing for "slowness" was advisable, or indirectly asking for help to end the pregnancy, should the sex be "wrong"? Was I missing an important subtext of the interaction?

Such encounters remain interpretively undecidable when based on a single formal medical interaction. In order to break the medical framework, and find out more about how women and their supporters discussed prenatal testing and its implications in the contexts of their daily lives, I chose to follow some test takers home. By deploying ethnographic techniques in which knowledge gained in one context is compared with knowledge gained in another, and its multiplicities, contradictions, and resonances richly overlapped at the site of analysis, I hoped to both query and observe amniocentesis as it played out in "real time," not merely in the chronology and location of medical interviewing. What I learned about the place of prenatal testing in their lives in the subject of chapter 5.

5
Waiting and Watching

So I was three months pregnant before I knew I was pregnant. Just figured it was change of life. The clinic kept saying no, and it's really the same signs, menopause and pregnancy, you just feel that lousy. So when they told me I was pregnant I thought about abortion. I mean, maybe I figured I was too old for this. But in my neighborhood, a lot of Caribbean women have babies; a lot of them are late babies. So I got used to it. But the clinic doctor was freaked out. He sent me for genetic counseling. Counseling? I thought counseling meant giving reassurance, helping someone accept and find their way. Wisdom, help, guidance, you know what I mean. This lady was a smart lady, but right away she started pulling out pictures of mongoloids. So I got huffy: "I didn't come here to look at pictures of mongoloids," I says to her. So she got huffy and told me it was about mongoloids, this counseling. So we got more and more huffy between us, and finally I left. Wasn't going to sit and listen to that stuff. By the time I got myself to the appointment [for the test], I'd been to see my healing woman, who calmed me down, gave me the reassurance I needed. I knew everything was gonna be ok. Oh, I wouldn't have had an abortion that late in the game. Maybe if it had been earlier. But not so late. I just got helped out by the healer woman, so I could wait out the results of that test without too much fussing. (Naiumah Foster, 43, African-American educator)

NAIUMAH FOSTER'S ALTERNATIVE counseling resources are not available to everyone confronting the anxiety that prenatal testing provokes. Some women find solace in talking with friends, family members, or religious leaders; others prefer to keep their feelings about the test to themselves. While a few women told me they were able to put the test out of their minds while waiting for results, the majority experienced this liminal period as fraught with concern.[21] Most of the women who ageed to speak with me during that long waiting period said that talking about the test made them feel better; a few reported feeling worse.

In this chapter, I try to parse the structure of the anxiety which the pregnant women I interviewed in their homes, and occasionally, their offices, reported while waiting for test results. While some of the anxious images and emotions we conversationally explored are surely linked to a widespread sense of liminality accompanying pregnancy as a time-framed, embodied passage replete with unknown dangers and possibilities, it is my contention that this older, perhaps universal response has now been given a technological boost and form. Highly educated users of amniocentesis are likely to report dissatisfaction with the gap between the possibilities of what they imagine to be the benefits of thorough biomedical surveillance and control of fetal health and the actual limited nature of amniocentesis results; those with fewer scientific aspirations are more satisfied with the possibilities of testing, but no less anxious about its outcome. And women from diverse class, ethnic-racial, and religious backgrounds all responded to the technological shaping of the fetus into a baby which was depicted by the interpretations of sonograms that accompany the test. Yet even as most women expressed deep pleasure at having "met" their babies on the sonogram screen, they also described layers of anxiety. For if sonographers can describe the ultrasound monitor's images in language that enables pregnant women to project fully imaginable babies, this encounter also underlines the dire consequences of potentially receiving a "bad" or positive diagnosis. The liminal period awaiting test results intersects anxiety on many levels.

Of course, the early medical and psychosocial literature on patient responses to amniocentesis picked up this test-provoked anxiety as the central theme of evaluation (Lipkin and Rowley 1974; Lippman-Hand and Fraser 1979a, 1979b; Lubs and de la Cruz 1977), and all the counselors I interviewed recognized the increased level of anxiety engendered by the test. As pregnant women said after counseling and test taking,

I *do* feel more informed. But it's like learning to drive, and getting scared of car crashes. You know you could have one, you really do. For a while it's too scary to drive. But you just have to do it, to turn the key and drive the car again. (Lacey Smythe, 38, African-American secretary)

The chances of miscarrying are not so big, as I understand them. But I'm 40, and throwing all those negatives on a person, it can be scary. (Merced Rodriguez, 40, Colombian homemaker)

I felt very bad after I had the test. I went to bed, I was so scared. But then the next day, I tried not to think about it. But sometimes, when I look down there, I see the spot where they put the needle, I see where it was. Otherwise, I try not to think about it. (Mari-Carmen Trujillo, 38, Honduran UPS parcel handler)

Some anxiety is materially grounded as well as existential: Women may perceive their jobs as threatening to their fetuses, as did a Puerto Rican hair colorist who had observed two miscarriages and the birth of a child with cerebral palsy among her beautician colleagues. As a matter of practical epidemiology, she came for genetic counseling in order to ask if the dyes and fumes with which she works might affect her pregnancy. "It sticks in your mind, those girls I work with. It makes you wonder." Less specific but no less burdensome is the time frame that work imposes on prenatal health care. One of the suggestions that counselors make is that women who have had an amniocentesis take the rest of the day off and avoid physical stress for a day or two, as most test-induced miscarriages happen within the first twenty-four to forty-eight hours. Inevitably, some women question that recommendation. While the cry, "But I can't afford to take the rest of the day off" may come from a busy lawyer, I also heard it from child-care workers, secretaries, and home health attendants. There are practical concerns at stake in undergoing the test.

Liminal Dread

But much of the dread that accompanies the test is existential, focusing on fear of causing a miscarriage, fear of learning bad news, and, perhaps, fear of having unbalanced the forces of nature which are presumed to be protecting a pregnancy. Such anxiety deserves a closer reading, for it is potentially composed of several layers. Most obviously, pregnancy is, by definition, a liminal state. In it, each individual woman slowly intertwines her own life with that of a simultaneously material, imagined, and growing other. Then, through a life-changing, physically and emotionally transformative labor process, the conjoined become two. This species-wide process of multiplication and transformation connects us all to natural life, providing a universal grounding on which historically specific symbolic, discursive, and practical activities are staged. Worldwide, the process of reproduction may be envisioned in many ways: as mimesis, a kind of "photocopier" of parental or other kinship material; as the unfolding of a spirit or soul destined to fulfill a cyclical mission; as an acorn, embryologically poised to unfurl into an oak; as a miniaturization of prior adult persons and their social relations or in some other fashion (Ginsburg and Rapp 1995; Jordanova, 1995; Strathern 1992). The interpretation of pregnancy has inspired responses in contexts as seemingly distant as Australian Aboriginal tribal ritual, Catholic art, and the development of Western reproductive medicine. Such institutionalized responses are highly gendered: whether one sees Australian ritual as "womb envy" (cf. Bettelheim 1954), envisions Mary's virgin birth of Jesus as "unique of all her sex" (Delaney 1986; Warner 1976), or pictures perinatology as a "male take-over of female creativity" (Corea, Duelli-Klein et al. 1987), pregnancy is clearly located on a terrain which is irreducibly female, but the need to control its outcome, thus ensuring members for a collective future, often fuels the activities of male specialists. The sexually embodied nature of pregnancy evokes a range of strong, and strongly culturally coded emotions, ranging from fear, awe, and dread, to hope, confidence, and attachment. Its anxiety is probably universal, as birth and death, maternal pain and accomplishment, and the many interests all societies hold in the recruitment of the next generation are inscribed in the rituals which pregnant women must follow.

Amniocentesis feeds upon this older, more universal state of liminal pregnancy anxiety, for it speaks directly to the personal and social aspirations embodied in producing normatively acceptable babies. The current generation of pregnant women is the first to be given an epidemiology of trepidation, and taught to live by the numbers. In place of "old wives' tales" and traditional wisdom, they have been given risk analysis. But its statistical powers provide only generalized descriptions for the specific concerns of individual women:

> You know, I kept thinking after the genetic counseling, the amniocentesis, they just keep upping the ante on you, they really do. Now, I'm not even allowed to pet my cat, or have a glass of wine after a hard day's work. I'm supposed to think that three cigarettes a day is what caused my first miscarriage. They can see a lot of patterns, but they sure can't explain them. But they talk as if they could explain them. I mean, they want you to have a baby by the statistics, not by your own lifestyle. (Laura Forman, 35, white theater producer)

Feminists have strongly criticized the "iatrogenic (medically generated) anxiety" which contemporary obstetrics in general, and amniocentesis in particular, produce (e.g., Hubbard 1990; Rothman 1986, 1989). As many historians, sociologists, and other observers of modern obstetrics have argued, the controlling preoccupations of prenatal and obstetrical health regimes turn pregnancy into a diseased state, sapping women's confidence in their own bodies' ability to produce healthy babies naturally. In that process, medical services, overwhelmingly controlled and practiced by male doctors, become indispensable (Davis-Floyd and Sargent 1997; Ehrenreich and English 1978; Kobrin 1966; Rothman 1982; Wertz and Wertz 1977). Yet as other feminist researchers have pointed out, the powerful critique of the medicalization of pregnancy should not obscure its potential to alleviate the material dangers and consequences that childbearing holds for some women: Historically, maternal suffering and death figured large in female consciousness (Leavitt 1986), and maternal and infant morbidity and mortality continue to plague poor communities, where improvements in both the quantity and quality of prenatal care could and should prevent needless affliction (Christmas n.d.; Kochanek et al. 1994; Queen 1994). Thus many women may experience the constraints of medical control, while others are still struggling to enjoy medicine's benefits. Both stories are "true" and embedded in the increasingly nuanced critique of the medicalization of pregnancy which feminist scholarship provides. Indeed, the same class of women who spawned the activism and scholarship that criticizes the social control of pregnancy are both the beneficiaries of its positive impact on maternal-newborn health outcomes and its controlling constraints. Additionally, many women reject this critique of medicalization, for they share American medicine's technocratic vision of controlling nature through cultural, mechanical intervention. Using technology to subdue natural processes in pregnancy fits well with their cultural worldview in general. For them, obstetrical interventions offer order and reassurance at the symbolic level despite the many practical, cogent criticisms leveled by feminists and other health activists (Davis-Floyd 1992). Thus, the anxiety surrounding amniocentesis expressed in the interviews I conducted mirrors a tension-fraught terrain: The acknowledgment of pregnancy's creative as well as frightening aspects, the desire to benefit from technological control as well as to reject it in favor of trusting natural processes, and the discomfort of making personal meaning out of statistics are all expressed in the concerns of pregnant women struggling to find reassurance through a medically monitored, culturally liminal, and contested state.

Communication and Miscommunication

A tension between the limited and specific nature of what an amniocentesis may reveal, and the more existential nature of pregnancy anxiety was the subject of many women's (and, occasionally, men's) evaluations of the counseling process itself. The literature on the evaluation of genetic counseling sessions suggests that counselors are usually quite satisfied with their communication with patients, but that patients have a far more varied response. In close to 50 percent of counselor-client interactions surveyed in one large study, neither side understood what the other wanted to discuss. In this study, more educated clients and those from higher socioeconomic groups fared better at communicating their questions and getting what they considered to be adequate responses (Kessler 1989; Wertz and Sorenson 1986; Wertz, Sorenson et al. 1986). My own data suggest a somewhat different shape to communicative evaluation on the part of patients: On the whole, and with significant exceptions, working-class and lower-middle-class clients appreciated their counseling sessions very much, finding the information to be very impressive, and the description of the test to be accurate:

> I think that's as close as they can get besides actually sticking you with one of those needles because they let you know what you're in for, what's actually going to happen. (Sandra McAlister, 41, African-American administrative secretary)

> She was very professional, she explained everything really well, we both understood this low MSAFP business by the time she got through. (John Freeman, 32, African-American computer technologist)

People from higher income brackets, especially if they were professionals, often considered the counseling unimpressive or insufficient:

> I found it to be mildly disorganized. I mean, those aren't great statistics. She didn't tell us how long ago was the sample, was it in New York hospitals or all over the country? Has the study been repeated. . . . How can you say it's an accurate study if it hasn't been repeatedly updated? You're required to sign consent forms right, left, and center, but that's for the protection of the hospital, not for your own information. . . . They're practicing defensive medicine. And they really don't give you as much information as they might. The questioning about our specific backgrounds should be vital, and I found it perfunctory. I

would have preferred to answer a questionnaire by mail, in advance. Then we could pinpoint the exact problems requiring testing. (Emily Pratt, 39, white lawyer)

Three themes of discontent are expressed in this evaluation, and all appeared frequently in professionals' responses. The first is the interrogation of the accuracy or efficacy of the numbers; the second is the criticism that genetic counseling is a protection device for the hospitals, not for the clients; and the third is that the specific circumstances of the pregnant woman (or, in this cohort, couple) have not been adequately taken into account. Over the course of several years of interviewing, I came to think that these three themes reflected class position and experiences, a point worth illustration.

"Fighting with numbers" is a strategy that frequently characterizes upper-middle-class client interactions, especially male interactions, with genetic counselors. A hospital-based psychologist, for example, challenged the counselor's expertise by asking about the patient population from which the Down syndrome epidemiology was drawn, asserting that his genealogy was full of older women having babies who would never have participated in such a study. When the counselor courteously corrected his notion of population sampling, he became quite aggressive and asked about the medical significance of diet as a contribution to birth defects. A biostatistician insisted that he and his pregnant wife had come to counseling for a decision-making tree, as he already had access to all relevant information concerning the incidence and distribution of birth defects statistics; he had no time for the counselor's rendition. Watching such interactions, it was hard not to make two judgments: first, that male professional expertise sits uncomfortably in a room with less-credentialed but more specialized female professionalism; and second, that male anxiety is commonly and acceptably expressed through rationalized hostility. The etiquette of counseling here permits behavior that would less likely be tolerated from those (like most women and/or minority men) who do not conventionally hold discursive authority. Professional women, too, can participate in the numbers game, but I have rarely heard them express overt hostility. When she heard about my research at a conference, for example, a white economist told me her own amniocentesis story. Pregnant with a third child at 38, she read extensively in the medical literature, and discovered that the birthrate of live born children with Down syndrome was 25 percent lower than the figures quoted for the prenatal detection of this condition. She reasoned that the test was less accurate (that is, that it produced 25 percent false positives) than what the geneticists were claiming, and rejected it on that basis. The difference between the two rates (at midtrimester, via amniocentesis; at birth, among newborns) is based on another "fact" which the economist failed to turn up in her reading: Chromosomally atypical fetuses remain vulnerable to miscarriage and stillbirth throughout the pregnancy; late spontaneous abortions and perinatal deaths of Down syndrome fetuses account for the difference in rates (Hook 1978). Her "informed consent" to reject the test was based on the upper-middle-class, highly educated strategy of "fighting with numbers." She was testing whether the discourse of genetics actually included a response to her own particular questions, based on a sophisticated but quite idiosyncratic statistical interpretation. Many professionals feel comfortable deploying the discourse of statistics, using this strategy to accept or reject the counselor's expertise.

Indeed, numbers loom large for professionals: Louise and Mark Peoples, a public school consultant and a college professor, were dismayed and discouraged to learn that their risk of carrying a fetus with Down syndrome had significantly increased in the four years since their first son's birth. They questioned the rapidity with which the incidence had gone up. Micki and Steve Schwartz, a real estate agent and a lawyer, felt bruised by the "callous way" in which such important numbers were offered:

> She gave us all these numbers and they were just scary and depersonalized. She never stopped to consider how we might feel hearing them. They ought to send you the numbers in the mail, so you could read it in advance, and get down to business, reacting, when you meet face to face.

Like Emily Pratt and Micki and Steve Schwartz, many professionals "want it both ways": They question the importance or the accuracy of the statistics when applied to their unique cases, while bemoaning what they perceive as counselors' insensitivity to the impact such frigid facts will have. This sense of entitlement to the best scientific data, personal, even existential, attention, and entitlement to control also strikes me as a class-based response to anxiety.

Many from this strata also considered the counseling session, especially the informed consent forms which they were asked to sign, as a protection racket:

> The genetic counseling was a drag. She gave me enough ifs, ands, and buts so that I would sign the consent form. Then I couldn't sue the pants off the hospital if something happened. I could have done without that. (Rita Newbury, 35, white real estate agent)

Many also indicated a dissatisfaction with the lack of individual, tailor-made testing, "as if" a more thorough interaction with the counselor would reveal additional tests that should be undergone:

> I think different people want different amounts of information. We got foggy-headed with her generalizations, we really wanted to talk about our own pedigrees. (Laura Forman, 35, white theater producer)

> No one walks around saying the numbers thing, like thirty-three out of one thousand have a miscarriage. They immediately say, "Which thirty-three? Is it me?" Hasn't she ever talked to thoughtful, educated women? Doesn't she know what our real concerns are? (Alicia Williams, 36, African-American public relations executive)

The generalizing nature of statistics, on the one hand, and the limitations of the capabilities of the test, on the other, left dissatisfied professionals in an existential dilemma. They could evaluate the limits of counseling information, but they could neither escape its indeterminacy nor acquire a more uniquely personalized reading of fetal health. Hamstrung, some reacted with anxiety or contemptuous dismissal. Perhaps this reaction is based in part on having experienced a relatively great amount of control over their life circumstances prior to choosing a late pregnancy. If my interpretation is correct, then, once again, the focus on control and the assumption that specialized services can enable greater control may also be linked to the middle-class, educated histories and worldviews including secularism, within which many late first pregnancies fit.

A few middle-class women who were (or were about to become) single mothers also told me they were uncomfortable at the counseling session because counselors request detailed information on paternal as well as maternal contributions to the pregnancy. Having chosen to carry a pregnancy without male social contributions, they saw little reason for evaluating male contributions to medical history:

> The nurses asked me a lot of intrusive questions about the father, questions I couldn't even answer. I was kind of adamant that I didn't want to discuss it. (Carol Seeger, 42, white museum curator)

> The counselor wanted to know why artificial insemination, and I was floored, I didn't know what to tell her. Finally, I just said, "Because I'm a single woman." I didn't know why she needed to know. (Enid Zimmerman, 41, white municipal service planner)

Both of the "out" lesbians whom I interviewed also reacted against the request for paternal medical information, but my sample is obviously too small to draw any interpretations. Its size may have less to do with the actual number of lesbian women using amniocentesis than with the decision not to reveal their sexual orientation in a bureaucratic, fragmented institution from which they must constantly seek services. The risk of hostility, derision, or other prejudicial reaction may condition a decision surrounding sexual and/or other reproductive information.

Nonetheless, counselors are persistent in seeking paternal health information. Their testing recommendations are, of course, based on information about both genetic contributors: A family history of mental retardation or spina bifida is as likely to run on the male as the female side. The responses of some middle-class single mothers and two self-identified lesbians thus reproduced the cultural assumption that women are solely responsible for the health of their fetuses, even as they contested the heterosexually coupled assumptions which ran through the intake interview. Clearly, they were also commenting on an ethos or norm of counseling: "When I got to the appointment, it was all for couples, like, for the fathers to be there: no room in that room for a single mother like me. Just imagine" (Naiumah Foster, 43, African-American educator).

Poor, working-class, and lower-middle-class single mothers were less likely to comment on normative coupledom as an aspect of counseling, and many counselors were skilled at making them feel comfortable, especially if their patient population often arrived without partners. Many single mothers from less privileged backgrounds simply told the counselor, "I don't know anything about his family" or "I can't tell you all that stuff," dismissing the counselors' probes for paternal health histories. But they rarely questioned why the information was needed. Professionals, once again, felt more empowered to question the framework within which their medical interactions were structured. "I've become more and more open to Western medicine, I basically think it's a good thing. Of course, you've got to stay in control, learn all about it, know your rights and needs" (Enid Zimmerman, 41, white municipal service planner).

Pregnant women and their supporters from less privileged backgrounds also expressed some dissatisfaction with the counseling process, but their reasons were quite different.

> You want to know my viewpoint? I was overwhelmed by that terminology. You could be more graphic, so people could understand. If you want to explain things, just make for example one circle with two lines,

then you can say more. There were too many words, too many pictures, I couldn't follow it all. [Asked if understanding would have been easier if the presentation had been in Spanish, he responded:] It's the same thing: In English or in Spanish, it's too dense. (Hubierto Lopez, 38, municipal worker)

How could I follow all that? She did her best, but it was a lot to follow. (Iris Hidalgo, 38, Puerto Rican homemaker)

I knew about mongolism. The rest of that stuff, I didn't quite get it, but I got the basic point. Otherwise, she would have had to slow way down and I could see she was busy. Too busy to explain it more. (Michelle Jeffers, 35, African-American nursing home attendant)

In each of the counseling sessions cited above, I had observed clients being unfailingly polite, and insisting that they understood the counselor's message when she asked for feedback. Yet in their home evaluations, there is ample display of the gaps across which counseling information did not reach. In thinking about why counselors don't always know whether their message is being received, I believe that at least two forces are at play. One is that even counseling materials developed for clients with low scientific literacy may often miss their mark; the other is that many clients from lower-working-class or working-poor backgrounds blame themselves rather than professional explanations when they do not understand something in a medical interaction. In other words, there is ample space for both improving the content of information, and increasing awareness of the role which class-structured etiquette plays. When some clients from working-poor and working-class backgrounds politely told the counselor they understood the information she offered at the hospital, but later told me that they did not, I was struck by the complexity of the problem of scientific literacy in a highly stratified society. Those on the top end of the scientific literacy scale often expressed dissatisfaction with the counseling process. Knowing more before they entered the counseling room made them less appreciative of the resources that counselors offered. Those from less privileged backgrounds expressed deep appreciation of the counselor's knowledge, but were sometimes unable to understand or use it. There is an obvious gap between the vast and rapidly proliferating font of information that genetics research is producing and counselors are shaping, and the communicative aspirations and frameworks that pregnant women and their supporters from diverse backgrounds bring to their interactions.

Acquiring Scientific Literacy

Of course, scientific literacy is forged in daily life, and not just in formal education or medical interactions. Because I wanted to learn about how women incorporated a new reproductive technology into their lives, and not only into their medical histories, one of my questions was how they first learned about amniocentesis. Their answers revealed that discourses of prenatal testing, genetics, and disability have permeated into sediments of public knowledge throughout the social spectrum. Many told me they had friends who had already used the test:

> I'm a big talker, I learn from all my friends. Nobody said, "Don't do it." (Diana Mendosa, 35, Puerto Rican nurse)

> My two sisters, they had it. Nothing bad happened. (Merced Rodriguez, 41, Colombian homemaker)

Virtually all middle-class women knew about the test from a dense and overlapping nexus of friends, medical professionals, and books. Working-class women more likely learned about the test from friends. But they and working-poor patients were also the only ones for whom a counseling session might be the first time they had heard of amniocentesis.

Sometimes, those without prior knowledge had to evaluate professional versus peer conversation: "At the clinic, everyone was talking about it, they say, 'Don't do it, my sister did it, they put the needle in the baby's head, it came out dead.' But I figured the nurse, she told me right" (Mari-Carmen Trujillo, 38, Honduran UPS package handler).

Networks of information (and sometimes, misinformation) abound throughout daily life. Many women in all social strata learned about both childhood disability and prenatal testing from mainstream magazines: *Glamour, Self, Savvy, McCalls, New York Magazine,* the *New York Times Sunday Magazine, Parents,* and *Good Housekeeping* all carried stories related to this technology during the years in which I was interviewing. Three times during the course of my research I found myself implicated when women I met said they had read about amniocentesis in articles in *New York Magazine, Discover,* and *Self* where my own research was quoted. During this period, activists from the Down Syndrome Parent Support Group in which I was an observer appeared on the *Donahue* show; I registered dramatic increases in the knowledge and the number of questions clinic patients raised at counseling sessions after that appearance. Middle-class women, especially professionals, were often unable to recall when and where they had first learned about amniocentesis; it was imbricated into their general fund of social knowledge. Well-educated women often arrived at counseling sessions with new questions on Wednesdays after the Tuesday science section of the *New York Times* reported on advances in genetic technologies. But women without privileged educational backgrounds were likely to remember and to mention specific media sources when I asked about their first encounters with this technology. Some learned from TV shows like *Jerry's Kids* (a telethon whose paternalistic attitudes make many disability rights activists livid), and from talk radio programs. Others found out about testing from soap operas and docudramas. During the late 1980s, *Dallas,* a melodrama of family wealth, sex, and intrigue, unfurled an amniocentesis story in three episodes, while the medical serial drama *St. Elsewhere* featured an abortion after a prenatal diagnosis of Down's. Increasingly, these and related issues end up in the science coverage of nightly news programs. And many science specials on Public Broadcasting Service and other channels featured programs on Down's and other relatively common disabilities, genetics, or new reproductive technologies:

> Besides, I saw this special on TV, it was a good special, about adults, they had Down syndrome, and they were institutionalized for many years. Then they were released, and two of them fell in love and got married. It was a very heart-touching drama. (Diana Mendosa, 35, Puerto Rican nurse)

In 1989, ABC showcased *Life Goes On,* a family series featuring a teenager with Down syndrome, which ran through the early '90s. Chris Burke, who played Corky, has also written a successful "as told to" autobiography (Burke and McDaniel 1991). The series provoked an enormous controversy in the genetics community: Many counselors and clinicians felt that his presence as a "high-functioning" Down's adolescent painted an overly romantic portrait of life with a disabled family member. But parent activists of children with Down syndrome greatly appreciated the show, for it normalized images of their daily lives and presented an optimistic portrait of their imagined futures. Chris Burke himself has made many activist appearances at events related to disability integration, and stands as an icon not only of normalization, but of economic success and social celebrity.

Pregnant women without privileged educational backgrounds sometimes also learned about amniocentesis through their workplaces. Bertita Coron, a Honduran building cleaner, listened to men discussing their wives' amniocenteses at the barber shop where she regularly swept up. When her clinic nurse suggested an appointment with a genetic counselor, she felt prepared. A child-care worker from St. Vincent came for amniocentesis at the urging of her employer, who had recently had a baby at the age of 38. She appreciated the suggestion.

Evaluating Amniocentesis

The overwhelming majority of the eighty women I interviewed (95 percent) were satisfied that they had used the test. Despite the anxiety it provoked, almost all reported that it was better to know than not to know. Even those reporting pain, or the side effects of cramping or exhaustion, were glad they had chosen to be tested:

> I'm a real coward for pain, I was scared to do this. And the cramping was bad, way worse than I anticipated, and I wondered a lot—we both wondered a lot—if it hurt the baby. She was moving around so much on the sonogram afterwards, we were scared we hurt her. But I seem to think not. I think she's ok. And soon we're going to know that she's *really* ok, and when that time comes, well, I'll be jumping for joy. That's what's so great about this test. (Carole Freeman, 33, African-American sales clerk)

> I cried at the test. The doctor, he said, "She came alone, that's why she's crying." But that's not why I'm crying. I'm crying because it's hard to think about these things. So I went to church for one hour, and then I felt better. This is an important test. We got a lot of women's problems, social problems, health problems, and this is an important test. (Merced Rodriguez, 40, Colombian homemaker)

But a few reported criticisms. The first set of criticisms had to do with social relations in the medical suite:

> The two girls [radiology technicians] and the first doctor [radiologist], they were nice. But this one man there, he was a Jewish man who don't say anything. I don't know who is touching my belly, pushing my belly. He puts something like a ruler on my stomach, he doesn't talk to me. He's punching, pushing, but he don't say anything to me. (Elena Lopez, 36, Peruvian homemaker)

He was cool, too cool, like, aloof. Like as soon as he finished with me, he didn't say anything to me, just pulled out the *New York Times* and sat down and started reading. I expected him to talk to me, but he never asked me one single question, not even my name. He just measured and poked me with his needles. (Angela Carponi, 33, white homemaker)

In these cases, basic courtesy or better "bedside manner" might well have augmented a woman's satisfaction with the test. But the second set of negative evaluations were more existential, indexing the burdens of "choice":

If something turns out to be wrong, maybe I'll be happy I've had it. But in some ways, I wish it wasn't available, I wish I didn't have to know. . . . I've had a couple of abortions before, so it isn't that. But there's something about this that's like playing God. (Nancy Smithers, 36, white lawyer)

I had to do this because of my husband, because of the drugs. But I don't think I'd recommend it to my girlfriends. No, I wouldn't tell them to have it unless they had to have it. I don't think a person should know all this stuff. (Sandra McAlister, 41, African-American administrative secretary)

This thing was stuck exactly where my baby is supposed to be the most protected. It was more intrusive that I ever imagined, having it there. I'm a tough old bird, and he [the doctor] just couldn't get that needle in. He kept trying and trying, and it went on a very long time, and all that time, I kept thinking, "This isn't right." My womb is a sheltered place, a protected place, the one place my baby should be safe and undisturbed. Yet here was this doctor with this thing, this needle, shattering it. I guess what was shattered was my image of my own womb. But it hasn't come back together again. (Carola Mirsky, 39, white schoolteacher)

In such comments we may detect the personal costs of extending medical control: A growing knowledge of maternal-fetal separation is implied in the use of prenatal diagnostic technology. The price of such knowledge of separation may include the transformation of maternal responsibilities from those of caretaker to those of quality control. Before the existence of such tests, pregnant women kept or ended pregnancies based on their life circumstances, but rarely on the anticipated quality of fetal life. But "information" is never neutral; in this case, it is bought at the expense of the pregnant woman's ability to accept her fetus "as is," rather than to achieve a psycho-medical distance from its growing presence in order to judge its quality.

But whether they were satisfied or dissatisfied with the counseling and the test itself, virtually everyone reported anxiety during the several weeks' waiting period before receiving results. Above all else, a close encounter with prenatal testing increases women's worries about the specific health status of the fetuses they carry. Generic pregnancy fears might once have crystallized around the desire to carry a "healthy" baby. For women having amniocentesis, there is now a focus on specific conditions: chromosomes and alpha-fetoprotein levels index a panoply of anxieties with newly medicalized names. The specificity and reality of childhood disability become exquisitely focused through prenatal testing, engaging a complex mix of science and superstition as pregnant women and their supporters encounter potential diagnoses:

> Down syndrome, I knew about Down syndrome. What I didn't know about was all that other stuff. There's more to worry about than just Down syndrome, now I know there's other heredity problems. And this spine business [spina bifida], I wasn't exactly acquainted with that. Something more to worry about. (Lacey Smythe, 38, African-American secretary)

> I remember thinking, "Oh, my God, it's like a message direct from inside." In the old days, our mothers certainly never knew this, the picture of the inside of their wombs, the small swimming thing. But we do. We're the first ones to follow pregnancy in books, day by day, with photos. We know exactly when the arms bud off, when the little eyes sew shut. And if something goes wrong, we know when that happens, too. (Pat Gordon, 37, white college professor)

> They called it "an error in cell division." It feels like the cells could have a car crash, and produce this wreckage, and that's the extra chromosome, that's Down's. (Pat Gordon, 37, white college professor)

> Suddenly, I'm starting to see all these kids with Down syndrome on the street. Who knows if they're really Down's kids, or if I'm imagining it. And now you're asking all these questions, and I'm trying not to think

about spina bifida. I never even knew spina bifida was a problem. But after counseling, I do. (Enid Zimmerman, 41, white municipal service planner)

Imaging the Baby

The power of the sonographic imaging which accompanies the test also has complex effects, funneling the pregnant woman's consciousness of her fetus into highly focused and routinized channels (Mitchell 1993; Oakley 1993; Petchesky 1987). But how are these channels constructed through imaging? The gray-and-white blobs of imagery it provides must be interpreted; they do not speak for themselves. As many sociologists and historians of science and technology have pointed out, the objects of scientific and medical scrutiny must be rendered, they are rarely perceived or manipulated in their "natural" state. It is their marking, scaling, and fixity as measurable, graphable images that enable them to be used for diagnosis, experimentation, or intervention (Fyfe and Law 1988; Lynch 1985; Lynch and Woolgar 1990). The power of scientific images may, in large measure, be attributed to their mobile status: They condense and represent an argument about causality which can be moved around and deployed to normalize individual cases and theoretical points of view (Latour 1986, 1990). Viewed on a television screen or snapped with Polaroid-like cameras, sonograms may appear to pregnant women and their supporters as "babies." But the particularity of the object they view is deeply embedded in the practices of its scientific representation:

The partial rotation of the beam and the electronic recording of the echoes as spots of light thus "renders". . . the internal two-dimensional structure of an organ or a limb or a test object in a given plane. The resulting image is certainly not artifactual. It registers features, like the fat-muscle interface, that really exit. Yet it picks out only those features that reflect ultrasound. (Yoxen 1989, 292)

But surely, neither pregnant women and their supporters nor members of the right-to-life movement are thinking about the embedded, reductive, and normalizing aspects of imaging technology as they "meet" a baby on a television monitor for the first time. Such uterine "baby pictures" are resources for intense parental speculation and pleasure, for they make the pregnancy "real" from the inside, weeks before kicks and bulges protrude into the outside world. The real-time fetus is a social fetus, available for public viewing and commentary at a much earlier stage than the moment of quickening, which used to mark its entry into the world beyond the mother's belly. Perhaps sonograms also enable fathers and mothers to "share" what was formerly an entirely female experience of early pregnancy, increasing and hastening men's kinship claims (Taylor 1993).[22] And surely, they increase the velocity of the recognition of fetal development as a process independent of the mother's embodied consciousness. As one white college teacher commented to me, "It put my pregnancy into fast-forward." She thus neatly aligned sonography with videotapes, that other near-ubiquitous forum for home viewing. One couple who disparagingly referred to themselves as "yuppies" brought their own video camera and tape recorder to the sonogram examination, for they wanted their own tape of the fetal heartbeat. The acceleration of a subjective connection to the pregnancy thus passes through, and is augmented by, a piece of technology external to the pregnant woman herself.

Of course, modern imaging technologies provide powerful framings for the health and meaning of a pregnancy which appear radically new and individualistic; but they do not hold exclusive rights to the air space in which the image of pregnancy is interpreted. Public commentary on pregnancy has ebbed and flowed with the development of religious discourse, the representational arts, and the history of science and medicine. Current biomedical interpretations pass through other "images that possessed power within their own time and to which other images and ideas clung" (Stafford 1991, xvii). In the process, pregnancy is constantly relocated as an object of speculation, investigation, and intervention.

While contemporary feminists have alerted us to a changing relationship among a pregnant woman, her fetus, and the social world indexed in reproductive medicine, they have also provided ample evidence for older representational politics. Sonograms reinscribe prior debates and interpretations about the meaning of pregnancy which have deep roots in Western history: Residues of those discourses shape what we take to be modern notions of sex and its biological embodiment. As I tried to indicate in chapter 4, the idea that women are responsible for the health of their fetuses but that men generate life itself has a long history in Western theology, the representational arts, natural history, and emergent biomedicine. Thus, public images of pregnancy are not new; but in earlier times, fetuses made their presence public slowly, over a period of months. A woman's physical and emotional state might reveal internal signs of pregnancy in hormonally induced swollen breasts, skin changes, energy loss, dizziness, or nausea, all of which were experienced kinesically and holistically. A midwife or physician might later pick up a fetal heartbeat through a wooden trumpet, stethoscope, or, more recently, a Doppler machine. But the passage from internal to external signs was slow, and almost all of the cues depended on the pregnant woman's reportage.

Now, sonography bypasses women's multifaceted embodiment and consciousness, providing knowledge of the fetus independent of her own framework (Oakley 1984; Petchesky 1987). Moreover, that framework reduces the range of relevant clues for whose interpretation women act as gatekeepers. A technology of exclusively visual signs which renders "a collection of echoes" into a representation of a baby now substitutes for embodied states. This reduction also sharpens the focus from a diffuse knowledge of women's embodied experiences to a finely tuned image of the fetus as a separate entity or "patient." This visual representation can then be described by radiologists, obstetricians, and technologists in terms which grant it physical, moral, and subjective personhood (Mitchell 1993). Indeed, one ethnographic study of sonographers and their pregnant patients powerfully described the code switching that medical professionals perform. Among medical peers, they describe sonograms in the neutral language of science, but when speaking to pregnant women, sonographers attribute motives to fetal activity and presence. A fetus that is hard to visualize is "hiding" or "shy"; an active fetus is described as "swimming," "playing," or even "partying." "Showing the baby" drives its personification (Mitchell 1993, 1994). In this case, the routinization of a new reproductive technology (or, more properly, a technology whose routinization is most powerfully occurring in the prenatal context; sonograms are also used to visualize the human heart and abdominal masses, but I doubt that these uses are personified) provides medical professionals with a "toy" through which they can simultaneously provide a compelling service, and stake their claim to authority. The need to both monopolize a new professional turf, and popularize its value here contributes to radiologists' and technologists' perhaps subconscious desire to personify the fetus (cf. Brown 1986).

Sexing the Fetus

Perhaps the most powerful aspect of that personification process is the sexing of the fetus. The technology often (although not always) allows radiologists to visualize fetal sex organs at the midtrimester examination which precedes amniocentesis. And whether or not the radiologist "can tell," the chromosome analysis always reveals fetal sex. And, as Barbara Katz Rothman's study pointed out a decade ago, knowledge of fetal sex increases the velocity of a pregnancy: In our culture, a sexed fetus is no longer a developmental imaginary, it becomes a "little slugger in a Mets uniform or a ballerina in a pink tutu" (Rothman 1986). Lost in the rush to fetal sexing is the slower process by which even a newborn may remain relatively unsexed, or, at least, episodically sexed in the experiences of new parents.

Not everyone wants to know the sex of the fetus. Genetic counselors report that about half their clients would rather retain the mystery. But in my interviews with pregnant women, less than a quarter didn't want to know, and they were almost always those bearing a second or subsequent child. For first-time parents, knowing the sex is a powerful lure. And in my personal case, it was difficult for my obstetrician to keep his mouth shut once chromosomal information had been entered into my chart during a pregnancy in which I explicitly said I didn't want to know about fetal sex. Genetic counselors often caution those who would rather not know to announce their preferences firmly when they enter the radiology suite. Otherwise, a loquacious medical staffer is likely to point out the sex.

Some of the lure of sexing is based on control of knowledge. To the question "Why do/don't you want to know the sex of your fetus?" many people (and virtually every Jewish person in the sample!) answered, "Because if the doctor (or technologist, or geneticist, or clinic secretary) knows, then I should know, too."

> I didn't like the idea that someone knew something about my baby that I didn't know. . . . I don't care whether it's a boy or a girl, it really isn't that, it's merely that information exists, and other people have it. (Laura Forman, 35, white theater producer)

> As long as it's known, I feel the parents should know, you know. I mean, we shouldn't be the last to know, it's that kind of a feeling. (Carola Mirsky, 39, white schoolteacher)

For such respondents, once technology exists to provide the information, ignoring it constitutes deprivation. Such a structure of sentiment surely drives the proliferation of knowledge generation and consumption. For some others, the need to know is cosmological:

> Just like that, because it's a miracle of science to know what God provides for you, that's why I want to know. (Feliciana Bautista, 37, Dominican factory worker)

They tell me it's a boy. After three girls! I still don't believe it. I'll believe it when I see it. I heard from a neighbor they sometimes make mistakes. I'll believe it when I see it. But knowing, that's a gift. (Cynthia Baker, 40, African-American homemaker)

And for some, fetal sex knowledge genderizes in conventional ways:

Because if it's a girl, you got to be more careful with girls. You can't just let anyone take care of them. (Rafael Trujillo, 43, Puerto Rican unemployed worker)

I want a girl, but my name is dying. If it's a girl, well, we'll just have to plan for a second. (John Freeman, 32, African-American computer technologist)

Let's face it, knowing the sex made it go from a fetus to a child. I can't tell you how, but now I feel more protective, it's more real. And because it's a girl, I feel more connected to it, to my mother, to my sisters. Jeremy asked me which sister I want to name it for. I don't know if I want to do that yet. But the possibility made her more of a baby, a full kid, a living child. (Marise Blanc, 35, white college professor)

Genderizing is not only conventional; it may be practical, as well. Several women from working-class families claimed they wanted sex information for practical reasons. "I figured at this point, financially, instead of buying all those different kinds of clothes, you just buy one specific set," said Angela Carponi, a 33-year-old white homemaker.

During the course of my research, I was invited to a baby shower for a pregnant genetic counselor with whom I worked closely. Her colleagues (who had analyzed her fetal chromosomes) had purchased appropriately pink items, but she refused to take them home, saying, "It's gonna cause a war in my family. My mother wants a girl. His mother wants a boy. They'll both be happy at the birth. But if they find out now, they'll tear each other apart."

Occasionally, differences arise in a couple. Then, a decision to know or not to know must be negotiated: "I want to know, but Frank doesn't want to know. . . . He doesn't want some doc, you know, telling him before he has the real experience, finding it out together, in life, not as information," said Marcia Lang, white psychologist, 37.

Like amniocentesis itself, which feeds on age-old pregnancy anxieties, the curiosity and mystery of fetal sexing is now reified and revealed through technology. Old cultural preoccupations with genderizing "who the baby will be" are thus put through the sieve of new technologies of knowledge.

Life before Birth

Many women are delighted to claim this new knowledge as their own, aligning their descriptions to what technicians and physicians orchestrate:

> It was wonderful. I said, "It's great, can I leave now?" I mean, I didn't want the amnio, I just wanted to see my baby. I saw the spine, the bladder, the orbs for the eyes, the penis, everything, I saw all of it, I loved it. That was very satisfying. Maybe they do it as bribery, so you won't jump off the table. I feel like there's not much discrepancy between the sonogram and what it feels like inside me. (Alicia Williams, 36, African-American public relations executive)

> It's a creature from the moment of conception. On the TV screen, I saw it all, a little head, a beating heart, even fingers and a backbone. It looked like a baby but indistinct, blurry....As it grows, it will get bigger, and more distinct, almost like tuning in the television. It corresponds to what's inside me now. (Juana Martes, 37, Dominican home-care attendant)

> It looked very alien, like a little space creature. It was clasping and unclasping its hands, and it had its fist under its chin....It was moving around, so I could see the arms and fingers, which was nice, then it kind of got up on its legs, kind of pushed itself up, and you could see the whole spinal column, and the heart and the eye sockets and the shape of its skull. It's like a halfway baby now, yes, it's a halfway baby, and it's an inside-out feeling. (Marge Steinberg, 39, white social worker)

Like the pregnant woman who used the video analogy, Marge Steinberg was drawing on the ubiquitous fetus-as-voyager imagery which moviegoers and television watchers recognize from films like *2001, A Space Odyssey* and the right to life's *Silent Scream,* and, more recently, the Volvo advertisement selling safety to pregnant couples and their "passengers" (Taylor 1992). The ad presents an ultrasound fetal image accompanied by the message, "Is Something Inside Telling You to Buy a Volvo?" It was withdrawn after public protest at capitalizing on a sacred terrain. Sonographic fetal images perform practical and aesthetic service in the world at large, where women get to know them long before they arrive in the obstetrics suite.

Many women also recognize that their viewing is orchestrated, and that their internal state has been interpreted:

> It was nothing, really, it looked like nothing. Then they showed it to me, and made it something. (Ileana Mendez, 37, Ecuador-born baby-sitter)

> To tell you the truth, it didn't really look like a baby. I couldn't really tell what it was, they had to tell me. (Letty Sharp, 36, white hospital clerk)

> You could see at certain points. Towards the end, I couldn't really tell what was what, and then there was the feet. I saw the legs crossed, and then it looked like a little baby, cute. After they told me what to look for, then I knew I was really pregnant. (Sandra McAlister, 41, African-American administrative secretary)

The voyager image provided by sonograms is compelling, ubiquitous, and hard to escape. When I asked women what their internal image of the pregnancy currently was, few found words that differed from the stereotypes describing fetal space creatures: "Like *2001*"; "Just like in *A Child Is Born*, you know, kind of pinkish-creamy"; "Floating," and "A little traveler inside me." Only a few women could imagine other descriptive referents, and they had luxuriant animals and vegetables blooming in their bellies:

> I could just imagine it like a little fish, you know, the one that jumps a lot, like a sardine, no, not a sardine, it goes uphill....A salmon, that's what I feel, this child goes so low sometimes it jumps like it's going to go through my vagina, that's how it jumps, all alive. (Angela Carponi, 33, white homemaker)

> It's got lumps and bumps, and they're growing, organic, you know, sort of like a cauliflower. (Marcia Lang, 37, white psychologist)

But for most women, internal images of their pregnancies had been refocused through the lens of sonography, eclipsing any alternative, less standardized embodied notions of what a fetus felt like. Their internal states were now technologically redescribed.

Moreover, this technologically assisted viewing is often a source of anxiety, as well as pleasure (Stewart 1986). If the fetus has become "real" through its imaging, as mysterious as an underwater documentary and as intimate as a videotape, it has also become vulnerable:

> I saw the sonogram of the twins, and I was thrilled. But I really couldn't read it, I didn't know what it meant. They had to interpret it for you, to say, "Here's a heart, these are arms." Afterwards, it made me queasy—they made the babies real for me by telling me what was there. If they hadn't interpreted, it would have just been gray blobs, and now, I'm more frightened to get the results of the amnio back. (Daphne McCarle, 41, white college professor)

> Because as soon as you see the sonogram, it's very real. They focused on the heart, and it was beating, and then you could see the head. . . . And the doctor was really terrific, like, there was all this excitement in the room, and she gave me a picture, and they're all very positive . . . but you're trying to contain yourself from feeling that way because you know the only reason you're having this test is because you're more likely than the average person to have a problem. So I walked out of there pretty high . . . but I really have been trying to hold back the feeling pending results. (Laura Forman, 35, white theater producer)

With sonography and amniocentesis, one *can* be "just a little pregnant." Laura Forman's comments on self-containment surely echo Rothman's analysis of the effects of having a *Tentative Pregnancy* (Rothman 1986). A woman's growing awareness of the fetus she is carrying is here reshaped by her need to maintain a distance from it "just in case" something wrong should be discovered, and she should be confronted with the necessity to choose to end or continue the pregnancy. Even as the sonogram personifies the fetus, the amniocentesis puts its situation in question. Simultaneously distanced and substantiated, the pregnancy is suspended in time and status, awaiting a medical judgment of quality control.

The intertwined technologies of sonography and amniocentesis underline the liminality of pregnancy, etching the burdens, as well as the benefits, of "choice" into the heart of the experience. Occasionally, viewing the sonogram enables male partners of pregnant women to articulate their own engendered anxieties:

> It's definitely a woman's choice, but it's heavy. I think guys should be there for the sonogram and the amnio. It's all very heavy. You really

see something moving, it makes it into a person for you. If something goes wrong, and she has to have an abortion, after that the guy should know what she's going through, take responsibility for that. (Steve Schwartz, 36, white lawyer)

After encountering his fetus on the screen, one father asked anxiously, "Where are all the other fathers? Why aren't they here to see this?" (John Freeman, 32, African-American computer technologist).

But most of the technological augmentation of anxiety is expressed by women, not only because pregnancies happen inside of women's bodies, but because most (perhaps all) cultural constituencies in contemporary America assign the benefits and burdens of making and raising babies to women:

So I went off to have the sonogram, and I had these two guys, lab technicians, I mean, we're all in a dark room, semidarkness, and they begin to refer to the fetus as "he," it's like there's a real ba . . . I mean, they were joking, but I was traumatized. It became a real baby. I didn't realize what a sonogram really was, what they show you up on that screen. All of a sudden, the baby, the fetus turned its face toward me. And, Rayna, there was a real face. Almost twenty weeks of face. And the technician said, "See it," and I thought for a moment, "He's look-ing right at me." He looked like that image from *2001*: I mean there was a person there, inside my body, looking out at me. It was too strange. And too traumatic to have abortion after that. That's what the sonogram did. (Carol Seeger, 42, white museum curator)

I was hoping I'd never have to make this choice, to become responsible for choosing the kind of baby I'd get, the kind of baby we'd accept. But everyone, my doctors, my parents, my friends, everyone urged me to . . . have amniocentesis. Now, I guess I'm having a modern baby. And they all told me I'd feel more in control. But I guess I feel less in control. It's still my baby, but only if it's good enough to be our baby, if you see what I mean. (Nancy Smithers, 36, white lawyer)

To tell you the truth, I had a sonogram with my first one at eight weeks, and it changed my ideas about abortion. We all say it isn't a human being, but that's no longer true. This pregnancy, I waited for the sonogram till the amnio. At sixteen weeks when you see it, every-thing is there. The heart is beating, the fingers are separating, the spinal cord is closed. It's your decision, it's your body, and you must do whatever is right because you must raise whoever you have. But it's a human being. You can't have this test without thinking about it like this. (Amana Owasu, 35, Nigeria-born hospital attendant)

If women have become the keepers of technologically assisted fetal health, they have also become our moral philosophers of "the private." Fetal imagery *is* changing the ways in which women respond to the anxiety of grading, normalizing, and controlling pregnancy. And our national political discourse on childhood disability on the one hand, and abortion rights on the other, is in part filtered through women's diverse and dense experiences with these anxiety-provoking images.

The anxiety about which I have been writing is thus multilayered. As I have tried to indicate throughout this chapter, it feeds upon older, more existential fears engendered in the liminality of pregnancy, and it is given new salience and medicalization through technological intervention. It is at once individual and private, and also public and political. Above all, this anxiety invokes dread because it confronts the issue of "choice." A diagnosed fetus is potentially an aborted fetus. And the fear of taking the responsibility for ending a pregnancy that one has desired is substantial.

Late abortion is thus the hidden or overt interlocutor of all amniocentesis stories. This technology turns every user into a moral philosopher, as she engages her fears and fantasies of the limits of mothering a fetus with a disability. It is this disabled fetal imaginary which forms the subject of chapter 6.

6
The Disabled Fetal Imaginary

I was on this incredible high, like I saw the head and the little shoulders and then I came home and I suddenly crashed because I thought, there was this little person, I mean, it looked like a little person. And I was more upset than I'd ever been because what would I do? You know, would I have an abortion? Because here I've seen it, and it looks like a little person. (Louise Peoples, 35, white public school consultant)

THE POSSIBILITY OF LATE ABORTION shadows the experience of having amniocentesis and is the barely hidden interlocutor of all prenatal testing. Its presence is particularly palpable when interviewing women at home, where the presence of family life—other children, and plans for where the new baby will sleep and the conditions of its care—are embedded. Should the news be bad, the disruption of daily life within which the pregnancy lives is tangible. In this chapter, I examine the anxiety, fears, fantasies, and phobias that a disabled fetal imaginary provokes. Anyone choosing amniocentesis necessarily confronts the limits of altruism, fate, and nature within which they picture parenthood, and their own values concerning quality control on the "reproductive production line."

While many women told me they "tried not to think about it" during the long period awaiting test results, more than three-quarters of those I interviewed were certain they would choose to abort, should they receive a diagnosis of Down syndrome. The rest were generally "uncertain" of what they would do; a few were clear that they would not choose to end the pregnancy.[23] While their stories are related to the discussion of women who declined to have amnio, which follows in chapter 7, it is important to note that the specific projected diagnosis often played a part in the answers women gave to my questions about attitudes toward abortion (cf. Press and Browner 1994, 1995). Virtually everyone recognized Down syndrome and recalled some of what the genetic counselors had said about this condition. They also felt competent to make a decision, should it appear in their test results. But far fewer recognized neural tube defects, for which the test is also used, and almost nobody recalled anything about other chromosomal conditions, including sex chromosome anomalies. Down syndrome accounts for only about half of all the positive diagnoses, the rest being made up of other chromosome anomalies and neural tube defects. Sometimes, women would tell me that they knew about a specific condition, only to misdescribe it as Down's. Once, for example, a woman awaiting results told me she would abort for a positive diagnosis of Down's because she had observed how difficult it was to get Down syndrome children at a program in her neighborhood to follow instructions or perform physical tasks. Unaware of the facility, I decided to track it down, only to discover that the center she had been describing actually belonged to United Cerebral Palsy, and served a rather different clientele than her imagined disabled child. A woman whose abortion story will be told in chapter 8 gave an adequate description of Down syndrome when I asked what the diagnosed condition for which she chose an abortion meant. But the condition for which she had chosen to abort was actually Turner syndrome, whose physical, especially hormonal, problems are accompanied by a relatively small risk of mental retardation.

Under such circumstances, what exactly is the meaning of "informed consent"? While more than half of those I interviewed said that they would terminate the pregnancy "if anything serious was wrong," many individuals distinguished among conditions, asserting that they would need to discuss the diagnosis with their partners, doctors, or trusted friends and family members. And some gave concrete, individual reasons for using the test, and deciding to pursue its consequences, should anything be wrong. "Of course I'd have amnio; it's so obvious. Doing it alone, becoming a single mother, is hard enough without special problems of a kid with a serious handicap," said Enid Zimmerman, 41, white municipal service planner.

Imagining Selective Abortion

In pondering the abortion attitudes that women (and, occasionally, men) expressed during home interviews, I was struck by three themes which make imagining late abortion of a desired pregnancy after receiving a positive diagnosis different from others. These themes also arise in discussions with women who have received what is medically labeled a "positive diagnosis" (chapter 9). Thus thinking seriously about the misfortune of bearing a fetus or child who is medically graded as abnormal connects users of amniocentesis with families into which disabled babies are actually born, separating them from the rest of the aborting population. The first clue I picked up as to what makes abortion after positive diagnosis different from others is that many of the women with whom I spoke had chosen to abort prior pregnancies, but they were still deeply ambivalent about the possibility of aborting their present one. It was not abortion in general which provoked their ambivalence, but selective abortion in all its specificity. This ambivalence is surely linked to the commitment they had made to being pregnant: Women who use or might use abortion services usually do so when they cannot make a commitment to a specific pregnancy at a given time. And, along with 95 percent of those American women who choose abortion, they abort at or before fifteen weeks of pregnancy (Epner et al. 1998). The lateness of the test and its results thus makes the abortion decision a much more difficult one, for most women understand that it will entail giving up a pregnancy that they had formerly desired and going through some version of labor.[24] Many also conider the fetus to be a baby or, at least, a growing presence in their lives.

Second, "selective abortion" is ethically different from abortion in general: Though we might want to argue that the fraught, contradictory, and technological spectacle of current abortion politics in the United States turns all aborters into moral philosophers, abortion after positive diagnosis carries specific ethical charges. Ending a pregnancy to which one is already committed because of a particular diagnosed disability forces each woman to act as a moral philosopher of the limits, adjudicating the standards guarding entry into the human community for which she serves as normalizing gatekeeper. She must make conscious the fears, fantasies, and phobias she holds about mothering a disabled child. And she frequently thinks in a vacuum, lacking much social context for what a particular medical diagnosis of a disability might really imply (Ginsburg and Rapp 1999). Thinking about selective abortion requires women to enunciate and sometimes interrogate their own stereotypes and biases. At the same time, women who use amniocentesis must also articulate their understandings of the ethical impact of a positive diagnosis on themselves, other family members, and the fetus, while describing the limits of how they want to live. These two tasks—an assessment of mothering a disabled child and the impact of such a child's existence on her most intimate social relations—are deeply intertwined, but they are not reducible to one another. Thus the question of what to do if the test produces upsetting results forced some women to cut across the grain of conventional, comfortable stereotypes they held of mothers as generous, self-sacrificing, and ready to love "whoever's in there." For others, it suggested judgment and failure in the face of a cosmic spiritual test. And for a few, such questions strengthened the resolve to bear the present pregnancy in all of its consequences. These are difficult topics to discuss. I often wondered if my questions forced an uncomfortable clarity upon women who might rather have consigned these attitudes to the shadows of their minds, should luck (or statistics) be on their side.

The third, related theme that my questions surrounding a potential selective abortion provoked was a direct discussion of knowledge, attitudes, and beliefs concerning specific disabilities. In asking pregnant women (and their supporters) to describe their prior experiences with children with various disabilities, I discovered that virtually everyone could recall a child with mental retardation, often caused by Down syndrome. Many commented that the retarded children with whom they were acquainted had reasonable lives; the price was paid, in their estimation, by other family members:

I was friends with the older sister. The kid with Down's did very well, but it was painful for Elizabeth, my friend. Susie was in and out of our house all the time, she loved to raid the cookie jar, she did just fine for herself. But all the other mothers on the block used to say how badly they felt for Mrs. Steiner, how ragged she looked, how she was very bright, she wanted to travel, but they couldn't travel, they had 200 percent full-time jobs, what with that child. They were on a short leash. The thing about human nature that amazes me is, we all rally when we have to rally. If I had a kid like that, I imagine I'd handle it. But when you have an option, well, I would take it. (Fern Horowitz, 38, white secretary)

When Lindsay was born, they decided to keep her at home, which was unusual for those times. So they found special schools, they really worked at it, there was this special training that she went through. The thing that I found horrifying was that in fact, now, I mean, she's probably 30 or roughly around there, and the mother is 70, and now what is going to happen to her? Actually, I think the mother gets a lot of pleasure from the relationship, I mean, she really loves her. By now, it's only the two of them left, there's companionship and caring and so forth. But it's horrifying to think about what will happen when the mother dies. I know what I would do, facing that choice, I just wouldn't do it. (Laura Forman, 35, white theater producer)

I have a cousin, my mother's sister's son, he's retarded and 38. Oh, it isn't Down's, it's something else. He's done fine, he's likely to live a normal life, to die at 80. But it's really messed up the rest of the family. My aunt gave up a lot of her life, it messed up all his siblings. I'm not that selfless, I don't want to live like that. (Nancy Smithers, 36, white lawyer)

My grandmother raised us. He was in the house with all of us, I knowed him really well, we still communicate. My grandmother didn't approve of his going to school. Each generation, we knowed him, and we all tried to be protective of him, even down to the grand-ones. I think I'd be like my grandmother—I'd be very protective—but I would sent it to school if I had such a child. But I'd worry, I'd be really choosy about which school—those people get taken advantage of. Even in the best of families, there's always a crooked member, and you got to look out, if you have such a child. If the baby's gonna be sick, be like that, if it can't help itself out, there's gonna be a lot of pain for everyone. So you know, I think I'd have another abortion. (Londa Wright, 37, African-American postal worker)

Some respondents voiced their objections to raising a child with Down syndrome in terms of the relationship they imagined they would have:

I would have a very hard time dealing with a retarded child. Retardation is relative, it could be so negligible that the child is normal, or so severe that the child has nothing. . . . All of the sharing things you want to do, the things you want to share with a child—that, to me, is the essence of being a father. There would be a big void that I would feel. I would feel grief, not having what I consider a normal family. (Philip Straughn, 28, white salesman, balanced translocation carrier[25])

I have an image of how I want to interact with my child, and that's not the kind of interaction I want, not the kind I could maintain. (Alicia Williams, 35, African-American public relations executive)

I'm sorry to say I couldn't think about raising a child with Down's. I'm something of a perfectionist. I want the best for my child. I've worked hard, I went to Cornell University, I'd want that for my child. I'd want to teach him things he couldn't absorb. I'm sorry I can't be more

accepting, but I'm clear I wouldn't want to continue the pregnancy.
(John Freeman, 32, African-American computer technologist)

Some people expressed a stereotyped horror of giving birth to a mentally
retarded child:

> So there I was trying to describe it nicely, nicely, saying I was having
> this test to avoid having a kid that was, you know, not all there, and my
> neighbor, she just cut right through, she said, "Oh, Rita, having a
> 'tard, what a bummer!" (Rita Newbury, 35, white real estate agent)

> It's devastating, it's a waste, all the love that goes into kids like that.
> (Chuck Francis, 53, white video technician)

> It's a feeling in my stomach, I guess, revulsion. Some of the thing is I'm
> not happy that I have the feelings that I have, but I have to be honest
> about them. I mean, the physical mess, excrement, food, things like the
> general look. I've worked with kids like that at summer camp, I don't
> want it. (John Freeman, 32, African-American computer technician)

Embedded Knowledge

When I probed for the grounds on which the projected rejection or acceptance of a fetus with Down syndrome (and other hypothetical disabilities) was
formulated, people gave a range of responses. Within this range, patterns of
justification emerged reflecting and refracting class- and ethnic-based experiences with disabled children. In analyzing these interviews, I came to realize
that such patterns are only tendential, for several reasons. First and foremost,
each individual and family has a particular history of encounters with disability in their most intimate and community settings. Thus, for example, the
incidence of sickle-cell anemia and cerebral palsy are higher in African-
American communities than among whites, and consequently some African-
American pregnant women spoke knowledgeably about these ailments
because they had lived with siblings, neighbors, or foster children who had
them. But others in the same communities knew far less, having observed
them only at a distance. Women and their supporters also have particular
reproductive histories which deeply influence a response to a perceived reproductive crisis: prior abortions, miscarriages, infant and child deaths all condition how a parent projects her (or his) desires and fears onto the current
pregnancy. Thus a white schoolteacher who held negative attitudes about

children born with mental retardation nonetheless strongly considered the possibility that she would keep a Down syndrome fetus because she had suffered through two miscarriages and a prolonged bout of infertility, making the present pregnancy particularly precious. As I have tried to stress, pregnancy is a necessarily liminal state; it makes parents and potential parents conscious of the turning points and unfinished nature of their own lives.

Secondly, as genetic counselors are quick to point out, a hypothetically projected decision may well be set aside when a "positive diagnosis" is delivered, or a baby is born with a diagnosable problem. Here, ethnic community, religious, and class-based differences clearly intervene in ways that will be elaborated throughout this and subsequent chapters. Women and their supporters may respond to an interviewer "as if" they had a rational plan (or an ability to avoid having to have one) for confronting bad news. But the resources and concerns that influence a real decision may be significantly different from a description offered in response to a hypothetical probe.

Finally, the generalizations about class and ethnic-racial themes reflected in the materials I am about to present concerning projected decision-making about disabled fetuses contain a significant bias. Despite my best attempts to avoid bias, my concentration on interviewing in Manhattan, Brooklyn, and Queens too easily leads me to conflate class and ethnic-racial descriptions. I offer a methodological self-critique as a preamble, focusing on questions of both general social theory and urban, regional history. As many theorists have pointed out, "class" is a gloss for the processes through which people come to their experiences in light of their relation to the means and meanings of their place in production (e.g., Roseberry 1990; Thompson 1963). Class-based experiences reflect influences as intimate as the educational values expressed in one's family during childhood, as distant as the structural forces reshaping the regional accumulation of capital, and hence, available jobs. Social science labels tend to flatten out class relations as "factors" or "variables" for categorizing individual and collective histories. But those histories—at both the individual and more communitarian level—are, by definition, open to revision, according to particular circumstances as well as structural patterns. Class experiences are deeply historical: In 1950, for example, modal working-class jobs still brought people in the eastern United States into factories. By 1980, secretaries, postal workers, food processors, and other service workers occupied the numerically dominant sector of the working class in the same region. And, to complicate matters, New York City is currently home to a richly polyglot immigrant population, much of it consigned to the informal and lower reaches of the service-sector labor markets. Moreover, immigrants of childbearing ages (even, in this case, late childbearing ages) are likely to be overrepresented in City Hospitals, where I conducted much of my research. Had I developed my sample through the patient lists of private physicians, I would know far less about recent immigrants, and a bit more about middle-class, assimilated "Hispanics." Thus, when I speak of Latina or Hispanic or Spanish-speaking women, I am often describing immigrants or their first-generation offspring, or those (usually, Puerto Rican or Dominican) who have remained in immigrant communities. Moreover, in speaking about Spanish-speaking immigrants, for example, it is too easy to gloss recently arrived Colombians and third-generation Puerto Ricans, both of whom may be working as hospital attendants, day-care providers, or secretaries. Both groups are much more likely at the current moment to be found among the working poor, or the stable working class, than in the middle class, as both an artifact of recent immigration, and position in a highly stratified labor market. While the two groups surely hold something in common, including a deep history of New World Catholicism and more recent Pentecostalist Protestant challenges to it, they are also quite different. By contrast, both the hospitals in which I worked and the relatively stable residential histories of those I interviewed make white women and their families appear more upper-middle-class than they might, had this research been conducted in another region of the country. In Manhattan, many of the white people I interviewed were professional members of the upper middle class who used private physicians, the "middle middle" was shifting toward HMOs, and white working-class respondents, served by either HMOs or public clinics, tended to live in Queens or the near suburbs, where I did less interviewing. In a smaller city, the white population might not have exhibited such a wide economic and social range of jobs, health care plans, or patterns of residential segregation. So "white middle class" becomes a gloss for mainstream, often professional American values and experiences, while "working class," including those who self-identify or are identified as white, is often conflated with vibrantly ethnic and, some-times, recently arrived ethnic communities. I have tried, to the best of my ability, to untangle and describe these differences in the stories I present. But the generalizations about patterned responses reflect the limits of my under-standings of how class and racial-ethnic diversity are differentiated and con-densed in contemporary New York.

Are White Women Selfish?

That being said, the patterns I observed focus on four themes: (1) white middle-class women's concern with their own selfishness, and, occasionally, the projection of selfishness onto others; (2) Spanish-speaking women's concern with fetal suffering and their responsibility to sustain or end it; (3) Latinas's and Latinos's articulation of a commitment to the project of migration and assimilation, if they are recently arrived in the United States, and worry about how a disabled baby would fit; (4) a multiethnic working-class concern with the impact of disabled children on the aspirations and needs of other family members. This last theme was consistently uttered by people from all ethnic-racial groups. These themes are overlapping and complex, and each deserves illustration and interpretation.

From the very beginning of the interview process, I was struck by the preoccupation with selfishness that white middle-class women consistently expressed. The word selfish and, occasionally, its apparent opposite, selfless, popped up spontaneously when talking with Catholics, Protestants, and Jews, whether lawyers, secretaries, teachers, social workers, or homemakers. Some women considered it selfish to have babies; some, to remain childless. Wanting a specific sexed fetus (or even wanting to know the sex of the fetus) was labeled selfish, as was the decision to abort for a diagnosed disability. White middle-class women queried their own motives, wondering at every turn in our conversations if they were being selfish. "Selfish" was also used by several white male partners in a fashion which I discuss below. To the best of my ability to monitor my data, I have recorded this concern with selfishness or selflessness only twice in the conversations of Latina women, and twice among African-Americans, once articulated by a woman, and once by a man.

> In a certain way, I think I'm selfish, having a baby, because it's a joy I want to experience. . . . I don't know, maybe it's selfish, but I don't want to raise a child like that, if I don't have to. (Fern Horowitz, 38, white secretary)

> I feel in many ways all these decisions are selfish decisions. I don't think that children and adults who have Down syndrome necessarily have such miserable lives. Some of them do, but then, so do lots of normal adults. So it's selfish, and I don't mean it as such a pejorative term, it's just that if I had a choice . . . (Marge Steinberg, 39, white social worker)

> Mostly, this must seem selfish, but when I had an abortion a decade ago, I knew I was killing. There was no other way to think about it, to describe it. . . . But I was killing a very small piece of life in favor of my bigger life. That's important, it makes you get your priorities straight. (Rita Newbury, 35, white real estate agent)

Often, white middle-class women compared themselves to women who had mothered disabled children, and found themselves lacking:

> Oh, I know I'd work really hard at it, I'd throw myself into it, but I'm afraid I'd lose myself in the process. I wouldn't be like her, she was a really great mother, so self-sacrificing. (Laura Forman, 35, white theater producer)

> My aunt was terrific. But she stayed home. I know I'm going back to work after this baby is born, and I can't imagine what it would take to do it her way. I'm too selfish. (Susan Klein, 37, white accountant)

What accompanied these she/me distinctions in the discourse of white, middle-class women was a running battle over the question of selfishness and self-actualization, a problem linked to the central importance of "choice" as a cultural value and strategy. "Choice," of course, is a key concept in the abortion controversy currently raging in our national political culture, and white middle-class women seem most vulnerable to its implications. But "choice" also figures large in the idea of women holding paid jobs outside of their households, ostensibly for reasons of self-development, as well as money. Virtually all of the women I interviewed from this group, whether Catholic, Jewish, or Protestant, provided critical exegeses on the tension between "selfishness" and "self-actualization," melding their right to abort a disabled fetus and their right to plan an adult, working life. Their discourse revealed something of the limits of self-sacrifice that mothers are alleged to embody.

> I just couldn't do it, couldn't be that kind of mother who accepts everything, loves her kid no matter what. What about me? Maybe it's selfish, I don't know. But I just didn't want all those problems in my life. (Linda Morgan, 37, white public school teacher)

> Maybe I shouldn't mention it, but I don't want to spend my time that way, taking care of a kid with a lot of insoluble problems. I imagine I could never get back to work, never get back to my own adult life. I think the technology gives me that possibility, even if it's selfish. (Louise Peoples, 36, white public school consultant)

> I share a lot of the feelings of the right-to-life movement. I've always been shocked by the number of abortion clinics, the number of abortions, in this city. But when it was *my* turn, I was grateful to find the

right doctor. He helped me to protect my own life, and that's a life, too. (Mary Fruticci, 44, white homemaker)

This self-interrogation over selfishness and self-actualization is mirrored in a counterdiscourse expressed by some male partners of white middle-class women having amniocentesis. Several went to some length to point out that a decision to bring a disabled child into the world knowingly was, in their view, "selfish":

But if you know it beforehand, it's cruel to bring a child into so much pain. And parents who will martyr themselves to do it are a bit puffed up, in it for their own self-image, is my estimation. (Mark Peoples, 40, white college professor)

If you have a child that has severe defects, the natural thing I think that would happen would be that it would die at a very early age, and what you're doing is you're prolonging, artificially, the child. And I think that most of the people that do that, do it for themselves, they don't really do it for the child, and it tends to be a very selfish thing for people to do. (Jim Norton, 42, white lawyer)

That child [who is mentally retarded] consumes their life in so many ways. Keeping him on in the family, well, it strikes me as selfish. (Chuck Francis, 53, white video technician)

Their inversion of selfishness neatly reverses the vector of blame which right-to-life imagery would pin on their wives.

Why are white middle-class women wrapped up in a discourse at once self-critical and ambivalently technological? Of the multiple threads woven into the fabric of their lives which might contextualize this discourse, three seem particularly suggestive.

The first is that the material conditions of motherhood really are changing, and changing dramatically within their lifetimes. White middle-class women who have jobs and postpone babies are constructing different life courses than many of the women in the communities from whom they learned to mother. In the 1950s and '60s, when many of them were girls, the ideal middle-class mother was a homemaker. If she worked outside of the home, it was usually part-time, and her work was not considered culturally salient. The white middle-class women I interviewed are thus drawn from a group for whom the emphasis on individual self-development through the world of work is a relatively recent cultural goal. In this, they differ from African-American women, for example. For many black women, working mothers are long-standing community figures, and motherhood is a culturally public role, enacted in churches, politics, and neighborhood networks; full-time homemakers were and are relatively scarce.

This self-conscious interrogation of the values and limits of motherhood also set white middle-class women apart from many Hispanic respondents, who painted images of sacrificial motherhood, and maternal-fetal fusion in response to queries about the test. For them, there appeared to be only minimal conflict about the normative responsibilities of motherhood, a theme to which I return below. While *all* Americans prize "choice" as a political and cultural value, large-scale transformations in education, labor-force participation, postponed marriage and childbirth have enabled many white middle-class women to maintain at least an illusion of control over their life circumstances to a degree unprecedented for other groups, and in other times. Their relative freedom from unwanted pregnancies, child illness and death is easily ascribed to advances in medical science. Medical technology transforms their "choices" on an individual level, allowing them, like their male partners, to imagine voluntary limits to their commitments to children. But it does not transform the world of work, social services, media, and the like on which a different sense of maternity and the "private" sphere would depend. Their ambivalence about the limits of the technological transformation of motherhood is thus structural.

Moreover, their private sphere and its commitment to childbearing is now being enlarged to include men. Fathers, too, can now be socially created through pregnancy regimes, birth coaching, and early bonding. While many African-American and Hispanic women told me about their male partners' plans to attend the birth or mentioned other signs of masculine involvement with children, it is white middle-class men who spontaneously speak the language of bonding and who declare the pregnancy "ours." These men may also claim the right to comment on women's motives for pregnancy and abortion in powerful ways.

Individually, white middle-class women may be becoming "structural men," freer than ever before to enter hegemonic realms of the culture from which they were formerly barred, but at the price of interrogating their traditional gender identity (Ginsburg 1989a, 1989b). Mainstream feminism exhibits considerable ambivalence concerning the transvaluation of women's nonnurturant activities: On the one hand, many and diverse women's projects and movements have celebrated women's contributions beyond the maternal. On the other, the insistence that "women's ways" of relating and caring be socially recognized comes with the historical territory of feminism itself, much, but surely not all of it theorized from white middle-class maternal experiences (Collins 1994; Ruddick 1989). The cultural meaning of motherhood is thus a contested terrain; modern, high-technology maternity is a small part of the gender relations now under negotiation. But it currently lies in a culturally ambivalent zone, a kind of "no-man's-land" between technological claims to liberation through science, and a mainstream feminist recuperation and romance with women's nurturance as a valued activity.

A second reason for white middle-class women's ambivalence surrounding prenatal diagnosis and abortion may well be, paradoxically, their close connection to the benefits and burdens of the increasing medicalization of pregnancy. While "everybody" now undergoes prenatal care including pregnancy sonograms, not everybody is as committed to the medical discourse, and its visualization in pregnancy primers, as this group is. For them, an emergent separation and reconnection to fetuses as relatively distinct and personified entities appears to be particularly powerful. Their images of fetuses tended to faithfully reproduce medical representations, and they picture the contents of their wombs as well-developed, autonomous babies. Paradoxically, white middle-class women are both better served by reproductive medicine and also more controlled by it than women of less privileged groups. They are more likely to be educated in the same kinds of institutions in which doctors are produced, and their own language closely approximates medical speech and its doubled critique in both the right-to-life's discourse of "selfishness" and mainstream feminism's "self-actualization."

A third reason for the articulation of complex and contradictory feelings surrounding prenatal diagnosis and abortion is not confined to white middle-class women, although the importance of individualism as a cultural and medical stance may make them particularly vulnerable to its effects. This reason concerns the shifting historical ground on which abortion practices rest. That point was made dramatically in one amniocentesis story:

For three weeks, we tried to develop further information on oomphaloceles and satellites on the chromosomes,[26] and the whole time, my mother kept saying, "Why are you torturing yourselves, why don't you just end it now, why do you need to know more?" She'd had an abortion between her two pregnancies. And my mother-in-law had even had a late abortion when she first got to this country, and she kept saying the same thing: "I put away one, just do it and get it over with." And I was so conflicted, and also so angry. So finally I turned on my mother and said, "How can you be so insensitive, it's such a hard decision for us, you can't just dismiss this." And as we talked, I realized how different their abortions were from mine. They were illegal. You've got to remember that: They were illegal. They were done when you worried about the stigma of getting caught, and maybe, getting sick. But you didn't think about the fetus. You thought about saving your own life. (Jamie Steiner, 33, white health educator)

Illegal abortions were dangerous and expensive. They were performed under the shadow of death—maternal, not fetal, death. Morbidity and mortality from the complications of abortion dropped sharply after 1973, in the wake of Roe v. Wade. Indeed, "Abortion-related deaths decreased by 73 percent within a decade of abortion decriminalization" (Petchesky 1984, 157). Criminal prosecution, morbidity and mortality were the fears attached to illegal abortions, not "selfishness." A variety of social forces, including medical reform and feminist political organization, led to abortion law reform. On the heels of its success, the right-to-life movement was quickly organized. It deployed the charge of "selfishness" against all women who would limit their maternity through abortion. White middle-class women seem particularly vulnerable to this criticism, given the contradictory changes in their recent experiences. They have internalized and articulated it as if "selfishness" were an accurate label for their behavior at the intersection of private and public life.

Fetal Suffering?

But perhaps there is a less culturally salient boundary, or a shifting boundary, separating public and private life for other groups of women, especially racially marked women who have often moved across the cultural boundaries distinguishing domestic and public life to serve in the homes of white middle-class families (cf. Glenn 1992; Mohanty 1991; Ruiz and DuBois 1994). In one ethnographic study, for example, Dominican factory and service working women often expressed a strong desire to protect the privacy of their family life from employers' questions or concerns. They did not want to view their family interests as located in a public domain (Pessar 1996; cf. Segura 1994). And a history of African-American women's community activism in churches, schools, and social service agencies suggests that the role of "mother" was and is a far more public or collective status than it is for most white middle-class women (Glenn, Chang et al. 1994). The roots of the white middle-class discourse on "selfishness" probably lie outside women's individual "choices," at the fluid intersection of culture, politics, and technology, where the meaning of "fetal life" as attached to both public policy and private values is being renegotiated (e.g., Ginsburg 1989a, 1989b; Hartouni 1992). At these shifting crossroads, race and class differences mark both the privileges and burdens that a new technology offers to women whose reproductive life stories have been constructed in varied communities.

When examining attitudes toward fetuses, disabilities, and abortions, there are, indeed, communities within communities to which racial-ethnic census categories hardly do justice. Early in this research, I noticed that many Spanish-speaking and bilingual Spanish speakers expressed a deep concern with the possibility that the fetus would be born to a life of suffering when we discussed potential diagnoses and the question of selective abortion:

> I would abort for Down syndrome because the child would suffer, it would suffer too much. Science can tell us important things. We don't have to have children born to suffer. (Feliciana Bautista, 37, Dominican factory worker)

> I know in my heart I can't raise something I feel is going to be born to suffer. (Diana Mendosa, 35, Puerto Rican nurse)

Sometimes, these concerns were articulated in Marian, religious overtones, as for example in the testimony of a Dominican woman who chose to terminate a pregnancy after a prenatal diagnosis of trisomy 18, a usually fatal chromosomal anomaly. While her story properly belongs in chapter 9, her reasoning links her to other amniocentesis users from Latin communities: "When they told me what the baby would suffer, I decided to abort. But it was Easter, so I couldn't do it; I just couldn't do it until after His suffering was ended. Then my child could cease to suffer as well" (Lourdes Ramirez, 41, Dominican house cleaner).

Many women from Latin backgrounds also claimed the maternal authority to fantasize and judge the feeling states of the unborn, perhaps another instance of the maternal-fetal fusion about which I speculated in chapter 4. Indeed, many women raised in Latino communities considered the judgment of the fetus's "quality of life" to be their responsibility, an obligation which might cut both ways:

> I made this baby, I accept it. If it's gonna have a problem, it's my responsibility to shoulder that burden. I'm the mother, it's my burden if the child should suffer. (Maria Acosta, 41, Puerto Rican homemaker, home day-care provider)

You ask me what to do if the baby is born sick? If the baby is born sick, very sick, then it is better for me to know now. If I know now, I can stop that baby from ever being born, born to suffer from being sick. (Sonia Perido, 36, Colombian hotel chambermaid)

This sense of maternal responsibility to evaluate and regulate the suffering of the fetus was deeply linked to perceived obligations to other family members, especially among those engaged in the project of migration. Recent immigrants often stressed that the reason to consider abortion was the need for the whole family to succeed in making a new life. They considered the constraints and resources of that new life in some detail:

A kid who is different, he does better here, people are kinder here than they are in my country. But that's not the whole story. Because we can't afford health care here, even through Jorge's job. We've got health care, and it still costs plenty. A kid with a disability, it would cost plenty, all the doctors' visits. I've got two other children, I can't afford one like that. (Remedios Borjil, 37, Colombian homemaker)

I'm so happy to be having this baby, I pray God will make it healthy and strong! I had five abortions before this: It wasn't time yet. Enrico and me, we had to put something aside, have something before we bring a child into this world. Even now, we couldn't manage if this child had a big problem. (Bertilda Flores, 37, Colombian waitress)

Here, it should be noted that abortion functions as a controlling element of the family economy, and not as an instrument of individual egotism or development.

Family Stress and the Fetal Imaginary

The focus on fetal suffering and maternal responsibility, sometimes in explicitly religious tones, may well be particularly Latin, but the need to locate the problem of selective abortion within a larger family matrix is not. On the contrary, it is widely shared across ethnic boundaries by many women and men from working-class and lower-middle-class backgrounds. This focus links the project of immigration (articulated with greatest density in my tapes by recent immigrants from the Caribbean, Central America, and South America) with the more general need to establish rational strategies for family survival under economic pressure. This latter theme appears continuously in the concerns of many of the working-class families with whom I spoke.

> With my other two, Lionel worked nights, I'm on days, we managed with a little help from my mother. When Eliza was 3, my mother passed on, then my sister, she helped out as much as she could. With this one, we're planning to ask for help from a neighbor who takes in a few kids. I couldn't keep a baby with health problems. Who would baby-sit? (Londa Wright, 37, African-American postal worker)

> We both work at the hospital, we drop Eddy at the early bird program at his school on the way to work. Evenings, my mother picks him up. Thursdays, she's at Sodality, Eddy goes home with his friend Reginald, we get him late, after dinner. When the new baby comes, I get six weeks. Then, my mother will help out until he's big enough for the sitter. What would happen to us if the new one was sick? So I took the test. Only the sisters at Eddy's school don't know. That's why I had you turn off the tape when we talked about abortion. (Letty Sharp, 36, white hospital clerk)

The aspirations of working-class women for themselves and their children were articulated in the context of stress-filled lives. Some middle-class women, of course, also articulated this focus on family strategies under stress, but I heard far fewer comments from them as a group on this topic. Perhaps the family economy and network figure so large in conversations with working-class versus middle-class women because middle-class women are much more likely to be having a first, delayed pregnancy after the age of 35. Because working-class women are apt to have other children at home, their sense of the stress involved in parenting children, ordinary as well as those with extraordinary needs, is better developed. Additionally, in a day-care-scarce society like this one, the middle class is more likely to solve its considerable child-care problems in the cash nexus, rather than within the family economy, as is so often the case for working-class women (Nelson 1994; cf. Chang 1994):

> The way we live is already too hard. We can barely manage with one child, what with Jed's traveling and my late nights at the office. Miranda [the sitter] stays late when we need her, but she isn't always happy about that situation. A second is going to be hard enough, without adding on problems like this. (Emily Pratt, 39, white lawyer)

I think it's kind of like triage, or like euthanasia. There aren't enough resources in the world. We'd have to move, to focus our whole family on getting a handicapped kid a better deal. . . . Why spend $50,000 to save one child? And what sort of a life would it have? What sort of a life would we have? (Rita Newbury, 35, white real estate agent)

Middle-class parents, too, are often distraught over child-care problems, but they rarely need consider their direct implications on extended families. But among those detailing the imagined impact of a disabled child on kith and kin, a few even described the pressures in terms of specific family members. They located their potential abortions in the love they bore for their other children:

If I had this baby at 44, and it had Down's, who would inherit it? Oh, not Alex, not Stephan—it's always the girls, the girls who get caught. If I had that baby, it would be Livia who inherited the family problems. When I think about it, I'm saving my daughter, I'm not just saving myself. (Mary Fruticci, 44, white homemaker)

If anything would happen to me, I'd be so worried for my daughters. I wouldn't want it to be a burden on them. Their life would be destroyed, if I had the baby with Down's and then I died. (Londa Wright, 37, African-American postal worker)

Revisiting Gender

Such encumbered fantasies are deeply gendered, for they assume a direct transmission of burdens from mothers to daughters, with no interventions by fathers or sons. But fathers and potential fathers do, in fact, play a significant role in using, refusing, and fantasizing the role of prenatal diagnosis and selective abortion. Although I was able to interview only fifteen fathers of fetuses, all but three of them white and middle-class, I have come to believe that men's attitudes toward the use of amniocentesis deeply influence women's decisions to use or refuse the test. As I tried to indicate in chapter 4, gender scripts are played out in many directions: While some men are controlling and others supportive, the mere fact of prenatal testing raises to consciousness and negotiation an aspect of gender relations not usually articulated. Here on a frontier of reproductive technology, gendered beliefs and claims are enacted; prenatal diagnosis provides a hot spot where we can see gender in the remaking.

Sometimes, men enforce the use of the test. Ecuador-born Ileana Mendez, 37, felt pressured into having the test by her U.S.-born husband:

> Maybe for single mothers, for very poor families, maybe even for women who wouldn't have the patience, this is a good test, but for me, this isn't a good test. I worked for two years in my country with children like that [mentally retarded]. I wouldn't want to end my pregnancy for that. I think it's almost a crime, having an abortion that late. My husband doesn't want to speak about it. He knows I wouldn't want an abortion, but he keeps telling me he would want an abortion. So now we just can't talk about it. I'm just praying that the results will come soon.

At other times, men demanded that women forgo the test. This strategy is not necessarily effective: Several women from Spanish-speaking communities told me they had never informed their partners about their decisions to use amniocentesis, once objections were raised. Now, they weren't talking about it and planned to claim a miscarriage, should unsettling results lead them to actually choose an abortion. Two African-American professional women reported that they had simply announced their decision to use prenatal testing over their partners' objections; women from many backgrounds told me, "He doesn't like it, but we just don't talk about it now."

Discussing amniocentesis seemed to present problems of policing the cultural boundaries between public and private life for many men. Few were willing to be interviewed, and several expressed discomfort, and sometimes downright hostility, at the thought of their female partners sharing amniocentesis stories with me. It is possible, of course, that they would have voiced objections to interviews on any intimate topic, but the subject of prenatal testing seemed to arouse substantial anxiety. Five women from varied cultural backgrounds canceled appointments to speak with me, claiming male objections, as one said, to "washing our dirty laundry in public." One, eager to talk, but afraid of her husband's ire, arranged a clandestine meeting.

While such stories suggest male manipulation of female experience and reflection upon it, gender-reversed stories were also told:

> I wanted Frank to get more involved. I didn't say, "Come with me to the first sonogram because it will make you more involved." I think I just said, "I'd really like it if you came with me to this sonogram thing." He's not that affective, he isn't really that connected to the baby yet. But he is connected to me. So I knew the sonogram would

get him more connected, through me. . . . And I think it was true because he seemed moved, emotionally moved, and for the first time, after the sonogram he started talking to people about the baby. (Marcia Lang, 37, white psychologist)

I was frustrated that so many women came alone. I brought my husband—it's important, very important. For good and for bad, it's women's burden, and her husband should know about it and share it. If there's a miscarriage, he should share the pain. It's his creature, too, and if he sees it on the television, he will know it as his own, love it from the very beginning. He will see God's work, marvel and share. The family should be united for the test, so that men share with women the power of God's work and the joy of a new baby. (Juana Martes, 37, Dominican home-care attendant)

I took my husband and my son to see it. I thought he was, you know . . . uncommitted. I thought it would touch home. That's why I did it. I had a feeling. Use a little psychology. My husband, he was amazed by what he saw. (Diana Mendosa, 35, Puerto Rican nurse)

In such stories, a new technology supports an old female strategy of attempting to heighten male involvement in pregnancy.

Three of the white, middle-class men I interviewed expressed their own opinions on amniocentesis, while also making clear their deep understandings of the dilemmas which women using the test faced:

It's definitely a woman's choice, but it's heavy. I think guys should be there for the sonogram and the amnio. It's all very heavy. You really see something moving, it makes it into a person for you. If something goes wrong and she has to have an abortion, after that the guy should know what she's going through, take responsibility for that. (Steve Schwartz, 36, white lawyer)

I'm against abortion; I really do believe it's life from the moment of conception. And once you think that way, getting rid of a baby just because it's going to have a problem is an act of extreme selfishness. But let me tell you, this is really Rita's choice. She's the one that's carrying this pregnancy, she's the one that's going to stay home and care for it, she's the one who'll comfort a sick child, or even a dying child. I don't get to choose; she does. (Jack Newbury, 39, corporate manager)

It's very interesting talking with you, but basically, what I say is irrelevant. I'm here to support Laura. She's the one who's facing tough choices. (Jeff Chase, 40, lawyer)

John Freeman, an African-American computer technologist, found the burden of shared fetal personification both enlightening and unexpectedly complex. "Where are all the other fathers? Why aren't they here to see this?" he nervously asked.

Both the boundary-policing and partner-supporting strategies of men suggest that pregnancy is widely viewed by men from various classes and ethnic backgrounds as women's domain. Many women from Spanish-speaking communities reported that their husbands said, "It's your decision," when asked for their opinion about using the test; others said, "It's my decision. I make my decision, it will be fine with him." Even women who might have wished otherwise identified their amniocentesis anxieties as their own concern:

I was shattered, just shattered; I cried for two days after I had the test. I guess I was identifying with universal motherhood, I felt like my image of my womb had been shattered. It still feels like it's in pieces, not like such a safe place as before. . . . Len was very supportive that first day, but he's not involved in waiting it out. He takes it for granted that everything will be ok. His head is in work, in business. Mine is in the house, the kids, in him. It doesn't work the other way around. (Carola Mirsky, 39, white schoolteacher)

The sexual differentiation of pregnancy's practical and affective burdens is, of course, materially based, for fetuses dwell in women's bodies. This is undoubtedly why it was difficult for me to persuade more men to agree to be interviewed on a "woman's topic." But the cultural consequences of assigning pregnancy exclusively to women include the reproduction of reproduction as a starkly gendered domain. While individual men from various backgrounds breached that cultural divide, both in support and in control of their female partners, the basic cultural framework remains intact. To the extent that notions of reproduction as a sex-divided domain are in play, the sexual division of parenting is off to a culturally resilient start, despite the objections raised by a wide range of feminists, educators, and psychologists.

This representation of reproduction as exclusively women's domain cuts in two directions, for it both empowers women's decision-making control over their pregnancies, and diminishes men's sense of responsibility, making their support of their partners' pregnancies an individual voluntary commitment, rather than a cultural obligation. Moreover, the exclusive assignment of pregnancy to women reveals a contradiction that runs rife through daily life and through feminist theory, as well. On the one hand, women's bodily autonomy, and the unique physical abilities and limitations associated with pregnancy are voiced and valued in picturing reproduction as an exclusively feminine domain: The value of female difference is stressed. On the other hand, the withdrawal (and, sometimes, exclusion) of men from considering the benefits and burdens of childbearing as their own leave them remarkably free to envision not only fetuses but also newborns, babies, toddlers, and older children as women's responsibility: Equality of responsibility is avoided. This tension between acknowledging difference and seeking equality is long-standing (Cornell 1993; Milkman 1986; Scott 1988, 1992; Vogel 1990). It is played out in our cultural categories surrounding disability (e.g., Minow 1990), as well as gender, a topic to which I return in chapters 9 and 10.

Family Histories

Of course, the family within which consciousness of childhood disability is formulated is not composed exclusively of coupled women and men, nor of parents and children. Consciousness is also shaped by a more capacious sense of family history, and the memories of kinship through which that history is constructed. Some women and men have had extensive experiences with disabled children, and they told richly detailed stories of growing up with affected siblings or cousins. Others recounted skeletons hidden in the family closet. A white college professor says about her consciousness of her links to a sister with Down syndrome:

> I always felt that Janey, you know, I guess that it could always happen, I supposed my womb was like my mother's womb. Well, even if it's not genetically linked, maybe there's more of a connection than we know. My father is less tied to Janey biologically. . . . He sees the future coming, he tries to prepare. But my mother said, "I can't leave her here, I don't care what happens after I'm dead, I won't know about it. As long as I'm alive, she stays with me." Janey is my mother's perpetual child, she is carried in the whole family. Let me tell you a story. My mother only found out when she was an adult visiting her own mother's grave, that there had been two other children, boys, buried in their twenties, and she was never told. I tracked down Cousin Maxine, who remembered them. They were both retarded. They would come to the house

on Sundays, always well dressed. But they were institutionalized. Nobody ever told my mother who they were. They were the older brothers of my mother's mother, that's who they were. And they were put away, retarded. Later, when Janey was born, my mother suffered endless guilt, thinking those boys were precursors to her daughter. She never visited her mother's graveside again, after she found out; she didn't want to discuss it with my father. Trisha [a younger sister] and me, we didn't know any of this. We just knew that my mother felt guilty about Janey, that it was in some way her fault. Many mothers feel this way. When I read about chromosomes in college, it was a great relief. I went rushing to tell my mother: I finally learned about Down syndrome, I knew that Janey wasn't hereditary. But my mother, she assumed the other. . . . My mother was a real activist, we changed houses, we changed school districts; we always got the best for Janey. Once, I remember my aunt invited us to Sunday dinner. She said, "Why don't you leave Janey at home?" My mother was so insulted— I'll never forget this—none of us went. If Janey wasn't welcome, we didn't cooperate. She belonged in the family. (Carol Seeger, 42)

Sometimes, families change their collective minds about hereditary problems. A genetic counselor from Florida sent me a copy of an extraordinary family document compiled by one of her patients.[27] It was addressed to his extended (and extensive) family. It opens as follows:

Dear Family: As many of you know, Maria Rosa and I initiated a genetic study of the bone defect in our family after the birth of our affected daughter, Antonia. The completed investigation cleared up many questions that we had concerning the family situation, but most important it showed us a way to identify those people in the family at risk and steps that those people could take to prevent having a defective child. We did not share the results of the investigation with the family because we felt there had been . . . certain resistance and there was no point in bringing a difficult subject into the open, a subject that would never have to be faced by the majority of members of the family. Also our primary motive was purely selfish to try to prevent our own children and grandchildren from suffering the painful situation that we had suffered. However we have reevaluated this attitude at the birth of our grandson born with a hand defect last August, whose genetic situation was known and understood by us. We mean to say that we knew that his grandmother carried a risk and therefore his mother most probably carried a risk as well. We feel it was perhaps self-ish of us to have sat on this information and not to have shared it with the family—even though our intentions were to save the family from painful information. This was not in the best interests of the family.

This introduction is followed by a four-page, single-spaced clinical history of the bone problem as it has been expressed throughout the family, informa-tion on its genetic transmission, and clinical evaluation, including the prob-lem of close-cousin marriages, and an insistence that family members confront the situation for the protection of their future offspring. It con-cludes, "We realize that this has always been a painful subject to bring up in the family and it is not our intention to cause additional suffering, but we feel that it is time to bring it out of the closet."

A genealogical secret whispered across the generations here prompted a self-conscious revision of family history, using the resources of biomedicine. Indeed, the existence of prenatal diagnosis may cause some people to recast prior familial knowledge:

My father has two brothers, and each one has a retarded son. I've always known that, but I never much thought about it. Now, suddenly, after my amnio, I'm seeing Down's kids everywhere, on the streets, all over the place. Those cousins, they suddenly came zooming into view. Like I needed to know what caused it. I knew all along, at least, I think I knew, that it wasn't Down's. But I've started to worry: Is my baby more likely to be retarded because of this family history? Mostly, I think not. But I needed to know what caused it. So I talked with my father and with one of my aunts, and I got the birth histories. Now, I think about them differently. (Enid Zimmerman, 41, white municipal service planner)

The realm of kinship is not always a source of support, as this story from a white working-class homemaker illustrates:

My husband's family, they're ignorant, they're Sicilian immigrants, they're poor, they never got any education or moved up in the world. When I had Paul [a child with neurological impairments] I wanted to know if this ran in the family. My husband's mother, she denied it, but his father's girlfriend, she told me the truth. "What do you mean," she says, "telling her there's six kids. Why don't you stop lying and tell her about the three that's gone now!" Two were boys; they were retarded, they died young in institutions. One was a girl, a perfectly formed girl except she had no female organs. They kept her at home, but she died, too. I don't know if this is connected to Paul's troubles. I only know they lie, and they deny, and they make it hard to find out for the sake of the children. (Angela Carponi, 33, white homemaker)

Kinship friction over amniocentesis may be profound, or nuanced. When Daphne McCarle, a white college professor whose description of the sonogram of her twins is quoted in chapter 5, told her sister about the experience, she expected a delighted response. But the sister, a right-to-life activist and mother of eight, reacted with outrage: "A sonogram this early: Why'd you have a sonogram this early? I bet you're thinking of committing murder!"

Letty Sharp, the white hospital clerk who asked me to turn off the tape recorder when we discussed attitudes toward abortion, never told her sister or parents about the test because she feared their judgments. Nancy Smithers, a white lawyer who expressed ambivalence about the quality control of babies through amniocentesis, confronted her sister's moralism when she announced her own test results. Marcia Lang, a white psychologist, said of her fundamentalist in-laws, "It crossed my mind to tell them I had a miscarriage, if it was really Down's." One couple analyzed their genealogy in some detail for me, speculating about which relatives would approve, and which disapprove, of prenatal testing: "My older brother would be horrified, aghast that we'd done this. My middle brother, he would understand. But my mother, she'd throw me out of the family if she knew" (Jim Norton, 42, white lawyer).

Many women and their supporters make fine distinctions among relatives, deciding with whom they can share their decision to have an amniocentesis. Sometimes, their reasoning is psychological, focusing on who can "handle it" and "give me support." Often, their concern is political: They judge the link between prenatal diagnosis and abortion to be so iron-bound that vociferously antiabortion family members would oppose them on both individual and social grounds.

Encountering Belief

Of course, I have been speaking of attitudes toward disability and abortion as if decision-making were familial and families were forged in the contexts of racial-ethnic and class-based communities. But there is another nexus of values, mores, resources and judgments that also frames these subjects. Much of that framework is provided by religion and religious affiliation. Throughout my hospital-based observations, and in many home interviews, I encountered a dense presence of religious discourses. Having embarked on a study of what I initially thought was the impact of scientific literacy and technology, I was often surprised to discover the daily inflection of religious language and practice within the experiences I was trying to map. I would, for example, arrive at Middle Hospital to translate for a Spanish speaker about to undergo an amniocentesis, only to find that the secretary who pointed me to the sonography suite wanted to discuss the Good News when I asked for directions. Moreover, about one-quarter of the women who agreed to home interviews were evangelical or Pentecostal Protestants. While their numbers at first struck me as disproportionately large, I came to believe that their presence in my sample was not random: Perhaps they agreed to be interviewed because they saw my visit as an opportunity to testify.

The clamorous nature of religious expression was particularly apparent among clinic patients. But like my earlier discussion of class and ethnic influences on attitudes toward disability and abortion, this observation requires unpacking. People from all social strata shared their religious reflections and, sometimes, objections to prenatal testing with me. But private, middle-class patients who refuse amniocentesis on religious grounds usually inform their personal physicians, and rarely accept an appointment with a genetic counselor. Their religious testimony was thus harder for me to collect. Clinic patients often voiced their religious concerns in the more public context of being offered amniocentesis in a hospital where I was observing, and were thus available to me.

My home interviews included the topic of religious background and practices, and probed for religious influences on decisions surrounding prenatal testing and abortion. My questions concerning this topic were placed in the second half of the interview schedule; often, however, the topic emerged dramatically and spontaneously early on in our conversations. It is obviously of central concern to many people. The answers to my questions about religion suggested two broad themes. The first is that religion and science continue to have an intertwined discursive relationship; the second is that religion provides not only spiritual direction, but social and material resources to many people. This is especially true for recent immigrants, but occurs for many others as well, as indicated throughout chapters 7, 9, and 10. I will discuss and illustrate each of these themes in order.

The intertwined nature of religious and scientific discourse deserves elaboration. Sometimes, the two fields of meaning collide and collude in reproducing conventional and comfortable images which too neatly sort practitioners and their beliefs by race, ethnicity, and class. This problem of religious stereotyping dogged me throughout my research, for I often found myself coding interviews as "typical": "Catholics use abortion services, but they suffer more than others for doing so" or "Pentecostalists can link anything, including a genetic intake interview, to God's miraculous presence" or "Jews are so committed to rationalism that they insert technology into God's benefits." Yet even as I echoed a kind of conventional and stereotyped denominationalism, I attempted to follow the steps by which a pregnant woman and her supporters actively produced meaning at the moral crossroads where amniocentesis had deposited them.

As I tried to indicate in chapter 5, the liminality of pregnancy and prenatal testing encourages women and their supporters to articulate their fears, aspirations, and values surrounding children and the future. The very realm of reproduction often invokes homegrown moral philosophy and a recognition of the mysterious and uncontrolled forces impinging on its outcome in particular, and the human condition in general. Many of the people with whom I spoke thus mixed speculations on pregnancy and spirituality quite spontaneously into their conversation, even before my questions turned to religion. Many also identified a self-conscious link between their religious background and how they viewed prenatal testing:

Basically, I grew up Catholic, I think it's tragic to end a pregnancy, to end a life. The only exceptions to me are if it was going to endanger my own life, or this one, if something could go profoundly wrong with the baby. But I'd have a hard time ending it. I'd rather carry the pregnancy, then see what develops. (Donna Straughn, 26, white homemaker, wife of a balanced translocation carrier)

I was raised Catholic, but I wasn't attending church, not like now. Since we joined the Assembly [of God], I go on Tuesdays for Bible study, Thursdays for meeting, Sundays for worship. They all know I'm having this baby, I'm having this test. They all pray for the health of the baby. They're keeping it healthy for me. (Mari-Carmen Trujillo, 38, Honduran UPS package handler)

Let the pope walk in my shoes. When the pope has to raise a kid with a tragic problem, then he can have a vote in what happens. Until then, I can't let an old man tell me how to deal with this stuff. (Marie Mancini, 38, white high school teacher)

God proposes, science disposes. When God gives you a problem, he also provides the cure. (Sonia Perido, 36, Colombian hotel chambermaid)

In line with the national statistics indicating the importance of church attendance in black communities, most of the African-American women with whom I spoke considered themselves religious:

I was raised Methodist, I went to church every Sunday, and to Sunday school. Back home, it was part of everybody's life. Now, I take my daughter sometimes, when she's bothering me for it. Methodist or Baptist, it's ok, I'm not a member, but I go sometimes. When I was coming up, we learned the Lord's Prayer, the Ten Commandments. I teach those to my daughter, I teach her at home. Especially, respect your elders, that's the most important. And then, respect yourself. If you don't respect yourself, nobody else will. (Lacey Smythe, African-American secretary)

I'm a Protestant, I don't go too regularly, it doesn't affect my decision. (Londa Wright, 37, African-American postal worker)

For women from mainline churches, belief and practice flowed easily into the acceptance of biomedical technologies. But for Pentecostal and evangelical Protestants, the intertwined nature of Jesus and genetics was more dramatic:

I had this vision: It was a girl. She was like me, only lighter. I lay my hands on her, and she went crazy. Only when we were in church. So I offered her to God, I dedicated her in that church. In my vision, God showed me everything, the crib, how she was dressed. But she had a problem, she had a hole in her heart. And she couldn't see. So God fixed it, he fixed the hole in her heart, and he gave her glasses. In my vision she was wearing little baby glasses, real cute. The Spirit warns us about everything, and the Spirit also heals. (Rafael Trujillo, 42, unemployed)

Could I abort if the baby was going to have that problem? God would forgive me, surely; yes, I could abort. Latin Catholics, we are raised to fear God, and to believe in His love and mercy. Now, if I were evangelical, that's another story. It's too much work, being evangelical. My sisters are both evangelicals, they go to church all the time. There's no time for abortion for them. (Maria Acosta, 41, Ecuadorian home-maker)

Many Catholics used the occasion of amniocentesis to articulate their own relation to the church's position on abortion; according to the genetic counselors I interviewed, Catholic women use amniocentesis as frequently as non-Catholic women, but they are more troubled by it. Many mainline Protestants pictured reproductive technology as occupying a space apart from their spiritual practices, for they saw both faith and reproductive medicine as private matters. But evangelicals and Pentecostalists often saw amniocentesis as a dramatic occasion for interpreting God's presence in their lives. Their religious beliefs and practices beckoned them to find spiritual clues everywhere, and their social landscapes were densely populated with signs of Christ's proximity.

Jews I interviewed had a "user-friendly" attitude toward medical intervention. All were positive about amniocentesis. Many expressed this sentiment: "Why not use the miracles of modern technology to make life better?" As one couple said, after terminating a Down syndrome pregnancy, "We're crying over our losses, it really hurts, but it's better this way. Modern medicine is a blessing, even when it brings you the hardest lessons of all." A secular Jewish woman told me this story:

The technology is there to help you out, I think you should use it. It's there to make life easier, that's why God invented it. So I was at Elite getting my Tay-Sachs test, and there was a Jewish Orthodox couple there. She was young, very pretty, she looked about 14. I was shocked. He was older but still young. Your stereotypic Hasidic man, shlubby, patriarchal, kind looking. The counselor said, "I'll take you together," and he said, "Oh, no. This is my daughter, she's getting the test, not me." Later, alone with the counselor, I just couldn't resist. I said, "Why's she getting tested, she's so young, just a baby herself, why are you testing her?" And the counselor said, "It's the So-and-so program. It's for arranging marriages so that no double Tay-Sachs carriers are matched up." I was floored, I almost died. There we were, the Tay-Sachs gang, an Orthodox arranged marriage and a 41-year-old, lesbian, AI [artificial insemination] single mother, both getting the same services from medicine because we're both Jewish. (Enid Zimmerman, white municipal service planner)

(Parenthetically, it should be noted that the Chevra Dor Yesurim Program ["Organization for the Generations"] was initially developed by an Ortho-dox rabbi living in Brooklyn who had lost three children to Tay-Sachs dis-ease. In his community, arranged marriages were the norm; stigmatized births and childhood deaths implicated linked genealogies, making marriage arrangements very problematic. The idea of voluntary testing developed so that couples deemed incompatible could be prevented from dating. The pro-gram now screens more couples for Tay-Sachs in the United States, Canada, and Israel than any secular public health program, working primarily through the community's religious high schools. Modern biomedical genetic technology here undergirds and enhances a traditional patriarchal practice.)

This compatibility of Jewish Orthodoxy and modern biomedicine was often demonstrated in the stories I collected. Indeed, one obstetrician who serves the Hasidic community responded to my research by describing the predicament of one of his clients who was married to a balanced transloca-tion carrier. She wanted a very early prenatal diagnostic test, as her rabbi's interpretation of Jewish law declared that a male fetus can be aborted only up to the fortieth day of the pregnancy (while a female fetus can be removed as late as the eightieth day). But no New York medical center offered chori-onic villus sampling and returned results within the religious time frame she required. The couple flew to England with the obstetrician's help to partici-pate as subjects in a cutting-edge experimental protocol testing the safety of extremely early intervention. Their contribution to science was also science's contribution to their religion. Three years after I collected this story, a con-versation with an advocate for Chevra Dor Yesurim taught me how quickly science and religion may march on: Now, the organization routinely sends known carrier couples with an "accidental" pregnancy to Philadelphia, where a world-renowned researcher is willing to provide extremely early test-ing and results.

The relationship between science and religion is thus both deeply inter-twined and open to interpretation when viewed through the eyes of individ-ual pregnant women. Not only do different religions hold diverse stances toward reproductive technologies,[28] but practitioners within religions may vary widely in their interpretations of official doctrine and personal adher-ence. Many Hispanic Catholic women, for example, reported multiple early abortions, despite church teachings. To them, *late* abortion was a mortal sin. They carved finely honed, female-centered theological distinctions and prac-tices out of a monolithic theology to achieve a reconciliation of religion and family life. Likewise, Protestants display a wide array of beliefs and practices. Some of these differences can be linked to specific churches. Evangelicals and fundamentalists are most likely to preach against the test, and one respondent (whose story will be recounted in chapter 7) beat a beeline to her Mormon roots when she wanted to be talked out of an abortion following a "positive" prenatal diagnosis. Mainline groups like Episcopalians, Dutch Reformists, and Methodists are either silent or supportive on the topic of amniocentesis.

But very often, women insisted they were expressing not an official church teaching but a personal interpretation. Lynthia Cato, Barbados-born and recommended for the test at the age of 41, refused it, telling me in a subsequent interview that it was against her belief. When I queried what that was, she warned me not to confuse her "denomination" (Seventh-day Adventist) with her "creed" (personal), in which a female deity bestowed healthy pregnancies on those whose behavior merited them. Two Latin American evangelicals who swore they would never consider abortion nonetheless underwent amniocentesis. In almost identical words, each told me she "wanted medicine to help know what miracles God had in store for me."

Religion provides one resource in the complex and often contradictory repertoire of possible identities a pregnant woman brings to her decision to use or reject amniocentesis. There is no definitive "Catholic," "Jewish," or "Protestant" position on reproductive technology, when viewed from the pregnant woman's point of view. Rather, each concrete, embedded pregnancy is assessed in light of the competing claims on maternity the individual acknowledges and to which she responds. Religion constitutes one powerful arena for such identity claims.

The Materiality of Spirituality

But religious affiliation also provides more than an orienting, discursive, ideological or personal worldview, for religious communities are often places of social solidarity and material connection. The resources they offer to families can be quite concrete, ranging from day-care services, Bible school, and parochial education to job recommendations from pastors and priests, leadership opportunities for women in church voluntary organizations, and visiting programs for the elderly and other homebound relatives. Where resources are available, their withdrawal through moral judgment or stigma can present a serious problem. Several Catholic women, for example, told me they were afraid to go to confession in their neighborhood parish churches after having amniocenteses. Sometimes, genetic counselors provided introductions to priests and other religious specialists who were sympathetic to such women's spiritual concerns. Letty Sharp (a white Catholic hospital secretary) and Angela Carponi (a white Catholic homemaker) were both active in their parish churches, and both asked me to turn off the tape when we spoke about abortion. In an extreme and institutional version of the same problem, several genetic counselors in Middle Hospital complained to me about the influence of the Catholic Church on their offices. The church owned the air rights (providing restrictions on future high-rise building in their space) over the building that Middle was constructing, and had explicitly asked that genetic counselors be barred from working in the new maternity service to be located there.

Churches may also provide the concrete moorings for problem solving in stressful lives. Indeed, the very reasons for accepting or rejecting prenatal testing are deeply embedded in different collective histories of social risk toward which neighborhood churches stand as interested witnesses. When I interviewed a 38-year-old Honduran UPS package inspector in a run-down neighborhood in Queens, for example, she seemed to have accepted an amniocentesis without great introspection. As the mother of two teenage boys from a former marriage, she "just wanted everything to be all right." During the course of an hour's home interview, my tape was filled with her disinterested answers, interrupted by the flamboyant and sonorous testimony of her fervently Pentecostalist husband. He described his vivid visions of the infant Jesus protecting his own infant-to-be, swore that the prayers of his co-congregants had already healed all manner of potential problems the child might have faced, and used the occasion of my visit to witness the benefits of faith. It was a stunning performance. Later, Mari-Carmen walked me back to the subway, and without the pressures of husband or tape recorder told me the following story: Pentecostalism was saving her husband, who had twice been jailed on drug charges, and from whom she had once separated because of his infidelities. He attended programs at their church several times each week. Her chief worries centered on her older sons, both having problems in school, one involved with a neighborhood gang. If "having a baby for him" would stabilize the family, she would accept the pregnancy, and the amniocentesis, and any other advice the doctor gave her. She said "The kids are excited about the baby. He is, too. He prays, he gets me to pray. The kids ain't running around now. Him neither."

It was in this spirit that she had accepted the Pentecostalist congregation. Pentecostalism here served as a poor man's rehabilitation program, providing structures for self-restraint, setting boundaries on acceptable behavior, and beckoning the tempted toward a normative, better life. And, in true Weberian spirit, it encouraged Mari-Carmen and Rafael to accumulate and shepherd their own resources without giving money away to close kin who remained Catholic. Without the benefit of this shadow interview, I might well have coded Mari-Carmen's answers as "medically compliant" and stereotypically religious. But the real risks in her life—a dangerous neighborhood, substandard schools, a husband involved in drugs, and other threats to family stability—were far more pressing, and external to medical definitions of her situation. For these, the Assembly of God offered some concrete resources.

Toward a Homegrown Epidemiology

Indeed, problems of social vulnerability and family stress run like a red thread through the home interviews I conducted. Many women and their supporters from diverse backgrounds experience stressful circumstances, but most of the stress stories I collected were told by working-class and working-poor women, for they are most vulnerable not only to the problems built into unsafe or run-down neighborhoods, inadequate medical insurance, or unemployment, but to the lack of access to private professional helping services which middle-class women and their families often use when in a predicament. Stress stories, like religion, frame the amniocentesis accounts of many women.

Most dramatically, involvement with illegal drugs on the part of male partners and, sometimes, pregnant women themselves, sends many to seek genetic counseling. Sandra McAlister, an African-American administrative secretary, was not thinking about Down syndrome when she had amniocentesis at the age of 41. Her husband was having a hard time kicking his heroin habit, and she feared it would affect the baby's development. She hoped that the new pregnancy would give him a reason to dry out, but was realistic in her awareness that it might, instead, create additional pressure. Mari-Carmen Trujillo, whose Pentecostalist husband's testimony is recounted above, was on her second marriage to a drug-involved man. His problems loomed far larger than the chromosomal anomalies described by genetic counselors in the story-within-the-story she told me. Lorraine Johnson, an African-American social worker, wavered about allowing amniocentesis at the age of 31, but finally took the test because she feared that the methadone she took in place of heroin would damage her fetus. Less self-destructively, but perhaps no less stressfully for family life, three women I interviewed reported husbands with recurrent histories of hospitalization for mental illness, and six mentioned partners who were depressed or withdrawn from their pregnancies as a result of unemployment.

Poverty imposes its own stresses. One woman changed the time and venue of our interview many times, describing her fight with her landlord about a fallen ceiling. She considered her housing situation too hazardous to risk inviting me home. At one City Hospital, 51 percent of the patients sent for genetic counseling reported having no telephone, and at another, which served a predominantly Afro-Caribbean clientele, I was almost never able to follow up with home interviews because the pregnant women either had no telephones or shared them with neighbors and relatives who could not be expected to transmit my messages about scheduling interviews. Telephones cost money, and many working-poor women reported family feuds over who could afford the service, or even stand in line to pay the bills, given the lack of a checking account. The lives of the very poor are extremely complex, and some of that stress derives from the personal work essential to keeping basic necessities and services available. Moreover, many of the working poor work long or irregular hours. I interviewed two home health attendants on the job, during the hours when their elderly clients were napping. Their work days, which often ran to seventy-hour weeks, were too long to permit a "home interview" at their own homes.

Under these stressful circumstances, prenatal health care in general, and amniocentesis in particular, plays a very small role in women's lives. Indeed, the very idea that risks are measurable and individual may be overwhelmed by other assessments women make about factors influencing prenatal health. For example, when a genetic counselor suggested that Londa Wright, an African-American postal worker, should convince her husband to stop smoking for the sake of the fetus, she laughed and said, "So maybe he won't smoke, and it won't make no difference. All the peoples around me at work, they're smoking all the time." She continued to describe her medical interactions: "So I go to see the blood pressure doctor, and he says to relax. Relax! How can you relax when they give you only a half hour for lunch, and then the supervisor's barking at you the whole time anyway?"

In light of the myriad health statistics suggesting that African-Americans suffer more stress-related illnesses than do whites (e.g., Kochanek et al. 1994; Queen et al. 1994), there is in such responses an incipient recognition of the social, rather than individual, nature of factors which put maternal-fetal prenatal health at risk. Indeed, many African-Americans spontaneously volunteered the knowledge that health problems ran in families. They were usually speaking of alcoholism or childhood seizures, although diabetes was sometimes mentioned. This melding of the biological and social, and, sometimes, the backgrounding of the genetic in favor of the community-based route of transmission is illuminated in a more dramatic and cross-cultural example.

When the research team seeking the causes of Huntington's disease began to interview villagers around Lake Maracaibo, Venezuela, where the incidence of the condition is elevated, and endogamous (in-village) marriage assures its continued presence in many genealogies, they discovered an indigenous explanation. Villagers believed that everyone in their community was at risk, only some would inherit the condition acutely, although all might fall prey to its ravages. Those decimated by Huntington's disease were well-treated, and their sufferings publicly acknowledged, perhaps because of this heightened consciousness of collective risk (N. Wexler, personal communication, 1992; A. Wexler 1995).

In highlighting this background theme of practical and collective explanation, I do not mean to underestimate the great importance of individual health-seeking behavior: Nonsmoking, healthy diets, and prenatal vitamins are almost universally recognized approvingly by pregnant women as crucial elements in responsible prenatal behavior. Indeed, several studies suggest that female intravenous drug users make their best attempts to quit when they are pregnant, for the sake of the baby (Chavkin 1990; Paltrow 1990). I am only attempting to point out that the wholly individual picture of risk (and its responsiveness to amniocentesis) which genetic counselors articulate may have to compete with more experience-near and collective concepts of risk in which, paradoxically, these are differently individualized risks to be considered.

Many working-class women, especially African-Americans, expressed not only this more social sense of risks to fetal health, but a stronger sense of collective responsibility for what happens to their children. Many mapped the contributions that close relatives and neighbors played in their child-care arrangements. In listening to their stories, I was often struck by how much less they focused on the pregnancy itself than middle-class women, and how much more they described the safety net into which they wanted the child to be born. We might interpret these practical strategies as illustrations of two threads that often run through working-class life: The first suggests that the risk discourse of genetic counselors falls upon a terrain already dense with other kinds of problems, medical as well as more broadly social. Chromosomes are relatively small and distant factors in the risks that many pregnant women understand themselves to face. Second, evidence of a more social analysis of risk and reassurance is occasionally prefigured in such responses. Speculations about this possibility appear in chapter 11.

This more practical epidemiology of working-class and working-poor women sometimes includes low expectations of and by health professionals. Many minority women, even if they are not poor, cannot count on support for their pregnancies, and pregnancy-related decision-making, from their health care providers. Frankie Smithers, an African-American schoolteacher, told me that when she got her positive pregnancy test results back at City Hospital, she was delighted, but the nurse automatically directed her to make an appointment for an abortion. It took considerable complaint to persuade the woman to schedule a prenatal care visit instead. Clinic patients Sonia Perido, Maria Acosta, and Juana Martes all expressed enthusiastic interest in being interviewed; they took my questions as evidence that somebody at the hospital actually cared about their well-being and evaluation of services during their pregnancies. Ironically, I could not convince them that my independent investigation was not a new follow-up benefit extended to them by the Health Department. It is, of course, important to add that middle-class women, too, may feel that their needs are unmet by doctors, nurses, and other staff members. And many working-class and working-poor women feel very well-served by their health care providers. Differences in what we might label the "culture of clinics"—including appointment protocol, staff stability, and the amount of health education outreach—vary dramatically among City and Middle Hospitals. These environmental factors influence not only women's general attitudes toward health care, but also their acceptance or refusal of the offer of amniocentesis.

Throughout this chapter, I have tried to situate the complex issues attending amniocentesis in light of the social relations and cultural resources within which each pregnant woman's life is embedded. The anxiety of pregnancy, attitudes toward childhood disability and abortion, and family history and religion all shape how a pregnant woman awaits the results of prenatal testing. These same factors also influence the decision not to undergo amniocentesis, a subject to which we turn next.

7
Refusing

I wanted to take the test, but then he said no. At the hospital, I was all gung ho, but on the way home, he expressed his feelings. That whole night, he expressed his feelings. We went back and forth. The next day, I called up so many people. I have this religious aunt, she's the one that made me see: Down syndrome, no need to take the test for Down syndrome. It's not necessary. Everything my husband said, she said, too. So I went, "Ok, I won't take it." And I didn't take it. (Catherine Judd, 35, African-American secretary)

WHEN I FIRST MET CATHERINE JUDD and her husband at a group counseling session at Middle Hospital, I was sure from her reactions and questions that she intended to use the test. But a few weeks later, when I called to see how she was feeling after an amniocentesis and to schedule an interview appointment, she told me that she had changed her mind. We met for lunch that week, and, tape recorder in hand, I learned that Catherine's decision not to use amniocentesis was made in the context of opposition from her close kin. It therefore at first appeared to be an entirely personal decision, mediated by the strength of her kinship community. But later in the same interview, she also said, "My husband didn't say much there [at the hospital] but he sure read those forms carefully. He didn't much like the parts about experimentation." At first, I intervened to say,

> You mean the consent form for the laboratory? What they mean by experimentation doesn't have anything to do with you, or your husband or your baby's body. It's about using the leftover amniotic fluid to check for other chromosome patterns, to compare it with other fluid, instead of just looking at it for a diagnosis for you. That's the

way they find out about general patterns, by comparing lots of left-over fluid. It won't even have your names attached, just a number when they use it for experiments, if you give them permission. And you can say "no" to the experimental use and still have the test for your own use, if you want that.

But as we talked, I realized the narrow, science-focused preoccupations of my own interpretation. Her husband was expressing strong feelings about experiments in a much wider context: his perception of the role of black people and medicine. And Catherine herself went on to say,

> Because I read something . . . I don't remember what magazine I read it out of, but I remember reading that the reason why we have AIDS was to kill off the blacks and the gays. . . . I don't know how true it is, but supposedly over in Africa what they did was they shot the children. They shot something into the immunization shots, into the people over in Africa, and that's how it started.

The Green Monkey experimental theory of AIDS in Africa purports to explain how a malevolent experiment ran amuck and spread a killer disease throughout that continent and then to the New World. In the late '80s and early '90s, it was much discussed in certain black-focused tabloids and talk shows. Though scientists have denounced such theories as "disinformation" or even as "paranoia," their staying power needs to be evaluated in light of a long history of indifferent, or even menacing experimental medical interventions for which black communities *have* served as guinea pigs: The infamous Tuskegee syphilis experiment, for example, and the chaotic conditions attending early sickle-cell anemia carrier trait screening have both been widely reported in the black-focused media (cf. Duster 1990). African-American consciousness of biomedical experimentation may thus be filtered through incompletely remembered, and, sometimes, media-shaped views of prior medical interventions (France 1998). It is not then so surprising that Catherine's husband read the informed consent form for laboratory work on the amniotic fluid sample with a critical eye. He joined at least five other African-Americans in the context of my research who expressed fear of experimentation in response to this form. Only two non-African-Americans raised any questions about descriptions of "experimentation" in the lab form by my count. Might we interpret this suspicion as a response to a structural position which black communities have historically occupied vis-à-vis medical experimentation in the United States?

Catherine Judd's change of heart thus raises an important theoretical issue for me: It seems to be at once the product of individual choice, contextualized by kin and community pressure, and also a response to racially differentiated sentiments and histories in relation to medical intervention and experimentation. The interplay of social history and individual volition, of collective position and personal choice, in short, the imbrication of structure and agency, continually perplexed me as I attempted to find out how people came to accept or to refuse prenatal testing.

As amniocentesis has rapidly diffused and become part of routine prenatal care for some sectors of the population, there are those who choose not to accept its complicated benefits and burdens. Their narratives may enable us to understand why a routinizing technology does not always stay en route. Are some groups more likely to opt against the technology than others? Do some reject it categorically, while others accept parts of the bundle of assumptions, values, and practices to which it comes attached? A woman may step off the conveyor belt of a routinizing technology at many points in its trajectory; but not all exits are used equally, nor are those who exit at specific points a random group, as I hope to show below. These questions provoked my interest in refusers. Initially I wondered if I might code them as "resisters," that is, as people who consciously opposed routinization. Or might their refusal be based on a lack of access to information and discomfort with biomedicine, thus also reproducing prior power relations between patients and providers? But my search for resistance and reproduction was, of course, too simple: The reasons for refusing to use amniocentesis are diverse and complex. And according to a leading epidemiologist of prenatal screening and birth defects, even the most perfectly accessible services are unlikely to yield higher than 70 percent utilization rates in this country (Hook 1989).

In prior chapters, I have tried to indicate that the communicative practices on the basis of which women accept prenatal testing are themselves highly structured. And in chapter 4, I foreshadowed a range of reasons some women give at counseling sessions for their decisions not to use amniocentesis. These include fear of miscarriage, suspicion of the accuracy of statistics and testing, discomfort with unbalancing the forces imagined to be sustaining a pregnancy, and religious beliefs. A refusal may also be based on a report of male opposition, as I have elsewhere indicated. Yet each individual refusal exhibits a complex amalgam of structure and agency—after all, male dominance, or scientific literacy, or religious observance, or prior reproductive history all express both individual and social characteristics. Moreover, the timing of an acceptance or a refusal—when and where one exits a new reproductive technology—may be structural as well. These patterns are the subject of the present chapter.

Class and Racial-Ethnic Concerns

Among the structural reasons for rejecting prenatal testing, class-associated differences loom large.[29] It is an axiom of genetic counseling that middle-class patients (disproportionately white) usually accept the test while poorer women (disproportionatel from ethnic-racial minorities) are more likely to refuse it. But that generalization needs interrogation. Private (i.e., middle-class) patients usually don't come for genetic counseling (to learn about amniocentesis) unless they are already determined to have the test. They are likely to have prior knowledge about the test, gleaned from books, friends, and private physicians, and to have already made up their minds. They inform their private physicians about their lack of interest in or opposition to the test, and never make an appointment with a genetic counselor. So refusers in this class rarely get counted. This was surely true for the economist whose story was told in chapter 5. Pregnant in her late thirties with a third child, she felt entirely confident about refusing amniocentesis based on her own (mis)readings of health statistics. Likewise, an education consultant who had suffered through several years of infertility before her first successful pregnancy at 34 rejected amniocentesis during her second pregnancy, at age 37. She was more frightened of the miscarriage rate than she was of the rate of detection of fetal chromosomal problems. It should be stressed that both these cases involve scientifically confident middle-class women who felt empowered to make a decision "against the grain" of their immediate peer group to forgo amniocentesis, while situating themselves comfortably within statistical, scientific thinking.

Some middle-class women and their partners also reject the test based on philosophical, ethical, or religious reasoning. For example, a nurse married to an epidemiologist in the New York City Health Department decided against amniocentesis after she and her husband had investigated the potential adoption of a "special needs" (disabled) child. Their Protestant church had directed them toward an agency that specialized in hard-to-adopt children when they had trouble getting pregnant again after the birth of their first child. By the time a second, successful pregnancy was established, they felt quite open to the possibility of raising a child with a disability. Another male physician whom I met through the Health Department wistfully described himself as a virtual conscript to my study: His wife, raised a devout Catholic, would not consider amniocentesis, despite his own professional interests in the test. But these stories—which mirror class-refracted versions of concerns also offered by clinic patients who reject amniocentesis, as well—came to me through personal networks of friendship and work; they were never entered into the medical ledger, for the rejections occurred in the context of private medicine.

But among clinic patients, an appointment with the genetic counselor may provide the first opportunity they have to ponder the significance, risks, and benefits of prenatal testing. In all hospitals, registers are kept detailing pregnant women's appointments and their outcomes; in some hospitals, those who refuse amniocentesis are also asked to sign an "informed consent" document attesting to their decision. They then make up their minds in a context in which their choices become part of hospital statistics. Moreover, many women from working-class and working-poor backgrounds, including African-American and Hispanic women, *do* accept the test. And refusal rates vary dramatically from hospital to hospital. At one Middle Hospital, for example, where the clinic serves primarily a Spanish-speaking, low-income population, acceptance rates are high: 70–80 percent. At City, with an Afro-Caribbean and Spanish-speaking population, acceptance rates are low: 30–40 percent (Hsu 1989). We could go fishing for a cultural explanation about pregnancy beliefs, medical attitudes, and so on. But a simpler observation is this: Middle's prenatal clinic provides a stable and welcoming environment in which women tend to be very comfortable, and to trust the nurses. Relative to many other hospitals, Middle has a lower rate of nurse turnover; clinic patients therefore have the opportunity to develop an ongoing relationship with a health care provider whom they are likely to see through the course of one or more pregnancies. By the time they arrive for an appointment with a genetic counselor, pregnant women have usually talked with a favorite nurse, often in Spanish, and feel competent to accept or reject the test.

City Hospital, by contrast, has been a site of struggle over services for many years, and the prenatal clinic is a difficult environment in which to receive health care. Women (and often their young children) feel imprisoned in uncomfortable waiting rooms where they routinely spend two to three hours before being seen. By that time, the level of anger and frustration, as well as the lack of professional-patient communication, makes it much more likely that a woman will break a counseling appointment or sit through it in a state of distrust. Far more than simply "ethnic differences" are at stake in the microsociology of access to respectful medical services which then condition acceptance rates. Entering into the ecology of prenatal clinics are the stability of residential neighborhoods; city, state, and federal health care funding and politics; hospital labor contract negotiations and issues of community control.

Even more complicated to evaluate structurally are the number of women who arrive too late in their pregnancies to be offered the test. In some City and Middle Hospitals, a woman's tardy entry into the prenatal care system is based on her prior experiences with pregnancy. In chapter 3, for example, I recounted the story of a woman who came too late to City for amniocentesis because she believed that the test, which she had accepted in an earlier pregnancy, covered all her pregnancies. And very experienced mothers from some pro-natalist, highly fertile ethnic communities do not seek much prenatal medical care. Hasidic women, for example, often do not register for maternity beds until the sixth month of their pregnancies, knowing full well that this is a hospital requirement. Prior to that point, many feel entirely competent to monitor their own progress, contacting doctors or nurses only if the present pregnancy feels different from their many prior ones. They are thus unlikely to visit a prenatal clinic in time to be offered an amniocentesis. Moreover, genetic screening in their communities is somewhat demedicalized and linked to marriage arrangements, rather than to prenatal care. Among Hasids and traditional Orthodox Jews, a genetic screening program for those diseases which run at elevated rates in Ashkenazi-derived communities (initially, Tay-Sachs disease; now, increasingly, other conditions like Gaucher's disease, for which prenatal screens have become available) works directly in the community, attempting to screen potential spouses before they meet one another, rather than relying on the screening of already established pregnancies. Ideally, the *Dor Yeshurim* screens yeshiva students anonymously, assigning each young person a computerized file. Before dating is approved by their families, the two file numbers can be called into the program; their match will be deemed "compatible" or "incompatible," depending on what has been learned about carrier status. Marriages among those deemed "incompatible" by the screening program are then avoided as families plan for their adolescents' futures. So members of the Hasidic community are not likely to use the same entry point to genetic screening, nor to include it in prenatal care, except under emergency conditions.[30]

But in a city where more than twenty thousand women give birth annually without ever having received any prenatal care at all, there are other problems endemic to the health care system which condition the likelihood that a woman will enter too late to be offered amniocentesis. Non-English speakers, especially if they are recent immigrants, may not know their entitlements: Medicaid will cover prenatal care, including prenatal diagnosis, but the paperwork necessary to get into the system is intimidating. A crowded, busy clinic may have a discouraging effect on women attempting to make an appointment, even though in principle, obstetric nurses are prepared to help anyone identified as being of "advanced maternal age" or as having had a serious problem in a previous pregnancy to jump the cue and receive prompt attention. But unless they have the confidence and ability to speak with the intake nurses, such women may well be dismayed by long appointment lines and complex paperwork.

In some City Hospitals, up to one-third of all the genetic counseling interviews I observed took place with women who had arrived at the end of their second trimester of pregnancy, too late for prenatal testing. Some were quite willing to sit through the counseling sessions in order to learn about chromosomes, birth defects, and amniocentesis "for the next pregnancy" or to "spread the word" to friends and kin. Others were disconsolate to discover that they were candidates for what they considered to be an important test of which they had no previous knowledge. One low-income Afro-Caribbean woman, for example, cried softly throughout the intake interview: She had discovered in her twenty-fourth week of pregnancy that both she and her partner carried the trait for sickle-cell anemia, and could have had their fetus diagnosed. She was very frightened to learn that there was a 25 percent chance that her fetus had a serious, life-threatening disease. Observing low-income women frequently entering prenatal care too late for amniocentesis made me wonder in each case if the woman would have used or rejected the test. My problem is moot: Despite the best efforts of many individual health care providers, the health care system had already structurally rejected her through its inability to make prenatal clinics adequately accessible.

In addition to late entry into the prenatal health care system, there are other early exit points from the conveyor belt of amniocentesis. Some women, especially in City Hospitals, refused the test indirectly, by missing one or more counseling appointments. "No shows" are a highly variable lot: Among private patients, the rate of those referred for counseling who do not keep their appointments is less than 10 percent. But their numbers run toward one-third of all clinic patients referred for counseling in some City Hospitals; in others, good communication between nurses and patients means that a pregnant woman can refuse the test directly, and no appointment will be made for her, in respect of her wishes. From a counselor's point of view, this latter strategy is obviously preferable: She can use her time to better purpose, rather than sitting in an empty room, speculating about whether her client is just late or not coming at all. Episodically, I would attempt to follow up "no shows" with a phone call. The reasons women gave for missing appointments were diverse. Sometimes, they would explain that the stresses of daily life—cancellation of baby-sitters, broken plumbing, bad weather without adequate coats—had kept them from an appointment. Sometimes, a woman had had a miscarriage before the time arrived for her scheduled counseling appointment. But often, fear of the test was reason enough to skip an appointment.

Reproductive Histories

Most refusals, however, happen during or directly after a counseling session at the prenatal clinics, and were therefore accessible to me. In such cases, I observed women making a decision based on the information at hand, to which they responded with the resources of their personal and cultural background. The most common reason that women from many social sectors and cultural traditions gave for refusing amniocentesis was fear of miscarriage. For them, any risk of causing the loss of the pregnancy, no matter how small, was unacceptable. While concern about miscarriage rates was the single most common issue raised in counseling, this fear was especially prevalent among women who had suffered prior miscarriages or bouts of infertility:

> After three miscarriages, I'm finally, really pregnant. That's more important than looking for needles in haystacks. (Susan Allison, 38, white social worker)

> I waited five years to get pregnant. I'm not going to risk it now. (Louise Bryant, 37, African-American secretary)

> My factory's almost closing. I can't afford to take any chances with this one. (Acantha Jones, 37, Afro-Caribbean secretary)

Likewise, a Haitian mother of four girls, age 38, who worked part-time in a child-care center debated having amniocentesis. She was eager to discover if number five would (finally) be a boy. She was enthusiastic about the benefits of testing at her counseling appointment, but after talking it over with her husband, she decided against testing: Any risk of miscarriage was unacceptable to them. Should the baby be lost through an "act of nature," she reasoned, they would accept the loss with peaceful consciences. But the possibility of causing a miscarriage was far more serious than the consequences of learning about fetal sex or chromosomes, from their point of view.

Reproductive history entered strongly into most, perhaps all, of women's decision-making. This is undoubtedly as true for women who accepted the test as for those who rejected it. Moreover, reproductive history was strongly intertwined with sources of knowledge that might be medical, or more broadly social. For example, one mother of a child with Down syndrome refused amniocentesis in a subsequent pregnancy because she had learned too much: "Down's is only the tip of the iceberg," she told me. "There's hundreds of birth defects. This test can only pick up a few. What's the point in getting false assurances?" Her fear of "lightning striking twice" would not be allayed by the incomplete information testing offered. Another mother whose second child had died of hydrocephalus wanted no part of testing: "Doesn't matter, I can't go home empty-handed again!" she exclaimed.

And reproductive histories are not simply individual; they are woven into family and community life. For example, Mercy Aguilar, an advertising executive, was sent for genetic counseling because of prior miscarriages, and because, at 34, she was borderline "advanced maternal age." Mercy had also been exposed to medical uterine radiation in the early weeks of this pregnancy, before she realized she was pregnant. She entered group counseling with a negative bias against amniocentesis: As a member of a large, close-knit and practicing Catholic Filipino family, she had helped raise a brother with Down syndrome.

> We are eight in my family, and we all know the joy he [the brother with Down syndrome] brought to us. When my mother gave birth to him, she blamed herself, but gradually, we learned you don't cause this. It's just part of nature. Now, my mother is only concerned with the danger to me of all this testing. She isn't concerned if I have a normal child. Of course, we all want a normal child. But if the child is retarded, well, my whole family will be behind me. They will help me; it's different than for most people in America.

Mercy went on to speak eloquently about the solidarity of large families, even when separated by migration. She also said that the prior miscarriages had made her even more determined to carry this pregnancy to term. And she added, almost as an afterthought, a liberal response when I asked about her Catholic background: "I would never have an abortion. It's ok for people who believe in it, but I don't believe. My husband agrees, we want this child, we don't want to endanger it. If there is something wrong, we accept that." Here, reproductive history is family history, as well: The stability of a large family which raised a disabled child successfully, and familial and religious acceptance of Down syndrome all condition the meanings of prior miscarriages and form a context within which a decision not to use prenatal testing was made.

Sometimes, reproductive history refers back to a community or culture from which immigrants have come, encompassing a fund of social information which is at odds with medical practices in their new host country. Katya Janos, a Hungarian painter, refused amniocentesis at 34, insisting with confidence that her family had no genetic problems and that testing wasn't offered before the age of 40 in her native country. If she wouldn't do it there, why do it here? she reasoned. Wilhemina Jordan, 40, told me she briefly considered having an amniocentesis when we met at City Hospital. But nothing in her Liberian background supported the test:

> My sister, she hollered at me, "We never did this back home," and she got a healthy boy when she was 36. She hollered, and she hollered, and she hollered. She made me remember about her births and our family's births. Here, everything is different: The babies get born here in the early morning; I never heard of such a birth at home. Perhaps they need the testing here, but not there. They want me to come back [to the hospital] to discuss it. I know they mean to help me, but I was brought up one way and not another. I'm afraid of complications, I've been through a lot of pain to have my children, that is how we do it at home. I never did this, we never did this, what do I need this for now?

Another immigrant said, "I don't want to know about the future. That's not how we think in my country" (Rose Clarion, 39, Haitian garment worker). And some people refer back to prior pregnancies, in which they consider testing to have been a mistake. Daisy Caruthers, 38, African-American, unemployed, said, "I had amenosynthesis [*sic*] with the last one. Now I'm a little beyond [i.e., late] for this one. I waited, I was kind of worried about the test. Oh, it was monitored and everything, but something can always go wrong. It was too scary. If I'd known, I wouldn't have done it then, and I won't do it now." When I asked what had made the prior experience so scary, she told me that no one had explained anything about it; she just arrived on the appointed date, signed the papers and had the test. Given the care with which counseling is handled at this particular City Hospital, it is hard to evaluate exactly what went wrong. Daisy's file includes an annotation about having received prior counseling. But in her own estimation, the test was insufficiently explained. This, too, becomes part of a reproductive history.

And, as I indicated in chapters 3 and 4, miscommunication is always a possibility. When I interviewed Marcya Milton, age 44, after she refused prenatal testing at City, she spoke eloquently at length about her belief that a female deity had given her a healthy baby girl the year before, and would protect her present pregnancy. As we were about to part, our conversation took a different turn.

> Marcya: Oh, and another thing. Now, before you go, there's one thing I really must tell you. When I went to counseling last year, it was a nice lady that counseled me, and the figure was one half. On the desk, she wrote that figure. It's a fifty-fifty chance the test will harm my baby.
>
> Me: She must have misunderstood your question: It's less than a *point* 50 percent chance of causing a miscarriage; fifty-fifty is a very big number, and I'm sure she intended a very small one.
>
> Marcya: I didn't ask any questions, I just sat and listened, and then I discussed it with my husband, and what with the chances so high, well, we were against it. Now, this time, she said that the chances of having a baby that's retarded was nine hundred. Do you know what I mean, when I say nine hundred?
>
> Me: Do you mean one in nine hundred? At 45, the counselors usually say, the risk of having a baby with a chromosome problem is one in nineteen.
>
> Marcya: Yes, it was only nine hundred, so you know what I mean now. We couldn't take a fifty-fifty chance of harming that baby.

This refusal of testing intertwines a doubled discourse: At the beginning of our conversation, Marcya expressed a strong personal faith as the reason for her confidence in a healthy outcome: This was experientially the most significant reason she gave for choosing not to have the test. But at the end of our conversation, she also revealed a profound misunderstanding of both miscarriage rates and the risk of carrying a chromosomally atypical fetus. The numbers given were not the numbers received; this problem haunts medical decisions based on statistical thinking, especially when multiple and intersecting probabilities are being explained to someone without a privileged scientific or mathematical education.

Thinking through the Gap

The gap between statistical risk figures and phenomenological experience also informs some refusals. At her City Hospital counseling session, Jeanette L'Oiseau impressed me as a very well-organized and intelligent listener: She took notes, and told me that she was currently supporting herself as a home health-care attendant but hoped someday soon to study nursing. She agreed to have amniocentesis without any hesitation. But when I called her back some weeks later to see how the test had gone, she told me she had canceled. In the week prior to her amnio appointment, she met three women who had lost pregnancies after the test. I have no way to evaluate the causes of their loss; doctors and researchers cannot account for most miscarriages, and the chance that she met three women in one week who had recently used the test and become part of its miscarriage statistics is infinitesimally small.[31] But their stories were impressive, concrete, and current; they displaced a more abstract biomedical picture of the losses and gains attendant upon testing. Caught between their existential concreteness and her own newly acquired knowledge of testing, she said, "I think I made the right choice, but now I'm scared, I'm really, really scared. I wouldn't be so scared if I didn't know, but now, I know."

Likewise, as discussed in prior chapters, many women without a high degree of scientific literacy have developed a practical sense of community epidemiology. Enfolding their own reproductive health into that of kin and friends, they say, for example, "I don't smoke, I don't drink, I don't do drugs. My mother had my sister when she was 40, my sisters, they all had late babies, healthy babies. My friends, they're all fine. I'm healthy, I don't need this test" (Veronica Landry, 36, Trinidad-born factory worker). To which a geneticist at City Hospital replied, "It doesn't depend on how you feel, on how you live. The only way to know for sure if your fetus has these problems is to have the test." But Veronica had made up her mind, and she had the last word: "I like surprises," she said.

Sometimes, pregnant women and their partners refuse amniocentesis because the test cannot pick up the problems about which they are concerned, and they do not find the conditions it can detect sufficiently disturbing to merit testing. For example, Latoya and Kalim Mullen, a young African-American couple, were sent to genetic counseling at City Hospital by the high-risk prenatal care program in which they were enrolled. Despite their youth, they had already had premature twins, and sustained two miscarriages and a stillbirth, possibly caused by cytomegalovirus. They felt well-served by City's many services, but were firm in rejecting the test, since it couldn't yield information about cytomegalovirus and its possible damages. That was the only thing about which they expressed concern. They opted, instead, for multiple sonograms, to check fetal development throughout the pregnancy. Mercy Aguilar also stressed that testing could reveal only a very small number of conditions: She didn't think it advisable to start down the "slippery slope" of searching for problems which might well be there, but not be discernible using current technologies. Sometimes, women discovered that the reason they had sought counseling—exposure to pharmaceuticals, street drugs, occupational hazards or other potentially toxic substances early in pregnancy—wouldn't show up in amniocentesis. Even when offered the test "for reassurance," they opted against it, since it couldn't allay their anxieties.

Some people also express a disbelief in the accuracy of testing. Statements like, "I don't believe they can *really* know all that stuff" or "Isn't that just baby's pee they're looking at?" or "No wonder they say it's '99 percent accurate.' That's for when they make their mistakes. Then you can't hold them to it" are most likely to come from those without privileged educations. But occasionally, highly educated professionals express similar skepticism or misgivings. A close social science colleague of mine who was attempting to get pregnant once told me she didn't believe in chromosomes: She thought that modern genetics had taken a wrong tack, and was insufficiently focused on the interaction of environment and organism. While sympathetic toward her abstract philosophical position, I pushed hard to find out what she thought chromosomes might be (or not be). Her response: "That squiggly stuff in the microscope? It's cellular material, I'm sure, but I don't believe it does half of what they think it does. I wouldn't trust what they say is in it all that much."

Misunderstandings or disbeliefs concerning scientific discourse and findings account for some decisions to forgo testing, especially, but not exclusively, among those women without advanced scientific education. But the incorrect "numbers crunching" of the white professional economist mentioned earlier in this chapter, and the "fighting with numbers" strategy prevalent among white professional men in chapter 3 should remind us that this interpretive tendency is not owned exclusively by those who come from working-class and working-poor backgrounds.

And not all rejection of amniocentesis comes from skepticism about scientifically based information. Religious beliefs provide another set of powerful resources from which a refusal may be drawn. Some women, like Marcya Milton, hold a personal or denominational faith in the health of their fetuses. Others, like Mercy Aguilar, meld religion and family history into their acceptance of Down syndrome as a possibility with which they could comfortably live. And some use religion as a way to make a clear, if difficult, decision. Pat Carlson, for example, was raised as a Mormon in the Southwest. Living in New York and working as the head of a secretarial department in one of the city's largest and most high-powered law firms, she hadn't attended temple in decades. At age 37, with one grown child and one divorce behind her, Pat found herself pregnant after a casual liaison. She was extremely pleased, despite the complex conditions involved in undertaking late, single mother-hood. She accepted an amniocentesis at the suggestion of her obstetrician without much concern. But when her fetus was diagnosed as having Down's, she was shocked. At that point, Pat made a beeline to her Mormon roots:

> Maybe if I was married, maybe if I had another shot at it. But this was it: Take it or leave it. So I took it. I called the Mormons back. Oh, I hadn't been to temple for years. But I knew in my heart of hearts they'd convince me not to have an abortion. And they did. One man, he just came and prayed with me, he still comes. Stevie [her son with Down syndrome] gets a lot of colds, I can't always make it to temple. But when we don't make it, he comes over and prays with us.

In this case, the Mormons have consistently provided personally tailored shut-in prayer service and tremendous social support for a woman who left their fold to swim against the current, but returned when she needed their help.

Religious beliefs and practices, and the concrete social resources that churches provide, are thus central to many pregnant women's orientations. And while many denominations are, in principle, accepting of genetic testing and even abortion, others are vociferously opposed. In either case, the women with whom I have spoken rarely "toed the line" of any particular church; they were much more likely to describe the complex accommoda-tions through which they tested and negotiated their faith. As I tried to indi-cate in chapter 6, when viewed from a pregnant woman's point of view, religious orientation is a complex matter: In their conversations with me, women did not so much reflect theological or doctrinal positions as exhibit the working out of an experiential trajectory through which profound exis-tential dilemmas could best be understood and internalized. This is no less true for the mainline Protestant medical professionals who decided not to use amniocentesis after exploring the possibility of adopting a "special needs" child with the help of their church, than it is for the Seventh-day Adventist clinic patients who thought that their respective deities would reward their faith and clean living with healthy pregnancies.

A Change of Heart

Sometimes, a woman who initially signs on for an amniocentesis changes her mind in the period between genetic counseling and the appointment for the tap. Many factors may influence a change of heart, as Catherine Judd's dilemma, which opens this chapter, makes clear. In the "first yes, then no" stories that I collected, two processes stand out with particular clarity. One has to do with the lateness of the test; the other, with the role of men.

Because amniocentesis is conventionally offered between the sixteenth and twentieth weeks of gestation, it comes at a time in which a commitment to a pregnancy has already been made.[32] As feminist sociologist Barbara Katz Rothman pointed out with both anger and poignancy more than a decade ago, the timing of this test forces women into a "tentative pregnancy" (Rothman 1986). Technologies for earlier intervention are under continuous development and testing, as I indicated in chapter 2. But they are not widely and safely available, nor are they likely to become so in the near future. If and when such experimental technologies become available, amniocentesis is likely to remain the most reliably available technology for women who get their prenatal care through HMOs and hospital clinics. For some women, the tardiness of the test looms larger and larger as they confront their scheduled appointments:

> I signed the forms, and then I said to myself, "Let me think about it." I decided not to have it: I didn't want to know now, no way, it's too late. In the beginning, I almost had an abortion, but then I decided to keep it. Once I decided, that's it. If anything's wrong, it makes no difference now. . . . I discussed it with my fiancé, he said it was up to me, but I don't want no abortion this late. The lady showed it to me [on sonogram], I seen it, it's really a baby there. It's hard to know what will happen, but I'm not having no test, not now. If it had been earlier, well, yes, especially when I was making up my mind [i.e., to keep or end the pregnancy]. (Charlene Gray, 38, African-American bookkeeper)

Charlene also mentioned the support of her large, loving Southern family. She had discussed the possibility of prenatal testing and abortion with her grandfather, who "spoiled all the babies" back in South Carolina. He volunteered to take the baby, should anything be wrong.

Acantha Jones, age 37, also mentioned family support and the powerful influence of having seen multiple sonograms when we discussed the reasons why she had changed her mind about testing. Friends introduced me to Acantha, an administrative secretary at a nearby university, because she had some questions about prenatal diagnosis. As a sickle-cell anemia carrier with a noncarrier husband, she wanted reassurance that this fetus couldn't be affected by the disease (true). She also wanted the test because she had read about the relation between folic acid deficiency and spina bifida, and was worried that her diet, as an anemia carrier, had not been healthy enough to protect her baby. Neither she nor her husband was particularly concerned about Down syndrome, or other chromosomal conditions. I made some research calls on Acantha's behalf to genetic counselors, and shared their knowledge about diet, fetal health, sickle-cell anemia, and testing; I also volunteered to accompany Acantha to the test. She was glad to have company, as neither of her two main supporters, her mother, a nurse, nor her husband, a construction worker, could take time off from work. Her mother was particularly in favor of this pregnancy, having married late herself and suffered with fibroids during the difficult, single pregnancy that produced Acantha. As a pediatric nurse, her mother was confident that the baby would be healthy. If not, she intended to take care of it herself.

When I arrived at Acantha's workplace on the morning of her scheduled test, she told me there had been a glitch. Her HMO had just called to say that she wasn't covered for testing at the site to which it initially assigned her. The secretary promised to call back with a new appointment. I went home, and kept in touch by phone. Several days later, the test site was still under negotiation, and the HMO wanted Acantha to see a new doctor; they had to declare her "high risk" in order to cover an amniocentesis. Acantha demurred, and returned to her regular OB/GYN, toward whom she felt great loyalty, attempting to reschedule the test herself. After more than a week of telephone tag, she changed her mind. Here, it seemed to me, was a structural impediment to testing: HMO bureaucracy delayed an already late procedure, tipping the scales against its use. Acantha's own evaluation of the problem was more personal and complex:

> I went to my regular OB, and now I have seen this baby twice already. Unless this baby is going to be a fish, I really couldn't do anything about it at this point. I have known it for eighteen weeks, and I don't want to part with it. I don't think I could really do anything about it now, so why torture myself? Oh, I think this test is a boon, a real boon for older women. I'm all for it. But I wish it had come earlier. If we'd done it when we first said we would, I'd be over the hump by now. But it's too late. I asked my doctor about the new test [i.e., chorionic villus sampling] but she felt it was too risky. Maybe later on, it will be a useful test, but it isn't useful to me right now.

Here, the slow pace of bureaucratic cost-effectiveness intersects her mother's own reproductive history and the offer of family support, as well as the experience of a growing and technologically mediated attachment to the pregnancy. All make testing too late. Like Acantha, many women who refused amniocentesis mentioned that they would have considered it, had the test come earlier.

A second reason for converting a "yes" into a "no" is also structural but is not connected directly to the technology itself: I have come to think of this reason as "The Man Question." As I mentioned in chapters 1 and 3, it was particularly difficult to interview men directly about their responses to the offer of an amniocentesis for their pregnant mates. But I came to believe that men strongly influenced women's choices, despite their frequent absence from the parts of the process that were visible to me. They did so in many ways, in part according to the gendered roles appropriate to their class and cultural backgrounds: by forbidding the use of the test, or pushing it; by picturing pregnancy as an exclusively female realm in which they had no decision-making interests; and sometimes, by "boundary keeping" conversations between their partners, health care providers, and nosy anthropologists. In these gendered scripts, confrontation, manipulation, and resistance might flow in either direction. What was revealed was not so much a single pattern of male dominance and female subordination, or male insistence on female difference, but the disruption of not-quite-conscious gendered assumptions which the offer of a new, morally fraught technology brought to the surface. Nonetheless, it was striking to me how often women said, "My husband won't let me" in response to the query, "Why did you decide not to have this test?"

Lucille Edwards, 37, offered one classic version of this narrative, a few weeks after our meeting at a genetic counseling group at City Hospital. She said she was very interested in having an amniocentesis but had reluctantly decided against it, and went on to elaborate:

> I was thinking of doing it, as my husband has diabetes in his family, and what with genetic problems, you never know. But then, he don't approve. I'm still interested, but he don't believe in it. I don't quite know why. When they explained it at the hospital, it was so interesting to me. And I was even thinking of sterilization, and going to get that done. I got to quit work now, waiting for the baby, and I don't want to. But he insist. My husband, he has seen people older than us having kids and nothing happen. I explain to him, most of the times, it's all right, it all works out. But then sometimes, just sometimes, it don't. In England, I know this lady, she had twins, one came out fine, the other came out a mongol. Because of her age. I don't know what I'd do, how I'd raise it. But my husband, he don't believe in it, no abortions, he

don't believe in that, either. Nor in sterilization. . . . I have a friend, she asks me, "What do you think about all this, about your husband and you?" I say, "My ideas are not similar to his ideas. But we have to live together, to raise our children." We've got three kids, it's time to plan for their futures, to sacrifice for their futures. I need to get back to work, not having any more babies, and certainly, no sick babies. But he won't permit it.

Contained in this story is a personal history of male privileged decision-making, and female peacekeeping across gendered values. Likewise, Catherine Judd was persuaded, but not commanded, to forgo an amniocentesis by her husband's racial-historical and religious concerns. And as mentioned above, the Haitian day-care worker (mother of four daughters who wanted a son) began with an enthusiastic interest in having an amniocentesis, but came to agree with her husband's assessment that any risk of miscarriage was reason enough to eschew prenatal testing. These cases seem to me to be on a continuum from command to suasion to influence. But in all, women's refusal is deeply responsive to their partners' opinion. In interpreting this continuum, my anthropological persona is here at odds with my feminist persona as I work through my own methodological relativism. On the one hand, family life surely requires compromise, and my narrow window on complex relationships does not reveal whether these instances of male privilege are (or are not) balanced against trade-offs in which women's wishes predominate. On the other hand, in a complex and highly varied gender system, certain enduring similarities stand out: Pregnancies happen inside women's bodies, yet in this country historically and unto the present, we know that men often control access to and use of the services and practices that might make those pregnancies easier, healthier, or more freely chosen. Moreover, women are too often the disproportionate bearers of the burdens of rearing children, especially children with health or other energy-consuming problems. A feminist ethic suggests that those most affected by the consequences of decisions should have the weightiest vote. Yet earlier, in chapter 6, I inveighed against male absence from the social relations of pregnancy and childrearing. But "responsible male involvement" as a social goal is not the same thing as male privilege. Ideally, men's involvement in childrearing would enable them to cast a contextually grounded vote in response to their partner's pregnancy. But gatekeeping around prenatal care, abortion decisions or, in this case, the use of amniocentesis without an equal commitment to the hard work of living with the consequences of raising the children strikes me as an instance of male privilege. In this impasse between relativism and feminism, I also realize that my position on "equal work, then equal votes" closely mirrors the modern bourgeois ideal of companionate marriage, revealing my own class position as well as my activist commitments. There is thus no way out of the dilemma of judgment involved in identifying male privilege.

Refusing Abortion

In this chapter I have thus far spoken about both structural reasons that influence women to forgo testing, and more individuated, personal concerns contributing to a decision not to use amniocentesis. I have noted the strong class influences on the structural positions pregnant women occupy in relation to the provision of medical services, and their comfort and confidence in understanding the risks and benefits of them. I have also plotted the points along the trajectory of technological use—before a genetic counseling appointment, during, and after one—at which the decision to opt off the conveyor belt may occur. But there is another, much rarer refusal of this technology, as well: Women who accept an amniocentesis, and, learning of "bad" or "positive" results, decide to continue their pregnancies. It is to the decision-making processes of such women that we now turn.

But first, three things should be said in contextualizing these decision-making stories. The first is that responses to the receipt of a "positive diagnosis" are the subject of chapter 9. Here, I only preview the topic, focusing on those who choose to continue their pregnancies, in effect, rejecting the next step in the use of a reproductive technology. The second caveat is that there is no way to evaluate the representative status of the stories I tell here: No records are kept either federally or by state on the outcomes of amniocentesis; New York and California probably have the best approximations of statistics concerning both the use of amniocentesis, and the birth of babies with chronic conditions (Meaney, Riggle et al. 1993; Cunningham 1998). In principle, those two sets of statistics could be studied in tandem, but the task is arduous and therefore expensive. In a world of health cost accounting and severe cutbacks, there is no incentive to undertake this particular, rather arcane task. Thus, my best approximation of numbers comes from speaking with epidemiologists and biostatisticians in those states, and genetic counselors, the front-line workers on these issues. According to all, the decision to keep a pregnancy after receiving the diagnosis of a serious condition is relatively rare. But it is not possible to evaluate precisely how rare, a point I take up again in chapters 8 and 9 (cf. Palmer, Spencer et al. 1993). A third and related point is this: The decision rests in large measure on the diagnosed condition. Most people hold firm opinions about Down syndrome long before they encounter amniocentesis; they thus feel entirely competent to make a decision to continue or end a pregnancy in which this condition has been diagnosed. When Down syndrome is diagnosed, abortion rates run high, 90–95 percent in local clinical studies (Palmer, Spencer et al. 1993). But most of the other conditions for which the test can provide diagnoses—chromosomal problems ranging from the severe and deadly, like trisomy 13, to the ambiguous, like the sex chromosome anomaly, Turner's syndrome—are usually unknown to a pregnant woman and her supporters before they receive the news that their fetus "has something seriously wrong." Response to disability news, couched at first in entirely biomedical discourse, is thus a complicated affair, engaging a lot of hard work toward understanding and evaluation on the part of both genetic counselors and their pregnant patients.

Pat Carlson, who enlisted help from her Mormon roots when she wanted to keep a pregnancy in which Down syndrome had been diagnosed, was thus quite unusual in deciding to keep her pregnancy after a positive diagnosis. But she was *not* exceptional in the way in which both prior reproductive history and religious resources entered into her decision-making process. Before coming to her decision, Pat did a lot of work. Her obstetrician suggested an abortion as he delivered the bad news, but Pat stalled for time. She left his office in a daze, and while walking around her neighborhood, she noticed a home for retarded adults. She immediately made an appointment to visit the place. She said, "You know, it was kind of nice. They looked pretty happy, they had jobs, they went bowling. It really made me think about it." Unmarried, a divorcee with a grown child who had survived two miscarriages and the death of a premature baby who lived only three days, Pat's reproductive history made her value this pregnancy as a "miracle." She used the Mormon church to sustain her decision to keep the pregnancy in the face of her obstetrician's objections. The rest of her story therefore belongs with the other parents of disabled children, in chapter 10.

Migdalia Ramirez's story also contains unusual elements. Sent for genetic counseling and amniocentesis at the tender age of 19, Migdalia, a Puerto Rican, was a devout Catholic who considered abortion to be "killing." But she was also the older sister of a girl with severe spina bifida whose disabilities had made a profound impression on Migdalia and her mother. As Migdalia described it,

> My sister, she can't walk, she can't see, they left her blind at City Hospital, my mother is still in a lawsuit. When I got pregnant the first time, I was very young, 15, 16 when I had my baby. I talked with my

mother, she really wanted me to have the tests, I wanted it too, she had such a cross to bear. God gave it to her, but it's a lot of work. It was hard for my mother to carry that cross, to take care of a child like that, especially when my father walked out on her. Oh, we love my sister, it's just that God made her special, it's a cross to bear. I was only concerned if my own baby couldn't walk or talk. I just talked it over with my mother, no one else, and together we decided about that test. The test wasn't hard, they explained it good, they took a bit of the liquid, I wasn't worried, I just didn't want my baby to be like my sister. I don't know what I would have done if it had been like my sister, I think I would have had an abortion. My mother and me, we're against abortion, so maybe I would have carried that cross, like my mother did. But then again, it's a case where I think I would have had an abortion.

Migdalia's fetus didn't have spina bifida, for which she had requested prenatal diagnosis. It did, however, have Klinefelter's syndrome, one of the sex chromosome anomalies involving growth problems, sterility, and possibly, learning disabilities and mild mental retardation. Migdalia's reaction to the news is instructive:

> I wasn't too concerned when they said he'd be normal. Just that he might be slow-minded, but he'd look normal in appearance. I have faith in God, I'll be there for my son. And I have my mother helping me all the way. He's gonna be normal, he'll see and walk. That's all I care about. As long as he looked normal, acted normal, I'll be there for him. And I didn't mind if he maybe was a bit slow. And as it turns out, he isn't, he's quick to pick up everything. Back then, I talked it over with my mother, she thought so too: What's the use of killing it if he'll be normal, he'll walk?

Like many other women for whom religion provided orienting metaphors and beacons, Migdalia's narrative is richly embroidered with her Catholicism; it also highlights her close relationship with her mother. In deciding to keep her pregnancy after Klinefelter's syndrome had been diagnosed in her fetus, Migdalia wasn't unusual; counselors estimate that less than half the women receiving this diagnosis choose abortions (cf. Robinson et al. 1989). Her decision has a very strong context: Intimate knowledge of one disabling and worrisome physical condition in her sister could be contrasted with a disability that "didn't show." It was the relative invisibility of the consequences of her son's atypical chromosomes that made them normal in her estimation. Indeed, "normal" was a concept she personally and actively produced under the shadow of her sister's condition. For Migdalia, both spina bifida and Klinefelter's syndrome have concrete, specific meanings.

Donna Moran's positive diagnosis was delivered by sonogram, not by amniocentesis. A 45-year-old mother of four and the emotional center of a breakaway Catholic commune in rural upstate New York, she saw a local midwife only episodically in her fifth pregnancy, and intended to give birth at home. Both she and the midwife felt that the baby was not moving properly; in her seventh month of pregnancy, she agreed to travel to a nearby town for a visit with an obstetrician who owned a sonogram machine. He quickly located the problem and delivered very bad news: The fetus was anencephalic, lacking a portion of its brain and skull. This condition, inevitably fatal, is one of the few bases on which an abortion can be obtained after the legal cutoff date (in New York State, twenty-four weeks). Most legal and ethical scholars are in accord: The suffering entailed by this condition for both mother and child merits abortion. But Donna was clear in her decision: She would carry the fetus to term and accept God's mercy in taking the baby quickly to Him. Her labors began in the eighth month and, since the fetus had no upper skull with which to push, ended after much stress in an emergency cesarian. The baby lived for several days; the mother's recovery was arduous and prolonged. Here, the meaning attributed to a reproductive tragedy was highly religious. Donna saw her own suffering and the suffering of the baby as a test of God's mysteries. Additionally, she was surrounded by a group of communards with whom she had constructed an alternative, rural, spiritual life for most of two decades. Donna's story and its interpretation came to me from one of those communards, who expressed awe at the spiritual strength and physical endurance of someone she saw as a true "earth mother." She also felt strongly that Donna had been exploited by an unself-conscious male bias present in her own commune: The role of mothering and maternal suffering was taken as central to a higher order. While I do not know enough about this case to venture an alternative or lengthier commentary, it strikes me that some of the same themes obtain—strong religious orientation, strong social support, prior (confident) reproductive history—that were present in other cases of women deciding to continue pregnancies marked by positive diagnoses.

In one case, I was present as a positive diagnosis was produced. Working in the lab one February afternoon, I observed a technician as he found something ambiguous on the #9 chromosomes of the sample he was scoping. After using the laboratory protocol to check twice and then three times the number of cells usually examined for a normal diagnosis, the case went to the head geneticist, who agreed: There was additional chromosomal material on the top, short arm of the #9s. She initially called it "9P+," 9 for the pair of chromosomes on which it was located, P to designate the short arm, and + to indicate additional chromosomal material. First, she scanned the literature for an interpretation. Then she phoned the head obstetrician at City's prenatal clinic, in charge of the case, and made an appointment for the woman to be called in. Over the course of a week's research, the geneticist located some clinical reports on trisomy 9, the closest known condition to which this case might be assimilated (her reasoning was not frivolous; a more elaborate description follows in chapter 8). In all those cases, babies born with trisomy 9 had physical anomalies and were mentally retarded. Armed with a provisional diagnosis, the geneticist met with the genetic counselor, who then counseled the mother. When the mother decided to keep the pregnancy, the genetic counselor asked the geneticist to meet with the mother. After a second consultative counseling session, the mother remained quite firm in her decision to continue the pregnancy.

The baby was born in early June, and in late July the geneticist contacted the new mother through her obstetrician, asking if she would be willing to bring her child to the genetics laboratory for a consultation. The mother agreed. On a Wednesday afternoon, the "trisomy 9" came visiting: He was a six-week-old Haitian boy named Etienne St-Croix. His mother, Véronique, spoke reasonable English and good French. His grandmother, Marie-Lucie, who carried the child, spoke Creole and some French. The two geneticists spoke English, Polish, Hebrew, and Chinese between them. I translated into French, ostensibly for the grandmother and mother. Here is what happened:

The geneticist was gracious with Véronique but after a moment's chitchat asked to examine the baby. She never spoke directly to the mother again during the examination. Instead, she and a second geneticist, both trained in pediatrics, handled the newborn with confidence and interest. The counselor took notes as the geneticists measured and discussed the baby. "Note the oblique palpebral fissure and micrognathia," one called out. "Yes," answered Véronique in perfect time to the conversation, "he has the nose of my Uncle Hervé and the ears of Aunt Mathilde." As the geneticists pathologized, the mother genealogized, the genetic counselor remained silent, furiously taking notes, and the anthropologist tried to keep score. When the examination was over, the geneticists apologized to the baby for any discomfort they had caused him, and one asked the mother a direct question: "I notice you haven't circumcised your baby. Are you planning to?" "Yes," Véronique replied, "we'll do it in about another week." "May we have the foreskin?" the geneticist queried. "With the foreskin, we can keep growing trisomy 9 cells for research, and study the tissue as your baby develops." Véronique gave her a firm and determined "yes," and the consultation was over.

Walking Véronique and Marie-Lucie to the subway to direct them home to Brooklyn, I asked what she had thought about the experience: from the amnio to the diagnosis to the genetic consultation. She replied,

> At first, I was very frightened. I am 37, I wanted a baby. It is my hus-band's second marriage, my mother-in-law is for me, not the first wife. She wanted me to have a baby, too. If it had been Down's, maybe, just maybe I would have had an abortion. Once I had an abortion, but now I am a Seventh-day Adventist, and I don't believe in abortion anymore. Maybe for Down's, just maybe. But when they told me this, who knows? I was so scared, but the more they talked, the less they said. They do not know what this is. And I do not know either. So now, it's my baby. We'll just have to wait and see what happens. And so will they.

Here, marital and kinship relations clearly influence the decision to continue a pregnancy after positive diagnosis; so does religious conversion. But at the center of this narrative lies another important theme: diagnostic ambiguity. Biomedical scientists work from precedent, matching new findings with old. When presented with an atypical case, they build a diagnosis in the same fashion, comparing the present case to the closest available prior knowledge in clinical archives. While the geneticists are confident that this child will share the developmental pattern reported in the literature for other children with very similar chromosomal patterns, the mother was quite aware of the idiosyncratic nature of the case, its lack of clear-cut label and known syn-drome. She therefore decided that the contest for interpretation was still an open one. This is a dramatic instance of interpretive standoff between bio-medical discourse and family life.

But in some sense, all positive diagnoses appear ambiguous to pregnant women.[33] An extra chromosome spells out the diagnosis of Down syndrome, but it does not distinguish mildly from severely retarded children, nor does it indicate whether this particular fetus will need open-heart surgery. A missing X chromosome indicates a Turner's syndrome female but cannot speak to the meaning of fertility in the particular family into which she may be born. Homozygous status for the sickle-cell gene cannot predict the severity of ane-mia a particular child will develop. All such diagnoses are interpreted in light of prior reproductive histories, community values, and aspirations that partic-ular women and their families hold for the pregnancy being examined.

This problem of ambiguity—inside of biomedicine and inside of family life—is one encountered by genetic counselors with a fair degree of frequency. Virtually all counselors I interviewed mentioned mosaic conditions when I asked about difficult cases. In mosaic diagnoses, cells are both normal and atypical in varying proportions. Roughly speaking, the greater the density of atypical cells, the greater the likelihood of disabling conditions which are known to geneticists, and can be described to potential parents. But some conditions may exhibit mosaicism in one cell line without profound clinical expression at the level of the whole organism, that is, the child. This is true for example, of mosaicism on chromosome 20, where the atypical findings may come from the amniotic membranes rather than from the fetus. Yet when experts find a single mosaic cell line they cannot know which organ system of the body will be affected or unaffected. And sometimes a known condition—for example, Down syndrome—may be present in mosaic patterns on the cellular level, producing a child who is "slow" but still coded by the relevant caretakers in her life as "normal." Mosaic diagnoses are thus hard to explain and harder to interpret. Their inherent ambiguity leads some women to continue pregnancies in which they have been diagnosed, especially if the number of atypical cells is relatively small or the genetic counselor can say of a particular condition with some degree of confidence, "It rarely has profound clinical significance." Women receiving mosaic diagnoses are among the most likely to stop the technological conveyor belt, preserving their pregnancy and preparing for the birth of a child whose cellular "fortune" has been read but whose clinical future they understand to be truly unpredictable (Robinson, Bender et al. 1989).

Existentially speaking, of course, we *all* live with truly unpredictable clinical futures; the existence of prenatal diagnosis has simply added a new twist to that impasse in the human condition. Now, it is possible, indeed, necessary for those who would have the chromosomes of their fetuses "read" to know something about possible problems and limits a coming child may face in vitro, without having encountered those problems and limits as they unfold in vivo. The difference between a biologically described organism and a socially integrated child is, of course, enormous. And it is within this gap between laboratory-generated descriptions of disabilities and potential disabilities and their consequences for family life as a child develops that some women receiving positive diagnoses choose to operate. Those who opt to continue a pregnancy after any positive diagnosis must consciously face what the rest of us confront only episodically: The hard work of redescribing and reinscribing a powerful biomedical definition into the more complex and variegated aspects of personhood, childhood dependency, and family life. In this situation, the structure of chromosomes initially looms large as a defining characteristic of what a child's future may bring. Women who continue pregnancies after positive diagnoses thus expend considerable agency reducing the significance of chromosomes in order to welcome a child on grounds other than biomedical normalcy.

As I have tried to show throughout this chapter, women with strong religious affiliations, strong kinship or other communitarian social support, or strong reasons anchored in their reproductive histories are most likely to decide against the biomedical information amniocentesis brings as a basis for accepting or rejecting a particular pregnancy. These patterns hold true across differences of income, lifestyle, and job description, which provide rough measures of socioeconomic class. But other patterns of amniocentesis use and rejection are highly class-structured: Access to information and respectful health care surely conditions how prenatal testing is perceived and valued. Moreover, those without advanced scientific education are most likely to reject testing altogether, although many women from working-class and working-poor backgrounds also choose to be tested. And the problem of male privilege or even male dominance in decision-making also intersects these patterns of use. Such socially structured trajectories cannot be reduced to a reflexive response to any particular diagnosis; in other words, they hold no automatic or predictable intersection with the biomedical diagnoses described in the course of laboratory life (to borrow a felicitous title from Latour and Woolgar 1979).

My use of the terms "in vitro" and "in vivo" in the preceding paragraphs, and my musings about the gap between biomedical diagnoses and the integration of diagnosed babies into family life have an intention that is far from innocent. Throughout these chapters, I have been writing about knowledge gained in conversation and observation of an essentially discursive set of practices: Counselors, pregnant women, and anthropologists all communicate and reflect on their communication as the central focus of their mutual interactions. In chapter 8, I add the complexity of material culture, interpreting what I have learned from watching clinical laboratory practices in action. In entering the laboratory, I hope to show how the daily material routines of biomedicine anchor one new reproductive technology, in the service of making diagnoses. In the process, such practices intersect the wider culture outside the laboratory and may be used to stake a claim on the nature of what it is to be human. It is to those lab practices that we now turn.

8

Culturing Chromosomes, or What's in the Soup

It's easy to recognize the 12s, 13s, and 14s. Head, shoulders, and hips, just look for the bands for head, shoulders, and hips. (lab supervisor training author to identify and pair chromosomes for karyotyping)

Why do we tryspinize the cells? We trypsinize to eat away at the protein, to make the patterns more distinct, and to get them growing in sync so there are a lot of them in metaphase when we lift the cell button off the flask floor. (Veronica Pele, lab technician)

Laboratories use the phenomenon that objects are not fixed entities that have to be taken "as they are" or left to themselves. In fact, laboratories rarely work with objects as they occur in nature. Rather, they work with object images or with their visual, auditory, electrical and so on traces, with their components, their extractions, their "purified" versions. (Knorr-Cetina 1995, 145)

IN 1986, WHEN I BEGAN an informal internship at the Prenatal Diagnosis Laboratory, I was both curious and anxious about my ability to learn the kinesics of chromosome analysis. Observing counseling and interviewing pregnant women or families had allowed me to focus on talk, a method with which I was both comfortable and experienced. In the lab, I imagined myself awkwardly perched at a microscope, unable to find and focus on chromosomes in cells, serving an apprenticeship in activities which I had found daunting in my pre-contact-lens high school and college days. Over the course of six months (two quite intensively), I participated in the life of the laboratory. Four years later, I interned for two summer months in another lab at Middle Hospital, to assure myself that my exposure to "laboratory life" was not entirely idiosyncratic. And in the summer of 1995, I returned to the second lab for ten days in order to update my understandings, as computerization had transformed some of the key tasks I initially set out to master. There were a few differences which characterized each lab: At the PDL, prenatal diagnoses of fetal cells were the exclusive work of the organization; at Middle, prenatal cases constituted the majority of the workload, but leukemic bone marrows, and parental and newborn bloods were also occasionally karyotyped. The PDL was a much larger laboratory: It had double the floor space and number of technicians as the Middle lab. Yet protocols at the two labs were recognizably similar. In these three apprenticeships, my curiosity was indeed rewarded; there is an ordered sociology to the construction of chromosome diagnoses, which I will here describe. And my sense of my own incapacity to scope slides was also confirmed: I *still* have trouble operating a microscope, despite the excellent tutelage I received. But I also learned that focusing on talk was no less important than focusing on cell boundaries. Laboratories, like clinics, schools, and home interviews are sites of simultaneous and imbricated material and discursive construction.

In this chapter, I describe cytogenetic laboratories (where chromosomal structure is analyzed) as workplaces. I am particularly interested in conveying the interplay of strict scientific regulation and interpretive freedom through which the dense interactions of highly skilled professional technicians, technologists, Ph.D. and M.D. geneticists and occasionally genetic counselors or, most rarely, their patients, negotiate the production of a work product: the karyotype, or chromosome map, of specific human tissue samples. Tissue culture enrolls biological material in the service of making relevant medical meanings, and a rich array of machines, technologies, and biomedical artifacts figures centrally in this production. In this analysis drawn from participant observation, chromosomes are work objects that must be deeply and scientifically manipulated before consensus on their interpretation can be reached.[34] Tracking the dense circulation of personnel, technical artifacts, reagents, biological tissue, and machines through a collaborative protocol whose outcome is a pictographic and alpha-numerological diagnosis eventually led me to think of the lab as a factory for fact construction. But this interpretive claim emerged slowly, as my initiation into hands-on laboratory life proceeded, and I came to partially understand, if not to develop full competence, in the performance of those protocols. My interpretation was also deeply influenced by developments in science studies, through engagement with a growing literature which has taught me to think about laboratory products as boundary objects incorporating and instantiating natural and cultural processes which cannot be logically or sociologically broken apart (e.g., Clarke and Fujimura 1992; Fujimura 1992, 1996; Heath 1994, 1998; Heath and Rabinow 1993; Knorr-Cetina 1995; Latour 1987; Rabinow 1992; Starr 1995). This chapter thus argues for a view of prenatal diagnosis which is, in Donna Haraway's awkwardly brilliant phrase, "simultaneously material-semiotic" (Haraway 1989, 1991; e.g., Haraway 1997, 11).

Working at Diagnoses

In the beginning, what distinguished the laboratory for me was the hustle and bustle of work life, in which technicians were at once highly individuated in their tasks, yet appeared instantly responsive to team-based initiatives. I was observing highly structured and rule-driven activities and individual variations in a complex choreography through which all actors seemed to play out their roles with only minimal cues from supervisors. If I was lucky enough to arrive by 9 a.m., or be around at 3 p.m., I might witness the set-ups for tissue culture by anywhere from one to ten technicians. If I came at 10 a.m., I would observe some technicians (or techs, as they refer to themselves) variously mixing reagents, heating, centrifuging, or cooling test tubes partially filled with multicolored substances, observing and transferring suspensions under the hood in rubber gloves, scoping samples, cutting photographs of chromosomes (or later, monitoring computers which "cut" the chromosomes), labeling specimens, writing in logs, or engaging in various record-keeping tasks. Throughout both labs, a friendly banter of joking and cooperative calls for help prevailed; timer bells punctuated the conversation, incubator and computer fans provided background noise. In both, music was likely to be episodically playing on radios, food was being stored, heated, and eaten in work spaces, and family photographs, plants, and calendars personalized and enlivened the space. How, I wondered, did people move among such a range of work stations, tasks, and cases without losing track of their purpose? And did they ever think about the individual or social consequences of the work they were doing when they delivered routine (and, very rarely, nonroutine) diagnoses from their lab to the front office, through which genetic counselors, physicians, and their patients were contacted? It was the desire to understand both the people and objects engaged in diagnostic cytogenetic work, and the relevance (or irrelevance) of its social consequences to the laboratory workforce that drew me to the lab.

One way I came to understand the formal structure and informal variation of laboratory work was to follow samples of amniotic fluid through the many steps to diagnosis: simply put, I wanted to know what happened to the body fluids that the women I interviewed were yielding. The fluids pass through steps that may be characterized in terms of setup, incubation, harvesting, staining (banding), chromosome analysis and its record-keeping inscriptions. All require a technological mobilization which is taken for granted by regular participants but dizzying in its detail to novice observers: Some technology is disposable (pipettes, test tubes, flasks, and biochemical reagents are continually discarded and renewed), while some is relatively permanent, requiring only repair or long-term upgrading (microscopes, photographic apparatus, computers, and, of course, the support technologies of telephones and fax machines). And all require the abstract kinesic mobilization of human agents, as well: Technicians and technologists exhibit a familiarity with a range of techniques at once deeply embodied and mentally regimented.

To provide an analytic and narrative structure, I here trace the amniotic fluid samples through official laboratory protocol; only after its routine and rigorous trajectory is described do I introduce the practical kinesic knowledge necessary to cytogenetic diagnosis in action. This continuous interplay of formal scientific discipline and informal interpretive craft is key to an understanding of laboratory life. Laboratory manuals mention only the former; technoscientific actors rely on the latter. And it is the blending of the two which produces and stabilizes consensus diagnoses.

In protocol parlance, fluids begin as labeled deliveries. They are transferred from pregnant women and their obstetricians by messengers, genetic counselors, or patients themselves. To an outside observer, the liquid appears variable in color, ranging from clear yellow to murky brown. On average, a pregnant woman "donates" about 20 ccs of it, which arrives in test tubes. Technicians are assigned or assign themselves new cases depending on their ongoing caseload. When my research began, the recommended international caseload was three per tech per week; at the PDL, they were supervising between three and six, depending on levels of experience and efficiency. Ideally, whoever is in charge of a sample will follow it through from the moment it is logged in until a diagnosis is signed out, although flexibility is occasionally imposed by workloads, vacations, and other vicissitudes of daily life. The tech will log the sample into the logbook, assigning it a laboratory number next to the patient's name and chart number. Each tube, flask, and slide that comes into physical contact with the sample will bear these numbers; many will be inscribed with the tech's initials, as well. These various indexes follow a sample through the lab, enabling and ensuring cross-checks for assigning accurate diagnoses to the correct patients.

Once a sample is multiply logged in, setup occurs. While large samples get more flasks and smaller ones fewer, the average sample requires three flasks. Using prepared growth media, sterile pipettes, flasks, and test tubes, and working under a sterile hood, the tech dispenses the amniotic fluid into prelabeled sterile centrifuge tubes. During the ten minutes that the sample is being centrifuged to condense and assess whether it contains the requisite 5 percent of fetal cell material in it, the case number, flask number, type of growth media, patient's name, date, and technician's initials are all written onto the flasks. When centrifuging is over, all but a small amount of the supernatant (the less dense fluid at the top of the test tube) is removed, labeled and refrigerated for alpha-fetoprotein testing.[35] The tech then taps the tubes lightly to break up the cell pellet and resuspends it with growth media, dividing it into three flasks. At the beginning of my internships, two kinds of growth media—chag and fetal calf—were used. Each contained a mix of preproduced commercial media products, antibiotics, and L-glutamine, and had to be prepared in the lab several times each week. One medium went into each of two flasks, and a combination of the two went into the third. This variation in environments increased the likelihood that some cells would eventually grow. By the time of my third laboratory stay, a single commercial media product, "amnio-max," was in uniform use: It produced slightly more rapid cell growth, perhaps because it contained a smaller proportion of antibiotics. Each flask was then gassed with carbon dioxide, capped, and placed in an incubator at 37 degrees centigrade (body temperature) for six days. During incubation, cell growth occurred, although not at a uniform rate. After that time, cells might be fed every three days until adequate growth for harvesting occurred.

When my internships began, harvesting occurred, assuming adequate cell growth, at the tenth to fourteenth day; now, it occurs at five to nine days. At the beginning of my research, harvested cases required one to three days of lab work; by the end, they never took more than one. The result of these compressions of work time for each case means that diagnoses are reported much more quickly: Whereas patients used to wait about three weeks for results, they now wait eight to ten days. These changes in turnaround time are both technologically and economically driven.

Like setup and incubation, harvesting, staining (so that the bands on chromosomes are made more visible), and chromosome analysis and its many record-keeping inscriptions proceed in accordance with a well-defined protocol that requires both the mobilization of technology and skilled human technique. On the day prior to harvesting, cells are again fed and gassed. Three hours prior to harvest, velban solution is added to break mitotic fiber and arrest cells in mitosis (chromosome replication or doubling). Various reagents are made and assembled; some are heated, others cooled. Slides are prepared and stored, then harvest begins. Patient case numbers are rein-scribed, velban-treated cells are gently placed in centrifuge tubes, and the flask is washed with trypsin, which is then added to the centrifuge. The trypsin eats away at the protein, enabling more cells to be lifted from the flask floor; it also "eats" the cell membrane, sculpting it for more visible banding and shape. But the enzyme's use must be carefully timed and moni-tored: A trypsin bath that is too short will leave too many cells behind; an overly long bath will digest the cells. Thus, after centrifuging, supernatant is once again decanted, cell pellets are tapped and resuspended, and hypotonic solution is added to the solution to counter the trypsin, and to swell the cells. After the test tubes are briefly bathed in body-temperature water, fixative is gently mixed in, centrifuging occurs once more, additional fixative is intro-duced, and the cell culture is refrigerated for at least one-half hour. Then cell suspension is dropped onto cold, precleaned slides, blown lightly to spread the cells, and quickly dried. Each slide is inscribed with its case number, cul-ture number, and slide number. Each is observed to see if the cell suspension is of the right concentration, and if an adequate amount of chromosome spread is present. Corrections for cell suspension and chromosome spread can be made at this point. If there are too few cells in mitosis (chromosome doubling, in which pairs of each chromosome are visible), then reharvesting, or occasionally, even replanting and regrowth is necessary. After initial obser-vation, the best slides are set aside for banding studies, in which the enhanced dark and light patterns on each chromosome can be scrutinized, matched, and judged.

After slides have been incubated overnight in a drying oven, they are stained in a technician-prepared solution of phosphate buffer, methanol, trypsin, and Giesma (or "G") stain. Technicians vary their proportions slightly; with experience, the "look" of a slide suggests the correct amount of stain needed to enhance banding. Slides are soaked, rinsed, dried, and checked. With optimal treatment, a range of dark, light, and intermediate gray bands will appear on all chromosomes, marking the patterned regions through which identification, pairing, and a judgment of normality or abnormality can be accomplished. Occasionally, alternative banding tech-niques, especially fluorescent quinacrine (or "Q") banding may be used, when regions of the Y chromosome or certain common polymorphisms require further observation and characterization.

The first step in chromosome analysis is to count the number present in a representative sample of cells. In selecting cells for chromosome counting, technicians try to find those that appear unbroken, and in which the spread of chromosomes on the cell is least ambiguous; chromosomes are three-dimensional objects reduced to two dimensions for visualization, and their overlap may make boundaries and bands murky or invisible. Once a cell is put under count, the technician's results must be recorded on a tally sheet; it cannot be exchanged for a "better" cell. Protocol requires that a minimum of twenty cells, ten each from two of the three incubated flasks, be counted. Thus the normal diagnosis of either 46 XX or 46 XY (normal chromosome count, female and male respectively) requires the counting and recording of twenty cells. Whenever a single cell with a numerical abnormality (too few or too many chromosomes) is found, the third flask is also harvested, and slides from it are prepared. If all twenty cells counted in two flasks (ten per flask) contain the same abnormality, ten additional cells from the third flask are counted: The diagnosis is then considered confirmed at thirty cells. But if the abnormality involves some cells from only one flask, the third flask must be used, and twenty cells from each must be counted. In this case, the diagnosis is based on sixty, rather than twenty or thirty cell counts. If the abnormal count is found in only one of the three flasks' samples, a diagnosis of pseudo-mosaicism (i.e., a "founder effect" of a small or insignificant anomaly multiplied through cell division in one small sample of tissue) is considered. If the abnormality is found in some cells harvested from two or more flasks, then true mosaicism is diagnosed. Similar counting protocols are in place concerning structural aberrations such as deletions, rearrangements of parts of chromosomes, or the presence of satellites signifying additional chromosomal material. Normal diagnoses are made by technicians and approved by supervisors who inspect karyotypes and tally sheets, but do not independently scope slides deemed normal. Cases in which slides show abnormal counts or arrangements are checked independently by at least one technician and one supervisor, and by the cytogeneticist in charge of the lab, as well.

Chromosome analysis requires pictographic as well as numerological evidence. Before a case is completed, three mitoses will be counted, photographed, and karyotyped, that is, arranged into a map in which chromosomes are paired and displayed numerologically, from largest (number 1s) to smallest (number 22s), with the XX or XY of fetal sex displayed in the right-hand column. In my first two internships, these photographs were taken through the microscope by technicians who then decided which were the best pictures for karyotyping. The karyotype itself was visuo-manually constructed by technicians sitting at a cutting table: Using scissors and rubber cement, they clipped magnified pictures of each chromosome and its mate, matching them by size, shape, and band patterns, arranging them on a worksheet and gluing them in place when they were satisfied that the map for that cell was entirely accurate. Now, much of this intense eye-hand labor is performed by computer: While the technologist still selects the cell, the computer karyotypes it. After visually scoping chromosome counts in twenty cells, the tech selects four to six to be karyotyped by the computer. On the computer screen, the tech selects and focuses an image of the cell, trimming it by moving a mouse over the space around the cell. The tech also visually corrects overlaps and splits from multiple images of the selected cell. When the technician is satisfied with the general parameters of the cell, s/he signals the computer to karyotype it. The "cytoscan" program aligns each chromosome from its centromere outward, sorts by size and shape, and arranges into the familiar map of twenty-two sized pairs plus sex chromosomes. A mouse is used for "enhancement options": The computer can be made to (re-) "align," "normalize," and "increase contrast" in banding. When the technician is satisfied with the results, prints of selected screens issue from the machine's printer on command. The hardware and software of computerization thus replaces manual microphotography, cutting table karyotyping and rubber cement. It does not replace the judgment of the technician, who still corrects, enhances, and commands the production of the karyotype image. But it dramatically shortens and eases the task. And it makes the diagnosis more aesthetically persuasive.

Once the chromosome analysis and its multiple inscriptions (on tally sheets, karyotypes, and in logbooks) are complete, in the case file are placed the tally sheets counting twenty or more cells, and the karyotypes picturing three or more cells in mitoses. These are brought to the lab supervisor (technologist) and from her to the laboratory director, a cytogeneticist, who approves the documents and sends them to the clinical geneticist, who signs off. After this, paperwork and phone calls are directed through the front office back to genetic counselors who contact patients (or sometimes, their obstetricians) and send final reports. Additionally, the lab archives each case. Two karyotypes and one metaphase print of each diagnosis are logged and saved for future reference. This task, on which no immediate biomedical judgment or service depends, is very low-priority, and case files usually accumulate until one or more technicians has the time and energy to handle them in batches.

So far, I have described the protocols of cell culture and cytogenetic diagnosis in some detail in order to illustrate the detailed uniformity and formality of procedures under which technicians and technologists operate. This uniformity and formality is highly significant when viewed from the perspective of laboratory regulation, a subject to which I will return. I have also

noted some degrees of freedom within which the practical skills and prece-
dential interpretations of technicians are exercised. But these descriptions
give a rather flat and limited sense of laboratory labor processes; one might
as well attempt to learn haute cuisine from reading a French cookbook, or
absorb jacquard or argyle knitting techniques from an illustrated stitchery.
"Hands-on" learning is a requisite aspect of laboratory life; indeed, geneticists and supervisors speak with admiration of those techs who have "good
hands" the way gardeners speak of peers with "green thumbs" (Heath 1994).
Much of the work of cytogenetics is nonverbal and requires attentive physical expertise: Cell buttons are flicked, cell suspensions are adroitly dropped
and blown across slides, test tubes are flamed as pipettes are unwrapped,
used for suctioning samples, and discarded with continuous and rapid movements. Chromosomes are recognized by shape, size, and bands, and are
manipulated into karyotypes by hand or by computer mouse. It took me several months of working in the lab two days a week before I could produce an
accurate karyotype from photographs of magnified mitotic cells. "You can't
learn to make karyotypes unless you go blind cutting chromosomes eight
hours a day," my trainers assured me, when I expressed frustration with my
own slow pace of learning.

It was this amalgamation of mental-visual precision and manual dexterity
which returned me to the idea of kinesic knowledge throughout my laboratory internships. And it was the constant fusion, mastery, construction, and
negotiation of artifacts by skilled agents which brought me to think of laboratories as factories for fact construction. Like many other embodied knowledge systems, cytogenetic analysis both requires and develops a merger of
"hand, brain and heart" (Rose 1983), a "feeling for the organism" (Keller
1983) like those detailed in classic feminist analyses of science and scientists.
Even in the most routinized of biomedical laboratory labors, the judgment
of an experienced and highly literate, numerically confident technician is
essential to the construction and affirmation of cellular diagnoses. As the
techs say, if you can't tell robust from wimpy chromosomes by spec, feel, and
slide spread, you are in the wrong field. And, as my invocation of the crafts
of gardening, cooking, and knitting, as well as feminist science analysis suggests, that field is majority female.

Laboratory Labor

In both the labs in which I worked, personnel totaling at least eighteen technicians, two supervisors, and four geneticists were more than two-thirds
female. By common perception, laboratory work is "women's work" because

it is service-sector work which has regularized hours and low pay. While this is most visible in the case of technicians, it also holds true for geneticists, who rarely rank near the top echelons of prestige or remuneration in clinical medicine. And in the cases with which I have the most familiarity, laboratory workers are often international, as well. The technicians from whom I learned came from the Middle East, Latin America, Eastern-Central Europe, and Asia; the five geneticists I observed had been born on four continents. While my perception that genetics services and laboratories are staffed by the international circulation of highly skilled scientific workers may be an artifact of my placement in New York City (which has a highly international and migratory population in general), it is also true that technoscientific skills travel better than some other professions—teaching or law, for example. Here, a combination of kinesic and manuo-visual skills, reliance on protocols and technologies which have general international comparability, and licensing practices that set rational, attainable standards all add to the mobility of a scientific workforce.

The multiple routes into that workforce may also make it more "friendly" to women and immigrants. When I began this study, technicians might be licensed in New York State on the basis of a B.S. degree from an accredited college after six months of supervised work; they might also gain a license after completing eighteen months of supervised work and successfully passing a state-mandated examination. Technologist-supervisors took a proficiency examination at a level higher than what is required of a technician after three years of work. And laboratory directors (usually qualified as a Ph.D., but possibly an M.D.) trained for three months under supervision. Since 1994, New York City's Department of Health has changed the certification requirements: Exams were discontinued in favor of supervised case work in genetics laboratories. Technicians must have completed at least one year of college-level biology; technologists require a B.S. degree. And laboratories are licensed according to state standards. In New York State, which arguably has the highest standards in the country, the number of cases per lab is regulated, but this is not a widespread practice. Federal regulations attached to CLIA (Clinical Laboratory Improvement Act of 1967, amended 1988) monitor the quality of some laboratory reagents, but their relation to the new DNA technologies is ambiguous. Proficiency of personnel as well as adequacy of facilities and standards are thus part of normalization as supervised by the state.

Geneticists are a highly trained and internationalized professional cohort. Most medical geneticists are postdoctorally trained M.D.s, both because the subject is complex and requires an undergirding in other specialties (e.g., cell biology, embryology, pediatrics), and because genetics continues to be under-taught in most U.S. medical schools (Touchette, Holtzman et al. 1997). Postresidency fellowships attract M.D.s whose basic training is most likely to be in pediatrics, where they encounter embryology, neonatology, and other subjects abutting on human genetics. And such M.D.s may well be drawn from other countries: In the shadow of the "revolution" in molecular biology, countries which do not have the resources or orientation to focus on DNA technologies export their elite students to metropolitan centers for additional instruction. And some of them make new lives for themselves in the country of training.

But training as an M.D. is not the only route into genetics, nor has it been the main route throughout the recent history of the field. In the 1960s, when cytogenetic technologies blossomed, the study of chromosomes was the laboratory arm of a congeries of other medical specialties: pediatrics, obstetrics, pathology. When faced with the clinical problems of miscarriage and dysmorphology (usually, anomalous births), M.D.s would turn to colleagues who were often laboratory-based Ph.D.-holding researchers for tissue culture studies. Such specialists were as likely to have been trained in plant or mammalian genetics as in biomedicine. By the early 1970s, developments in banding technique made the characterization of chromosomes by regions much more precise: Some pathologies could be mapped to specific chromosomal areas via linkage studies. At the same time as cytogenetics was flourishing, great strides were also made in the identification and naming of genetic syndromes, that is, groups of symptoms that traveled together in babies born with birth anomalies. For example, varieties of albinism, retinitis pigmentosa, and collagen disorders were all classified during this period. Teratology (etymologically, the study of monsters; but in sanitized biomedical terminology, the identification and classification of transplacental substances and processes that produce abnormal fetal development) also expanded, as research focus shifted toward biochemistry: Inborn errors of metabolism, enzyme deficiencies and the hemoglobinopathies (literally: pathologies of the blood component hemoglobin like sickle-cell anemia and thalassemia) all became central objects of investigation in laboratory studies. Increasingly, a division of labor was imposed as medicine "took over" genetics: M.D.s engaged in patient management, relying on Ph.D. laboratory-based researchers to supervise the cytogenetics and biochemistry on which diagnosis was based.

Into this divide, the profession of genetic counseling was born (cf. chapter 3). But her lineage is in dispute: When Ph.D. geneticists of the senior generation tell the story, they tend to take credit for the development of genetic counseling. As non-M.D.s, they felt committed to conversations with family members as they calculated the odds of anomalous recurrences, and were not likely to arrogate to themselves normative judgments concerning reproductive choices. That is, value neutrality emerged as researchers explained what was known of hereditary anomalies and their statistical patterns. But when senior M.D.s tell the same story, they are likely to see genetic counseling as a daughter of doctoring: From their point of view, laboratory-based technicians are less likely to worry about the ethics of medical decision-making and informed consent. For them, helping families to understand a syndrome and its recurrence rates belongs to clinical medicine. Despite the standoff in origin stories, both groups agree: Genetic counselors were cheap labor, trained to explain risk figures and informed consent, as prenatal diagnosis flourished. And, under the shadow of the DNA revolution from the 1980s on, the division of labor became more stark: The current generation of molecular biologists is mainly composed of Ph.D. holders stalking "interesting" genes which may well cause specific conditions, but they do not necessarily have direct experience with patient populations who live with specific medical syndromes. Their purview is laboratory-based; they are much more likely to develop expertise around PCR machines which amplify the amount of DNA available for laboratory analysis, or transgenic mice which can provide models of human conditions, or protein biochemistry where the relation between gene alternation and the product it produces is tracked than they are to have hands-on knowledge of patients, their syndromes and symptoms. This work belongs to medical geneticists who work closely with genetic counselors, and sometimes with obstetricians and neonatologists: Ideally, they are patient and family-oriented, placing the genetics of a diagnosis in its larger clinical context. Interactions between these two research and clinical specialties occur in scientific journals and at professional meetings, as well as among members of interdisciplinary research teams, and some M.D.s or M.D.-Ph.D.s embody these interdisciplinary crossovers in their individual training and work. But the nature of the interactive transfer of their knowledge bases is up for grabs, especially under the expanding shadow of the Human Genome Project.[36]

This increasing and interactive division of labor may also be influencing the international circulation of laboratory geneticists, and their distribution across basic research and the applied service work of diagnosis. The arduous and highly accurate microscopy required for proficiency in cytogenetics is no longer fashionable as more than a way station on the route to molecular biology in many U.S. doctoral programs: Under the shadow of the DNA revolution, it has become technique. But it remains a highly skilled specialty in its own right in some countries that do not have the resources or orientation to compete in the "molecular biology sweepstakes." Consequently, demand for professionals trained abroad in cytogenetics remains robust; as one laboratory supervisor commented, "Pretty soon, it will be South Asians running the show in every New York lab." Of course, neither the United States in general nor New York City in particular are the only sites of international professional cytogenetic circulation: Two U.S.-born technicians with whom I was working, for example, had recently completed a two-year, well-paid employment contract in Saudi Arabia. There, their services were needed in the diagnosis of leukemic bone marrows and the chromosomes of couples experiencing infertility, rather than for prenatal diagnosis. This internationalization of geneticists and technicians may also be influencing the role which science plays as a kind of Esperanto or Lingua Franca among those with multiple, polyglot origins who find themselves as close collaborators in metropolitan labs.

Imagistic Knowledge

The collaborative scientific discourse in which technicians, technologists, and supervising geneticists engage is at once organized by highly formal rules, and the site of informal imagistic elaboration. While the pairing and organization of human chromosomes on a karyotype is governed by the Paris Convention of 1972 which standardized an international map on the basis of normal morphology, for example, informal images and stereotypical reductions abound in daily description. Techs taught me to identify chromosomes by personifications alleged to be carried in the contrastive bands: the 7s, 8s, and 9s are deemed to have distinctive and recognizable noses, glasses, and beards; 12s, 13s, and 14s sport heads, shoulders, and hips; and the X-Y sex chromosomes are stereotypically identified by bikinis and chests, occasionally characterized as "wimpy."

This reduction of chromosomal description to culturally recognizable images is not a contamination of scientific process, but lies at its heart, as social analysts of many branches of science have commented (e.g., Hacking 1983; Knorr-Cetina 1995). Indeed, it intersects larger questions concerning the role of language in human cognition that currently rest at the boundaries of neuroanatomy, psychology, linguistics, and philosophy, but that is a story which cannot be engaged here. For purposes of this study, it is sufficient to note the linguistic density with which metaphors fly through the lab. Both cells on a slide and chromosomes inside a cell, for example, can be located using the image of a clock. Thus a cell formally sited by its numerical slide coordinates may be conversationally resting at 6 o'clock; so, too, may the number 4 chromosome which a technician is inspecting within that cell. Descriptions of these clocks-within-clocks are heard throughout the lab, as techs informally confirm one another's perceptions: "Take a look at the cell at 11 o'clock for me. There's a weird 6 at 9 o'clock" is common shorthand. And techs are confronted by an onslaught of ambiguous material which they need to describe as they ask a colleague to verify what they are scoping: Nadine confirmed her own judgment, for example, by beckoning Leila to her microscope when she called, "Come here and look at 2 o'clock for me, will you? Does it have a centromere?" For an outside observer, there is a fine line between confirming what's "out there" inside the cell and constructing it in such a conversational interaction. But this collaborative coconstruction of material interpretations is science as usual.

Cellular descriptions are mapped using metaphors in the world outside the cell. Throughout my apprenticeship, I kept wondering if the internal world on the slide under the microscope would have meaning without reference to these prior and external images (Keller 1992a, 1992b; Lakoff and Johnson 1980). But my question is not meaningful when interpreted through the powerful and routinized practices by which diagnostic work takes place, for it posits the destabilization of a world to whose material stability technicians are, of course, committed. They must hold the vexing language-borne questions of how to describe material reality apart from metaphors at bay; otherwise, their consensus descriptions could not be animated with the power of persuasion, indeed, the power on which biomedical intervention must be based.

Indeed, producing that stability is tantamount to producing routine diagnoses; without an agreement on the norms of chromosome recognition and the boundaries of normalcy, cytogenetics would be meaningless. All concerned parties must begin from a consensus which anchors normative descriptions of the material world inside a cell's nucleus, while taking the known variations and aberrations within it into account. Yet the material on which technicians work must be foregrounded through this normalizing grid against a background which includes murky or broken cells, in vitro accidents, and uneven growth rates. All of these constitute normal processes; it is up to the tech to abstract readable cells from the soup in which they are incubated. All techs recognize this background ambiguity, and the active work entailed to reach consensus: Learning to muffle background noise in favor of the normalizing grid is a central skill of their work. At the same time, they must highlight each entity which differs from the norm, investigating its potential to move from background insignificance to foreground significance. This continuous process of normalizing, highlighting potential abnormality, and renormalizing is governed by rigorous procedural protocol. The discovery of a single anomalous cell, for example, kicks the machinery of fact construction into overdrive: When a technician finds a single extra chromosome, s/he groans in anticipation of counting thirty or sixty cells in order to rule in or out certain interpretations. At the same time as s/he submits to the rigorous discipline of tripling the cell count, there is also an acknowledgment that the most likely (and best) outcome is the diagnosis of "in vitro accident," or "pseudo-mosaicism." As a lab supervisor said, "We're all probably running around with a little mosaicism in our cells. But the question is, in what proportion? Go to sixty [cells], then we'll see."

Laboratory workers tolerate a high degree of ambiguity in the process of reaching consensus diagnoses. But once that process is complete, they must also accept the closure of disambiguation. For example, I was present one morning when a general buzz started to resonate through the lab. Jila had found what appeared to be a deletion on the Q-arm (bottom arm) of an X chromosome. To my untrained eye, it looked like a small white spot. And it was present in only one of the twenty-three cells she had counted. She called for help, and when a second technician also spotted the problem area, they began to debate its significance. If it were a P-arm (top arm) deletion, and if it were real (i.e., found in a significant proportion of cells, not just one cell), it might eventually be labeled mosaic Turner's syndrome. When I asked for an explanation, one tech said, "A P-arm deletion would inactivate the X, so that means it's X without a second X chromosome, so that's Turner's. But a Q-arm deletion, well, that's not so clear." The other said, "P-arm or Q-arm, a deletion is a deletion." To which the first replied, "I don't think so." After ten minutes of microscope consultation to which the lab supervisor was recruited, the team decided to replant the sample in flask B, to double the number of cells which were not drawn from flask A, where the single X deletion was found. In augmenting the number of cells drawn from a different sample, they hoped to discover whether the deletion was an artifact of laboratory procedures, magnified by tissue culture technique in a single flask, or a real event, present across varied flask samples. By awaiting cell growth in the extra sample, and counting sixty cells, they hoped to resolve the presence of one ambiguous cell. But they also understood the chain of command through which ambiguity would be taken out of their control, and disambiguated elsewhere. "Real or not real, that's for her [the chief geneticist] to decide," said one. To which the other quickly countered, "No, it's not. Real or not real, that's the headache she'll give the parents to decide."

The majority of ambiguous preliminary findings resolve themselves through additional staining, scoping, or testing. That is, they both arise and resolve as artifacts of the culturing process, through which their significance is judged. A few XX chromosomes in a case otherwise counted as an XY fetus can be resolved through Q-banding, for example, which makes the lower portion of the "real" male Y sex chromosomes appear more highly contrastive to the presence of maternal cell contaminants which have added extra Xs. And small, consistent areas on single chromosomes which look odd to the technician can be checked against parental bloods. If one parent carries the same small anomaly, it is most likely a polymorphism, that is, a variation on the banding patterns of normal chromosomes. Certain chromosomes are known to be highly polymorphic, i.e., the number 9s and, to a lesser extent, the number 16s. When such small regional variations are found on chromosomes not usually associated with polymorphism, the case merits greater attention. As one technician told her story:

> So I found the smallest blur on the top of the 18s, and it was in every cell. But you could almost overlook it, is was so small. So I looked at it for a long time, and then I took it to Doctor H., and at first she didn't agree with me. But the longer she looked at the slides, the more she thought I might be right, [that] there was a blur on the 18s. But she didn't think it was real. So we called the parents in and we cultured their bloods and then it turned out that the mother had it too. The same small blur on the 18s. So that's doubly good: It's good that I found it, and it's good that she had it.

Thinking as a formerly pregnant woman awaiting amniocentesis results, I hardly coded the call for parental bloods as "good"; a panic attack undoubtedly accompanied the request from the lab. But with my rudimentary training in cytogenetics, I understood Marita's point. Although the discovery and its prolonged resolution was anxiety-provoking for the parents, it ruled out possibilities that would have been much more serious. Prior to the development of banding techniques, which made different regions of the chromosomes more highly contrastive and visible in the 1970s, of course, this "double good" would have been neither possible nor necessary.

But sometimes a variation which is not carried by either parent is located in the fetal tissue. Then, technicians, supervisors, and geneticists intensively scope an increased sample of cells, attempting to decide upon the reality status of the variation, and consult the medical literature, to determine whether this variation, or one surpassingly like it, has been reported before. I will return to the presence of the "invisible college" (Crane 1972; Spanier 1995) constituted through the literature. But here it suffices to say that this de novo (new or unique) event is more worrisome because it has neither known significance nor known insignificance. That is, the rule-out procedures of biomedicine cannot (yet) be applied.

During the winter, spring, and summer of the year in which I undertook my first laboratory apprenticeship, I was present for an extended prenatal diagnosis of a de novo anomaly. While an account of genetic counseling and the mother's decision to continue this pregnancy was given in chapter 7, the story of its discovery and diagnosis in the laboratory belongs here. When Veronique LaCroix, a 37-year-old Haitian immigrant, had amniocentesis, the results were ambiguous: Additional material was found on the number 9 chromosomes in the sample of her 46XY fetus. The extra material on the 9s had banding patterns suggesting that the top arm was reduplicating itself. The geneticists therefore provisionally labeled it 9P+ to indicate the location of the extra material. At the time, the mother's blood was examined, but the father was "too busy" to give a sample. In examining parental bloods, laboratory staff were attempting to rule out a balanced translocation (that is, an even exchange of material from two distinct chromosomes, which creates two new hybrid chromosomes). If one of the parents were carrying a balanced translocation, that parent would have the normal complement of genetic material present in atypical banding patterns because of the exchange of chromosome pieces. One of those atypical parental chromosomes might have transmitted an abnormal amount of chromosomal material in unbalanced form to the fetus. But the mother's chromosomes did not carry this aberration; there was no way to know if the father's did. When the baby was born, the geneticist received umbilical cord blood to confirm the diagnosis. She also contacted relevant researchers by telephone and scanned the literature. There, she discovered no reports of 9P+, but almost one hundred reports worldwide of trisomy 9. This very rare condition, which includes distinctive craniofacial features, stiff joints, and mental retardation, was the closest characterized pattern the geneticist could find, although it was based on a fully present third number 9 chromosome, rather than on an extra P-arm piece. She therefore asked to examine the baby, and to keep the foreskin tissue from his circumcision for laboratory studies.[37] By combining laboratory tissue culture studies with clinical inspection, she hoped to produce a more powerful diagnosis and possibly, prognosis. By using the resources of the "invisible college" of colleagues and their internationally published reports, the geneticist also decided that the extra material at the top of the 9s could be interpreted as the chromosome partially reduplicating itself. She therefore assimilated her finding of 9P+ to trisomy 9.

The move to transform and stabilize a diagnosis was not frivolous; at the outer reaches of knowledge, medicine, like law, works by precedent. The development of this child will be closely watched, his anomalies potentially linked to findings in tissue culture. The "invisible college" here demarcates the limits of collective clinical experience. Through the formal and informal channels of communication available in scientific communities, the geneticist grounded her anomalous case in prior findings which provide a template for further study and publication. She also normalized a rare abnormality, tethering it to the ground of prior interpretation.

The process by which diagnostic consensus is reached in the face of ambiguity is a powerful aspect of biomedical scientific practice, involving a complex and often innovative choreography of researchers and clinicians, who may for some specific diagnoses serve as combined researcher clinicians. Ideally, all cytogenetic findings need to be constructed such that expert audiences drawn from an appropriate set of constituencies agree on interpretation (cf. Knorr-Cetina 1995). Yet the reality of ambiguous or rare diagnoses is often one of negotiation. There is a great deal of flexibility in the process of anomalous diagnosis, as illustrated by the interactions of the technician who found the blurs on the number 18 chromosomes that were ultimately carried in parental bloods, and by this story of the 9P+ assimilated to a trisomy 9. Research papers can and will undoubtedly be based on these case histories, affecting future interactions across the permeable membrane separating laboratory research and clinical practice. But the need to stabilize a consensus is also built into the diagnostic procedure, and the consensus must be a powerful one, where routine laboratory services are offered to patients.

As a consumer of health care services, I have certainly benefited from that staged certainty. And as an observer of contemporary American political economy, I am aware of the statutory-juridical pressures which drive the training and certification of geneticists, technologists, technicians, and their laboratories, assuring and coercing their ability to reach consensus. If expert audiences do not agree on the laboratory results of diagnosis, licenses may be lost, business may dwindle, and lawsuits may be filed. But as an observer of science as a congeries of social practices, I also feel compelled to point out the continuous construction of stable interpretations in the face of material ambiguity.

Stabilizing Diagnoses

This problem of stabilization and disambiguation is well-known by all scientific practitioners. Provoked by my presence at the cutting table, for example, one technician grumbled, "There ought to be a better way of teaching the objective differences among chromosomes." To which I queried, "What makes you think the differences are all so straightforward and objective?" A second technician, overhearing our conversation, partially agreed with me, adding a metaproblem of her own: "The problem is in our language: There must be a better way to describe these patterns." When I asked, "What if there is no perfect description? What if they are a little variable and inherently ambiguous?" the first technician replied, "Then we're all in trouble, bigger trouble than I thought."

Circling around a philosophical black hole, the technicians wanted to place the trouble in the world of descriptive language, meliorable through more cumulatively powerful terminological distinctions. I wanted to provoke a discussion of the material world as more variable and full of surprises than routinized laboratory work allows; and to signal the inherently open nature of scientific knowledge fields, where workers collaborate among themselves by using conventional descriptions which then sometimes reflect back on the gaps, mysteries, and uncertainties of the very field on which they stake their knowledge claims. We were here necessarily at an interpretive standoff.

Likewise, the technologist who runs the rocket gel electrophoresis for alpha-fetoprotein measurement in the centrifuged supernatant of amniotic fluids described one variant of the analysis as "a bad test." Electrophoresis entails running an electrical current through segments of DNA; the timing and length of DNA molecule motion patterns can be precisely read, enabling abnormally long or short amounts of a given molecule (in this case, alpha-fetoprotein) to be identified when compared to the normal responses of the rest of the tested set. But the technician considers the fetal hemoglobin electrophoresis portion of the test quite difficult to read. When I asked, "Do you mean that it's ambiguous?" he quickly backed off, saying, "No, I don't want medicine to get a bum rap in your report." Among insiders, the acknowledgment of ambiguity, uncertainty, and stabilizing judgment calls is part of normal and normalizing cytogenetic practice. So, too, is its containment through limiting the recognition of its potential impact: When questions are raised about the status of a scientific fact, they need to be resolved by expert agreement for routinized diagnoses to proceed. When they cannot be resolved through standard or more creative protocols, a new research question may be provoked. But self-reflexivity is ruled out at the heart of diagnostic procedure, although it surely exists in the intellectual and interactive conversations and speculations of scientific workers, and is occasionally shared with nosy outside observers, a point to which I return below.

Of course, when viewed from inside normalizing scientific protocols, much of the ambiguity I have been describing can be technologically ascribed. Scientific progress is widely viewed as cumulative; its practitioners and many of its social analysts depict and predict the limits of scientific knowledge as inherently advanceable as human abilities to invent and harness new technologies evolve (cf. Cantor 1992; Cornwell 1995; Gilbert 1992; Horgan 1996; Judson 1992; Kitcher 1996). The debate about the potential limits of cumulative scientific knowledge is ongoing, and progressivists have much data to support their position, especially with regard to recent advances in molecular genetics: *Science* magazine, for example, has published an impressive annual chart since 1990 in which advances in knowledge of the human genome achieved through sequencing and mapping are chronicled. And when we descend from the Olympian heights of triumphalist histories of science to the trenches of routinized laboratory work, it is apparent that the fusion of human practice and its technological products is very powerful and currently quite dramatically expansive. Many of the advances in cytogenetics described above are less than a quarter-century old (Hsu and Hirschhorn 1977; Judson 1992; Olby 1990b). To an outsider, they often appear to be magic potions. But their existence is obviously a product of human ingenuity. As I worked in the labs, I kept wondering: Who invented and tested each variety of growth media? But as techs would say with a good-natured laugh as I pondered these minutiae, "We don't always know why it works, but as long as it works, we use it. And if it doesn't work, why, we'll try something else. If that works better, we'll use it, too." The technicians are here describing their own craft expertise; successful technicians are flexible experimentalists who tinker in order to produce more persuasive results. And, like the "invisible scientific colleges" constituted by researchers and their journal reports described above, successful biomedical technicians develop protocols that enable technology to transform quickly, setting evolving norms which are rapidly communicated, becoming highly portable across laboratories.

And the portability of technology is international, as well. On the day I decided to survey lab technology, the scores of reagents and machines I listed came from the states of California, Delaware, Illinois, New York, Massachusetts, and Pennsylvania, and the countries of England, Germany, and Japan. Bottles bore the insignia of multinational corporations like Corning and Kimberly-Clark, and the "home brew" labels of small laboratories in suburban New York and Boston. The DNA technologies which are currently bidding to surpass cytogenetics in manufacturing prenatal diagnostic kits come from the sector of national and international venture capital, but that is another story (cf. Juma 1989; Kornberg 1995; Natowicz 1997; Rabinow 1996).

Describing Actants

All these technologies and techniques can be labeled "actants" in the parlance of science and technology studies (Latour 1987), for they are constellations of people, processes, and artifacts which collectively represent and intervene in specific contexts. In using the term "actant" I am indexing a long-standing sociological debate concerning the importance of machine-human imbrications in modern society, and the limits of human agency independent of the material world that humans have built and in relation to which their actions are always predicated. Actants are always already congeries of people, techniques, and technologies about which no linear origins tale can be told: The inventions and discoveries of technoscience may conventionally be attributed to Great Men (or anonymous laboratory workers), but they depend on prior combinations and recombinations of practice (cf. Callon 1986; Casper 1994a, 1994b; Latour 1987, 1994; Pickering 1995). Actants are therefore amalgamations of persons, things, and practices which represent semiotic functions. They have consequences in a material world from which the actants themselves derive and which they help to define.

Abstracting from a cantankerous literature, I would underline two "actant"-related ideas: First, machines are constructed by humans' consciousness, ingenuity, and intent, but they take on a "life of their own"; people and their potent objects have no clear-cut boundaries, as they mutually invent one another, transforming the tasks, meanings, and knowledge bases they collectively produce and accomplish. Second, in that transformative process, technologies, techniques, and "their" humans mutually set the directions and limits on their past, present, and future composite accomplishments, fusing the techno-human parameters and characteristics of their collaborations. Technologies, techniques, and people combine to wield agency. There is no bounded entity which is a technoscientific agent apart from these negotiated and fluid properties of human and nonhuman agents in powerful interactions and productions.

In the laboratory, techno-human actants wielding active objects abound. Some combinations, like sterile hoods, microscopes, and the vitreous cornucopia of pipettes, tubes, flasks, and slides which undergird the routine work of dexterous technicians, hail from the age of "classic" laboratory science. Others, like the Bunsen burners, refrigeration, or logbooks on which technicians depend are so low-tech as to be taken for granted by all who use and observe them. Current successful diagnostic work relies on the invaluable mergers accomplished in these older and low-technology actant alliances. Their routinized contributions now stabilize, rather than transform, a field.

Once, it was otherwise, as standard histories of science fruitfully illustrate: New and destabilizing scientific knowledge in its applied form conventionally produces technologies which quickly "reduce" to practical techniques (Bernal 1965; Bijker 1995; Bijker, Hughes et al. 1989; Feenberg and Hannay 1995). But some technologies define and occupy cutting edges and boundaries of fields. Computerization and informatics, for example, are hand-in-glove technologies without which it would be impossible for gene hunters to conceptualize and carry out current DNA sequencing and mapping (Cantor 1992; cf. Haraway 1979, 1981–82, 1983, 1989a, 1997). Polymerase Chain Reaction (PCR) machines enable the replication of genetic material at a speed and accuracy which would have been unimaginable even a decade before their invention (Olby 1990b; Rabinow 1996).

Cytogenetics technology builds on the classic tools of microscopy and tissue culture prefigured from Leeuwenhoek on, and invented in modern forms during the first half of the current century. But it shares a space with new, destabilizing, and transformative technologies, themselves the products of scientific interventions developed in molecular biological research: quite literally, Middle Lab had a PCR machine on loan from its manufacturer in an office down the hall during a period when one geneticist tried (unsuccessfully) to raise interest and cash for a pilot project in cystic fibrosis screening. And DNA analysis provides a moving frontier for the development of an expanding array of prenatal diagnostic kits linked to hereditary diseases, which range from the relatively common (cystic fibrosis; sickle-cell anemia) to the extremely rare (familial dysautonomia; Williams syndrome). The most obvious "new" actant on the cytogenetic scene, however, is the computer bearing the "cytoscan" program, which karyotypes chromosomes from slides.

Returning to the lab after a five-year absence, I saw the "cytoscan" program as miraculous: Not only can it cut and pair chromosomes, it can "see" overlaps when two or even three metaphase cells are bunched together in a droplet on a slide. Of course, this work is the product of human-machine interaction, not only in the initial writing and development of the program, but in the selection of appropriate slides by technicians. If there are overlaps in pairing and aligning chromosomes in size order that the machine cannot read, it deposits them in a pile at the bottom of the computer screen. There, with a mouse, techs "hand cut" those chromosomes the machine finds illegible, dragging them to appropriate locations on the chart. The machine can align, enhance, and generally aestheticize a karyotype. While I was awed by the presence and capacity of this machine, it should be stressed that the technicians were much more blasé. Intimately attached to this software, they do not feel mastered or out-thought by its speed of chromosome recognition, perhaps because they are the first generation to use it, and are therefore still actively debugging its many glitches, or perhaps because a large amount of human decision-making is still built into the technology. That is, it is semi-automated. Or semi-informated.

But "cytoscan" is only the latest actant in a panoply of technologies which enable expert workers to purify and thus construct a powerful and persuasive work object made from human tissue. Laboratories do not accommodate objects like human chromosomes in their natural forms; they are not bound by their locations in the wombs of pregnant women, or their natural chronology (in this case, metaphase cell cycles). All are transported, transformed, and manipulated, as laboratory workers "improve upon the natural order," upgrading it, and relocating it firmly within a social order in which it can be studied (Knorr-Cetina 1995, 145). When viewed through the lens of the laboratory, the "chromosomes" produced by cell culture are not natural objects but cultural ones; perhaps, in the interests of dispersing dichotomies which abound in and mystify science as a way of practicing and knowing the world, we would best label them natural/cultural or socialnatural objects (cf. Haraway 1997). Chromosomes in drosophila, mice or "men" have powerful effects in constituting an organism, but they become knowable only through the myriad sociotechnical interventions which enable and produce them as objects of scientific investigation. In this sense, "tissue culture" has a doubled meaning: It is at once a technique for growing cells, and an enrollment of biological material for making human meanings.[38]

Professional Reflections

As I have tried to stress throughout this chapter, the professionals who work in the field of medical/prenatal cytology are highly accomplished diagnostic disambiguators and boundary keepers. They are at once much more fluid in their interpretations of what genetics and chromosomes are and might mean than is the general public, and much more rigorous in their collective practices. They know that something must be diagnosed for each case, but they also know that mosaics and minor ambiguities are common occurrences. They therefore worry, as one technician put it, "What are we doing to the mothers? One bad cell, and we feel compelled for legal reasons to tell them. This is more information than they need or can use." They also know that mistakes are possible, despite the strict protocol that laboratories employ to prevent them. In the first decade of the PDL's practice, out of fifteen thousand cases, three mistakes are known to have occurred (Hsu 1989). Two involved a discrepancy of lab-reported fetal sex versus observed sex at birth. From the lab's point of view, one of these cases was not a mistake at all—the baby probably sustained testicular feminization, an abnormality of prenatal hormone development, but not an abnormality which is visible in the sex chromosomes. The other may well be attributable to maternal cell contamination, which would be unnerving to parents expecting a girl who "got" a boy, but is of no medical consequence. Only one of the three could probably be credited to true technician error: A fetus diagnosed as normal was later born with severe congenital anomalies; intensive restudy of the slides suggested that there may have been a very subtle deletion which no one—not the tech, supervisor, or laboratory director—initially discovered. As the laboratory director said, in discussing this case, "People think this work is routine, and mostly it is. But it isn't *just* routine. This is a tough business. We often don't know exactly what we are looking at. We work hard to get it right, but really, we're just very lucky that there have been very few mistakes."

Yet these same protocols, and the extreme professional division of labor which they accompany, also distance many practitioners from thinking about the larger, more long-term social consequences of the field in which they are operating. When querying technicians and technologists about their thoughts on the social impact of the field, I often heard responses like these:

> The mother? No, I don't think about the mother. Oh, I feel sorry for her, if I should find something. But if I stop to think about her feelings, I wouldn't finish my work. (Jila H., technologist)

> Of course, we are glad that almost all of our work gives good news. But really, we aren't here for good news, we are here to get the job done. And if the news is bad, well, that's the reason you want to have this test in the first place. (Nadine P., technician)

At the same time, professionals are generally aware of the expanding space their field plays in contemporary culture. And many are quite focused in their queries and criticisms: One of the geneticists I interviewed described the dilemma of the rapidly expanding field of prenatal diagnosis thus:

> We are in a fast-moving train and we manage to learn how to eat in the train, even sleep in the train. But I don't think we think very much about where the train is going. Or, at the least, we are very simplistic. . . . Of course, geneticists are the ones creating the technology. But it is being created without too much thought. . . . When I began,

this work belonged in academic medicine; now it is rapidly commercializing. Pretty soon, it will just be profit-making labs offering kits. They'll have a roving genetic counselor to pay lip service to malpractice insurance. This is not what geneticists wanted when we insisted on genetic counseling.

This problem of commercialization should, I believe, be closely linked to a discussion of two other problems: geneticization and genetic discrimination. Geneticization is an historically consonant ideology linking individual attributes and social problems as if they could be effectively reshaped or eliminated only in the realm of biomedicine now reduced to genetic diagnosis (Lippman 1991, 1993). As more and more human variation is attributed to genetic difference, it becomes easier to foreground the biological and background the social, as if they were separable, reproducing and sustaining classic nature/culture dichotomies in popular as well as scientific thought. A worldview of genetic differentiation as the most meaningful way to describe human problems and ascribe their causes to biological bases flows easily from this ideology.

In the shadow of this worldview, genetic discrimination makes sense. Although much of the data is still anecdotal and spotty, some insurance companies and employers (and, in the case of self-insured employers, these are the same) are interested in obtaining information on genetic predispositions in order to exclude or not hire those deemed to have a potential for costly ailments in their futures (Billings, Kohn et al. 1992; Draper 1992; National Institutes 1993; Natowicz and Alper 1991, 1992; Resta 1992). At the time of the present writing, the legal situation is quite fluid: The EEOC issued guidelines in 1995 suggesting that those with known genetic predispositions are protected by the Americans with Disabilities Act of 1990, but this ruling has yet to make its way through the courts. Many states have "genetic privacy" legislation in various stages: enacted, pending, or proposed; genetic privacy clauses have also been attached to several of the "health reform" bills currently before Congress. Whether these protective statutes will survive various legislative challenges and compromises, and if so, in what form, is, of course, unknown. My point is twofold: First, the issues of geneticization and genetic discrimination, and growing popular consciousness of both are closely linked, and they are unevenly evolving at the present time. Second, these sociocultural worldviews are only roughly linked to the practices of laboratory life, which are at once messier and more rigorous than is suggested by a geneticizing ethos, its commercial possibilities, and legislative constructions.

Popular consciousness of geneticization is nurtured in many domains.

Among the most powerful is the pervasive use of a discourse of "triumph and tragedy" provided by media representations of genetics as a frontier of biomedical research. When I began this study, stories about genetics were relatively infrequent, but by now, there is a newspaper or television report of a genetic "base" for a dramatically expanding list of traits each week; some of these initial reports are substantiated, but many remain in dispute. This pattern of announced advancement and skeptical challenge and retreat is inherent in the practice of normal science, as analysts are quick to point out in debates as wide-ranging as the search for the "cause" of manic depression, or verification of the degradation of the ozone layer, or evaluation of unconventional treatments for cancer (Gieryn 1995; Hess 1997; Hubbard and Lewontin 1996; Lewenstein 1995; Nelkin and Lindee 1995; Yearley 1995). Yet popularized reports rarely discuss retractions, elaborations, or failures of new theories: "Brilliant scientific careers are not built on failure," Spanier writes (1995, 30). Thus, only the heralding of a new "breakthrough" usually enters popular consciousness through highly visible journalistic and public relations media reports; its retraction or diminution rarely receives comparable publicity. At the same time, real advances in gene hunting are being made via molecular biological technology, and these are continually reported. Such successes fuel public expectations of a future in which many undesirable traits will be eliminated, despite the present lack of success in any gene therapy (Hubbard and Lewontin 1996; Marshall 1995). Abortion following the prenatal diagnosis of a known genetic or chromosomal problem is the only technology of elimination currently available. Problems that now appear intractable in the development and delivery of gene therapy may be ascribed to either "standing on the threshold of a new era" and its growing pains, or to the need to rethink how cellular components uptake and interact with the entities we introduce into them (and, of course, the two may be intimately related; this, too, is part of normal scientific research).

And genetic researchers no less than lay constituencies are deeply affected by these processes: A Swedish colleague married to a population geneticist told me of her resentment at how genetic discourse is being introduced, shaped, and molded as it leaves the lab and travels into media spaces, often to the distortion of daily scientific practices. She feels increasingly coerced to attend panels and workshops on bioethics in which researchers are being tutored in a preformulated discourse of "problems and possibilities," "tragedies and triumphs," and "costs and benefits" as a language in which they will be required to speak to the public about the Human Genome Project. That "public" is, of course, heterogeneous in its capacities, powers, and aspirations; in the United States, it includes venture capitalists, congressional regulators, HMOs and other service providers, as well as potential patients and their supporters. Listening to her complaints, I had an image of the field of bioethics as a giant modem, connecting the research informatics of the Human Genome Project to a fascinated if under-literate public.[39]

As these complex successes and limits of research and therapy filter and float across multiple contexts, and as more traits are prenatally or presymptomatically diagnosable without necessarily increasing our treatment options, we should expect an intensification in both geneticization and consciousness of its potentially discriminatory effects. That is, we are living out a "history of the present" in which genetic discourse plays a powerful, contradictory, and currently expansionary role.

But if geneticization poses both ideological and practical problems, so too, ironically, does lack of access to the specific benefits of genetic technology (King 1992; Nsiah-Jefferson 1989). At the same time that "molecules of the year" appeared on the cover of *Science* and *Newsweek*, governmental defunding of medical genetic services proceeded apace. Public health surveillance of genetic disease is minimal; funds for its monitoring and the provision of services were hit hard in the Reaganization of the budget beginning in 1981, which turned health monies over to the states, effectively removing federal impetus for their provision or evaluation. Maternal-child block grants are highly competitive, and genetic services, understandably, rarely count as major players when compared to more widespread and pressing needs. Reaganization also enjoined congressional funds from being used to collect health statistics: This increased the invisibility of class inequalities in both access to services and health outcomes. In the wake of this federal hostility to monitoring health statistics, representatives from the fields of public health and genetics founded CORN, the Council of Regional Networks for genetic services. CORN organizes the meta-statistics of the ten regions within which participating state health departments have organized themselves to assemble their comparative information on genetic services; its task is a daunting one. Underfunded and reliant upon the regions and state health departments, many of whom do not have the resources to provide a state director of genetic services or a registry of birth defects, CORN is attempting to do voluntarily what national health services do by government mandate throughout the rest of the developed world (Meaney 1992; Meaney and Chang 1991; Meaney, Riggle et al. 1993). CORN's initial minimal data set (MDS) suggests that only GENES, the Genetics Network of the Empire State (N.Y.), is providing genetic counseling and amniocenteses for a low-income and minority population to any significant degree. But the MDS is not yet representative in any statistically meaningful sense. And more

recently California has been compiling comprehensive records which indicate that their maternal serum screening program (which may lead to
amniocentesis, but is much more widespread and less expensive as a form of
prenatal diagnosis) reaches a population whose racial diversity is representative of the state's demographic profile (Cunningham 1998). Almost a decade
later, we would expect to find both stronger outreach programs affecting the
underserved, and stronger statistics describing those programs. Access outside of New York and California is underdocumented, and there are good
reasons to believe that this represents a problem in the provision of basic services, not solely a problem in reporting.

But if genetic services seem hard to come by for the underprivileged, they
are flourishing in the commercial sector for the well-to-do. While academic
research protocols often offer genetic testing for rare diseases to affected families gratis or at cost, debates are currently raging about the provision of controversial genetic tests like the breast cancer screen by for-profit labs (Collins
1996; Hubbard and Lewontin 1996; Koenig 1996; Kolata 1996; Seachrist
1995).[40] And increasingly, routine screening and diagnostic tests are available
in the corporate sector: Metpath now provides a significant percentage of
routine amniocentesis and/or MSAFP services. But it is impossible to know
how widespread for-profit provision of genetic services is: No national or
state statistics are kept. Some enterprising scientists-scholars have attempted
estimates based on examining the annual reports of biotechnology corporations (Natowicz and Ard 1997). Whatever the percentage is, it is surely growing. And while free-market advocates might praise the cost-effectiveness of
shifting unwieldy and expensive academic medicine to a more competitive
sector, research geneticists point out the downside of that slide: Even routinized tests require collaborative lab work and interpretation which is cut to
the bone when time budgets are cost-accounted; unusual conditions require
greater research and collaboration than usual ones, yet these are the very
ones for which the biotechnology companies are developing kits (Milunsky
1993). The consequences for patients are sobering:

> Commercial laboratories have made direct arrangements with practic-
> ing physicians and have targeted non-teaching hospitals, health main-
> tenance organizations et al. to short-circuit academic genetic clinical
> and laboratory services, opting for "quicker" services and conve-
> nience. However, the patients' interests have not been well served by
> these arrangements. Many clinical geneticists can attest to patients
> with "abnormal" genetic test or screening results who are frantic
> about the implications and seek appropriate consultations at the

eleventh hour. . . . Frequently, after commercial reports of an abnormal karyotype, repeat cytogenetic analysis (and more cost) is required for optimal interpretation in academic centers. . . . To serve the best interests of their patients' genetic care needs, physicians must practice considerable circumspection when selecting laboratories and consultants, to avoid becoming the victims of hype, hubris, and hucksters. (Milunsky 1993, 629)

When corporate labs advertise speedier results, they do not necessarily report whether their test kits are as accurate as more traditional cytogenetic methods. Nor are they as likely to insist on the provision of genetic counseling for patients, although many corporate labs do employ counselors on an elective, fee-for-service basis. And, according to technicians at the PDL and Middle Labs, the older, hospital-based nonprofit genetic laboratories feel constrained by these corporate moves quite directly: They are under competitive pressure to decrease the turnaround time per diagnosis without the ability to control the number of employee hours available per case, or investments in automation. In both academic and commercial molecular biology laboratories, advances are being made in automating diagnoses: Microchip technologies with "high through-put" may well be the wave of the future. The need for highly efficient molecular diagnostics is also driven, in turn, by the push for greater cost-accounting in our transforming system of health care. Caught in the interim, laboratory technicians worry about case overload, even as they respond to competitive pressure by becoming more efficient. The precarious trade-offs between efficiency and overload, accuracy and profit status all condition the environment of laboratory work.

These are some of the historic, economic, and ideological transformations which surely influence the environment in which cytogenetic technicians peer into their microscopes, read a cell with a chromosome count of 47, discover the extra chromosome to be the number 21, and increase their cell count to thirty before logging a diagnosis of Down syndrome. This ordinary laboratory occurrence sets off an extraordinary reaction in the hearts and minds of the pregnant women and their supporters to whom it is shortly reported. It is to their experience that we now turn in chapter 9.

9

An Error in Cell Division, or The Power of Positive Diagnosis

When we walked into the doctor's office, both my husband and I were crying. He looked up and said, "What's wrong? Why are you both in tears?" "It's our baby. Our baby is going to die," I said. "That isn't a baby," he said firmly. "It's a collection of cells that made a mistake." (Leah Rubinstein, 39, white homemaker)

THE SHOCK OF RECEIVING BAD NEWS is never routine, no matter how ordinary its contents may be for the diagnostic laboratory. The discovery of an extra number 21 chromosome in fetal cells on a slide produces the cytogenetic technicians' most common positive diagnosis of Down syndrome. But every woman with whom I have spoken recalls the delivery of this, and every other diagnosis, vividly. The receipt of a diagnosis shatters the routine of daily life:

In my mind the tape repeats endlessly. I can hear the genetic counselor saying it again and again, "I'm sorry, Adrian, I'm calling with some bad news. Are you alone? Would you like to get your husband to the phone?" (Adrian Miller, 39, white medical science writer)

Everything slowed way down. I don't get hysterical, I get methodical; under stress I just, you know, get very quiet. I asked him, "How sure are you? What are the odds? Do we need to repeat this test?" I didn't flip out until I found myself in the car, going to pick up my husband, sobbing on the highway. (Margaret Thompson, 34, white psychologist)

When bad news arrives from the cytogenetics lab, it is usually delivered in pieces. Many women told stories of being called by genetic counselors, or by obstetricians, who would not divulge the exact nature of the problem over the telephone; they preferred for the pregnant woman (or, ideally, the couple) to learn the relevant details in person. Many women also complained about this protocol; while acknowledging the competence, and often, compassion, of the counselors, they would have preferred to have the diagnosis named on the phone, rather than ruminating while waiting for an emergency appointment, often a full day away. Some counselors and doctors do, of course, "tell all" in the first conversation. While some women found this to be a relief, others had the opposite reaction. Of the fifty women receiving positive diagnoses whom I interviewed, at least two complained about the insensitivity of having counselors call and "blurt out" such deeply disruptive news: They would have preferred to hear it more gently from a private obstetrician with whom they had an ongoing relationship. The obvious point of these different stories is easy to spot: There is no good way to get bad news. And the circumstances of its delivery are indelibly etched into the memory of everyone with whom I spoke.

These circumstances are particularly dramatic when they entail a diagnosis made by ultrasound, rather than through chromosome studies.[41] Visualizations are presented on a monitor quite similar to the ubiquitous television screen, and their impact is instantaneous. They hold a powerful place in women's narratives, and are recalled far more vividly than the "caterpillar stick figures" of karyotype photographs (cf. Drugan, Greb et al. 1990). In the cases where spina bifida, anencephaly, or life-threatening heart, lung, and kidney problems were visualized, women from diverse sociocultural backgrounds seen at the full range of New York's hospitals told virtually the same story:

> Pretty soon, it was a regular doctors' convention in there. At some point, I must have had eight doctors muttering over that screen. I said to myself, my God, something is terribly wrong here, because they keep calling other people to come in and take a look. I know they wanted their opinions. But they wouldn't say anything to me. (Marilyn de Soto, 34, Puerto Rican social worker)

> He just kept looking and looking, and the area that I noticed that they looked at most basically was the heart. They just kept focusing on that. The technician called the doctor, the doctor called more doctors.

I asked, I kept saying, over and over, "What's the problem?" Because I told my husband, I says, "With Leona, I was in and out in half an hour, this is all wrong." I kept asking the technician, but you know, they don't tell you anything, because they're not really allowed to. . . . Finally, when the doctor came in, I begged and begged, and she said, "Well, we're noticing a little fluid in one of the baby's lungs." And I said, "What can that be from?" And she said, "We really don't know at this point. We're going to go ahead with the amnio, and when you get upstairs, you just tell your counselor, and she'll talk to you." When she told me that, I knew at that point that she already knew. She just didn't want to be the one to tell me. (Nivia Hostos, 26, Puerto Rican administrative secretary)

Then when the radiologist came in she called the other one, the clinician, and they started looking more and more, and focusing on more and more places. Not that I knew what was going on, but I knew that it looked ominous. You could feel something hanging in the air in there. And suddenly there were more and more people in the room, and they're changing positions around the screen, and they're highly focused, but they never talk to you. Then, they turned off the machine, and they all left the room. And they sent me out of the room without telling me what they had seen. (Tamara Levkovitz, 34, white private school teacher)

Sometimes, women intervene in hospital protocol, attempting to gain access to information which they desperately need. Marilyn de Soto, for example, opened the sealed envelope containing the ultrasound report while waiting to deliver it to the genetic counselor. "It's my body, I have a right to know," she told me. She thus read the diagnosis of fetal polycystic nephrosis—a fatal kidney condition in this case associated with the diagnosis of trisomy 13. Later, crisis-racked, with her veterinarian husband at her side explaining the second sonogram, she "saw for herself": "I'll never forget seeing the black hole where the kidney should have been. And a lot of damage to the other one. That's something that you could see. That's what did it for me."

Forced Choices

The delivery of a positive diagnosis inevitably forces the pregnant woman and her supporters to make a decision to continue or end the pregnancy. The full impact of that decision-making process is, of course, multifaceted and complex; it provides the subject of this chapter. But one of the first things that struck me when I began interviewing women who had been through this painful process was that my sample divided dramatically into two groups: those who more or less knew that they would choose abortion if a serious condition were diagnosed in their fetuses, and who therefore "decided" instantaneously upon hearing bad news; and those who needed to work their way through the problem step-by-step, arriving at the abortion decision as the conclusion of a more protracted process. The two strategies condense multiple differences, including the very significant difference between understanding common and arcane or ambiguous diagnoses, discussed below. But in addition they reflect sociocultural influences on women's comfort and trust in biomedicine, including diagnostic technology, and the prior knowledge, attitudes, and beliefs that pregnant women and their supporters hold about specific disabling conditions, as well as about childhood disability in general.

The use of abortion after a serious positive diagnosis seems almost automatic, if nonetheless painful for some women, especially under two conditions. One is the diagnosis of Down syndrome, with which they feel familiar. This diagnosis is the single most common one made through amniocentesis, and accounts for almost half the chromosome problems detected. While there are no national figures for abortion rates following positive diagnosis, epidemiological and biostatistical experts estimate that more than 90 percent of women receiving this diagnosis go on to abort (Drugan, Greb et al. 1990; Hsu 1989). One Midwestern study found that 93 percent of the women receiving what the physicians characterized as "severe" prognoses, including all autosomal (nonsex chromosome) trisomies, of which Down's is the most common, decided to abort (Drugan, Greb et al. 1990). These suggestive studies correlate well with data collected in England, where national statistics on abortion following a positive prenatal diagnosis are kept. There, 92 percent of those receiving this diagnosis chose to end their pregnancies (Alberman, Mutton et al. 1995). The second factor which seems to influence an "automatic pilot" response to a serious diagnosis is attachment to an upper-middle-class, or middle-class, Jewish background:

Decision, what decision? It comes with the territory. If you're having amniocentesis, you're having an abortion when they find something wrong. (Leah Rubinstein, 39, white homemaker)

We talked it over before deciding to have amnio. If I was going to have it, we would already know that I was going to have the abortion. People always have their opinion, and people were saying, "If it's Down syndrome, you don't want to have to live with that for the rest of your life." I can tell you a lot of compassionate stories about friends with mentally retarded kids. And I know if we just had a kid with that problem, with no testing, we'd do the right thing, we'd love that child and raise it well. But the bottom line is, we agreed that we want to avoid this problem if we can. (Fran Goodman, 34, white nonprofit community service worker)

And, of course, while virtually every Jewish woman in my sample had this response, they were not alone. Many others also told stories in which decision-making was instantaneous, almost always with Down syndrome, and sometimes, with other conditions, as well:

And when the doctor told me, that was the first instance when I knew that I was going to have an abortion. I made up my mind instantly, I checked in the hospital right away. . . . It was the only thing I could have done. I mean, it was the only thing I could have done. (Nancy Tucker, 36, white college professor)

An unambiguous decision does not entail less suffering:

Sure, it was the best decision I could have made under the circumstances. It was a perfectly right, clear decision, but an enormously painful one. (Diana Morel, 28, Puerto Rican secretary)

I feel fine about the decision, I'm fine with it. Nothing could have been more obvious. It's just that my heart is permanently broken. (Donna deAngelo, 38, white homemaker)

Most of my respondents had prior knowledge about Down syndrome gleaned from neighbors, friends, and kin who had children with this, or another, form of mental retardation. Seven were teachers or social workers whose professional life had brought them into contact with families with disabled (usually, mentally retarded) members. Sylvia Lin, 43, Japanese-American special-education teacher, said, "I told my husband, 'Down's, that means practically nothing.' Because I've seen them very retarded, and I've seen them practically normal."

Other women also had more nuanced understandings of this, and other disabilities:

I knew enough to know not to worry about Down's babies. They're cute, they get by. But you really worry about what happens when they grow up, when you get old, when you die. Who takes care of Down's babies then? (Harriet Genzer, 41, white editor)

I had an autistic brother. My mother put everything she had into him; it ate up her whole life. Maybe the kid would do well. But what about me? (Megan Johnson, 41, white writer)

And some expressed self-criticism of their own aversion to keeping a child with the diagnosed disability:

I'm not proud of this, but to be honest, I don't want to cope with a mentally retarded child. My mother did volunteer work in the schools, with MR kids. She's deeply against abortion. But she's not against abortion for this. I guess some of her attitudes must have rubbed off on me. The thing that entrances me is having a smart child. (Sally Hart, 38, white college professor)

The Chosen Loss

Knowing (or thinking one knows) about a condition undoubtedly strengthens the resolve of decision-making. But it doesn't lessen the pain of loss. Ending a wanted pregnancy is a multifaceted, complex process which all the women with whom I spoke consistently identified as a profound loss. The emotional recovery after what is medically labeled a "selective abortion" is lengthy. Women and their supporters experiencing this process share an existential territory with all who survive the death of loved ones; they also have much in common with those recovering from any pregnancy loss or stillbirth. But their experience is also distinct because it is a chosen loss (Black 1994; Kolker and Burke 1994). The idea of "choice" is one to which women returned again and again, especially highly educated, middle-class women. Said Pat Gordon, a 37-year-old white college professor, "I felt like a voice in a Greek chorus, chanting, 'Your choice, your choice, your choice is upon your shoulders.' I felt like a minor figure in a major tragedy."

Yet for some, the very notion of "choice" is unbearable and must be abolished from the vocabulary of grief: When I asked about decision-making, I heard again and again, from women of diverse backgrounds, "I had to have an abortion" or "It was a forced choice." Some were even more explicit:

I'd prefer the doctor told me the baby was dead. I kept secretly hoping it would die before we got to the hospital. Then I wouldn't be part of causing this loss. (Nivia Hostos, 26, Puerto Rican administrative secretary)

Don't speak of it as an abortion, that's disgusting. This was a loss. I did what I had to do, I couldn't help myself. It's a loss, not an . . . (Harriet Genzer, 41, white editor)

Others acknowledged their ambivalence about what one woman who identified herself as "a rabid pro-choicer" nonetheless called "being an accomplice to a murder." And some spoke of the pain in having to have a choice at all:

When I was going to Dr. R's office to have the laminaria put in again and again, I kept thinking: No one is forcing me to do this. I'm making my own choice. This is awful. It's the single most awful thing that's ever happened to me. But it's my choice, and I'm making it. (Michelle Kansky, 38, white public school teacher)

Indeed, the seriousness of "choice" was a theme that occurred repeatedly as women spoke about decision-making:

Because I had a very serious relationship with that child, and to be carrying it around, wondering whether I was gonna kill it or not was just very serious, I mean, it's feeling like you're going to murder something that you're very close to that's inside of you, when you have the choice not to, and you're choosing to, you know, you're choosing the most difficult thing. (Margaret Thompson, 34, white psychologist)

Many expressed gratitude about having had a choice, despite the deep pain that accompanied its exercise. Knowing about a profound problem in a fetus and being able to choose to avoid bringing it to term was, in their estimate, better than living with the consequences of its birth. "It's better to know than not to know, better to have the choice rather than not to have the choice at all," said Marilyn de Soto, 34, Puerto Rican social worker.

Yet contained within this discourse of choice are the seeds of at least two other themes which bear mention. One is the subtle, perhaps fetishizing aspects of individualism implied in the concept of choice. Because the fetuses who are diagnosed grow within individual women's bodies, the sociodemographic circumstances of their development—older mothers, accessible, new reproductive technologies, the "background rate" of "birth defects" in all populations—may be harder to spot. This theme was brought home to me in the words of an African-American nonprofit education administrator who was also a single mother. Much of our conversation concerned the benefits and burdens of being on one's own as a professional and a mother. Yet when I used the language of "choice" to her, Doris Paul immediately responded, "'Choices, choices.' 'Decisions, decisions' would be more like it. Because we're always called to crossroads and tests, they aren't things we seek, they're situations that befall us. And we go on, just the same."

Her reminder of the matrix within which individuals find themselves confronting decisions is apt, for it turns down the volume on individual volition, beckoning us to also attend to the structured situations over which individuals have very little control, but within which they regularly operate and compose their lives. This message was likewise echoed by a medical professional who wrote about her experiences with abortion after early prenatal diagnosis. For Rose Green (a pseudonym), the "choice" masked the non-choice of having produced an unhealthy child (Green 1992).

It is this second theme of "having produced an unhealthy child" against all odds and desires that also bears discussion. When I spoke with her a few weeks after she had terminated a pregnancy upon learning that her fetus had Down syndrome, one white lawyer quoted a recent popular book on pregnancy loss which includes a chapter on abortions after prenatal diagnosis: "The father was speaking of a double whammy of grief [in Kohn and Moffit 1993]. That's right. First you've produced this defective child, then you've gone on to have a devastating abortion. Who could possibly understand?" And others went on to speculate about the meaning of making a fetus that couldn't live, or couldn't live normally, especially when the diagnosis included mental retardation, a profound dilemma for the many constituencies who value normal intelligence:

I feel pity for my husband. All he can think about, the thing that torments him is: He's smart. I'm smart. The other kids are smart. How could this have happened to one of our children? (Donna deAngelo, 38, white homemaker)

After this, I really understood adoption much better. Because it can't be predicted how your child will be from getting your genes. And you don't need your kids to be genetic copies, they might be unlike you anyway. After all, there we were, two perfectly accomplished, intelligent, competent adults. And we'd made a baby who could never grow into those things we most valued. For some, I know it's guilt. For me, it was astonishment. And overwhelming grief. (Pat Gordon, 37, white college professor)

And there was anguish expressed at having produced the "wrong" child, a theme which reappears in chapter 10. For example, Fran Goodman, 34, white nonprofit community organizer, said, "I always wonder when people hear (that we aborted a fetus with Down syndrome), there's still this thing like, 'Can't you have a healthy baby?' There's just a little piece of me which thinks they're wondering."

Diana Morel, a young Puerto Rican secretary, suffered a doubly devastating loss: First, she experienced the stillbirth of her first child from spina bifida, closely followed by an abortion when her next pregnancy was revealed on sonogram to be carrying a fetus with Epstein syndrome, a rare and inevitably fatal heart insufficiency. Yet she spoke to almost no one about her disorientation, grief and depression: "I'm ashamed. I'm ashamed that they'll blame me for the damages I made."

Taking Responsibility

The grief accompanying an abortion following prenatal diagnosis is thus multilayered. It condenses the pain of all pregnancy loss; the frightening fantasies accompanying the knowledge (but not the mediating and potentially resolvable phenomenological experiences) that one has reproduced in an unhealthy or otherwise problematic way; and the sense of responsibility attendant upon choosing to end a pregnancy which had been deeply desired.

It is this last point—the desire for a pregnancy that one is also ending—which haunts many of the narratives I collected:

Oh, I was so all right with that child, it was just me and that baby, I didn't want anything else. I was so contented that fall. Then, in one minute, it all turned around. I heard the doctor's voice, and the baby disappeared. Even though it was still kicking. And I was numb, I was a zombie. And I haven't recovered yet. (Nancy Tucker, 36, white college professor)

I spent five months doing everything right, nurturing that baby, eating right, trying to slow down and take good care of myself. Not one drop of alcohol. And on the night we found out, I wanted nothing but sleeping pills. Me who had never once taken a sleeping pill in my life!

"I can't stand the kicking." I remember crying that to Shelley (the obstetrician) when I asked for a prescription. "Have a drink, it will put the fetus to sleep," she told me. "A drink!" I said in horror. "I can't drink, I'm pregnant!" (Pat Gordon, 36, white college professor)

It was hard, it was just too hard. Because I really, really wanted that baby. I try not to think about it now, to maintain a positive attitude about the next one. If I think about it, I'll just start crying all over again. Because I really, really wanted that baby. (Carolyn Williams, 36, African-American postal worker)

Few studies assess the impact of receiving a positive diagnosis. Those that exist describe great grief and personal and interpersonal stress accompanying the experience (e.g., Black 1984, 1994; Blumberg, Golbus et al. 1975; Furlong and Black 1984; Kenyon, Hackett et al. 1988; Kolker and Burke 1993, 1994). This disorienting pain and intimate upheaval are particularly pronounced in the case of women who have received ambiguous diagnoses.

In some sense, of course, all diagnoses are ambiguous: No matter how clear-cut or relatively common a diagnosis is, one always can fantasize that the test was wrong or mislabeled; one can believe that *this* potentially fatal heart defect or *this* case of mental retardation will be outgrown. A few of the women I interviewed took the potential variability of their fetus's condition very seriously, undertaking what I have come to think of as social research to better comprehend the range of difficulties assocated with the diagnosis. Of the fifty women receiving positive diagnoses whom I interviewed, five reached beyond medical experts to learn about the family and community lives of children with the conditions they knew their fetuses to have. In these cases, the women found obstetricians and genetic counselors compassionate toward their dilemma, but fundamentally unprepared to assist in a social, rather than a medical, assessment of the situation. Several commented that they had volunteered or been recruited to act as "peer counselors" after the genetics team learned about the decision-making work they had undertaken. Like Pat Carlson (chapter 7), who visited a neighborhood home for retarded adults before deciding to keep her Down syndrome pregnancy, such women moved beyond the medical network, where a richer picture of life with a disabled child can be gleaned. Jane Butler, for example, asked the genetic counselors to find her a parents support group for parents of children with Down syndrome (her fetal diagnosis). She and her husband visited one classroom and spent an hour with a family:

I talked with this couple who had a kid with Down's, and I thought they were terrific. The kid was nice, and they seemed like a fine family. But they'd been married almost twenty years when it happened, had raised three other kids, and were confident of their commitments. Stu and I have only been together for two years, and it's our first baby, and what if the strain were too great? What if we never got the chance to have a normal kid? What if we broke up over it? (Jane Butler, 35, white secretary)

She thus contextualized the differences in marriage and family life which led to her abortion decision. And she and her husband felt satisfied that they had "done their best."

Margaret Thompson's fetus was diagnosed as having a neural tube defect biochemically, but the lesion could not be located on initial sonograms. She carried the fetus for a month, visiting schools and clinics where children with spina bifida received services. She found the nurses, teachers, and mothers "very upbeat," but she was also overwhelmed by the amount of work and the medical crises which punctuated the daily lives of the children and their families. "I really wanted her [the nurse] to tell me not to have the child, but she couldn't do that. She made it quite clear that it would be a full-time job, and not easy, but very rewarding, that this child would accomplish a lot." When the lesion became visible many weeks later, she and her husband chose to end the pregnancy:

The thing that stood out in my mind the most when I saw that second sonogram where it didn't look like there was anything wrong was, I remember seeing his little penis—it just tickled me, it was so tiny and so straight up. [Later, when the spina bifida was visible], [k]nowing that my child could never have sex, and he'd never be able to have an erection, which was pretty clear once we saw where the injury was to his spine, well . . . that did me in, more than anything else. (Margaret Thompson, 34, white psychologist)

Conscientious research and familiarity with services were not sufficient to balance the sense of grief and loss she and her husband assigned to the imagined future their fetus would have.

Some women must cope with not only the existential dilemmas entailed by any prenatal diagnosis, but the problems inherent to an ambiguous diagnosis. Some conditions are so rare as to be interpretable only through "guesstimate" from the viewpoint of biomedical experts; others have potentially variable consequences—some acceptable, and some unacceptable—to the pregnant woman and her supporters. Under these circumstances, decision-making may be protracted, as pregnant women visit additional experts, undergo additional tests, and live with additional stress. Marie Mancini's fetus, for example, was diagnosed with satellites (additional, patterned genetic material on the ends of chromosomes) in a configuration so rare that the geneticist supervising her case at a major research center could locate only fifteen other clinical reports of the same condition. She tried to follow the outcomes of those fifteen, which were highly variable, and included both "normals" and infants who were profoundly neurologically impaired. Her abortion decision was made in part because there was so little medical information, and even the "normals" in the literature had been followed only through infancy. Jamie Steiner, a white health educator who chose to have amniocentesis at the age of 33, received a doubly ambiguous diagnosis: A sonogram revealed a large fetal oomphalocele, a midline closure defect, in which gut organs protrude and abdominal muscle is missing. The chromosome study also revealed satellites. The geneticists were hesitant to link the two problems, one of which might well be correctable by neonatal surgery, but with unknown success rates, the other of which might or might not have clinical consequences.

> The whole time they were doing more sonograms, checking the chromosomes, confirming their diagnosis, that whole time I kept thinking, "I'll keep the baby, I'll go to the hospital, I'll nurse right there. Who knows, in a year, two years, this baby might get better." I just kept romancing that, wanting to believe that I could be that kind of mother.

Alternating between hope and despair, with no definitive biomedical pronouncement of the seriousness of either condition, Jamie and her husband took a month to make their decision to abort. Likewise, white artist Sybil Wootenberg took a month to undergo extensive sonogram studies and to visit the neonatal surgery unit at Elite Hospital in another state, after her fetus was diagnosed with an oomphalocele. She consulted everyone—including her family pastor, a couple whose child had had an experimental oomphalocele repair, and the local feminist medical anthropologist—before deciding to abort. "I want to be a mother, I really do. But I'm 41, on a second marriage, it isn't all that I want. My mother died in her forties. There's got to be more to life than this!" After she finally ended the pregnancy, I asked Sybil how she had tolerated a month's delay in reaching a decision while the fetus kept growing and kicking. She said: "Maybe it's sick, but having all those sonograms, consulting with all those doctors, having this big problem on my hands—it made me into an interesting case. And it kind of replaced the baby. If I was losing the baby, at least I was becoming an interesting case." Here, expert interpretation of the technological inscription and reinscription of a fetus provided some of the benefits of "specialness" which she had felt as a pregnant woman. A technological substitution thus masked some of the pain, inventing a new biomedical status for pregnancy loss.

The Burdens of Knowledge

Sometimes, diagnosed conditions are inherently slippery from a social or cultural perspective. This is surely the case with sex chromosome anomalies, a collection of atypical diagnoses involving too many or too few sex chromosomes. People born with such conditions may well never be diagnosed, as their appearance may fall within the range that they and their peers code as "normal"; their only presenting "problem" may be infertility due to un- or underdeveloped reproductive organs (either visible or invisible). Some sex chromosome anomalies may not even have been coded as "biomedical problems" until relatively recently. For example, one genetic counselor told me that the first time she encountered XYY chromosomes was in the karyotyping of a doctor at the hospital where she worked. After a prolonged period of infertility in his marriage, the doctor had sent both his own and his wife's blood samples for chromosome analysis. The condition had obviously not affected anything else in his life sufficiently to require this clinician to seek biomedical help. Men with small penises or no sperm in their ejaculate also *may* have such chromosomal conditions and never know about them. But the range of syndromes accompanying sex chromosome anomalies is wide, and includes substantial risk of learning disabilities, mild mental retardation, growth and stature anomalies, and in the case of Turner's syndrome (XO, a female with a missing X chromosome), atypical neck, fingers, and possible heart problems. Additionally, men with extra Y chromosomes (XYY) were thought in the 1970s to be at risk for antisocial, violent, or even homicidal behavior. While such an interpretation has long been ruled scientifically spurious (Duster 1990; Green 1985; Hook 1973), it has had a lurid half-life in popular media and fantasy. And when genetic counselors describe sex chromosome anomalies as part of the range of potential findings in amniocentesis, it is not uncommon for couples to ask if these conditions are related to homosexuality, as I indicated in chapter 4. Widespread phobias and fantasies thus intensify the meanings attached to the interpretation of sex chromosome problems.

Throughout previous chapters, I have narrated several stories of those receiving sex chromosome anomalous diagnoses; some women chose to end their pregnancies, while others continued them. About half of the women receiving this diagnosis continue their pregnancies, according to New York counselors (cf. Petrucelli, Walker et al. 1998; Robinson, Bender et al. 1989). In my interviews with women or couples who had received such diagnoses, I was struck by the burden of knowledge: All of them wondered whether they could bear to raise a child with a "hidden" problem that would unfold in adolescence, about which the child would initially know nothing but the parents would be informed.

> Would he blame us for this, blame us for knowing? (Rosaria Lugones, 29, Colombian homemaker)

> I thought to myself, if you didn't know these things that would be one thing, but knowing this, how would this child feel, knowing that you knew? My husband was very clear; he's a man, and he started explaining psychology to me. It's rougher on boys. . . . The kid will be teased to death because boys are more . . . Ending up as a male with a small penis and sterile, it was hard to sort it out, about the kid feeling so bad. If he ended up mentally retarded, my husband would be furious, but *he* might not mind. But if he ended up normal, *he'd* be so furious, "How could you have let this happen to me?" There was no good answer. (Sylvia Lin, 43, Japanese-American special-education teacher)

The burden of knowledge forced potential parents to articulate their own submerged values as they debated their fetuses' futures. One genetic counselor, for example, encountered two patients who chose to abort a fetus after learning that its status included XXY sex chromosomes (Klinefelter's syndrome). One professional couple told her, "If he can't grow up to have a shot at becoming the president, we don't want him." A low-income family said of the same condition, "A baby will have to face so many problems in this world, it isn't fair to add this one to the burdens he'll have." And a young lawyer who very much supported his wife's decision to end a pregnancy in which Klinefelter's had been diagnosed mused about his own parenting skills:

> So he would have had this sex chromosome thing, he might have been slow, and he was going to be aggressive. I didn't know how to handle a kid like that. When he got rowdy and difficult, could I be a committed parent, or would I have thrown up my hands, thinking, "It's in his

genes"? [Author: What if you hadn't known through prenatal diagnosis?] I'm sure if it had just happened we would have handled it. But once you know, you're forced to make a choice. (David Kass, 35, white lawyer)

Diagnoses may be socially as well as biomedically ambiguous. I was present at Genetics Rounds one Thursday at Middle Hospital when a case of fetal chromosome breakage was presented. In this instance, a high percentage of broken chromosomes (present in thirteen out of thirty-three cells examined) were found in one sample; such a finding might indicate a rare underlying genetic syndrome including, in the worst cases, fatal anemias. But it might also well indicate that a transient infection had broken the chromosomes; once the infection passed, the next sample should reveal a growing percentage of unbroken chromosomes. In that case, the fetus might well be normal. The staff discussed the case extensively, understanding that a pregnant woman might be panicked by such an anomalous situation, and abort because she could not know what the outcome was going to be. They therefore decided to recommend a second amnio, in the hopes that it would lend weight to the "transient infection" hypothesis. They also considered and set up a more experimental (and hence, riskier) procedure, PUBS (percutaneous umbilical blood sampling), which would draw fetal umbilical cord blood directly, in the hopes of securing a faster and more definitive diagnosis for the mother, who was already eighteen weeks pregnant. They set in motion the cumbersome bureaucracy, both at the pregnant women's HMO and at Middle, to get rapid approval for the procedure. They additionally recommended high-resolution sonography, and a karyotyping of a maternal blood sample, to rule out other less likely anomalies that might be responsible for the breakage.

With these multiple strategies in mind to preserve the pregnancy in the face of an ambiguous diagnosis, Rena Coron, a 43-year-old social worker from a Dominican background, was called in. She had already spoken once with a genetic counselor, and knew that there was something anomalous in her fetal results. I was present at the counseling session, and spoke with Rena many times over the course of the next several weeks. The initial counseling session was dramatic. After the head geneticist had gone over the findings and offered both a second amniocentesis and PUBS, Rena erupted in consternation and anger:

I cannot wait emotionally another ten days to see if I can look at kid things and maternity clothes, or see if I am considering abortion. I'm a single mother, I've got a 14-year-old son, I'm a professional. I have to let my job know right away if I am taking maternity leave or not. I simply cannot wait.

Various members of the genetics team tried to bring the conversation back to the possibility of a normal, or near-normal outcome, encouraging Rena to have both an additional amniocentesis and high resolution sonogram that very day. But she interrupted their medical discussion once again, saying, "My fiancé had another woman who got pregnant for him, and the fetus died during labor. What is 'fetal distress'? Is this in any way related?" Trying to reassure her that "fetal distress" was a broad-spectrum label, and not a genetic diagnosis per se, the team explained PUBS, hoping that even a high-risk procedure would be more appealing than an automatic fetal death. But Rena went on:

> I must be honest with you. If, after the sonogram, I choose to end this pregnancy, are you saying you will still want to study the fetus? I was very excited about this pregnancy, I really wanted this baby. But I'm 43, I'm reconsidering. I'm not sure that pregnancy is really the direction in which I want to go. I work with learning disabled; with emotionally disabled, this is taking its toll. . . . My fiancé and I are pulling apart; we may well not be together by the time this situation is resolved.

At this point, the chief geneticist interrupted the consultation, ostensibly to consult with the radiologist about the impending sonogram. But he asked the head genetic counselor and me to accompany him. In the hall, he organized an emergency meeting, saying, "I do not think this woman wants to continue this pregnancy at all. Things have changed in her life, the boyfriend is easing out of the picture. She has a right to end it if she wants to. Aren't we imposing our values on her, keeping her pregnant for longer and longer, to study a case?" Our "team" was thrown into consternation; counseling needs for the woman clearly superseded fetal diagnosis. After a few minutes, we reentered the room, repeating that the sonography team was ready to examine the fetus if she wanted. But we added that she might like a few minutes in a quieter location to consider the stressful "facts of the case." Alone with me and one counselor, Rena was quite explicit:

> I've prayed over this case. I'm a strong person, I've gotten through other difficulties, I'll get through this one. My relationship with my

fiancé is going downhill. The more I tell him, the less he responds. This may lead to a parting of the ways. My son really wants this baby; he's going to be miserable. But I have decided to end it. Here and now.

The counselor took a deep breath, abandoning chromosomes in favor of abortions, and started to describe the possible procedures. For several weeks, I called Rena back, inquiring about her abortion experience, her recovery, her support system. I learned a great deal about her mother, son, and women friends, and a bit about her (by now ex-) boyfriend. What I never learned was the salience of broken chromosomes: The ambiguous diagnosis, so central to the work of a conscientious genetics team dedicated to setting up cutting-edge services to diagnose Rena's fetus, had receded into the mists. It had kicked off a decision-making process in which social ambiguity—of appearance, professional commitments, and, above all, the status of a love affair—far exceeded the weight of genetic material.

Late Abortions

However clear-cut or ambiguous a positive diagnosis may be, the circumstances of late abortion are always difficult. In the United States, 89 percent of abortions occur in the first trimester; only 6 percent occur between the thirteenth and fifteenth weeks of pregnancy, and only 5 percent after the sixteenth week, including virtually all amniocentesis-related abortions (Epner et al. 1998; Koonin, Smith et al. 1996). The larger share of second trimester abortions are performed on teenagers, young women without adequate social and financial support, or women with extremely irregular menstrual cycles who didn't gauge the onset of pregnancy correctly. For these women, the grueling process of ending an unwanted pregnancy between its fourteenth and twenty-fourth weeks (the legal limit for termination in the state of New York) brings unambivalent relief, even if the abortion procedure is difficult. But for the women receiving positive diagnoses through prenatal technology on wanted pregnancies, the situation is different. They describe their abortions with great ambivalence, often contrasting themselves with the teenagers and other "misfit mothers" they are likely to meet in the hospitals and abortion clinics where their terminations are performed.

This distinction between "good mothers in bad situations" and "girls unfit to be mothers," that is, between "good aborters" and "bad aborters," was one I initially resisted. As a longtime reproductive rights activist and someone who had done volunteer abortion counseling during the period directly before and during its legalization, I knew that an abortion decision is always a complex matter. Yet I was forced to recognize the *cultural* judgment that many women with positive diagnoses make about their own circumstances: They considered themselves to be appropriate mothers, and therefore, tragically, appropriate aborters. While they often expressed compassion for teenage girls "in trouble," they did not want to be identified with them in any social sense:

> These girls, they just don't want their babies. And it's a good thing; What kind of mothers would they make, anyway? They're here for a second, maybe a third, abortion. They can't be worried to do the right thing. Later, maybe later they'll understand. But it's just craziness for us, being put into a cattle car with them. It's a real mill, and what makes it worse is, the rest of them just don't want their babies. (Marilyn de Soto, 34, Puerto Rican social worker)

> You know, I was the biggest one there. You could really see my stomach, and I kept saying to myself, I'm not just here having an abortion, I'm here taking out a child that needs to be taken out because of a reason. Some of the women, the girls, they're just there to take it out because they don't want it. It was hurting me more, and I was like, I was sure it was because that's something beautiful to me, having the baby, that's why I'm crying over it. (Iris Lauria, 29, Puerto Rican hospital housekeeper)

> This was something I had to do. For these girls, it was just a lousy method of birth control. (Doris Paul, 43, African-American nonprofit education administrator)

> And what stands out in my mind is that there was this very young, beautiful teenager, a young Asian girl, and while I was resting, you know, recuperating, waiting to go downstairs, she got up from the cot and stepped on the scale, you know, to see if she'd lost any weight. I just about died. I felt so bad for her, Oh, Jesus! I just felt bad like, she'd missed the whole point. Maybe she's lucky to have been, you know, so stupid. But it's a fucking tragedy to be so stupid about something so valuable. (Margaret Thompson, 34, white psychologist)

Satisfaction or dissatisfaction with delivery of abortion services—on maternity wards or in clinics (often referred to as "mills")—were tied closely to the care women received: Some found the nursing "fantastic," "compassionate," or even "very important—like, they made it clear this was a tragedy, I wasn't having a baby, even though I was on the maternity ward. I'll never forget them for that" (Nancy Tucker, 36, white college professor).

Others were appalled by the negative judgments of nurses who hadn't read their charts and therefore assumed they were being "irresponsible" to have waited so long to abort; or nurses who made their personal disapproval of abortion in general known. Some doctors were praised for their compassionate and professional manners: One obstetrician/gynecologist used by several of the women I interviewed reaped especially high praise because he called at home frequently after the disturbing results were forwarded to him, and after the abortion. He was explicit in his symbolic dissociation from the abortion procedure, sending his patients to a "real pro" who "only did abortions," so that he himself could continue to "only bring life into the world."

This physician's words alert us to the symbolic issues involved in late abortion after prenatal diagnosis: Many women wanted a clear-cut boundary established between pregnancy-leading-to-life and pregnancy-leading-to-death. While some decried "impersonal" or "anonymous" doctors, two women who had received private abortions at Elite and Middle Hospitals appreciated the good care but wished they had attended a "mill." There, they reasoned, the reality of making the pregnancy "really gone" or "a faceless mistake" would have been clearer, unlinked from "regular" pregnancy care. Moreover, laboring to give birth to death, when a woman wanted to be birthing a healthy baby, was a situation described again and again throughout these interviews. The symbolic dimension was also brought home to me in the complaint of Doris Paul, whose longtime HMO obstetrician/gynecologist personally performed her late abortion. Instead of feeling well-attended, Doris protested the confusion she felt about breached boundaries: "He delivered my daughter. I mean, how can he do both things, deliver Liza one year, and kill it [the fetus] the next? It was confusing. After that, I didn't want him to be my doctor anymore. I actually changed to the nurse practitioners at the HMO."

This conflation of labor with abortion is material as well as symbolic, as it reflects a common experience, depending in large measure on the method of termination used. There are three basic methods for terminating second-trimester pregnancies; two require the woman to go through active labor to deliver the fetus. Traditionally, an installation procedure requires the transabdominal injection of either saline or urea directly into the uterus. These substances cause the placenta to separate, killing the fetus, which (eventually) brings on labor. To hasten labor with installation procedures, or as a substitute for them, hormonal (prostaglandin) vaginal suppositories are used in the majority of late abortions. The timing and intensity of labor are easier to control with prostaglandin, but it often produces side effects like fever, chills, nausea, and diarrhea. Prostaglandin-induced labor without transabdominal installation is safer for the laboring woman, as it removes the slight but potentially fatal risk associated with shooting lethal chemicals directly into her abdominal cavity, if the uterus is missed. But in addition to the potential side effects, prostaglandin-induced abortions include a 5 percent risk that the fetus will be born alive. In either case, and usually (but not always!) with pain medication, women labor on average ten hours to deliver a dead fetus. The third method of late abortion, less widely available in the United States (but quite available in New York City, depending on a woman's health care provider services) is the D&E (dilation and evacuation). It is safer for the pregnant woman, but requires much more active work on the part of the physician and her or his operating team of anesthesiologist and nurses. Prior to the procedure, the woman has laminaria—thin sticks of specially prepared seaweed—inserted into her cervix. As they absorb moisture, the cervix is dilated. This causes cramps which may range from mild to extremely severe. Twenty-four hours later, while the woman is under general anesthetic or heavy sedation, the fetus is removed surgically in an operation lasting from fifteen to forty-five minutes. Recovery is usually rapid, and there are few complications.

While I have described these procedures in medical and objectifying language, all carry a heavy load of physical and emotional suffering for the women involved; D&Es are also described as unsettling for some of the health care providers who perform them. As both a researcher who directly collected fifty late abortion stories, and heard countless more from counselors, and as a woman who has endured this experience, I have a strong bias in favor of D&Es. They are over more quickly, and do not involve the physical and emotional toll of labor. But the fetus is usually dismembered, a fact which was problematic for some women and their supporters. Several worried about the exact moment at which their fetus died, and whether it felt pain. And one Orthodox Jewish woman who aborted after a sonogram diagnosis of anencephaly told me she found the description of the D&E too stressful, choosing labor induction instead: "What decided my mind was no remains. I needed to take home the baby, even in a coffin, to bury it properly. I couldn't live with the idea of no remains, no one to visit in the cemetery" (Tamara Levkovitz, 34, white private school teacher).

But several women who were given no option to going through labor to deliver a dead fetus railed bitterly against their service providers for not giving them a "quicker way out." Despite their safety and "relative" ease, D&E

procedures are sometimes rejected by physicians, for they require additional training and active intervention from the medical staff, who may object to the grueling work, or suffer OR burnout.[42] Moreover, labor-induction procedures require little work on the part of the physician, who need only be present to administer the initial drugs; after that, the doctor can depart, leaving the nurses completely in charge of highly variable labors. Differences of status and skill in the medical hierarchy may thus influence the available procedures. Moreover, a dismembered fetus is harder to study for pathology; some doctors thus suggest that their patients choose labor-induction abortions in order to better preserve fetal tissue as a "contribution to science." But many women resented the punitive nature of laboring to bring forth death when other alternatives were possible. Once again, the message is simple to interpret: There is no good way to exit the bad script of late abortion.

Fetal Remains

And for those who choose (or are given only the option of) labor-induction abortions, a relationship to the external fetus (as opposed to the internal fetus) must be worked through. After delivery, women and their partners may choose to see or not to see, to hold or not to hold. Some, like Tamara Levkovitz, may want to bury, but this raises a complex political issue which I will describe below. In my research, those who chose to hold or examine the fetus described many feelings: grief, pity, admiration for miniature but visibly normal features of babies whose abnormalities they may have feared and had certainly rejected.

> I never decided, but when he took the baby out, I immediately said, "Can I see it?" And he was a little doll, seven, eight inches long, perfectly formed, a little tiny baby doll. He was beet red, and I couldn't see anything wrong but the nurse knew, she came forward, she showed me where the signs of Down syndrome were. And then the doctor stepped in and he showed me, too. And I think they did it well, so I could be at peace with the little doll of a baby, so I would never think that just because he looked so well-formed, I'd never think there had been a mistake. (Meeta Cabron, 39, Nicaraguan photographer)

> They wrapped her up so I wouldn't have to see the head [where a portion of the skull and brain were missing], and she didn't look so deformed, she just looked beautiful. And peaceful. (Tamara Levkovitz, 34, white private school teacher)

> They [the nurses] were great, only I didn't want that little baby whisked away so fast. God, it was so small, such a tiny baby, such a great loss. I started weeping immediately. (Johanna Gertz, 36, white community organizer)

A few women who chose not to hold their dead fetuses later expressed regrets.

The remains of fetuses are a highly political matter (cf. Casper 1994a, 1998). In New York State, aborted tissue must be checked by the hospital's pathology department. This regulation has medical utility, enabling diagnoses to be made or confirmed and monitoring abortion services. But it is also a symbolic statement claiming political turf in the abortion controversy at the state and city levels: Here, fetuses are not babies, they do not receive birth certificates or death certificates below twenty-four weeks, the legal limit to abortion and a few weeks short of what is now considered "viability."[43] While such regulations keep right-to-life movement activists at bay, they make retrieval of fetal remains for cremation or burial a daunting, usually impossible, task. Several women mentioned how distressed they were by sending the fetus to pathology:

> When the doctor took a tissue sampling I asked him why, and he said, "To send to pathology to confirm the diagnosis." And I started howling, I was just screaming my head off: "If there's anything that even possibly needs confirming, what am I doing here?" (Michelle Kansky, 38, white public school teacher)

Several women, including Tamara Levkovitz, managed to circumvent those regulations, retrieving their dead fetuses for burial, usually with the help of sympathetic obstetricians. But others had to find symbolic alternatives. One described burying ultrasound images of the fetus, and another told this story in her letter to me:

> We baptized our little son in the delivery room. We put the sonogram picture in the family Bible. No one can tell us we did the wrong thing, no matter how much they don't believe in abortion. He's gone now. But he *was* real. And abortion is real, and sometimes necessary. (Lena Jarowlski, 36, white homemaker)

The reality of family mourning, the demands of ceremonial closure, the rituals of transition so salient to intergenerational connection, all require what biomedicine cannot here provide: A material anchor with which to locate and condense the end of a desired pregnancy.

The Calendar of Grief

The grief and mourning which come with the territory of what is so antiseptically labeled "selective abortion" require more than ritual closure: They also require time. The particular work of mourning a desired pregnancy which one has chosen to end shares much with other forms of pregnancy loss, like miscarriage, stillbirth, and neonatal death. Its markers thus include the secret calendar of failed anniversaries: Due dates, the date on which a woman first learned she was pregnant, the celebrations that never got to happen are all present in the stories women told:

> Rosh Hashonah was my due date, so I was wondering, "Will I be home for the holidays, will I go to Schul, or will I be in hospital?" And then, after this, I was totally disoriented when the holidays came around. I didn't understand where I was supposed to be. . . . Sometimes, when I go to the cemetery, I take Shera [her daughter] with me, as a comfort blanket. Now I'm waiting until I can put up a permanent stone [in the Jewish calendar, one year after a death]. Maybe then, I won't need her to come with me anymore. (Tamara Levkovitz, 34, white private school teacher)

> One of my best friends was pregnant, due two days after me, and we had such great fantasies of pushing strollers together, raising them as friends from birth. When I ended my pregnancy, I spent a lot of time working it through, so I could welcome her baby, whose birthday would always, forever, not be my baby's birthday. (Pat Gordon, 37, white college professor)

The calendar of grief may extend across a whole social generation. Genetic counselors at Middle showed me an eloquent letter they received from a woman whose son was born with multiple congenital anomalies more than a decade earlier and died two hours after birth. At the time, the mother was so distraught that she could not bring herself to hold the baby, whose appearance she found frightening. Thirteen years later, she wrote to ask whether the genetics team still had the photographs that were taken as part of the pathology report. As a Jewish mother, she felt the need for closure at the season in which her anomalous non-son would have made his bar mitzvah and been accepted into her religious community as a young adult.

And mourning is quite embodied: Many women recalled the discomfort—indeed, pain—when their milk came in, preparing them to nourish the baby they didn't have. "It was like such an insult, those rock-hard breasts, like pouring salt on the wound," said Megan Johnson, 41, white writer.

Others recalled how they obsessed about the return of their menstrual cycles, wanting to reclaim their nonpregnant bodies. Many needed cyclical markers to try to imagine or establish another pregnancy, a subject that became an obsession for some women:

Now I'm on hold; I'm just waiting for the next period, the next pregnancy. Only he [husband] wants me to get my tubes tied. I need to complete this, he needs to end it. So we fight a lot. (Marilyn de Soto, 34, Puerto Rican social worker)

I'm selfish: Having and raising babies is the center of my life. All the great moral and ethical moments come to you, they shoot right out at you, as you watch a child unfold. This one was unfinished ethical business. I needed to replace it, to finish the cycle. (Leah Rubinstein, 39, white homemaker)

Unfinished business, that's what it is. I try to maintain a positive attitude, but it's just unfinished business. Maybe I'll be better once I'm pregnant. Again. (Nancy Tucker, 36, white college professor)

Some women interviewed after a subsequent pregnancy recalled the fear attendant upon waiting for a "healthy" outcome:

I was just on automatic pilot. Like I knew too much to be happy no matter what the tests said. I knew that something could always go wrong. And at the birth, Shelley flipped the baby over the screen, she said, "Look, Pat, ten fingers, ten toes. Now you can relax. Go to sleep." And I did. (Pat Gordon, 37, white college professor)

We just ate up the telephone lines, me and Hannah [a woman who had experienced a stillbirth]. No use talking to Paul, he couldn't get it, how panicked I was. Once the amnio was clear, I guess I expected that second baby to die during labor. Like there was no end point to worrying. I only started believing she was alive about two weeks into nursing. (Lorelei Kruger, 36, white homemaker)

Other women used the return of their menstruation as evidence that they were definitively done with childbearing: "When I finally got my period, I told Denny, I said, 'Let's have a garage sale.' And we did, we sold it all: The crib, the maternity clothes, the stroller, everything. We conceived it with our hearts, not our heads. And now, it's over" (Donna deAngelo, 38, white homemaker).

Becoming Un-Pregnant

Recovering from the late abortion of a fetus which was desired until a positive diagnosis transformed its status into undesirable entails the work of mourning with a double twist. Women poignantly described the difficulties of becoming an un-mother of a specific baby, a rather different process than simply becoming nonpregnant:

Friends kept telling me I was lucky to be free of such a difficult pregnancy. But you see, I had never planned to be free again in my life. I was planning to be a mother, not a free woman. It's a death. I had a little baby; it was alive, it was kicking, now it's gone. (Megan Johnson, 41, white writer)

I just didn't want her to disappear, she was my baby. It's dumb that knowing the sex of that baby really did me in, but it really did. I have a wonderful son, it isn't that, but somehow, I wanted a girl so badly. But I wanted a healthy child even more. (Marilyn de Soto, 34, Puerto Rican social worker)

Even though I have four healthy kids, and my youngest was there, delicious, playing superman, when I came home from the hospital, at that minute it didn't make a bit of difference. It was this one, *this* one I wanted. And I cried, and I mourned. (Leah Rubinstein, 39, white homemaker)

When I asked Doris Paul, eighteen months after her abortion following the diagnosis of Down syndrome, if she considered herself healed, she replied, "Never healed. No such thing."

Women also described a range of feelings concerning their responsibility for the death of a desired fetus. While some stressed an achieved understanding of responsibility described above in the discussion of abortions (like Green 1992), others felt guilt.

> I can't help thinking I brought this on myself. First I made the damaged babies, then I killed them. (Diana Morel, 28, Puerto Rican secretary)

> I keep asking, why did God do this to me, give me this terrible thing, allow me to kill it? I'm not a bad person, I know I'm not worse than the other ones having abortions. So why me? (Iris Lauria, 29, Puerto Rican hospital housekeeper)

Reactions like these were particularly likely to come from women from Catholic backgrounds, a finding I discuss below.

The problem of taking responsibility arose starkly for some women who—either voluntarily or without volition—immediately threw themselves back into work. I heard about this issue across the class spectrum, from professional lawyers and social workers, from freelance writers, secretaries, and hospital housekeepers. The return to work usually implied having a story of the pregnancy's end, a problematic issue in boundary maintenance. This problem of drawing a line between those who "deserved the truth," and those who "just needed to know I was hurting" was an issue that arose in all the interviews. It is deeply linked to attitudes about politics (most obviously, abortion politics) and religion. It is also linked to questions of social support and isolation. Both themes are discussed below. And it reflects the shift of "women's work" into the social service sector, where many jobs are highly public or visible. Many of the women I interviewed were teachers, social workers, secretaries, or hospital employees. They worked in busy offices and classrooms, where they encountered scores of colleagues and members of "the public" every day. In such circumstances, pregnancies are highly noticeable, and frequently discussed. So, then, are their unexpected endings. A story thus had to be constructed in which was condensed a statement about a dense range of issues: Individual attitudes toward disability, abortion, responsibility (or guilt?), and the relatively private or public nature of grief and mourning. Some women spoke openly about their diagnoses and abortions; others spoke only of a "loss." And most used a "mixed strategy" of elaborating the story for one circle of friends and relations, while giving less detail to a wider group:

So I took off two weeks, and they told my kids [in the classroom] that the baby came out too early and died. And that week, they showed a film about the Ethiopian famine, and one of the kids asked if they could buy a starving baby and give it to Mrs. Kansky. They had to be told something, you can see it really affected them. (Michelle Kansky, 38, white public school teacher)

I told my boss, and he told a few others, and they told the rest. Mostly, we just referred to my loss. I knew who knew. And I wanted them to know. But for months, the others, the others who didn't know, they kept asking me, "What'd you have, what'd you have?" It was hard having to keep saying that I lost the baby. (Marilyn de Soto, 34, Puerto Rican social worker)

One other problem involving boundary-keeping narratives also arose in women's stories of mourning and recovery. Women who had other children took them into account throughout the decision-making process and the termination of their pregnancies. Indeed, one of the strongest differences among those I interviewed occurred between women expecting (and thus losing) their first child, and those with children at home. Childless women tended to fantasize perfect babies; their loss included the loss of an imaginary experience of new motherhood. They thus mourned the loss of a romantic motherhood, along with the specific pregnancy. Women who had children were less romantic in imagining life with the child who would have resulted from the diagnosed pregnancy; they already knew the burdens of caring for perfectly ordinary, healthy offspring. The mothers recovered more rapidly from their grief, in part because they had child-centered responsibilities which kept them moored to the earth; they could rarely find the time to focus on their own pain.

Another Voice?

Their attentiveness to the needs and reactions of other children should be underlined: Too often, the politicization of abortion is inscribed in a discourse of individual "selfishness" (a theme elaborated for white women in chapter 6). But in the interviews I collected, women usually positioned their abortion decisions in relation to the way they imagined their intimate others would be affected. The most salient of these were their other children. Many expressed fear that a sick baby would absorb an unfair share of the family economy of love and time. Others were quite explicit about how having a disabled child would affect their families:

> When the decision came through I told my husband, I just said, "We cannot take the time. We're working parents, that's what we are. We'll never see Antonia again if we have to take care of this sick baby. We've got to end it, and end it now." (Iris Lauria, 29, Puerto Rican hospital housekeeper)

> Some people say that abortion is hate. I say my abortion was an act of love. I've got three kids. I was 43 when we accidentally got pregnant again. We decided there was enough love in our family to handle it, even though finances would be tight. But we also decided to have the test. A kid with a serious problem was more than we could handle. And when we got the bad news, I knew immediately what I had to do. At 43, you think about your own death. It would have been tough now, but think what would have happened to my other kids, especially my daughter. Oh, the boys, Tommy and Alex, would have done ok. But Laura would have been the one who got stuck. It's always the girls. It would have been me, and then, after I'm gone, it would have been the big sister who took care of that child. Saving Laura from that burden was an act of love. (Mary Fruticci, 44, white homemaker)

Such comments provide a healthy antidote to the discourse of "selfishness," substituting a more embedded sense of maternal responsibility and relationality in its place. But they also suggest that altruism toward other household members is the reason for the decision to end a diagnosed pregnancy. This important corrective then performs invisible work of its own, muffling cultural attitudes toward disability and the voluntary limits of maternity. But as we have seen throughout these chapters, standards for acceptable and unacceptable children, and the meaning of specific disabilities, are always culturally constructed. Though public support is strong for keeping abortion legal when "defective" or "damaged" fetuses are diagnosed, far less consensus exists on which disabilities are grounds for abortion (Drugan, Greb et al. 1990; Goldberg and Elder 1998). For some women and their supporters, the mental retardation accompanying chromosome trisomies is reason enough, while for others, physical stigmata are more upsetting, as indicated in chapter 5. In some times and places, infanticide or fostering is prescribed for babies born with socially inadmissible conditions;

in contemporary America, a medical procedure appears to offer a cutting edge in defining the limits of what women and their families are willing to accept. A discourse of "altruism" toward others thus masks an important discussion of whether, and under what conditions, women feel entitled to refuse specific pregnancies as a way to refuse specific disabilities in their children, and to refuse the surplus labors entailed in caring for them. At the same time, the possibility of positive effects—the acceptance of difference, the learning of compassion—which siblings of a disabled child might experience is never imagined. "Maternal altruism" thus papers over a terrain carved out by political demands for both reproductive rights and disability rights, even as it provides a more realistic portrait of the complexity with which many women approach an abortion decision.

In addition to including their other children in the constellation of decision-making factors, women also had to find appropriate ways to discuss the end of a pregnancy with them. Age-appropriate stories were constructed, with young children often being told some version of, "The baby was sick, and it died, and mommy went to the hospital to take it out." Older ones might be told more specifically what happened, such as, "We found out the baby was going to be retarded and might die from a heart problem. So the doctor helped us to end this pregnancy. Daddy and I are very sad, and we miss the baby. But its life would have been very difficult, and that would have made it hard for all of us."

In the small literature on the social impact of abortions after positive prenatal diagnoses, other researchers have commented on the "transient but real signs of distress" which the ending of the pregnancy—whether officially discussed or not—invoked in young children (Goldberg and Elder 1998; cf. from a child's perspective, Schrimshaw and March 1984). Conversations reported back to me included children's comments such as:

Mommy, what happened to your breasts? They're not so nice now. (3-year-old boy)

My son, now he takes his friends to his room, I hear him saying, "In this house, we are not happy, we are very sad. Because our baby was sick, and it died. And my mother had to get it taken out, and we all really, really wanted that baby. So we're sad." And he's 7. (Donna deAngelo, 38, white homemaker)

My little one only wants to know, "Will I catch that?" and I have to explain that it happens before you're even born, and no, she can't catch that at all. The big one is more concerned with me: She sees me crying, she wants me to stop crying—and to have another baby. (Carolyn Williams, 36, African-American postal worker)

Some parents are obviously more comfortable explaining their abortion or their grief than others. But all who had children felt the impact of their situation on them. As "Rose Green," who published her "letter to a genetic counselor" after choosing to end a Down syndrome pregnancy put it,

> I tell the children that the way I am acting now is normal, and that it *will* end (though sometimes I hardly believe it myself). When T says, "Mommy, I just hate it when you cry," I tell her I have ten thousand tears to cry about the baby, and I can cry them now, or I can cry them later, but they *have to be cried*. (Green 1992, 63)

Regimes of Truth

The work of mourning a voluntarily ended pregnancy may well include one other specific aspect: coping with the existential loss that accompanies entry into a "regime of scientific truth." Biomedicine offers "control" and "choice" at the individual level even as it normalizes outcomes, removing some unacceptable biological differences from the human community. Such normalization thus makes it both possible and plausible that some sectors of the population take partial responsibility for the genetic quality of their fetuses and children. This regime of scientific quality control is echoed throughout these interviews, as women regularly stumble over whether to call the ended pregnancy a "fetus" or a "baby." The first accords with a worldview in which genetic information leads to medical intervention to regularize the well-described and calibrated "products of conception." But in the second word, grief, desire, and human connection are more palpably present. Caught between the benefits of modern medicine and the emotions of pregnancy loss, many women cannot find a linguistic path, slipping back and forth between the two. When I queried this ambivalence of terms, one college professor answered, for example, "It just isn't clear." For her, the focus of loss was simultaneously a biomedical entity and a mourned child. Sometimes, women find themselves taken over and redescribed by the language of biomedicine under stress:

> So I was in labor for twenty-four hours and absolutely nothing happened. I mean nothing. A dead fetus, but it wouldn't come out. So I

called Dr. X at 8 a.m., and I guess I must have sounded crazy. "Hello," I said, "I'm a demised fetus and a failed prostaglandin. "Oh no you're not, honey," the nurse said. "You're a lady that's losing a baby, and you'd better stop talking and start crying." (Sandra Larkin, 36, white direct-mail consultant)

"Living by the numbers," "becoming a statistic" are fantasized in responses to genetic counseling (chapters 3 and 4) and actualized here: For many with whom I spoke, confusion and anger accompany the necessary choices imposed by submission to the benefits of technology:

We're lucky to have this technology even though we're unlucky that we had to use it. How did we get caught? (Michelle Kansky, 38, white public school teacher)

I'm so sick of being a statistic. How do you get meaning off of a statistic? (Doris Paul, 43, African-American nonprofit education administrator)

This anger at statistical "unluckiness" seems particularly dramatic in those few cases where the amniocentesis itself, rather than a positive diagnosis, led to a pregnancy loss. I was able to locate only two people whose miscarriages seemed to be linked to testing, that is, which followed directly upon complications like leaking, cramping, bleeding, and fevers, right after having amniocentesis. And I was able to interview one woman whose amniocentesis led to what I can only label an iatrogenically induced abortion: Continuous leakage after the tap produced an extremely rare complication in which the fetus continued to grow in a "dry" environment that could no longer support its development. After weeks of attempting to save the pregnancy via bed rest and fluid replacement, sonograms revealed total, life-threatening lung degeneration. Pamela Meinhardt, a 35-year-old white librarian, frantically sought medical consultations throughout the city, and only reluctantly ended her pregnancy when a geneticist gently convinced her that the situation was already hopeless. Later she told me, "I'm so angry at this technology for having gotten me into this position when I was hoping I could be a beneficiary of it." Committed now to "living by the numbers," Pamela told me she surely intended to use amniocentesis in her next pregnancy, despite the grievous loss it had caused in this one. After all, the risk of this having happened in the first place was less than one in four hundred (this is a number calculated from the rates of general amnio complications leading to miscarriages, and not based on any reported statistics for this particular rare event). Thus, she reasoned, the risk of having it happen twice was infinitesimal. And in all my interviewing, I never found a woman who had received a positive diagnosis who was willing to forgo testing in subsequent pregnancies. The "bottom line" for women from all social backgrounds who used the test was that it was better to know than not to know: "If the technology is there, it's better to use it. Better to live with the benefits of modern science, cry over your losses, but use every means science gives you to have a better life" (Michelle Kansky, 38, white public school teacher).

Learning to live inside of biomedicine may entail the loss not only of polysemic language possibilities, but of a concept of "fate," or the meaningfulness of being "chosen" to bear a particular problem for mysterious reasons. These strategies of explanation haunt memoirs of parenting ill and dying children, elevating familial suffering as a lens through which to view the entire human condition (Gunther 1949; Rogers 1956; Trautman 1984). The burden of "innocent suffering" can be reconfigured as a lesson in existential significance. This religious or philosophical quest for transcendental meanings is a subject on which biomedicine is, of course, silent.[44] As I indicated in chapters 5 and 6, religious discourse is richly connected to speculations concerning pregnancy in history, as well as in the present. Such connections are especially dense when discussing maternal/fetal pain, abortion, and death replacing birth. In looking at positive diagnosis, I was again struck by how quickly the women I interviewed turned to philosophy and religion in narrating their experiences with selective abortion and recovery. Often, they would describe convictions and confusions in explicitly religious or moral terminology long before the section of my interview schedule invited such considerations: The ethical standing of a disabled fetus was of enormous concern.

In one week of interviewing "positive diagnosis" cases, for example, the three women I encountered all began by framing their dilemmas in explicitly religious terms. Sylvia Lin opened our lunchtime conversation with a description of the Buddhist closure ceremony she had recently performed for her aborted fetus. A "returned" Buddhist from a thoroughly secular Japanese-American family, she had read about such ceremonies as a way to free mother and fetus from their linked cycle of rebirth: she therefore organized close friends to collectively enact one. Tamara Lefkowitz, daughter and sister of Orthodox rabbis, consulted three Jewish ethicists during and after the decision-making process which led to ending a pregnancy in which anencephaly had been diagnosed. "Without a brain, there is no question, you must do what you must to do," two of them told her. The third knew of one anencephalic child who had survived for several months in an institution on Long Island. "If it's going to live less than thirty days," he said, "it needn't count as a life. But one that survives for several months, in principle, that changes everything." Nonetheless, he also offered the opinion that she was free to end the pregnancy. Mulling over the range of rabbinical consultations, Tamara's mother offered an explicitly religious statement which echoed one I had heard from virtually all the Jewish women that I interviewed: "When God sends bad news, he also sends us the medical progress to cope." And when I arrived at the publishing office where Nivia Hostos worked as an administrative secretary, the first story she told me concerned her participation in a Project Rachel support group. Founded in the late 1980s under the auspices of Milwaukee's liberal Archbishop Rembert Weakland, Project Rachel now has chapters in all fifty states. While the groups remain embattled in national and international Catholic politics, bucking official doctrine and attitudes toward abortion as sin, grass-roots chapters offer a range of counseling, confessional, and support group services (Rubin 1992). Raised a devout Catholic and the mother of a child in parochial school, Nivia was guilt-racked by having chosen abortion after the prenatal diagnosis of Turner's syndrome. Nonetheless, she believed that she had made the right decision, and was optimistic that the group would help her to resolve her bad feelings.

Nivia's responses underlined a powerful thread which runs through the stories of women who abort wanted pregnancies after positive diagnoses: Catholic women do not use abortion services less than non-Catholic women. Indeed, national and regional surveys suggest that Catholic women obtain about 32 percent of all abortions in the United States, a figure somewhat higher than their representation in the population at large (Goldberg and Elder 1998; Henshaw and Kost 1996; Rubin 1992, 41). While they thus regularly fall into the population aborting after positive diagnosis, my strong impression is that they suffer more guilt and frame their suffering more explicitly in terms of sin and the need for absolution. Of the thirteen women interviewed for this chapter who identified themselves as Catholics, eight considered themselves to be practicing, and all spoke explicitly of the problem posed by the confessional. Two described elaborate journeys to churches they had never attended before abortion, in order to secure absolution from a truly anonymous priest. One, angry as well as pained, said of her abortion decision: "Let the pope stand in my shoes. That's what I told the father that confessed me, 'Let the pope just stand in my shoes. Then we'd see what he'd decide'" (Marie Mancini, 38, white high school teacher).

The other, quite philosophical, made a distinction between ideal values and the actual conditions of her personal history:

> I was raised to take what you get in life, any life you get. If I had stayed at home in Granville, if I hadn't gone to college, if I hadn't married Joe [who is Jewish], I'd still feel that way. I do feel that way. But even though I was brought up Catholic to believe abortion is murder, I also believe in a woman's right to choose. In people's right to choose. And that choice is a big part of me now, just as big as my religion. I'm not the same girl who went to Catholic school and thought that suffering would be redeemed. Now I'm suffering my own guilt. But it's in my own world, it's a bigger world, it includes more than just the sin of abortion. (Terry Hartz, 34, white homemaker and part-time bookkeeper)

In such statements, and in the projections of the Catholic women who used prenatal diagnosis without receiving bad news (chapter 6), we see a larger ethical self emerging, one which includes but is not entirely bounded by Catholic ethics. There is a precipitate of liberal, individualist Catholicism separating out of official doctrine: These women uphold a general ethical worldview which is deeply Catholic, and personally accept its emotional consequences. Nonetheless, they reserve the right (and accord it to others) to choose abortion under certain circumstances. Navigating between the universalist claims of Catholic education, and a kind of secular ethical particularism, they worked very hard to philosophically justify their actions. Ten out of the thirteen also believed that their Catholic backgrounds had made it harder to recover from abortion than they imagined to be the case for non-Catholic women. And several genetic counselors and geneticists were explicit in their statements concerning Catholic women's guilt and the need to provide sympathetic clerical references. I should stress that every woman with whom I have spoken experienced enormous grief after choosing to abort a diagnosed fetus, and most expressed concerns about the moral standing of a disabled fetus in their families and their communities, and their responsibilities in deciding to end the pregnancies. But the Catholic women seemed to carry an additional burden of guilt.

Contextualizing Selective Abortion

Although the problem of guilt was construed in these interviews as an individual and philosophical burden, some abortion stories also alert us to the larger realpolitik within which abortion decisions occur. Two women who live in small, upstate communities told me of their struggles to obtain abortions after diagnoses of fatal conditions in their fetuses. In both cases, Catholic and right-to-life influences on the local health care centers had made abortion unavailable. One spent a month unsuccessfully trying to get approval for the abortion of an anencephalic fetus through a specially convened hospital ethics committee, before transferring to a City Hospital. In another upstate case, members of the obstetrical and genetics staff tried to persuade a woman who had just received the diagnosis of Down syndrome to attend a local Down syndrome convention. "You'll accept this pregnancy, after you meet the other parents," they told her. No one mentioned abortion as an option, and several were extremely discouraging when she insisted on information and pursued her plans. When she made abortion arrangements at a hospital seventy miles from her home, her own health care providers refused to cooperate with the complex paperwork.

Such attitudes and behaviors among powerholders are, of course, punitive; under the guise of upholding "disability acceptance" they also attempt to coerce women into continuing pregnancies which they have already decided to end. There is, as the reproductive rights movement has continuously pointed out, a great difference between counseling that provides information on a range of options, and coercive directives. This problem is particularly clear when women are confronted with demonstrators attempting to dissuade them from receiving abortions. Two of the women I interviewed spoke of picket-line harassment at the abortion clinics they went to. "Go ahead," one of them screamed back at the right-to-life demonstrators. "You go raise this baby without a brain I'm taking out!" I was struck by the bravery and enforced activism of women who lived in places where abortion access was highly contested.

The links between legality, access, and the social and political climate within which abortion decisions are made was also brought back to me in a story told by a white health educator who had received a double and inherently ambiguous diagnosis which she researched intensely before coming to her abortion decision. While her story was more fully told on p. 231, it bears repeating here: Both her mother and mother-in-law expressed impatience and incomprehension when Jamie Steiner and her husband spent weeks weighing the meaning of the prenatal diagnosis they had received.

So finally I turned on my mother and asked her, "How can you be so insensitive? It's such a hard decision for us, you can't just dismiss this."

And as we talked, I realized how different their abortions were from mine. They were illegal. You've got to remember that, they were illegal. They were done when you worried about the stigma of getting caught, and maybe, getting sick. But you didn't think about the fetus. You thought about saving your own life. (Jamie Steiner, 33)

Illegal abortions were dangerous and expensive. They were performed under a different shadow of death—maternal, not fetal, death. The secularization of fetal personhood is a relatively new idea, condensing a variety of social forces which include the medical and technological objectification of fetuses, abortion reform, and right-to-life politics. Paradoxically, increased social consciousness of women's existence as a person apart from her maternity here coincides with a more independent focus on fetuses, too. In prior eras, mother and fetus were more culturally and materially fused; illegal abortion was a dangerous procedure, the major cause of death for women in their childbearing years (Garrow 1994; Gordon 1976; Petchesky 1984). Under these circumstances, religious hegemony was diffuse: It denounced the sin or crime of abortion, without a public focus on the fetus itself. The diverse movements which coalesced in support of abortion reform in the United States focused on maternal, or maternal/child health. It was the secular and medical authority of doctors which was posed against church doctrine in many of the successful court challenges which culminated in Roe v. Wade (Garrow 1994). In the wake of that historic decision, "Abortion related deaths . . . decreased by 73 percent" within a decade of decriminalization (Petchesky 1984, 157). By 1985, they had decreased fivefold (Council on Scientific Affairs 1992). Fear of criminal prosecution, and the morbidity and mortality of aborting women were thoroughly grounded in an older social matrix (Gorney 1998; Joffe 1995; Risen and Thomas 1998; Solinger 1993, 1998). On the heels of legalization, the right-to-life movement was quickly organized. We cannot analyze an emerging discourse of "fetal personhood" as it combines both religious and secular elements until we locate the meaning of abortion at the historic intersection of culture, politics, technology, and social change (Duden 1993; Ginsburg 1989a; Michaels and Morgan 1999; Petchesky 1984; Feminist Studies 1997). This intersection depends, in large measure, on struggles carried out among different power-holding sectors: The A.M.A., the right-to-life movement and its close ally, the Catholic Church, and various legal and governmental constituencies have all dominated national, state, and local struggles for and against abortion services. This power-laden struggle is reflected in the personal and quite philosophical concerns of the women I interviewed, as well in more public and literate debates.

Yet however nuanced and clear their ethical, philosophical, or scientific convictions, virtually all women who ended their pregnancies after positive diagnoses described a profound sense of social isolation. Part of the isolation undoubtedly stemmed from the social ambiguity of "selective" abortion: Many find it morally permissible, but no one is prepared for the conundrum it entails. How can one grieve so deeply when you got the results you "wanted"? This chosen, personal grief is technologically, that is, socially, produced. Yet we have, as yet, no social acknowledgment or etiquette in which to contextualize it. I remember poring over the medical literature a month after my own abortion for Down syndrome, trying to find any indication of how women survived this trauma. After I got used to finding myself described in terms of "posttermination morbidity" and as experiencing "sequelae," I discovered that there were (then) only two articles describing the "psychosocial" impact of this experience. Both were quite frightening from a user's perspective. (Was I headed for a nervous breakdown? A divorce? Or both?) And both were based on very small, biased samples. In the biopolitical order within which prenatal diagnosis currently occurs, there is very little significance attributed to the personal and social consequences of positive diagnosis: It isn't a socially significant topic for research, hence, the comfort which such research might bring to relevant women (and their service providers) is nobody's high priority.[45] As I set about finding others who had survived this disorienting grief, it was almost a decade before I met anyone who had met anyone but me who had also sustained this particular experience. So the literal oddness of one's circumstances is considerable, as nobody else one knows is likely to have "been there."

> I feel like I fell off the edge of this earth, like there's no one down here but me, like Alice down the rabbit hole, I've been falling through space so long I don't remember which end is up. Who could possibly understand this? (Pat Gordon, 37, white college professor)

> Forgive me, but unless you've lost a parent, you can't tell me anything about what it was like. All the ones who helped me then, my cousin, my husband, my best friend, they can only go so far with me on this one. Meeting you, it's the first time I've talked to anyone who has anything to say about getting over this. (Leah Rubenstein, 39, white homemaker)

I never met anyone, anyone who's been through what I've been through. It's lonely, it's sad and lonely. That's why, when the genetic counselors called me, I was so curious to meet you. (Iris Lauria, 29, Puerto Rican hospital housekeeper)

Over the last decade, a small popular literature on the grief involved in ending desired pregnancies has emerged. It often includes direct quotations from letters, poems, and accounts written by parents going through this difficult experience (e.g., Fertel, Holowinsky et al. 1988; Ilse 1993; Minnick, Delp et al. 1990). Much (but not all) of it is self-published, and/or distributed through small counseling services. It is thus not widely available, although many genetic counselors do distribute copies to those who seek them out as part of their recovery. Though some of the women I interviewed had read this literature and found it very comforting, most had never heard of it. I know of one videotape produced by and about a support group for those receiving positive prenatal diagnoses distributed through a medical center in California, (Loma Linda School of Medicine, 1984), but I have never seen it in use in New York. There is thus no obvious cultural space which has, as yet, been created for healing this technologically produced form of chosen suffering. Only three of the women I interviewed had participated in support groups for those experiencing pregnancy loss; none had found a support group specifically designed for her kind of chosen loss, rather than general pregnancy loss. The difference between pregnancy loss due to miscarriage and stillbirth and *chosen* pregnancy loss is substantial: One woman found the groups set up by hospital social workers or community organizations helpful, while two others felt that they became targets for anger. After all, they'd *chosen* to end a pregnancy, while the women in the group had been the "victims" of miscarriage, stillbirth, or neonatal death. Thus, the focus on individual choice—a quintessentially American cultural value—here again disrupts the commonality of pregnancy loss.

Cultural notions of privacy may also erect barriers against seeking collective support: For the many years since my own abortion, I have made my name and telephone number available to all the genetic counselors with whom I have worked, in case someone wishes to speak with another woman "who's been there." While counselors call at least once a month to alert me to the fact that they have recently given someone my name, only a handful of their patients eventually call me. Among those with whom I have spoken, some women mentioned more extended sessions with professional psychotherapists or social workers as particularly helpful. While most of these

were professional middle-class women used to purchasing counseling services, some came from less privileged backgrounds. One hospital housekeeper dropped in to see her genetic counselor quite regularly, and two
secretaries mentioned church-related loss groups that had been helpful.

Secrecy and Support

But most of the support women received came from close friends and family
members. To my queries of "Who did you tell first?" and "Where did you
feel support or criticism for your abortion decision?" the women I interviewed usually named mothers and sisters, with best (or close) friends following close behind. Sometimes, fine discriminations were made among family
members: Marilyn de Soto found her mother-in-law's grief and distress par-
alleled her own, while Nivia Hostos was careful to describe her abortion as a
"loss" or "miscarriage" to her own mother. Both these senior women were
deeply pious Puerto Rican Catholics. Iris Lauria, also from a traditional
Puerto Rican family, found the closeness and support offered by all her kin
enormously helpful; no one questioned the abortion decision. When Tamara
Levkovitz returned to her suburban home, shaken and in tears from the
sonogram diagnosis of anencephaly, her parents were already in the living
room, running interference with her children: Her brother, an Orthodox
Jewish rabbi, had reached them by phone before she did. And writing this
chapter, I recalled vividly that my own parents flew a thousand miles just
hours after they received our call, determined to do anything they could to
help us through a crisis. But other women had to hide their situations from
families which were hotbeds of antiabortion sentiment. And friends sometimes made mistakes in their efforts to help: Margaret Thompson took a
month to decide about ending her pregnancy after the biochemical diagnosis
of an invisible spina bifida. During that time, she became enraged with anyone who articulated a clear opinion on what she should do. Megan Johnson
had worked through an infertility crisis with a close friend some months earlier. After her own selective abortion, the friend failed to return phone calls
for several weeks. When she finally reconnected, the friend told Megan, "At
least you were lucky: You're able to get pregnant." Less dramatically, many
women reported that friends, trying to be helpful, would say, "This is just
helping nature along" or "It's all for the best." "They get me so angry when
they say that stuff. This isn't 'all for the best.' It's rotten. It's just rotten" (Harriet Genzer, 41, white editor).

People make comments intended to help which actually hurt. Meeta
Cabron's son's baby-sitter expressed great support for the affected pregnancy,

offering the services of her church's prayer circle: "We all believe your baby can be healed," she repeatedly proclaimed. But help and insight may also come from less obvious sources. For example,

> The next week, this father of my friend, he's Catholic, he didn't know a thing about what I'd done, he just starts in on this conversation with me about how much he admires Geraldine Ferraro [one time Democratic senator from New York who ran for vice president in 1988], her stand on abortion, and everything. He says, "What does the pope know? He's an old man like me. Better to let the women decide on this for themselves." And I felt very comforted by that, like even Catholics might understand. (Michelle Kansky, 38, white public school teacher)

Pregnancy loss is culturally located in the realm of "the private" (Layne 1990, 1992, 1997). Likewise, abortions are not usually widely discussed and are socially fraught. Abortion after a diagnosis of a disabling condition is still a relatively rare occurrence and morally ambiguous: Some commentators denounce it as neoeugenics, while most Americans still consider it to be a justification for legal abortion (Goldberg and Elder 1998). Yet because the experience was "chosen," many people do not code it as a "loss." For all these reasons, women undergoing selective abortions after positive diagnoses usually feel isolated and find the support they receive, no matter how well-intentioned, insufficient.

The ambiguity of this experience resonates through women's social lives, affecting all intimate relations. This resonance was particularly present in the stories women told concerning their partners' reactions. If, as Jessie Bernard told us, there are "His" and "Hers" marriages (Bernard 1972), then there are surely "His" and "Hers" abortions, as well. The overwhelming majority of women I interviewed felt that their husbands or partners shared deeply in the pain of ending a wanted pregnancy. They told many moving stories about men's wishes for healthy children, and concern for their own misery and safety in undertaking a late abortion. Three said that their husbands felt angry that only women got sympathy for this traumatic event; they, too, wanted some social recognition of a grievous loss. And the overwhelming majority of women also reported that men recovered much faster and needed to put the experience behind them much sooner than they did. Much of this difference is, of course, an embodied one: As long as a woman still carries milk-filled breasts, extra pregnancy weight, hormonally modulated emotions, and awaits the hormonal changes reestablishing her menstrual cycle, her memories of recent loss are inscribed in flesh. But many women from diverse social backgrounds also attributed gender differences in recovery to male psychology:

> I think it's real for him, but there's just a real difference in how experience feels. I mean, he doesn't experience it in the same way, it wasn't as much of a personal loss, it was a different kind of loss for him. He's very closed off about his own emotions, and it's something that he doesn't articulate, and he doesn't want to articulate, he prefers to get away from it. He grieves differently. . . . I kept a journal the whole pregnancy, and I wanted to burn that journal, to finish it that way . . . and he couldn't do it, he just couldn't do it. The most he could do was read it privately—he absolutely had to do it by himself—and then he had to put it away, he couldn't burn it. . . . We approach life differently; I just have to respect his way of doing things. (Margaret Thompson, 34, white psychologist)

> It was like he was, well, it happened, and that's that. He put it away on a shelf. I didn't want him to do that. . . . He didn't ever want to talk about it, got kind of uncomfortable when I brought it up. Then a month later, it all came out. . . . I mean, he just . . . let it all out, and I was so surprised. . . . I wished he could have, we could have sat down together and just cried our hearts out. . . . But I guess being brought up in a Latin household, it's very hard for him. (Nivia Hostos, 26, Puerto Rican administrative secretary)

> He got very upset about it. He didn't speak about it, but I know he did. He does have feelings, he's a human being. He kept to himself, but I know he felt it. (Iris Lauria, 29, Puerto Rican hospital housekeeper)

Their sympathy for their partners' seldom-expressed pain extended to interpretations of differences which they coded as similarities:

> Even though he wasn't talking, I think he may have taken it a little bit harder than even I did, because he seemed to be more afraid to try again. . . . I was more optimistic, and I guess he was still grieving, and I was already on to, "Ok, let's try this again." But he wasn't ready, he was more afraid. Even when he's not talking, I know what he's feeling. (Marilyn de Soto, 34, Puerto Rican social worker)

In the hospital he was great, he was 100 percent there, and then a few days later . . . he just couldn't understand my pain, he denied that he had the same pain, and so this was, he said, you know, it was a fetus, and that was that, and it's over. . . . And I was seeing a psychiatrist, and I was hysterical, and I only wanted to talk about trying again, but I realized my reaction was hysterical. And then I realized his reaction was hysterical, too. Because he couldn't discuss this, he couldn't talk about trying again, he couldn't sit down with me and just talk it out. This was his hysteria, right, this big, giant denial. (Nancy Tucker, 36, white college professor)

Many women experienced marital stress in the forms of anger, arguments, or alienation. When I inquired about the reactions of her husband to her own longing for a replacement pregnancy, Tamara Levkovitz said, "To Martin, life is Atlantic City. We were ahead, we had three healthy children. Now we're losing. Ok, if you're smart, you walk out of the casino." One obstetrician told his patients who expressed anger at their husbands for being less grief-stricken than they were, "The Orthodox say, 'God forgives anything said by a woman in labor.' She's allowed to be very, very angry. So go ahead, curse God out. He'll understand. He knows better than your husband." A very few women told tales of gender reversal and gender pressure surrounding their abortion decisions:

My husband is very stalwart, I mean, he wouldn't do anything less than rational ever. He's an investment banker, that kind of says it all. But when we first found out, he was the one who considered keeping the baby, he really did. And I was the one who flipped around, I had to get it over with, I had to get it out immediately. (Nancy Tucker, 36, white college professor)

Carey Morgan, a white interior decorator, found abortion "morally repugnant" but acceded to the wishes of her lawyer husband and her obstetrician after a fetal diagnosis of toxoplasmosis. Sylvia Lin dreamed a conversation between herself, her husband, and her Klinefelter's fetus in which the baby told her he wasn't afraid of dying, if that would bring peace to the two of them.

But sometimes, gender conflicts are not reconcilable. Two women attributed the breakup of their marriages to the stress surrounding this experience. Additionally, one African-American and one Dominican professional, both in nondomestic relationships where their pregnancies had been warmly welcomed, said that their partners had drifted away. "The partner? There's not always someone very involved," one said to me, as she described his lack of support around the time of the abortion of a pregnancy about which he had initially expressed great enthusiasm.

Thus the stresses and pains associated with choosing to end a wanted pregnancy after a positive diagnosis are more than individual and physical. They ripple through a woman's intimate network of partners, children, relatives, friends, and coworkers, spreading both disruption and reflection. I was continually reminded of the intense pain accompanying this experience, as my questions often provoked tears for which I was always apologizing. As the interpolator and mirror of that pain, I would often find myself returning home to pull the covers over my head after conducting "positive diagnosis" interviews. Although we feminist researchers who explore the terrain of miscarriage, childhood disability and death, and infertility often refer to ourselves ironically as mavens[46] of reproductive grief, it was only in the course of rereading these transcripts that I considered the implications of my own first live born child's standing as a "replacement baby," conceived in the aftermath of this painful experiece. And in analyzing the data for this chapter, personal history shadowed my analytic framework, complicating as well as enriching the issue of authorial voice throughout. The pain provoked by positive diagnosis, its aftermath, and its reanalysis on the part of both those receiving it and their anthropological interviewer is thus considerable. As I have tried to indicate throughout this chapter, this experience shares the hidden anniversaries, private losses, social separations and disruptions, and philosophical conundrums entailed by other forms of pregnancy loss, while also bearing its own unique and painful markings. But women and their supporters experiencing the pain of positive diagnosis also have much in common with those who give birth to children with disabling conditions, the subject of chapter 10 to which we now turn.

10

The Unexpected Baby

So they diagnosed Amelia right away, on the delivery table. She was barely out, I barely got a chance to catch my breath or marvel at my first baby when this doctor pours this bad news all over us. "She's got Down syndrome," he says to us, very coldly. And after he tells us about blood tests and confirmations and all this stuff, we say to him, "But what does that *mean*? What should we *expect*?" And just as coldly he says, "Don't expect much. Maybe she'll grow up to be an elevator operator. Don't expect much." So we clung to each other and cried. (April Schwartz, lawyer, mother of a 4-year-old with Down syndrome)

My doctor was so angry with me. He couldn't believe I didn't take that test. "How could you let this happen?" he yelled at me. "You're 40!" But I think something else: Even though he's mentally retarded, he could be a good person. . . . It's just like finding out you have a new job. You just do it, and you accept it, that's all there is to it. (Ivana Maldonado, nurse's aide, mother of a 7-year-old with Down syndrome)

In humans, the twenty-first chromosome suffers nondisjunction at a remarkably high frequency, with unfortunately rather tragic effects. . . . These unfortunate children suffer mild to severe mental retardation and have a reduced life expectancy. . . . We have no clue as to why an extra twenty-first chromosome should yield the highly specific set of abnormalities associated with trisomy-21. But at least it can be identified in utero by counting the chromosomes in fetal cells, providing an option for early abortion. (Gould 1980)

> The smiling face of the Mongolian Imbecile suggests the possession of
> some secret source of joy. . . (Sutherland 1900, 23)

THE BIRTH OF A BABY IS AN EVENT rich in material and symbolic connections: the recruitment and transmission of kinship obligations across generations; the promises and problems of caretaking, nurturance, and support
through lengthy periods of dependency; and the transformation of roles and
relationships in the constellation of those who become the baby's parents,
siblings, grandparents, and intimate community members. A birth is at once
the most ordinary and most extraordinary of events, as virtually any new
parent will attest. But the birth of a baby with a diagnosed disability transforms its kindred's experience of the ordinary and extraordinary, shattering
some expectations, and opening up others. It was this transformation that I
wanted to understand when I set out to interview families whose children
had hereditary disabilities, especially Down syndrome, the most common
positive diagnosis produced via amniocentesis, and the iconic reason that
medical professionals explain and offer the test to pregnant women. I also
wanted to understand how family experience is both shaped and described
to illustrate the difference between an exclusively medical view of a genetic
or chromosomal disability and its social consequences as children are integrated into daily life.

As I hope to argue throughout this chapter, parents of children with
hereditary disabilities often tell their stories as narratives of enlightenment,
describing a journey from fear or even loathing toward a state of acceptance
and appreciation. But this generalization requires contextualization: Such a
narrative emerges repeatedly as a journey freshly undertaken by each individual and family confronting disability, but it is, of course also deeply social
and historical, reflecting at least three prior traditions. One is the long-
standing Judeo-Christian narrative, which provides powerful models for
overcoming adversity and recognizing the goodness of individual essences
or souls. A second, which readily twins with the first, is a secular narrative of
social progress most powerfully embedded in biomedical discourses of scientific discoveries, clinical interventions and cures. The third is the recent history of disability policies in the United States and elsewhere, and its
complex imbrication with an emergent and morally compelling disability
rights movement which offers both language and vision to some parents
struggling to raise children with stigmatized differences.

Yet even in contextualizing family stories of disability in their larger and
quite historical religious, scientific, and political narrative traditions, impor-

tant caveats should be stated: Not everyone subscribes to a narrative of enlightenment, and I will endeavor to describe the social circumstances within which such metaphorical journeying arises or doesn't arise. Moreover, my own research focuses on those disabilities for which prenatal testing is now available. Heritable conditions therefore stand at the center of the stories I asked people to tell me. But life with a disabling condition cannot be so neatly contained: In some ways, hereditary conditions are specific as they immediately invoke questions of continuity and difference among kin. But in other ways, all people with disabilities are set apart from other members of their communities and societies, and hierarchies of disabling conditions are widely recognized and discussed in many strata of American culture, including the disability rights movement. Within such hierarchies, those disabled from birth or in earliest childhood stand apart from those who acquire their conditions through accident or illness after having experienced the normal benefits and entitlements of able-bodiedness. The content of a disabling condition, as well as the time of its onset also has implications which are sorted within relevant communities: Being or becoming blind or deaf, for example, has different consequences for the affected person and her or his closest allies than does mobility impairment. And mental retardation, a condition closely linked to Down syndrome, is particularly stigmatized in most, if not all, communities. Down syndrome, with its permanent, visible markings and socially obvious mental retardation, cannot therefore "stand for" all disabilities, or all hereditary conditions. Yet most of what I learned about children with disabilities comes from families and a wide range of professionals deeply involved with Down's. Throughout this chapter I will therefore try to indicate as best I can the particularities which characterize the social construction of Down syndrome and other hereditary conditions, and their relation to more general issues of disability.

Irregular Entries

When parents narrate the natural history of learning to live with a child's hereditary disabilities, they almost always spontaneously begin by describing the birth, and whether or not a diagnosis was quickly made. As the first two stories which open this chapter suggest, the birth and diagnosis of a newborn with Down syndrome is an event which is vividly remembered not only by the birthing woman and her partner, but by medical practitioners, as well. Indeed, the third and fourth quotations point toward a lengthy medical commentary on the mysterious nature of births gone awry: Doctors may have strong personal and professional responses to delivering and treating babies who cannot be seen as normal, and whose ills cannot be cured, investing them with symbolic meaning which sometimes supersedes their individual characteristics. Birthing mothers recalled their attendants' words and deeds in great detail, judging the quality of response:

> So I had a section, and my doctor came in seven hours later, and I was still pretty wiped out, and he stood there with me, and he says to me with tears in his eyes, he says, "Well, you have a Down's syndrome child." And I didn't know what he meant. I says, "Is it a cold, does it go away, what the hell is it?" And he says, "Patsy, the baby is mongoloid." I mean, it hits home, it's like, "Are you for real?" And then he looks me square in the eye and he says, "We have some papers. You could award him to the state if you don't want him." And I looked at my doctor that just delivered my son, my doctor that I loved, we had such a friendship, and I says, "Get the hell out of this room." (Patsy DelVecchio, white bus driver, mother of a 6-year-old with Down syndrome)

> So my husband didn't make it home for the delivery but he called from the airport, and the doctor got on the phone right away and gave him all this bad news. But you know it's like the doctor was more upset than we were, like he couldn't bring himself to say, "Here's this baby, and we don't know for sure." It's very hard for professional people not to see the down side, you know, to see the worst possible, this could have been the Down's kid that was going to have an IQ of 100 and make it to Harvard. We don't know the future when it's first born. But the doctor was seeing maybe his next-door neighbor's kid who can't do anything, or something, so it was very hard that he painted this gloomy terrible picture. (Lydia Sellers, white homemaker and dressmaker, mother of a 9-year-old with Down syndrome)

> She was tiny, but she was great, like she was just the cutest thing. And then my husband came in, and he looked weird and immediately he said, "The baby, something's wrong . . . " And all I could think of was that she's blind, I guess that was probably the worst thing I could ever have imagined. But the doctor had just called him and told him that Rose was mongoloid. It took a half hour to get it out of him, like he couldn't finish telling me the story, and then the doctor came and said, "What your husband just told you is right." He was, like, very down on the whole thing, very negative. He said, "The only blessing is they don't tend to live very long." So he thought it would be a good thing if

our new baby would die. What more can I say? (Flora Taglitone, white homemaker, mother of a 6-year-old with Down syndrome)

As such stories indicate, Down syndrome babies are "wrong babies" marked almost from the moment of birth by medical scrutiny as incurably damaged. Many women across class lines and from diverse ethnic backgrounds told similar stories of medical dismay at their children's births. It is not hard to spot the despair at having delivered a child most people consider frighteningly marred, a child who cannot be cured within the framework of medicine. Nor it is hard to pick up (as Lydia Seller's words suggest) the attitudes toward mental retardation expressed by many medical professionals. Likewise, most mothers commented on the speed with which information about putting the child up for adoption was conveyed. I will return to this point below.

But first, I should note that while the majority of birth stories I collected pointed an accusatory finger at awkward, cold, or downright insensitive obstetricians, a few families felt very well-served by both OBs and pediatricians, whose calm discretion they recalled with appreciation:

We're so lucky we had Robin at the Birthing Center, and not in the hospital. I mean, in a hospital, he would have been examined to death by a cast of thousands, they surely would have picked it up. But at the Center, they missed it. So I got to take him home, to nurse him, we stayed at home for four days quietly, all together, and then we took him to meet the pediatrician. And he made the diagnosis immediately. He was excellent, really excellent. It's such an important thing, how the professional handles it, the initial comment, I can't emphasize how important it is. Because I have since then talked to parents who have had that experience where the obstetrician or the pediatrician has been very negative, and it has really colored their whole impression of the child. And never once did Dr. E, I mean, there wasn't ever the implication that we wouldn't keep him or that there was something horrible about our son. He was just very positive and sensitive, he just said, "I have to tell you this, there are some things I'm concerned about." And I said, "Well, what?" and he said, "Well, let's look at his eyes and, of course, there's this crease in his palm. It's a simian crease." I don't know how I knew that, but I just knew what he was talking about, so I turned to my husband and I said, "Do you know what he's talking about?" and Paul said, "No," and I said, "Well, he's talking about Down syndrome." So I guess he didn't really ever have to tell me, he just got me to the point where I knew for myself. And then he hooked us up with all sorts of people, genetic counselors, heart specialists, and we always felt he just wanted the best for our son. (Polly Denton, white actress, mother of a 5-year-old with Down syndrome)

Laura and Dan Schulmann were quite satisfied with the straightforward explanation their pediatrician offered when he made the diagnosis of Down syndrome one hour after Ashley's birth:

He caught Dan at the telephone, calling everyone, and stopped him. "Don't make any more calls till after we've had a moment to talk," he said. And once he was done explaining, he warned us, "Don't touch the literature. It's badly out of date, it will only scare you." And he got us some other parents to talk to.

Several women went out of their way to describe the sensitivity and compassion within which nurses, rather than doctors, embedded a diagnostic situation:

Like the nurses all knew immediately, but they didn't say anything. It was a holiday weekend at Elite, there wasn't an OB to be found for two or three days, and the nurses were particularly nice, particularly attentive. They took over my life, they wouldn't let anyone come near me. In retrospect, they knew, but they didn't want to say. It wasn't until Tuesday morning, when we we'd had a pretty good weekend, that the pedes and geneticists and social workers came in. They whisked Ronnie out, they rushed back in and began to talk Down's. And it became an avalanche. (Nancy Haliday, white homemaker, mother of a 4-year-old with Down syndrome)

I was feeling so alone, like I lived at the bottom of a dark well, like I was the last person left on earth. So the nurses found another nurse, she worked on another floor, and they brought her in to speak with me. She had pictures of her little girl, a 6-year-old with Down's, and the kid was cute, and the nurse was the happiest and calmest mother I'd ever seen. And she really gave me a pep talk, I mean, she just said, "You can do it, you can make a great life for your little boy." And after meeting her, I started to think it would be all right. Whatever happened, it might be tough, but it would be all right. (Faith Weiner, white special-education teacher, mother of a 2-year-old with Down syndrome)

In the realm of biomedicine, newborns diagnosed with Down syndrome are intensively scrutinized for specific conditions that range from mild to potentially fatal. Their regulation is considered key to normalizing the survival of babies and young children with Down syndrome. Whether the individual story of diagnosis is coded as negative or positive, virtually all parents of a newborn with Down syndrome find themselves stitched into medical networks. Because babies with this condition are at high risk for heart problems, intestinal blockages, and a host of less life-threatening disabilities, a diagnosed baby is a medicalized baby, tied to appointments with specialists, and scheduled for high-technology testing from the moment a diagnosis is tentatively made: Geneticists, pediatric cardiologists, neurologists, and pediatric surgeons are all likely to see the baby shortly after birth; audiology, ophthalmology, podiatry, and behavioral psychology are among the services to which most parents of children with Down syndrome are routinely introduced. Two generations ago, of course, most of these services barely existed as specialties, and babies born with Down syndrome were sometimes allowed to die, or were counseled into institutions. Now, their future is highly medicalized. While some new parents find this attention reassuring, others find it invasive and disheartening: "Then they send you to the Heredity Department, that's when they give you the lowdown, when you're at your lowest. That's when they say, 'Heart problems. Leukemia. The works'" (Johnella Cornell, African-American hairdresser, mother of an 18-month-old with Down syndrome).

Diagnosed babies and their parents are also likely to be "social worked," connected to early-intervention services (of which more, below). One of the main introductory functions of the social worker is to make state law concerning fosterage and adoption clear to parents of disabled newborns: A child may be left in the hospital and made a ward of the state, once separation papers are signed. Virtually all mothers commented on how offensive they found this information:

Isn't Hershel my son, the same as the other two? What makes them think we'd give him up? (Gloria Hurwitz, white bookkeeper, mother of a 2-year-old with mosaic 18 syndrome)

Heredity kept talking about how I could give Aleem up. And they sent the director to me, and I told her . . . "You are all very cold and very cruel people," I said, "because the first thing you should ask the parent is, how do you feel about your child being born that way? You don't ask the parents that! The first thing, you shove it up the parents' nose with a paper to take the baby for adoption. Not for foster, to give you time to sit back and think, but immediately to put your kid up for adoption. Like, you should listen to the parents first, get to know how they feel, see if they can handle it. Then, only then, should you present the alternatives. Adoption should be the last thing you mention." (Johnella Cornell, African-American hairdresser, mother of an 18-month-old with Down syndrome)

While the immediacy of adoption information is shocking to most parents coping simultaneously with both a new baby and news of its serious problems, hospital social workers are also operating under constraints: Many disabled babies *are* abandoned and end up in the adoption system; the system works best in placing newborns, and once the child leaves the hospital in its parents' custody, the legal situation is more complex. They therefore offer an "adoption map" because they believe it is in the child's best interests. Yet such information is hardly neutral: It is never offered to the mother of a "normal" newborn unless she requests it. Moreover, adoption services have layered and complex histories: Emily Purl Kingsley, a Down syndrome activist who integrated her own son with Down syndrome into the early scripts she wrote for *Sesame Street,* founded the Adoption Committee of the National Down Syndrome Congress in 1979. There, flexible and informal respite fostering is often available to shell-shocked parents who need some time to decide if they can raise their disabled newborns. There is also a waiting list of families willing to long-term foster or adopt Down syndrome babies; often, they already have a child with the condition, and are eager to provide a "look-alike" sibling whom they imagine will have similar interests, capacities, and personality traits. The perception that children with Down syndrome resemble one another more than they resemble their families of birth has a long history and many familial implications to which we will return, below. But we should also note that voluntary arrangements for fostering and adoption within the Down syndrome community are a direct response to widespread public dismay at the wretched conditions confronting "hard-to-adopt" babies and older children who end up in public institutions. While many institutions have been closed in response to the combined legal, medical, and activist international movement for deinstitutionalization which has flourished since the late 1960s, it remains the case that disabled children are overrepresented in institutions (Shapiro 1993) and are harder to place in adoption (DeLeon and Westerberg 1980).

And the very practice of adoption has deeply historical resonances. An African-American welfare-dependent mother of three told me this story about the birth of her son with Down syndrome. She had been planning to put the newborn up for adoption, a decision she had reached shortly before his birth, due to the domestic stress and violence with which she was living. When the baby was born and diagnosed, a white social worker came to see her about placing the child. The mother asked what would become of her baby and was told, "We'll probably find a rural farm family to take him." "Then what?" she queried. "He'll grow up outside, knowing about crops and animals," was the reply. "Then what?" the mother repeated. "Maybe he'll even grow up to work on that farm," the social worker replied. "Sounds like slavery to me," answered the mother, who decided to take her baby home. This imagery and its legacy contrast strongly with the stories many white mothers tell, in which they fantasize a peaceful, rural life "in nature" as the perfect placement for their children with Down syndrome.

Despite their almost universal aversion to what they found to be insensitive adoption information, many mothers of newborns with Down syndrome recalled praying that their babies would die:

> So I really wished he would die because I thought that if he would die this would be very, very sad, but number one, I didn't know him, because he was asleep for the first twenty-four hours after he got born. He wouldn't even feed off the nipple, the bottle, nothing, he was like semi-comatose. Number two, I didn't want a Down syndrome child. I didn't know any except for your stereotype two-hundred-pound schleppy person walking along the street with their parents at 35 years old. So I felt like, well, if he would die, that would be the perfect solution. We would mourn this baby, but it would let me completely off the hook, I wouldn't have to raise him. [Asked if she had ever thought of giving him up for adoption rather than thinking he should die, she answered:] "No, never, I could never consider giving him up." (Judy Kaufman, white nurse, mother of a 5-year-old with Down syndrome)

The usually fleeting death wish expressed on behalf of newborns with serious disabilities is the flip side of the mourning process which parents also experience. As social workers and other professionals are quick to point out, mourning is complex: One mourns for the fantasized normal child replaced by this "wrong" baby; one mourns for the imagined and known changes in family life that a child with "special needs" entails. As mothers put it:

> You mourn for the future that was snatched away when this baby got born. (Polly Denton, white actress, mother of a 5-year-old with Down syndrome)

I'm always mourning a little bit for how hard everything is for her,
how long everything takes her, even though I admire her pluck. The
mourning just goes on, along with the love. (Linda Hornstein, white
special-education consultant, mother of a 6-year-old with Down syndrome)

In addition to intensive medicalization and social work scrutiny, diagnosed babies are networked into education services including early-
intervention programs, and physical, occupational, and speech therapies for
young children. Funding for such interventions comes through the family
court (in New York State, where my research was conducted), tying families
into a bureaucratic web of services and paperwork from the moment of
diagnosis. Though all newborns are conscripts to modern bureaucratic
record keeping and discipline via birth records, immunization schedules, the
establishment of contracts, wills, and the like, diagnosed babies are fused
with public services at a much more intense and often bewildering rate.

For many of the families with whom I spoke, recommended services provide reassuring resources for dealing with what at first feels like an overwhelming dilemma: Being able to "do something" to help an intensely
vulnerable child sheds some rays of hope during the early weeks and months
following the birth and diagnosis of a baby with Down syndrome. For some
families, learning to speak the highly medicalized physical therapy language
of hypotonia, proprioception, and subluxation provides a vocabulary around
which early interventions may be effected. And exposure to the range of helping therapists available through early-intervention programs also provides aid
for families coming to terms with how to handle and what to expect from a
"different" or "wrong" baby. As one physical therapist who works extensively
with developmentally delayed newborns and young children put it, "With a
handicapped baby, we now know how important it is to go all out, to shoot for
the moon. That way, the kid will achieve whatever is best for them."

The optimistic energy and realistic sense of possibility expressed by such
therapists are usually extremely beneficial to family members. Yet early-
intervention services also have shadow effects. When I praised the high-quality services available to parents of newborns and infants to the director of an
early-intervention program, herself the mother of a teenager with Down
syndrome, she told me this story:

When Debbie was born, the pediatrician said, "Well, she has mongoloid tendencies." I knew what he meant. He knew that I knew. But
no one talked about mental retardation or heart defects all the time. I

went for weeks without anyone mentioning it; it was a keen eye that picked up Down's in babies then. I had a couple of years to grow into my baby, to grow with her. Now, every parent that's referred here is waiting for the results of chromosome studies, hoping it's "only mosaicism," and thinking about facial surgery. What kind of information do you really need to handle a 6-week-old? I didn't look at my daughter every day and say, "She has Down's." Today, they get more services and more support. But they've got less ability to forget it, to just get on with knowing the child.

Alienated Kinship

In both positive and negative terms, I have been describing a system of continual interventions marking difference in medical and kinship language. In the shadow of such difference, establishing the child's bona fide presence inside a system of connections, that is, as a family member, is a major cultural accomplishment. For, as I hope to show throughout this chapter, there are many barriers—both subtle and overt—to normalizing kin ties with disabled children. Medical and other professional language may constitute the first barrier, for it often separates Down syndrome and other hereditarily disabled newborns from the category of normalcy, imposing descriptions which create distance. Remember, for example, the Haitian mother whose visit to the genetics laboratory was described in chapter 8. There, geneticists discussed the oblique palpebral fissure and micrognathia of her 6-week-old son, diagnosed with trisomy 9, while she genealogized his features, assimilating them to various aunts and uncles. Likewise, one white mother of a baby boy newly diagnosed with Down syndrome kept insisting that his father was black and had the same low-hung ears as the baby, linking the child to his familial heritage over the pathologizing discourse of the pediatricians. An African-American mother said of her newly diagnosed baby, "They wanna talk about trisomy something, I need to deal with a sick kid. My kid's got a heart problem. Let me deal with that first, then I'll figure out what all this Down's business means."

When mothers of children with Down syndrome tell the story of their pregnancies, births, and diagnoses, one common theme is explicit disconnection, or lack of familial resemblance, as orchestrated by medical attendants:

So I had a home delivery, and the midwife was very cool. Like she suspected something, but she didn't want to say anything, she just wanted me to enjoy the birth, to bond with Laney. But he was too sleepy, so she knew something was wrong. She called the doctor, and the pedia-trician came, and she said, "I hate to bring this up, I just have the vague suspicion he doesn't look like he's related to anyone in this fam-ily. I just don't think he resembles any of you.". . . At first, I just blocked what she was saying, and then I looked, and well, I had this uneasy feeling because he didn't look like us. He looked like he belonged to some other family. (Judy Kaufman, white nurse)

The first thing the doctor said was, he said, "If you had a lot of Irish moon faces in your family, I'd be happier about seeing this child. But she doesn't look like you, she doesn't look like she's from your gene pool at all." Then he explained why he thought it was Down's. (April Schwartz, white lawyer)

And a woman whose story concerns a positive diagnosis of Down's also invented a trope of alienated kinship when she said:

I had my abortion on June 30th, and I was a mess. I was weeping all the time, I was inconsolable, and we went away for the 4th of July, and I couldn't calm down at all. We were watching the parade on Main Street in Hamlet, at my in-laws' cottage, and a family with a kid with Down's was standing in front of me. Right there at the parade, honest to God, like a sign direct to me. And the thing was, I really looked at the kid, how she dripped her ice cream all over, how she couldn't be made to do what the other kids wanted. I looked at her and thought, "She doesn't belong in that family." She didn't look like them, she looked like someone else. Like a lot of someone elses, not quite from the same race, if you know what I mean. And it made me feel, well, that I'd done the right thing, that the one I aborted wasn't quite from my family, either. (Emily Lockhardt, 37, white antiques restorer)

The labeling of children with Down syndrome as alien and racially other is powerfully conveyed via medical terminology. One activist couple who were parents of a child with Down syndrome interrupted our interview in midstream when the mother exclaimed, "Shit! I just told you that Leslie doesn't have all the stigmata associated with Down's! There I go, sounding just like them [i.e., the medical professionals]!" The father commented that it was almost impossible to avoid pathological language, despite their pride in their daughter's accomplishments. And many families noted that the lan-guage used to diagnose and describe Down syndrome includes references to a "simian crease," obviously grouping its bearers with apes rather than humans. We will return to this problem of animal identification and evolutionary "throwback" or "degenerate" language below.

The claims of kinship must be articulated not only against the technicist diagnostic discourse of biomedicine, but sometimes against other kinsfolk, as well. Faith and Bert Weiner, both special-education teachers, didn't tell many relatives that Benjamin had Down's. Instead, they invited various aunts and cousins to their home in Queens and placed the newborn in their laps, leaving the room. Crying in the bedroom, they waited with trepidation to learn who would make the discovery for themselves. Inevitably, relatives fell in love with their adorable baby; only after they were sure of this newly forged bond would the parents emerge to deliver the news. Likewise, Linda Hornstein, a special-education consultant, felt that three out of four grandparents were quite accepting of Amy when she was born with Down syndrome. She immediately took the holdout grandparent with her and the baby to an annual Down syndrome picnic, where he became enchanted with Down syndrome softball teams and the cheerful attitudes of other families.

Sometimes, other family members blame mothers for giving birth to "wrong" babies: "My husband would have left me if I'd done that," said the mother-in-law of one mother of a newborn with Down's. Two African-American fathers believed that their babies caught mental retardation from retarded neighbors from whom they had warned their wives to keep a distance during their pregnancies lest it "mark the baby." Gloria Hurwitz, an Orthodox Jew, told almost none of her relatives that her baby had been diagnosed with mosaic trisomy 18. Beyond initial medical evaluations, she mainly consulted a geneticist who belonged to the same synagogue. "Jewish people don't accept mental retardation," she told me. But she expected to send Hershel to Hebrew school, along with her other children. Susan Lee, estranged from her parents after a religious conversion and marriage to someone of another faith, didn't initially tell her parents that their first grandchild had Down syndrome. "What's the point? They were already set to reject her. This will only make it worse," she reasoned. Marilyn Trainer, whose widely published journalism on life with a Down syndrome son presents a consistent message of acceptance, never told her elderly parents that her fourth child had this disability. She didn't want to burden them with what she expected to be sorrowful news (Trainer 1991). Some women without privileged educational backgrounds had to convince their partners and other family members that they'd done nothing to "deserve" or "cause" the "wrong baby."

Indeed, the existential problem of what causes hereditary disabilities haunted many in the early days of parenting anomalous babies. Susan Lee, newly fundamentalist Christian and antiabortion, thought her prior abortion was being rebalanced by a Down syndrome birth; Patsy DelVecchio, a recovering alcoholic, believed that she was being punished for earlier drinking habits. Johnella Cornell told me she was refused amniocentesis at five City Hospitals because she was too young; but in her recurrent dreams she gave birth to a damaged baby again and again, and she wanted the test to confirm the vision. When her son was born with Down syndrome, she considered it a sign and was relieved to have discovered the root cause of the dream. Having worked with mentally retarded infants and watched her mother foster a dozen children, she felt prepared to accept the dream baby. Pat Carlson, whose decision to keep a Down syndrome pregnancy after a positive prenatal diagnosis was discussed in chapter 7, believed that her son Stevie was put on earth for a mysterious and only partly revealed reason: She considered him to have been protected through a series of miraculous escapes, and expects his mission to become clearer as he grows up. Many practicing Catholics and churchgoing Protestants told me, "God only gives burdens to the strong."

The problem of interpreting misfortune is expressed not only in religious language. Some parents used medical language against itself, to explain the specialness of their children:

> I think it's like something positive; they're always feeding you all this negative stuff about the extra chromosome, all these disabilities, but I think it's something positive. Maybe the extra genetic stuff carries some mutation that causes positive things, too. I think that all that heart, that generosity, the lovingness, the feeling one with the world, those qualities, that's the positive side they never talk about. And it's got to be genetically built into them. Those are traits, too. (Judy Kaufman, white nurse, mother of a 7-year-old with Down syndrome)

> My son just has a different brain; it's got different inhibitors built into it. The point is not that he's stupid, that he can't learn; he learns really well, but really slowly. The brain connections are just different: He doesn't inhibit, he isn't limited, his brain just doesn't inhibit certain emotional expressions the way the rest of us do. His feelings are much more available to be expressed by this brain. What's so bad about that? (Bonnie d'Amato, white social worker, mother of a 5-year-old with Down syndrome)

This idea that children with Down syndrome share physical, cognitive, and emotional traits, resembling one another more than they resemble their families of origin, is enunciated by a wide range of relevant guardians—not only by genetic counselors and pediatricians, but by pregnant women and by the parents of children with this condition. Indeed, the notion that people with Down syndrome could be removed from the kinship nexus that was theirs "by birth" and relocated inside their own separate tribe, made me wonder if we might describe their symbolic predicament as a "kinship of affliction" (cf. Edgerton 1993 [1967]).

The attribution of alien kinship does more than separate Down syndrome children from their genitors and genitrixes; it also provides an alternative kin group into which they can be placed.[47] As the sister of an adult with Down's said,

> When she's at home, she loves her family, she really loves us. . . . But as soon as you bring her back to her workshop, or to her group house, she forgets you, she forgets you're there. She's with her people, her own people. You can't really talk to her about it, but you can see it. She's with her own people. (Carol Seeger, white museum curator)

Alternative kinship may romanticize difference. "You know, you can think of Down's people as another beautiful race that the Lord created on this earth," said Bonnie d'Amato. Alternative kin connections can be used to build freshly imagined families: "There's a place in Pennsylvania where they adopt these kids with Down's. They've got twenty-four right now," said Irena Gotchalk, a white accountant and mother of a 10-year-old with Down syndrome. Asked if she was referring to a school, Irena said, "No, it's a family, it's a new family for people who fit there."

Inventing counterdiscourses through medicine and kinship helps some parents to make meaning out of difference. This capacity to imagine a positive resolution to the existential dilemmas posed by misfortune is exercised by many parents of youngsters with hereditary disabilities.

Transformations in kin connections develop along with the disabled child. While many of the families with whom I spoke offered vivid descriptions of birth and diagnosis, as well as the intense activity surrounding services for newborns and preschool children, special-education and health professionals also alerted me to the evolution of alternative kinship dilemmas which comes with the territory of Down syndrome, and many other lifelong disabilities. A second flurry of activity occurs when children age out of preschool court-mandated infant services; the problems of surveillance by the Committee on the Handicapped [now: the committee on Special Education], through which an Individual Educational Plan is established, sets parents through the bureaucratic maze of Board of Education placements (or legal suits challenging Board of Education placements). If a child is well-placed, s/he may experience a relatively uneventful and stable service environment until aging out of public education. Then, families confront the issue of whether their adult retarded offspring will live at home or use independent living centers, habilitation programs, sheltered workshops, or residential facilities. And as siblings and parents of the disabled family member age as well, the ultimate future of the nonindependent member must be confronted: Who will take care of the disabled member of the family when the parents die? How will siblings and other close relatives apportion responsibilities? Thus, the individual life cycle as well as the familial domestic cycle of all those intimately connected with a disabled member are affected.

The Work of Kinship

But these abstractions pertaining to domestic cycling and kin continuities are, of course, experienced concretely. Mothers who spoke with me estimated they spend on average 25 percent of their time accessing services for their disabled young children; parents of older children assured me that the time constraints diminished as the child got older. But medical crises and failed placements requiring renewed research often punctuate childhood and adolescence. Moreover, classical gender divisions of labor were in place in many of the families with whom I visited: The mothers were far more involved with daily maintenance and transportation of disabled children than were the fathers. I do not mean to imply that fathers were uninvolved: There is obviously a wide range of marital coping strategies to this, as to any, family problem. And often, fathers described their own valued relationship with a disabled child: "We're very proud of Leslie, we think she's extraordinary," said Tylor Harris, college professor, father of an 8-year-old with Down syndrome. "I love taking her out with her bicycle, riding to the library. She's a great kid, she tries harder than any kid I know."

And a white museum curator who has an adult sister with Down syndrome described her parents' marriage in great detail, noting that her mother did all the physical caretaking, but that her father taught Janey to read:

> My Dad's like me: He finds Janey's mind interesting, I mean, he finds it really interesting. He thinks very philosophically about her, about how she processes the world. When she was little, I remember there wasn't much, the school board would send a tutor, but it was pretty minimal. Dad would sit with her for hours, patiently getting her to

spell, then he'd say, "What's the word, Janey?" and she'd say it, and he'd repeat it, and they'd go on again and again. He wanted her to have access to books, to enjoy the things we enjoyed. And she does. In her own way, she does.

In describing her aging parents' continued, close involvement with Janey, Carol Seeger also differentiated their respective tolerance for giving over responsibility. Although Janey now lives in a habilitation center, she comes home almost every weekend, and the mother visits her at the center many times during the week. These visits are viewed as intrusive by program staff, who have established routines and instructed Janey in the skills of semi-independent living. In Carol's view, her father was planning for a future in which he would no longer be around to care for Janey, while her mother was committed to the present: "My father, he sees it all coming. He's looking for long-term homes, he talks to me and Diana [other sister] about wills and stuff. My mother says, 'As long as I'm alive she stays with me. When I'm dead, I won't know what happens, but as long as I'm alive she stays with me.'" And she added,

> Janey's kind of the focal point, the center, of their lives. I mean, she has a lot of power. With her, there's a level of truth to every mother's wish to keep a child at home, to have one you never lose, who never leaves you by growing up and going away. And I think it's there some-where, deep in my mother, and unacknowledged. And the upsetting thing to me is, she's not really thinking about Janey's welfare.

The traditional division of labor by gender makes all children, and per-haps especially, disabled children, mother's work (see Fisher 1998; Ingstad and White 1996; Seligman and Darling 1989). According to conventional wisdom, it also places a strain on the marriage bond, as men sometimes feel overwhelmed by their wives' commitment to the children, to the exclusion of their own needs. While I will refrain from mounting a feminist polemic decrying a sexual division of labor that empowers men to imagine their own needs as autonomous from "the family" while women are denied such fan-tasies, it is important to point out that there is actually very little data on the effects of disabling conditions on marriage stability. And those studies we have are contradictory (Seligman and Darling 1989). Many social workers and special-education service providers commented on the stress and strain that disabled children add to family life. Sylvia Lin, a special-education teacher, said, "Oh, the activists, they're doing great. But mostly, the other

ones have marriages which fall apart: The guys walk out. Those are the kids
who are acting out in my class."

Four of the thirty-eight mothers I interviewed attributed the breakup of
their marriages in part to the pressures of life with disabled children. But
Lydia Sellers, mother of a 9-year-old with Down syndrome, said, "My marriage got stronger after this kid got born. I mean, it's fundamentally a boring
marriage, but we've worked very hard to keep it together. How could either
of us cope with him on our own?" And the scanty research on this topic suggests that this stress, like any other, polarizes couples: Those who would have
split under protracted pressure divorce; those who grow together stay married (Seligman and Darling 1989).

Siblings as well as parents are central to the transformation of family life
with a disabled member. Carol Seeger remembers her sister Diana as "all
messed up about Janey," jealous and judgmental of the time her parents
devoted to a life she found "worthless." Now, the two adult siblings cooperate, with some tension, as they try to help their aging parents and plan for a
future in which they are responsible for Janey. In another family, a 10-year-
old named Patricia says of her 6-year-old sister with Down's, "We share
some germs [genes]. Only Amy's got more germs, too many germs, that's
why she's different than me."

Nora O'Day remembers her retarded sister, Allison, as a very happy child.
But as the three other siblings grew up and moved out, she became morose.
Nora has recently found a way to communicate with Allison by computer: she
hopes to use Allison's e-mail messages to convince their parents that they need
to set up an independent living placement for the "permanent happy child"
who has become depressed as her closest peers moved away.

Caretaking issues are deeply influenced by familial resources. In families
who are comfortably middle-class, issues of estate planning and financial
resources divide able-bodied and disabled siblings: Disabled members must
be disinherited or their benefits will stop after their parents' deaths, when
their inheritance is counted against their Social Security income. And in one
wealthy family, the mother described the need to set up separate trust funds
for each child. She thus imagined that the able-bodied siblings would care for
Ronnie, a brother with Down syndrome, "voluntarily" if their own finances
were not taxed by his needs. This strategy stands in stark contrast to the
training Bonnie d'Amato is giving her 10-year-old daughter vis-à-vis her disabled 5-year-old son:

> I teach her to care for him, I make her responsible. Maybe it's too
> much responsibility, I don't know, what with all the feeding and paying

attention to him in the street all the time. But I'm a single mother, and let's face it, I'm not going to be here for him forever, and she is. What else can I do?

This situation contrasts with several African-American mothers who retained strong family ties in the South: They were confident that extended kin would take their disabled children after their own deaths.

Imagining a future for disabled family members as all intimates age is a complex conundrum: As Bonnie d'Amato pointed out to me with some anger when I queried her aspirations for her son Adam, parents of "normal" children are rarely asked how they imagine their kids will cope. Yet normals, too, are likely to run into significant social, personal, and medical problems as they grow up and assume independence. But the necessity to plan for a disabled family member is widely viewed as more explicit.

The futures which I asked parents to imagine for their disabled children included their aspirations for companionship and living contexts. Activists were most likely to imagine independence and peer dependence:

What do I want for Brian? I want him to live in a Center for Independent Living, to have a job, to have friends. I can imagine him marrying another person with Down's. Parents don't always think about this stuff; they have a hard time thinking past their own lifetimes. And you don't necessarily want your baby to leave the nest. But they have to leave the nest, and they have to do it before it collapses around them. (Marilyn Steiner, white social worker, founder of an early-intervention program and a parents support group, mother of a teenager with Down syndrome)

Marilyn went on to tell me the story of how she had "kidnapped" her mildly retarded adult brother, removing him from her aging parents' home in New York in order to supervise his placement in a group home near her own residence in Michigan.

While some of the working-class and working-poor mothers with whom I spoke aspired to keep their Down syndrome children living at home with them forever, many others, and most middle-class parents, *do* imagine independent living situations. Moreover, many fantasize marriages uniting young adults with Down syndrome; such arrangements are also discussed in the growing literature authored by people with this condition (Burke and McDaniel 1991; Kingsley and Levitz 1994). Such aspirations open up a range of issues: the problems of peer companionship outside of families for disabled adolescents and adults; parental concern and social stigma surrounding the sexuality and potential fertility or sterilization of the mentally retarded[48] (Angrosino and Zagnoli 1992; New York Times 1993); and, from my point of view, the reproduction of a kinship of affliction. Yet they also surely normalize the person with Down syndrome, imagining her or his membership in a community of adults, including those with the rights and responsibilities of a marriage contract.

Disability in Community

Normalizing stigmatized differences is an achievement which surely belongs to parents, but it is also dependent on larger social groups and forces. Johnella Cornell's dream of a disabled baby, and her strong criticisms of "being sent to Heredity" after her son's birth should also be contextualized by her longstanding residence in Harlem. There, her mother received a White House commendation for having fostered twelve community children, many with disabilities. There, too, Johnella had dense interactions with neighbors who had nonspecific mental retardation or cerebral palsy, both of which are diagnosed at high rates in poor communities. This working knowledge of disability gave Johnella pause to worry about how her son with Down syndrome might be teased as he grew up; but it also gave her confidence in his ability to survive as a member of his community. Likewise, three of the parents I interviewed through the Down Syndrome Parents' Support Group were teachers of special education; they had considerable professional knowledge of mild mental retardation. Professional knowledge doesn't necessarily imply acceptance, as the abortion stories of several special-education teachers who received positive diagnoses in chapter 9 should recall for us. But it does suggest that when babies are born with developmental delays, those with prior knowledge are likely to be quite resourceful about how to cope:

> I spent the first month on the telephone. By that time, I had Amy connected to every retarded service in the Bronx and lower Westchester. There was never any question: My kid was going to get the best special services the whole world had to offer. (Linda Hornstein, white special-education consultant, mother of a 6-year-old with Down syndrome)

Paradoxically, those with the most professional resources may also have the strongest barriers to overcome: Mental retardation in a child may be particularly frightening or sad in families where expectations for educational and professional attainment run high. This is a point to which I return below.

Religious beliefs and practices may also condition acceptance. When Susan Lee's daughter Leah was born with Down syndrome, many congregationalists at her fundamentalist church quoted Bible scripture: The blind man exists to show God's mysteries and not as punishment for the sins of his father. Estranged from her family of origin, Susan found that the woman sent as a homemaker by Retarded Infant Services was also Christian, and together they often engaged in prayer and Bible study. "Mrs. Sampson from Retarded Infant Services is like a mother to me. More than my own mother. She helps me, she prays for me, and for Leah. Even though she's black, she's the mother I need," she told me. Likewise, Polly Denton found solace and peace in her relationship with God during her Down syndrome son's many hospitalizations due to heart problems. Her Protestant church was a constant source of support, members providing encouragement, child care for her other youngsters, and company to her and her husband during long hours in hospital vigil. When Robin died at the age of 5, church members saw the family through. Bonnie d'Amato joined a Bible study group shortly after her son Adam was born with Down syndrome. She sees him as a messenger of God, "a minister of love," in her own words, a catalyst for spreading knowledge of God's compassion for all creatures. Many Christians with whom I spoke described their disabled children as "special angels" or "God's innocents," particularly valuable for the purity of their love and spirit. Some, especially those raised as Catholics, spoke of "special children" and "special tests" for parents (especially mothers) which God bestowed. I will interrogate this religious notion of specialness and innocence below. But for the present, it is useful to stress that Christianity seems to provide a dense landscape of figurative possibilities as well as communities of support for believing parents of disabled children: They are alien creatures, but benign, even mystical aliens who bring additional value to life. Indeed, throughout this research, I was continuously struck by how fortunate believers seem to be in the face of adversity, when compared to "secular humanists" like myself: Statistics offer cold existential comfort as a meaning system, when contrasted with the rich imagery, parables, and eternalizing models available in many religious traditions.

But religions do not necessarily orient their members toward acceptance. Although I was able to interview only two practicing Orthodox Jews with disabled children, both went out of their way to tell me that they didn't discuss the children with other community members because they feared their judgment:

I haven't discussed it with the other mothers at the Hebrew school [where the other two sons are students]. Jewish families can be cruel— they can ostracize a child for being slower, they can tell their own children not to play with him. I would have done that, too. Now, I just want Hershel to fit in.

Asked if the other kids wouldn't learn something about fitting in by knowing Hershel and his different way of learning, the mother replied, "Maybe, perhaps. But really, they will be cruel, and I understand it. For us, we need our children to do excellently in the schools" (Gloria Hurwitz, white bookkeeper, mother of a 2-year-old with mosaic trisomy 18).

The emphasis on reading Torah, on religious literacy (especially for sons), is deeply implicated in a survival strategy which has a long history in Jewish communities: Mental retardation therefore constitutes a deep threat to family and lineage. Moreover, in those Orthodox communities where marriages are arranged or at least carefully shepherded, connection with a family that has retarded members is shunned. Hospital social workers, always good sources of stories, told me of the shame and secrecy surrounding the birth of visibly disabled children; their presence may make alliances very difficult for their immediate and extended families. Some Down syndrome babies from Orthodox families have been sent to Canada and Israel, where their American parents use the SSI payments to which they are entitled to aid in their care. In this case, "acceptance" may include responsible caretaking, without the claims of proximate kinship.

Yet many other (non-Orthodox) Jews with whom I spoke also insisted that the Talmudic tradition provided ample philosophical room for contemplating God's purpose in creating suffering on earth. And many quite secular Jews offered philosophical ruminations on the possibilities for enlightenment that mentally retarded children brought as a gift to their families. Nonetheless, Jewish families (as well as Chinese families, who also stress achievement in education as a survival mechanism) give up Down syndrome infants for adoption at what appear to be high rates. Given the legally protected privacy of an adoption decision, there are, of course, no methods for determining objective figures. But Down syndrome activists who specialize in fostering and adoption consistently reported this pattern to me, as did one article published in *Lillith* (Axelrod 1990). The two mothers whose stories of giving up babies with Down syndrome for adoption I collected were both Jewish. One had had an anomalous prenatal diagnosis in which a fetal chromosome had a small deletion; she felt that the encouraging attitudes of the geneticists she consulted "robbed her of her choice." With the certainty of retrospect, she continued the pregnancy because she was influenced by their reassurance. She gave birth to a son who is deeply visually impaired, at high risk for childhood cancer, and developmentally delayed. Angry at the medical counseling she and her husband received, she shocked the accepting grandparents by giving the child away. A second birth mother who chose adoption told this story:

> So at first I didn't want to give her the baby. Who was she? Just some old maid, over 45, single, not what I wanted for my baby. What I wanted for my baby was the whole nine yards: White picket fence, dog, big brothers or sisters. A normal family. Then I realized, that was *me*, that was my family I wanted. And I couldn't bear to keep this baby. So who was I to judge her, when she had the heart to take him?

Neither of these birth mothers considered their Jewishness to be a factor in the adoption decision. But given the patterns into which their actions fit, I interpret their consciousness as having been forged in an environment in which mental retardation is particularly difficult to accept. Moreover, I am *not* suggesting that Jews find disabling conditions *in general* more difficult than non-Jews: The long-standing activism and support in Jewish communities around Tay-Sachs disease and, more recently, around Familial Dysautonomia and Gaucher's disease, all transmitted through Ashkenazi Jewish lineage, suggest that patterns of cultural as well as genetic connection are complex.[49] Rather, it is mental retardation which I believe to be at issue in communities which have learned defensively to "live by their wits." And of course, mental retardation is highly stigmatized in many sectors of the U.S. population, not only among Jews.

Activism and Support Groups

The communities within which parents form alliances and receive support or judgment are not only geographically, professionally, or religiously based: Some are associational, as well. Throughout this chapter, I have referred to some parents as activists; their particular activities, orientations, and aspirations for their disabled children are powerfully reorganized by participation in support groups. Parents are encouraged by a host of professionals—geneticists and genetic counselors, pediatricians and social workers—to join voluntary family support groups. Such groups are historically rooted in several intersecting traditions. One historic precursor to these groups lies in the tradition of immigrant self-help groups of the late nineteenth century. These shared with Alcoholics Anonymous, a WASP invention of the 1930s, certain practices of what might be labeled "early identity politics." A strong belief that "it takes one to know one" or, in this case, "to help one" was present in the birth of both those social movements. Endemic to this tradition is the valorization of "experience" (cf. Scott 1992) and the (often justified) skepticism of the availability or goodwill of public agencies to solve what are widely perceived to be intractable problems and recurrent crises.

A second source of strategy and expertise initially emerged from the needs of disabled veterans with service-related chronic conditions. Many early charities and later research and service groups arose in conjunction with the Veterans Administration. Four major wars in the twentieth century have left the VA with both an enormous constituency and a powerful, highly politicized budget-making process. Expanding demands for medical care, pensions, employment, and shelter have all been fueled by veterans groups and the army of professionals who serve them (Young 1996). Developments in post–World War II medicine also contributed dramatic resources: Widespread use of antibiotics and rapid technical evolution in surgery and blood banking made survival after serious injury a common outcome. As these military experiments became successful, they diffused rapidly to the general population. There they had immense impact on survival rates of accident victims (which affects young adults in disproportionate numbers), and of babies born with hereditary conditions.

While many of the traditional service-related charities and organizations were fed by a decidedly masculinist ideology inflected through national military service, many of the caretakers and activists were mothers and wives, first of disabled vets, and then of disabled children. As married women entered the paid labor force in greater numbers throughout the century, their voluntary and family-based caretaking became more visible; eventually, women became central activists in the movements which led to legislation guaranteeing not only medical but also educational resources for the disabled.

Additionally, national public interest in mental retardation was surely amplified by the well-publicized stories of the Kennedy family, beginning in the 1960s: An elder sister with mental retardation, and a child who died young with the same condition are part of the family legacy. So, too, are the scores of centers for research and clinical services to mentally retarded Americans which are found coast-to-coast. Many have been generously funded by the Kennedys, and some bear variants of their name. Legislative transformations in the Kennedy-Johnson years also affected the increase of Social Security coverage in the 1970s; and Section 504 of the National Rehabilitation Act of 1973 mandated that states cover an appropriate education for all handicapped children. The Americans with Disabilities Act of 1990, now winding its way into enforcement via federal and state regulations and court-based challenges, provides the most comprehensive protections to date.

Lay support groups clearly grew out of and responded to all these legal, medical, and social developments. Self-help organizations for those with specific physical and mental health concerns (rather than generic veterans groups, or research-service charities like the Easter Seal Society) are a relatively recent phenomenon, a product of the 1950s and 1960s, and becoming increasingly specialized as more differentiating and disabling conditions take on specific medical nomenclature (Weiss and Mackta 1996). In this newer tradition of grouping and differentiating support groups and networks according to diagnostic categories, genetic labels and the activism of kin are an expanding aspect of the social terrain. Nationally, the Alliance of Genetic Support Groups office in Washington collects and networks two hundred national and local groups whose identity is based in genetically identified conditions; parents of recently diagnosed children can turn to the alliance for information on relevant voluntary health organizations in their region and condition. There are at least four important national organizations, and scores of state-based and local associations, which grow from a fusion of familial and professional concern with Down syndrome. The two largest national organizations offer toll-free telephone help lines. The National Down Syndrome Congress was founded in 1971. It maintains a parent hotline, publishes a newsletter, holds conventions, and lobbies on national policy issues. The National Down Syndrome Society, founded in 1979, raises funds to support biomedical researchers whose work will enrich the understanding of Down's. Both groups offer pamphlets, videos, and other resources which are widely available to parents of newly diagnosed children. Local chapters of the ARC (formerly, the Association of Retarded Citizens) and Down Syndrome Parent Support Groups provide informal networks for parent-to-parent peer counseling. Most early-intervention programs have social workers and psychologists on staff who specialize in the nuts and bolts of family support, and who can negotiate the maze of medical and education evaluations and paperwork that accompanies access to the SSI and Medicaid funding to which most disabled children are entitled. They also point parents toward the local support groups (cf. Black and Weiss 1990). Ideally, by the time a newly diagnosed baby leaves the hospital, the family should be hooked up to such associational groups and services, where other parents and professionals with long-standing experience will begin the process of socializing them to life with a disabled child.

Local support groups offer rich and reassuring resources for parents learning to normalize a child as a family member, not only as a medical diagnosis. Paradoxically, medical worldview and resources figure large in the repertoire of such groups, even as these groups contest medicine's exclusive dominion over definitions of disabled family members. New identities as well as new knowledge of services are modeled by parent activists for their recently conscripted peers. During the two years in which I attended meetings of the Down Syndrome Parent Support Group of Manhattan and the Bronx, and occasional meetings of groups in other boroughs, I was particularly impressed by the many levels on which parent peer support was mobilized and extended. For purposes of this chapter, at least three should be mentioned.

First, as its public face, the group maintained a newsletter in which summaries of recent meetings and announcements of future ones were publicized. In its pages, parents might request specific information or help. The group also held monthly meetings, where the resources of cutting-edge biomedical research and scientific information were regularly made available to the group. Researchers working on chromosome 21, on the connection between Alzheimer's disease and Down syndrome, on neuroendocrinology, all addressed the group. So did a host of clinical specialists and allied health professionals: neurologists, orthopedists, pediatric dentists, audiologists, speech therapists, physical and occupational therapists. Computer specialists in learning stimulation programs, behavioral psychologists, and representatives from state and municipal departments of education were among the invited speakers. With the aid of an array of professionals, activist parents tackled many problems. Lists of relevant medical and technical services were drawn up and evaluated. In several cases, local doctors deemed excellent by the group were called upon to "straighten out" medical colleagues or even institutions whose attitudes toward children with Down syndrome parent activists found demeaning or out of date. The Education Committee spent several years conducting a survey of Down syndrome family needs, and evaluating special-educational resources in some of the city's many public school districts and private schools. They forged alliances with activists on the Committee on the Handicapped, coaching families through the bureaucratic maze as children made the transition from early-intervention services to individual educational placement. And they succeeded in mobilizing a local parochial school to set up a "special needs" classroom for children with Down syndrome who were mainstreamed for selected activities. The group also sent representatives to various national conferences, sporting events, and technology fairs from which they thought their membership could benefit. And they regularly heard reports on national legal and health policy issues affecting their families.

Of course, such projects involve far more work than can be accomplished by a few individuals at episodic meetings. In addition to countless hours clocked at subcommittee meetings, projects were also backed up by the existence and active use of a host of publications, including local newsletters, and nationally distributed, highly successful magazines like *Exceptional Parent* and *Exceptional Child,* and more vulnerable activist pulp magazines like *Disability Rag* and *This Mouth.* The armamentarium of activist parental support increasingly involves the use of technology ranging from the most routinized—telephones, televisions, and fax machines—to the more elite— on-line services including chat groups, cyberspace newsletters, bibliographies, and bulletin boards where regional, national, and international conferences are announced (e.g., Ferguson 1996). In all this work, the language of activism became deeply imbricated with that of science and technology.

Second, this public face of technoscientific and policy activism was supplemented and transformed by "human interest" meetings: Adolescents with Down syndrome reporting on their aspirations for adulthood; a bar mitzvah videotape of a boy with Down syndrome whose successful speech therapy enabled him to participate in this congregational rite of passage; and a meeting on how to start a parent support group. Many parents who would not find the time or interest to listen to molecular biological research reports were enthralled and encouraged to hear about "down-to-earth" success stories involving youngsters with their own children's condition. As several core activists told me, their own passionate concerns might lie in science and policy issues, but the crowd-drawing events were more likely to focus on uplifting experiences and accomplishments.

The third transformatory activity of the group was not open to me directly, but I learned about it from the grateful stories that parents of newly diagnosed babies told me: "Old hands" were quickly mobilized whenever a social worker, relative, colleague, or parent called for help. Using telephones, home visits, and occasionally the offer of respite care, families who had made a successful adjustment to raising a child with Down syndrome offered empathic peer counseling to the newly afflicted. The first few weeks and months of family life with a diagnosed baby can be grim. Medical problems, some life-threatening, are likely to loom large. Until the advent of antibiotic drugs and infant surgery, 50 percent of children with Down syndrome died before their fifth birthday; 20 percent still do, more than 10 percent during their first year of life (Julian-Reynier, Aurran et al. 1995). In addition to the stress and strain of "living on a medical roller coaster" (as several parents described it), there is the emotional strain of coming to terms with a child with a stigmatized difference. Peer counseling teaches parents how to cope with the ups and down of this transition. Using "been there" stories, gallows humor, and the deep appreciation which comes from having survived something one could not otherwise have imagined, many parents provided a buddy service for newborns and their shocked families, making themselves available in creative ways. The presence of young Down syndrome children at support group meetings (with a paid child-care worker in attendance so that parents could focus their attention on adult activities) also provided dramatic and optimistic evidence that families could thrive after a difficult diagnosis had been delivered. Collectively through their activism, parents of children with Down syndrome developed, deployed, and transmitted a worldview in which difference could be accepted and a new identity as parents of a different kind of child could be formulated and assumed. In the process, many families established a new site for the construction of community, finding first solace and then friendship with others who had sustained similar experiences. Thus, children socially stigmatized as alien could be embedded not only in their own families, but in a wider activist community, an extended family of affliction.

Indeed, the importance of forging new communities was forcefully brought home to me when one mother evaluated the extensive material disruptions which the birth and development of her daughter with Down syndrome entailed on prior social relations. The child's older sister, Patricia, came of age within the local web of kin and community that an extended Bronx family and neighborhood could provide. But Amy's infant stimulation program, special-education classrooms, compensatory services, medical interventions, and sports teams were all dispersed across three boroughs and four counties. Normalization required massive transportation. And as Amy grew, her slower development meant that she held less interest for the "normal" children in the extended family network. In the process, old ties were sometimes sacrificed: The family had less time to socialize. And new connections were forged: The family met others through intervention services and support group activities whose needs and perspectives closely resembled their own. New notions of community were thus built out of necessity as well as choice.

Imagined Communities

New notions of community are poignantly manifest in the collective uses parents make of kinship connection to stake claims for their stigmatized children. Earlier in this chapter I noted the linguistic constructs through which some parents (and biomedical service providers) imagine genealogies of affliction which work to exclude disabled members, placing them outside their families of birth and inside imagined communities of difference. But activists may also use the rhetorical power of kinship language to include their children in a universal "family of man."

These imagined communities of extended kinship take on much broader significance when evoked by parent activists in the service of disability rights. Relatedness and connection are rhetorically restored by the kinship discourse of activists. During my two years of participation in a support group for parents whose children had Down syndrome, I was struck by how frequently members articulated an inclusive, collective sense of parental responsibility:

> You also feel a sense of parenthood for everyone's child, there's a sense they're all my children, you know. Which I don't think you feel with your normal children. (Bonnie d'Amato, white social worker, mother of a 6-year-old with Down syndrome)

> Our kids need special classrooms in caring schools. Our kids need speech therapists and physical therapists who know their special needs. But most of all, our kids need respect. As a mother, it's my job to get those things for our kids. (Linda Degracia, white secretary, mother of a 5-year-old with Down syndrome)

The restitution of kinship here serves to enlarge the human family, claiming a natural base for a social challenge against discrimination.

In attending public meetings, hearing uplifting success stories, participating in peer counseling, and forging new kin and community connections, parents who rely on support groups often come to speak a doubled discourse of both difference and normalization. On the one hand, they must individually come to terms with a baby who wasn't expected, a baby whose developmental trajectory is largely unknown, and known to be different from other family and community members. On the other hand, families in the support group are given a rich array of resources for the acceptance and incorporation of their Down syndrome children, and taught that they should have high aspirations for their children's success.

In describing a doubled trajectory both of accepting difference and normalizing it, many parents told me a story that I first heard from activist Emily Kingsley at a parent support group. Some said an obstetrician or pediatrician first recounted the parable, while others attributed it to a sympathetic nurse or social worker. It is copied and distributed in many hospital pediatric wards:

Imagine you have planned a vacation to Italy, to see the rose gardens of Florence. You are totally excited, you have read all the guide books, your suitcases are packed, and off you go. As the plane lands, the pilot announces, "Sorry, ladies and gentlemen, but this flight has been rerouted to the Netherlands." At first you are very upset: The vacation you dreamed about has been canceled. But you get off the plane, determined to make the best of it. And you gradually discover that the blue tulips of Holland are every bit as pretty as the red roses you had hoped to see in Florence. They may not be as famous, but they are every bit as wonderful. You didn't get a red rose. But you got a blue tulip, and that's quite special, too.

This parable of acceptance glistens with metaphors of organic growth, planned and unplanned travel, representational and contrastive colors, and evolving perception. Many parents shorthanded this parable when referring to something their disabled child had said or done, referring to "blue tulip" rewards. Nonetheless, even parents who accepted the language and constructs of "blue tulips" could also express their losses.

I go along from day to day, marveling at what Stevie accomplishes. As long as he's home with me, I don't think he's slow; I just think he's growing and talking and learning. Now, he's counting to ten. Pretty soon, he's bound to be potty trained. Then once in a while, I'll take him to an office party or somewhere with other kids, and I really get slapped in the face. Blue tulips, again and again. (Pat Carlson, white secretary, mother of a 6-year-old with Down syndrome)

The parable of the blue tulip opens up for me a discussion of "doubled discourses," in which recognition of difference is substituted for judgments of abnormality, and enlightenment occurs. Like all metaphorical journeys of enlightenment, the one which many parents describe is time-consuming, fraught with tests and challenges and, of course, leads to great rewards. It entails a movement away from focusing on abnormality in their children to accepting differences variously described as physical, mental, emotional, and, some would say, spiritual. Thus the eye and facial bone structure, or low muscle tone so characteristic of Down syndrome becomes perceived as adorable and appealing rather than stigmatized in infants and toddlers; their eagerness and good humor are valued as signs of openness to experience rather than as simple minded; their affectionate presence, gift for mimicry, and ability to appeal to strangers are resignified as special "gifts" of a disabled child. In journeying narratives, doubled discourses provide maps, metaphors, and images of the normal and abnormal, sometimes described in terms of sameness and difference; human and animal; or even innocence and savagery. Doubled discourses inform not only parental perceptions, but professional attitudes and activist aspirations, as well.

As I became aware of these multiply sited doubled discourses expressed by a wide range of people among whom I worked in the course of this research, I initially tried to parse their grammar. But they proved to be quite slippery. Their value statements may at first appear to be starkly negative or positive, but explicitly or implicitly, they contain a polarity marking the opposite value, as well. They primarily rest on a contrastive and exclusionary pair of images or processes in which ordinary common sense or hegemonic assumptions are embedded, marking one element as normative and the other as abnormal. Intelligence in children, to take an obvious example, is desirable and normal; mental retardation is undesirable and problematic. Such polarized referents or processes are highly malleable, providing linguistic resources for a wide range of ideas and actions: Mentally retarded children may be prized for their "lack of guile" (to cite one parent). Most obviously, they may be invoked to express dominant or hegemonic values like loathing or disgust ("That child behaves like an animal!"); they may also be inverted to mark an elevated, exceptional, or romanticized status ("She's such an innocent angel!"). At the same time, if less commonly, doubled discourses may provide the material from which resistant or new images are forged. This is especially true when parents of disabled children use the inclusive language of kinship to stake claims for their excluded children's rights, as I indicated above. And doubled discourses are flexible enough to tip in favor of difference, providing space into which human alternatives may be imagined.

For this reason, mainstreaming is viewed by many parents and educators as a two-way street, of value to the nondisabled as well as the disabled. A commitment to mainstreaming entails including disabled children in a range of environments: most notably, schools, but also, play groups, religious education, community celebrations, and much more. Disabled children are described by most families in the support group as having a special lesson to teach. It is a lesson of acceptance and love of difference, a replacement of "less than" by "other than."

> Our kids are very musical, they sing from their souls. When Kenny was a toddler, he couldn't speak; people would get so frustrated with him, he'd get so upset. But he would dance and sway to the music, and you'd see the light of love in his eyes. I read somewhere that there's a

community for retarded people in the mountains, somewhere in Europe. They play music, and they run a farm. Kids like this are very loving, they're good with animals; it's like the music of the universe is inside of them. If only the rest of us could listen. Maybe they could teach us to hear it better. (Judy Kaufman, white nurse, mother of a 7-year-old with Down syndrome)

I want Adam to be a messenger of God's love. God made him for some reason; it's not ours to know, but everyone who meets him learns a little more about it. You can never get angry at people who are sincere, who really try, once you meet Adam. It's not being smart, it's being loving that makes you a human being. (Bonnie d'Amato, white social worker, mother of a 5-year-old with Down syndrome)

There are some benefits from having a child like this. Robin will never show guile, he will never be deceitful, he will always give and return love completely innocently. I would never say that about my other children. (Polly Denton, white actress, mother of a 3-year-old with Down syndrome)

My ideas pertaining to doubled, hegemonic, and resistant discourses are highly abstract, but the processes they describe are quite concrete.[50] Nature/culture oppositions, for example, are commonly found in the ordinary language with which mentally retarded hildren are described by parents and professionals alike. Even those most committed to nurturing and serving developmentally delayed children spontaneously deploy nature/culture oppositions when they use the language of animal imagery to merge them with other species:

Aleem was born with a lot of hair. I said, "Nurse, is this going to fall off before I bring him home from the hospital?" Because I didn't want nobody to look at Aleem and think he was a little monkey, not a boy. (Johnella Cornell, African-American hairdresser, mother of an 18-month-old with Down syndrome)

Having him in the house, it's like having a gorilla. (Cynthia Foreman, white law professor, mother of a toddler with a chromosome anomaly)

Among the ten common characteristics used for medical diagnosis of Down syndrome in newborns and infants is the presence of a simian crease, a single deep fold which runs across the palm, common among people with Down syndrome, in contrast to the multiple angular folds which most people without this condition carry. The medical use of the term "simian" carries with it a devolutionary implication: People with Down syndrome share some physical characteristics with monkeys. Like the racial label of "mongol" to which I turn below, "simian" indexes similarities in its bearers which group and segregate them from people without this characteristic, recategorizing them as closer to the nonhuman primates than to their immediate human kin. It is a frankly degenerative label. Several parents alluded to the problem of "monkey business" in labeling this "stigmata" (another word still widely used in medical texts and practice to describe the signs of Down syndrome, and one which barely conceals its religious origins in describing Christ's signifying wounds). One mother, however, inverted the discourse, resignifying the simian crease:

> He's all heart. Like he's such a lovely person, even now, he'll make me stop the car if his brother is crying, so he can get out of the car seat to hug him. He's pure love. He's right there in the moment, all 100 percent of him, which most normal people don't have that capacity. . . . The simian crease—well, according to palmistry, there are two lines, the head and the heart. The two lines should go across, one's the head, one's the heart. And they [kids with Down syndrome] only have one. So it's like they're merged, the head and the heart, all in one line. And I think that's true of all Down syndrome people, right across the board. They're all heart. And it shows in the crease. (Judy Kaufman, white nurse, mother of a 5-year-old with Down syndrome)

In her view, the purity of Down syndrome children's love, vested in their "heart," corresponds to the single, deep crease, when read through the counterdiscourse of palmistry. A covertly negative label is thus reprocessed through an alternative grid to yield a positive attribute. The simian crease becomes a desirable trait.

Evolutionary Thinking

The idea that children with this condition are less evolved, hence closer to animals and to the "savage races" has a long history. This view was held by, most famously, John Langdon Haydon Down, for whom the condition was medically named. Down served as the medical supervisor of the Earlswood Asylum for Idiots in Surrey, England, for a decade beginning in 1858. Later, he ran a private home for retarded adults in Teddington until his death in 1897 (Brain 1967). In keeping with the humanist scientific fashions of his era, Down devoted considerable time to observing and categorizing his patients, whom he divided by what he perceived to be their similarities to various ethnic races. Some were classified as "Ethiopians," some as "Malay." But the largest group contained "Mongols," and Down's reasoning is worth considering at some length:

> A very large number of congenital idiots are typical Mongols. So marked is this that, when placed side by side, it is difficult to believe that the specimens compared are not children of the same parents. . . . The ethnic classification of idiocy which I indicated is of extreme interest philosophically as well as of value practically. Philosophically because it throws light on the question which very much agitated public opinion about the time of the American Civil War. The work of Nott and Glidden labored to prove that the various ethnic families were distinct species, and a strong argument was based on this to justify a certain domestic institution [slavery]. If, however, it can be shown that from some deteriorating influence the children of Caucasian parents can be removed into another ethnic type, it is a strong corroborative argument that the difference is a variable and not a specific one. (Down 1877, 1866, 217, 213)

Down's classification thus exhibits a doubled discourse which is still widely, if less consciously, held: On the one hand, "defectives" and "idiots" resemble races which are ranked (here, by the English) as inferior to Caucasians. Retarded people and exotic races are thus condensed together as evolutionary throwbacks to a prior, intellectually inferior stage. This is the dominant message of the racial classification of retarded patients, and the one which continues to be projected whenever the label of "mongoloid" is used, as it was in this country in medical books through the 1970s, and through the '80s in analogous texts in England (Gould 1980; Lippman and Brunger 1991). While most educated people no longer use the term, it is widely recognized and carries with it the condensation of racial exoticism and mental inferiority. On the other hand, John Down's argument is entirely in the liberal universalist tradition, for he used the fantasized racial classification of his patients to argue for monogenism, a theory, then in decline, that the human race was singular and unified. "Mongoloid idiots" (as he labeled them) illustrate a principle that weakens the justification for racially based slavery because those who appear to belong to a different race are actually offspring of Caucasians.

When viewed from the end of the twentieth century, racial hierarchy dominates this scheme, and pressing reasons remain for extinguishing the racial epithet "mongoloid" as inaccurate as well as deeply biased. But from a contemporary perspective, humanist inclusion also lay behind the racial connections Down traced out.[51] Likewise, other medical writers from the third quarter of the nineteenth century onward commented on the affectionate personalities and amiable humor of people with Down syndrome. Such commentary suggests that scientific practitioners and authors were no less heir to deeply held cultural imagery than were their less educated contemporaries, for they stressed both the mystery of innocence—why are "idiots" happier?—and a universalizing appreciation of their likeable temperament.

If people with Down syndrome are metaphorized as closer to animals, "lower races," and mysterious innocents, they then also illustrate an older grand narrative scheme concerning the childhood of the human race. Elements of this narrative date back to the Greeks; aspects were reprocessed through the sieve of science to yield "ontogeny recapitulates phylogeny" in the nineteenth century. Particular organisms can then be viewed as representing immature stages in a wider scheme of development. Metaphorically, certain adult groups may represent humanity's infancy: Arrested in their development like fossil flies in amber, they are then thought to characterize a "purer" or more "original" state of being human. Pathological adults who are members of the dominant races may then be viewed as "throwbacks" to prior developmental stages (Gould 1980). Like the "primitive societies" which fascinated nineteenth-century armchair anthropologists, infantilized populations condense many Western preoccupations: Innocence before the Fall; or, in more secular parlance, pure feelings and perceptions rather than world-weary sophistication; or even states of permanent and childlike dependency rather than the painful trade-offs involved in growth and development.

While I am claiming that the problem of infantilization is linked to pervasive evolutionary paradigms in the history of Western intellectual thought, many authors and activists concerned with disability rights contest a present-day version of this problem. They have objected to the infantilization of disabled people in general: Criticisms have been leveled against a wide range of "disabling images," including "Jerry's Kids"-style telethons; poster children as fund raisers; more grimly, the rigid and punitive practices of enforced dependency encoded in more than a century's history of institutions designed to both "protect" and contain disabled citizens; and in policies and laws limiting the autonomy and choices (in education, jobs, housing, and even sexual, reproductive, and marital relations) (Finger 1990; Shapiro 1993).[52] This discourse of infantilization in all its complexity is particularly salient in polarized representations of mentally retarded children as either unworldly in their innocence or menacing in their bestiality, especially as they grow to puberty and sexual maturity (Angrosino 1986; Angrosino and Zagnoli 1992).

Parents of disabled children fall heir to this complex discursive heritage, for they spontaneously speak a doubled discourse of both accepting difference and actively working for normalization. Indeed, as many of the stories recounted in this chapter suggest, activist parents are particularly articulate in deploying both sides of this worldview.

Another View

But support groups do not reach or represent all parents of Down syndrome children. Indeed, during the two years in which I attended support group meetings, participation ranged from a "handful" of parents to perhaps thirty or forty adults in the room. Mothers from two-parent families were most likely to be in attendance; fewer fathers, and by far fewer single parents regularly came to meetings. Organizers told me that a core of about ten families did the work of the group, maintaining mailing lists of several hundred families who had requested information. At the time I conducted field research, similar support groups were active in three of New York City's five boroughs. But most parents of children with Down syndrome do not participate in support groups. In New York City, active members are likely to be middle-class, white, and parents of first children, or parents with the financial resources to use a host of commercial services, including nannies and baby-sitters. Far less likely to rely on the support groups are parents whose child with Down syndrome is a younger sibling; who do not have much discretionary time or income; or who come from community backgrounds with strong church or ethnic-group affiliation. As these issues of discretionary time and income suggest, class-based differences surely figure in support group activism. But class is here mediated (and sometimes, contradicted) through other, more "experience near" (Geertz 1967) sensibilities. As several social workers involved in Down syndrome services suggested, middle-class and professional parents are far more likely to take on a "voluntary" associational identity on behalf of their children than are working-class families. Perhaps middle-class comfort with "associational identity" is strengthened by prior professional experiences, or the proclivity to seek intellectually rational solutions to intractable personal problems. Some social workers, more comfortable than I am with a psychodynamic explanation, rendered the judgment that "those activists are too involved" with the issue of how Down syndrome has transformed their own identities. "Why don't they just get on with it?" was a question asked by several.

Several marginally active members of parent support groups offered social analyses of their own, describing both the class leveling (of misfortune) and the class privilege (of resources) which united and separated them from many activist leaders:

> You know, I just go to a few meetings a year, not too many. First of all, it's geared for new parents, the ones with babies and toddlers. I know all that stuff already. But second, I like to go because it really blows my mind, you know, if you think it was hard for us to accept a different kind of kid, imagine if you were like some of these people who thought you were gonna have a boy or girl with their lacrosse shirts, you know, that would go to Ivy League schools, that's how you always pictured it, and then this happened. . . . I kind of like to be in a room with them once in a while because I think it changes them for the better. It's not that I would hate them or despise them, it isn't that at all. But if this thing that happened to them hadn't happened, well, we'd have absolutely nothing in common. Now, I think their values have changed in a positive direction; they're not looking down anymore. I think it's changed my life in a positive direction, too, but I was never a person who put that much stock in my kid going to Yale or, you know, looking a certain way. I wasn't so oriented toward a certain lifestyle like they were. Maybe it's stupid of me, but I didn't expect rich people to have Down syndrome children, and it helps me to remember that they do, too. (Judy Kaufman, white nurse, mother of a 5-year-old with Down syndrome)

Patsy DelVecchio, a recovering alcoholic, offered both a class polemic and a commentary on the coercive, identity-encompassing aspects of support group membership.

> I'm very critical, you know. I cannot see myself sitting with a bunch of petty little women, talking about their children like they were some kind of topic of conversation. This is just life. You don't have to publicize, nor to condemn. You get a lot of mothers that's behaving just like in AA, like, "Yeah, I'm an alcoholic." "Yeah, I'm the mother of a Down's child that doesn't walk, doesn't talk, doesn't do this or that, and I have no time." You make time, lady, I say, you just make time. As far as going to meetings for parents with Down syndrome children, it's

ludicrous. You get these Park Avenue high-society women with charge accounts saying, "I have my daughter at the institute, I have a private tutor for my daughter." Just like they say, "I go shopping at Bloomies" [Bloomingdale's]. Lady, I wish I could afford your nanny. Meanwhile, they sit at meetings talking, "I have a Down syndrome child, Oh my child has slanted eyes, well, my child's tongue curls." He's not a freak, you're talking about a human being. Right, wrong, or indifferent, it's just life, and I wouldn't treat it any differently.

Patsy DelVecchio has, in addition to considerable class resentment, a resistance to what she takes to be self-promotion through identifying with difference. It is normalization through acceptance, not emphasis of difference, that she favors in this commentary.

Several working-class nonactivists also expressed a rather different sensibility concerning aspirations for their children with Down syndrome. Unlike those who strategize for what they consider to be the best educational resources, nurse aide Anna Morante replied to my questions concerning her son's future:

What does it mean to have this child? That I will be a mother forever, that this one will never leave home. That's ok, I'm glad I'll have him with me forever. Only I worry if I die before he does. I don't want anything else from the schools, there's no point in that. He's happiest right here at home, where I can take care of him.

And Leila Robertson, an African-American welfare mother of a 7-year-old with Down syndrome, was quite explicit in her critique of the mystification which she thought optimistic public images of disabled children brought to political life:

All those groups, those films and stuff, I don't know if that really helps Malik. In fact, it *don't* help Malik. What good does it do to put all those fancy white kids on television? Oh sure, it's an inspiration, I bet the Reagans, they sit home nights watching it. Gives them a good excuse not to worry when they cut the social services back. Those films don't say that the kids got parents who can pay for speech therapists, foot doctors, special computer tapes in their homes. Not my son. Why don't they put my son on the television? Then people would see what it's really like.

The discursive and material resources available for families of disabled children vary greatly along the social fault lines set up by race, class, religious, and ethnic differences in contemporary America. While all children with diagnosed disabilities are entitled to important benefits via public funding (like early-intervention services and basic health care), the intensive and costly extras (like specialized educational computer programs and the machines to run them; or home-based physical therapy equipment; or extra speech therapy or physical therapy sessions to enhance the work of early-intervention classrooms), as well as the transportational and other family support systems needed to access them are not randomly distributed. Disability thus is socially constructed, reflecting not only the hegemonic claims of medicine and counterclaims of families and activists, but crosscutting differences within the very category of "disability" as well.

Moreover, there is, of course, no simple relation between access to cutting-edge or expensive services and outcomes.[53] Patsy DelVecchio's son was among the "highest-functioning" children with Down syndrome I encountered in my research. Yet he attended a school rated as substandard by many other parents and by Patsy herself, who also criticized two infant stimulation programs from which she had previously removed him. Spending the day in Patsy's Staten Island home, I was struck by the rich, nonstop stimulation provided by the environment in which Jeffrey lived: A matrifocal extended family moving between two connected row houses provided hugs, shouts, and fisticuffs at all hours; the kitchen was a constant site of informal coffee klatches and half-consumed meals; a retarded adult uncle lived next door and was often left to supervise Jeffrey while other adults completed their chores. And though Bonnie d'Amato described her son Adam as a "messenger of God," I saw him as a lightning rod collecting attention, love, and discipline at the myriad evangelical church functions to which his mother brought him each week. He responded with an engaging social competence which included the ability to deliver lovely mock sermons and religious testimony. Mimicry and performance are skills often attributed by parents to their children with Down syndrome. Surely, a range of biological capacities and predilections exists for children with Down syndrome, as it exists for those without this chromosomal difference. But there is also a range of social environments within which developmentally delayed children are challenged to grow, and environmental stimuli come in many forms.

And all parents do not imagine that educational resources are key to their disabled children's futures: Both an African-American welfare mother and a white secretary told me they didn't want help struggling with the Board of

Education's COH and school placement: "Not everybody wants to fight City Hall," the secretary told me.

In offering these descriptions from the margins of parent activism, I should stress that the majority of nonactivist parents remained deeply appreciative of support group resources. And they were as concerned about the health and happiness of their disabled children as their activist peers. Their strongest reasons for not attending meetings or participating in informal networks with other parents of children with Down syndrome overwhelmingly focused on time constraints. But they were also far less likely to express mainstreaming aspirations for the futures of their Down syndrome children, and also less comfortable with the idea of representing themselves as parents of disabled children.

Biosociality

Throughout this chapter, I have been particularly interested in how a language of science (and social science) and creation stories harkening back to nineteenth-century evolutionary thought and forward to molecular biology are incorporated, and occasionally contested in the fund of social knowledge which families of children with Down syndrome develop. I have tried to show how modern community-based public institutions like early-intervention programs and parent support groups offer powerful resources for parents to become scientifically literate as they seek the best possible services and outcomes for their children. In the process, they also normalize biomedical definitions of the problems and solutions within which a disabling condition is assimilated into family and community life. Parents (and children) who resculpt their identities using the resources of peer support groups are participating in a process which Paul Rabinow (building on Foucault) has labeled "biosociality," the forging of a collective identity under the emergent categories of biomedicine and allied sciences (Rabinow 1992). Throughout this chapter I have also tried to describe older and deeper traditions of doubled discourses through which children labeled abnormal or anomalous can be reconfigured and integrated into social life. Biomedicine provides discourses with hegemonic claims over this social territory, encouraging enrollment in the categories of biosociality. Yet these claims do not go uncontested, nor are these new categories of identity used untransformed. Religious orientations and practices, informal folk beliefs, class-based and ethnic traditions as well as scientifically inflected counterdiscourses also lay claim to the interpretation of extra chromosomes. Moreover, not all families of children with Down syndrome rely on support groups, nor are all families equally likely to traffic in scientific worldviews and categories. At stake in the analysis of the traffic between biomedical and familial discourses is an understanding of the inherently uneven seepage of science and its multiple uses and transformations into contemporary social life. Of course, in a more general sense, this problem has informed my entire study. What, finally, has an examination of the social impact and cultural meaning of amniocentesis from multiple angles taught us? What might be the conclusions?

11

Endings Are Really Beginnings

IN THE PRECEDING CHAPTERS, I have attempted to analyze the social impact and cultural meanings of prenatal diagnosis from the perspectives of many different kinds of people: pregnant women and their supporters who used or refused the test; genetic counselors, geneticists, lab technicians, and others involved in the provision of relevant health services; parents of children with some of the same disabilities that can now be diagnosed prenatally, and professionals who work with those children. I began by describing salient aspects of the intersecting histories of human genetics, eugenics, and relevant legal formations within which the development and routinization of amniocentesis and its associated technologies came to "make sense": The seemingly intimate and private realm of contemporary women's pregnancies and their outcomes converge with these international, national, and local developments. It was against this sociohistorical background, and the escalating geneticization of the "history of the present" that pregnant women's entry into genetic counseling and the offer of prenatal testing were situated. Following a highly diverse group of New York women through counseling, their decisions to use or refuse amniocentesis, and home visits during the waiting period for its results engaged me in their fears and aspirations concerning fetal health and what specific disabilities might mean to them and their families. I also described the highly skilled technoscientific laboratory labors involved in producing and stabilizing diagnoses, and the impact of receiving a "positive" diagnosis on women who then chose to end their pregnancies. Finally, I reported on what I had learned by working with families whose children had Down syndrome (or some other hereditary conditions) about the disparity between a medical diagnosis and the social integration of a child with a stigmatized difference.

The fieldwork for this study was conducted among seven constituencies:

genetic counselors, geneticists, laboratory diagnosticians, pregnant women who accepted amniocentesis, those who refused it, women who received a positive diagnosis and chose to end their pregnancies, and families with children who have conditions that the test can now reveal before birth. While much of my research was conducted in hospitals, laboratories, and prenatal clinics, I also worked through two early-intervention programs for developmentally delayed children, several support groups for families whose children had Down syndrome, and visited with families at home, and parents and potential parents wherever it was convenient to meet them—in offices, restaurants, parks, playgrounds, and, occasionally, in my own home. I roamed as widely as possible in order to map the cartography of a new reproductive technology, situating it in the densest social landscape that I could imagine and visit.

Yet even as I plotted these overlapping constituencies and locales where emergent and diverse meanings of prenatal diagnosis were being constructed, I discovered other sites which I had neither the time nor the resources to explore. I did not, for example, focus on the basic research scientists whose experiments define the cutting edges of current gene hunting and mapping, although they surely would have contributed additional, valuable perspectives on the future possibilities for prenatal testing. Nor did I meet with pregnant women committed to home birthing or other countercultural reproductive strategies who are most likely to stand at a distance from the use of pregnancy technologies in general, and prenatal testing in particular. Their orientations might have added to my understandings of the contested nature of "nature" among some women deemed "medically appropriate" for amniocentesis. And I limited my investigations of the social meaning of Down syndrome to participant observation with families whose young children had this condition; I did not expand my work to include adults with Down syndrome who surely have important perceptions of their own to report (cf. Angrosino 1986, 1994, 1997). In a post-Freudian world, we have come to believe that all grown children tell stories which differ considerably from those narrated by their parents; this is all the more true when life stories focus on disability, so often fraught with issues of infantilization and dependency. Other renditions thus cry out for expression from the point of view of both young and mature adults living with Down syndrome and other chromosomal anomalies. Likewise, in a postantibiotic world where infant surgery and life-saving prostheses have become routine, the healthy cohort of people living successfully with these stigmatized differences is expanding; now, they occasionally write their own books (Burke and

McDaniel 1991; Kingsley and Levitz 1994; Linton 1998; Mairs 1997; Saxton 1987; see also Seagoe 1964 and Berube 1996, 263–264). Yet such voices were not queried as part of this research.

I mention these terrae incognitae to make an obvious point: Complex cultural objects, in this case the reproductive technologies of prenatal diagnosis, have neither methodological nor theoretical boundaries. They may be examined from multiple, and sometimes competing points of view. Like a hyperstack constructed and multiply bookmarked and hot-linked on the Internet, this object of investigation constantly recomposed itself in relation to the angle from which I was viewing it. And each shift of perspective brought additional aspects of the technology into focus. Thus, the constituencies I chose to engage shaped my understandings of the technology, augmenting the importance of some problems and muffling others. Had my own theoretical predilections been rooted in the anthropology of special education, for example, I surely would have constructed a different analysis (see McDermott and Varenne 1995, 1996); likewise, emergent science studies by anthropologists have strongly influenced my work, but were not the entry point of my initial investigation (cf. Franklin 1995; Fujimura 1992, 1996; Heath 1998; Heath and Rabinow 1993; Traweek 1992, 1993). Because I began from my own experiences with both amniocentesis and women's health movement participation, I privileged the voices, choices, and ethical conundrums that this technology poses for women, concentrating on the diversity of a gender set.

Moral Pioneering

Indeed, as my research became more layered, I came to think of the women who submitted to the discipline of a new reproductive technology in order to reap its biomedical benefits as moral pioneers. At once conscripts to techno-scientific regimes of quality control and normalization, and explorers of the ethical territory its presence produces, contemporary pregnant women have become our moral philosophers of the private. A classic feminist analysis might begin by noting that women have long been relegated to the sociocultural domain of the family, intimacy, and the private; thus important cultural and political tensions concerning the limits of individualism, privacy, and bodily integrity have been represented by and played out on our potentially reproductive bodies. While most (perhaps, all) cultures constrain women's individual reproductive relations in favor of social control, not all have as elaborate a heritage of labeling sexuality and baby-making as "private" (cf. Ginsburg and Rapp 1991). In the United States, multiple iterations of our sex/gender system index our medico-legal system: We have normative and deviant reproducers, just as there are justified and selfish aborters, or good women and bad women. Sexuality and maternity are terrains fraught with controversy and subject to public scrutiny, on which our most conventional and challenged gender representations are continually repeated. Under the shadow of such scrutiny, decisions surrounding sexual orientation and activity, birth control, abortion, the use of the new reproductive technologies, and maternal caretaking practices involve hard-won, unstable, and contested individual as well as collective rights. Women are thus culturally positioned to think about their reproductive capacities, desires, and decisions as a private dimension of public life.

It is a major finding of this study that once constrained and empowered by that privacy, women really think. No one enters the decision to undergo amniocentesis trivially; genetic counseling is too sobering an experience to permit a casual use of this technology by any of the women among whom I have worked. In addition to its discursively enunciated risks, the counseling process is shadowed by the fears, fantasies, and phobias which pregnant women and their supporters hold about childhood disabilities, and their pain at considering the possibility of ending a pregnancy to which they have already made a commitment. As I have tried to show throughout, the decision to use (or refuse) prenatal diagnosis engages deeply held values concerning the acceptable limits of maternity or parenthood, the importance of biomedical control over "nature," and the justification of abortion. While many upper-middle-class, professional women and/or couples may take it for granted that they will undergo amniocentesis in a pregnancy if it is deemed "medically appropriate," and working-class and working-poor women and their supporters may express only polite silence to obstetricians and genetic counselors when the test is explained to them, all hold firm and complex opinions concerning these topics when interviewed outside of an overtly medical framework.

Moreover, no woman I interviewed ever aborted for superficial reasons: Though I may have disagreed with some of the decisions women took with regard to specific fetal diagnoses, none entered those decisions lightly, nor did they recover without substantial emotional, interpersonal, and ethical work. Many women from a rich variety of backgrounds made a distinction between themselves as tragically "good aborters" and the "bad aborters" (usually, very young women) they encountered during their termination procedures. As a former abortion counselor, I initially resisted that distinction. But I came to recognize that the women I was interviewing were enunciating a nuanced ethics of reproductive control: Under circumstances of extreme misfortune, they reasoned that the burdens of motherhood tipped against the present, diagnosed fetus in favor of their commitments to other children, adults, and themselves. Selective abortion after the diagnosis of what they considered to be a serious condition was thus justified. Latina women were most likely to describe their reasoning in terms of the prevention of a child's future suffering; recent immigrants saw a disabled child as an impediment to survival in a new homeland; and white women of all classes worried about selfishness even as they protected themselves and other dependents from the imagined life-transforming obligations entailed in raising a child with congenital disabilities. Yet all enunciated a "philosophy of the limit" (Kittay 1997).

My initial questions focused on the variety of reasons women gave for these limits. But I came to think that the very fact that women had to set the limits required some explanation. Women judge the acceptability of specific fetuses for entry into their communities because there are so few limits on women's responsibility for the quality of life that the child would have. In other words, our gendered responsibilities for producing acceptable children (Collins 1994; Ruddick 1989) as well as our embodied responsibilities for the pregnancies that produce them overdetermine our need to think deeply about the consequences of knowing about and possibly eliminating disabled fetuses prenatally. Knowing in our bones (or in our wombs) that we will bear the major responsibility for whatever child we birth, we react with deep concern and thought. Because pregnancy and motherhood are culturally marked as such totalizing female responsibilities in the contemporary United States, women's decisions surrounding prenatal testing take on a weight they might not have if the burdens were more widely and socially distributed. The limits women individually placed on normalcy for entry into the human community varied considerably according to how they interpreted the severity of the specific diagnosis, and how they imagined their own responsibilities, powers, and aspirations as mothers. Thus, a limit might be drawn by articulating individual experience and values as, for example, when the mother of a child with spina bifida accepted the possibility of bearing a second one with the same condition with confidence and determination, but refused the possibility of Down syndrome or any other condition involving mental retardation. A limit might also be shaped as part of a recognizable near-consensus, as is seen in the high abortion rates following the prenatal diagnosis of Down syndrome. And some limits seemed ethnically or culturally shared, as, for example, the concern expressed among many recent immigrants from Spanish-speaking backgrounds about impairments of mobility or what they considered to be other highly visible physical stigmas, and their relative equanimity about mental retardation, especially when we consider the negative consensus Jews and Chinese placed on that condition. But for each pregnant woman accepting the test, the need to imagine a justifiable limit to maternity under the ethical conditions of choice was established. The very fact of imagining (and more rarely, enacting) a limit comes with the territory on which gendered responsibilities encounter reproductive technologies. Acting as a philosopher of the limit was thus an experience to which women came individually, one by one, in the privacy of pregnancy care and family life, under the shadow of their normative responsibilities as mothers and potential mothers.

When viewed collectively, all the women using or refusing the test can be seen as moral pioneers. Some explored the cartography of accepting a differently abled child, while many fashioned an understanding of the limits they and their intimates set on normalcy when they underwent an amniocentesis. In considering whether or not to accept prenatal testing, all were participating in an impromptu and large-scale social experiment: Whether as willing conscripts or draft resisters to biomedicine's technicist promise of more control over pregnancy outcomes, all made conscious a set of values, ethics, and choices which were located in the realm of the private but were shaped and in turn helped to shape a more social terrain. Those values were, of course, influenced by earlier traditions within which women had come to adulthood and to their ethics of reproductive choice: Most women spoke eloquently about the meaning of religious background, and sometimes, contemporary practice, in affecting their amniocentesis decisions. Yet even among the practicing Catholics and Orthodox Jews, evangelical Protestants, and Mormons with whom I spoke, none desired to limit the choices of other women. When someone felt she absolutely could not abort (at all, or for a specific disability), there was a strong tendency to leave open the door of possibility for other women: "Oh, I couldn't do that . . . but she might," was a formulation I heard frequently. Of course, I was not meeting many women who were so absolutely opposed to abortion that they never spoke with an obstetrical nurse, genetic counselor, or me about the existence of the test. I met many refusers who mentioned religious objections to abortion, but were highly nuanced individually in their interpretations of how absolute those objections were, especially when a "damaged" fetus was at issue. Perhaps the ones I was able to interview should be viewed as part of a strong liberal individualist consensus concerning abortion under certain limited circumstances, including a strong consensus on this one. In this sense, many contemporary religions participate, willy-nilly, in their own modernization into the realm of private values, rather than public norms. My sample may also be particularly "liberal," given its New York City origins, where religious organizations and voting loyalties have rarely been distinct during the present century. And perhaps it also (accurately) reflects the bourgeois individualist roots of modern feminism whose claims on the extension of personal rights, privacy, and bodily integrity to women are particularly potent when viewed through the lens of reproduction. Moreover, it is highly American in its nuanced but strong support for abortion rights, and judgments of what justifies the use of those rights. Whatever the reason, I rarely encountered pregnant women whose negative views of abortion were framed as universal social norms which they believed should affect others.

At the same time that the offer of prenatal diagnosis forced women to consider the concrete limits they might individually place on atypical maternity through selective abortion, it also forced an engagement with disability consciousness. This might be articulated negatively through the refusal of specific fetal problems or positively through imagining what diagnosable conditions one might accept, but in either case, a new cultural conundrum became highly visible. No woman who entered genetic counseling exited unchanged by this encounter. All participated—through acceptance or rejection of the test—in the meeting between reproductive consciousness and disability consciousness which technoscientific advances are helping to shape. One of my strongest analytic conclusions concerns the coproduction and social segregation of these two funds of social knowledge: Although the biomedical discourses and practical interventions of prenatal diagnosis are socioculturally separate from the hard-earned familial and professional knowledge which comes with the territory of integrating children with disabilities, technoscientific advances have played a strong role in both. And both are increasingly present and highly mediated in American popular culture. In other words, the new reproductive technologies and disability consciousness share a medical, legal, and social terrain, cultural boundaries to the contrary notwithstanding[54] (cf. Ginsburg and Rapp 1999).

But of course, women do not enter this regime of technoscientific pregnancy choices and disability consciousness equally: As I have tried to show through a cascade of examples, women's prior fund of knowledge concerning these issues is both individually and socially mediated by differences in class position and scientific literacy and racial-ethnic and religious backgrounds. It is also crosscut by individual, familial, and community histories with reproduction and disability. Thus those from middle-class professional backgrounds feel particularly self-confident in speaking the language of biomedicine, even when they enunciate criticisms of it, for they live in social milieux not entirely removed from the health care providers and prenatal services under interrogation. Those from less privileged backgrounds may be correspondingly less willing or able to articulate their concerns in the framework of biomedicine, but on their home turf they, too, evince aspirations for affecting the health of their fetuses. Attitudes toward specific disabilities or disability in general are influenced by both the aspirations pregnant women and their supporters hold for their children, and the knowledge—stigmatized, accepting, or an amalgam of both—they hold about children and adults with disabilities.

Stratified Reproduction

In speaking about the social funds of knowledge with which each pregnant woman enters her encounter with prenatal testing I am, of course, describing stratified reproduction (Colen 1986, 1990, 1995; Ginsburg and Rapp 1995). Reproductive futures are embedded inside other forms of hierarchy: Access to respectful, competent prenatal care, eugenic attitudes toward "excessive" or "wasteful" pregnancies, and financial and social resources for differently abled children are socially stratified in familiar patterns. Thus, for example, an African-American public school teacher had to convince the staff at her local City Hospital that she wanted an appointment for prenatal care, not abortion, when a late, unplanned pregnancy was diagnosed; a sibling of an adult with Down syndrome felt pressured into having amniocentesis by her obstetrician's attitude toward mental retardation; a white lawyer likewise felt that prenatal testing was being indicated because her health care providers were worried about lawsuits although she was "borderline" for the test just before her thirty-fourth birthday. Put starkly, pregnancies are not conceived, medically managed, or delivered on equal social terrain. Stratified reproduction is reproducing far more than individual babies: It is a lens through which we can see how representations of pregnancy and parenting, gender relations, socioeconomic futures and collective as well as familial aspirations for the next generation are also being reproduced.

The offer of amniocentesis is just one small fragment of a massive social project, the project of stratified reproduction through which children are born into a hierarchically organized world. Like any small fragment, its importance varies with the constituency whose aspirations are being addressed. I came to this research as a white, middle-class college professor whose own amniocentesis experiences had been life-transforming. But I had to learn that not everyone views this technology in the same way. As the story in chapter 6 concerning the UPS package handler whose evangelical husband was "in recovery" from antisocial behavior suggests, amniocentesis was just a tiny part of a wife's strategy to stabilize family life. Likewise, the special-education teacher who chose an abortion after an anomalous finding of chromosome breakage despite the best efforts of the genetics team at Middle Hospital to contextualize and minimize the problem taught me that the health of the fetus was only one small factor in the larger picture of that pregnancy's acceptance. The fact that such a high percentage of the women who agreed to be interviewed at home after their amniocenteses were evangelical or fundamentalist Christians suggests that testifying about religious miracles rather than exploring the impact of prenatal testing was the reason for their participation in my social scientific research. While I have tried to make a case for the social significance of this biomedical technology in action, the flip side of the cultural coin also needs description: The importance of amniocentesis and its associated technologies must be contextualized in the complex and highly stratified lives within which women undertake their pregnancies. My focus on a new reproductive technology opens up this dense social terrain for an investigation of stratified reproduction, but it isn't equally important to everybody who encounters it.

In large measure, I have come to see the variegated importance of amniocentesis as an index of differential social risk. Prenatal diagnosis was designed and continues to be developed from a biomedical perspective that takes hereditary risks and their potential elimination as its starting point. Many pregnant women from all social backgrounds are grateful to have this test, while some refuse it. But in accepting or refusing, all its potential conscripts are exposed to risk analysis, and given specific risk figures based on their age and medical pedigree. For those who can and do "live by the numbers," the idea of risk reduction through technological control of testing and possibly abortion "makes sense." For a 36-year-old professional woman undertaking a first pregnancy, the epidemiology of chromosomally anomalous births describes a universe into which her experiences in trying to control the world may well fit. But ironically, the very populations most at risk—less privileged "older" women having more pregnancies with more partners; experiencing more reproductive, perinatal, and infant mortality; and higher death rates throughout their life cycles—may be least likely to live by the numbers precisely because they understand their risks to be spread over a greater territory than chromosome analysis in pregnancy describes. Chromosomes and their potential aberrations may be "experience far" when compared to how some groups define persistent risks to pregnancy and children and their alleviation. For example, minority participation in movements against hospital and clinic cutbacks, and for electoral and school board reforms may be interpreted, too, as statements about what constitute "experience-near" risks to family life. Perceptions of the political economy of risk are thus culture- and community-specific. No matter how powerfully chromosomes may loom in the matrix of biomedicine, they offer only one possible explanation of risk and its potential reduction in the shifting and multicultural world of the contemporary United States.

Emergent Epidemiologies

These highly differentiated notions of risk were present in the comments of some African-American women who "talked back" to genetic counselors' very sensible advice concerning reduction of smoking, or increased bed rest, or reduced-salt diet during pregnancy: For them, individual control was hard to attain and largely irrelevant in the face of social stress on the job, at home, and in the community. Their aspirations for healthy pregnancies were consonant with the model that health professionals were espousing, but they did not expect the locus of control to rest so exclusively with the individual pregnant woman. Likewise, Doris Paul, an African-American nonprofit education administrator corrected me gently but firmly when I spoke about the *choices* involved in prenatal testing and abortion: For her, *decisions* was a more appropriate word. She was insisting that the intersections at which pregnant women act are not so much "chosen" as constructed by forces much larger than women themselves. "We" then act as decisively as we can. In such cases, a less professional and more populist model of social epidemiology is emergent: The reduction of fetal risk involves far more than chromosome or DNA testing, for it rests on the highly stratified social terrain within which their mothers and other potential caregivers live. Indeed, precise biomedical notions of risk are constantly put to empirical challenge by the encompassing and uneven life chances through which women and their supporters encounter them.

This emergent and episodic social epidemiology as expressed by some pregnant women and their supporters should be located in relation to a lengthy history of statistical thinking, and the contests over its meaning. As I tried to indicate in chapters 2 and 3, learning to live by the numbers is a cultural accomplishment which was produced inside European ideas about gambling and insurance long before it settled into the framework of health and medicine in the nineteenth century in many parts of the world (Asad 1994; Daston 1987; Hacking 1990, 1992; Porter 1995). In fields as diverse as accounting, government reports of housing quality and prices, the caliber of military recruits, and, of course, the surveillance of causes of death, the technology of statistics has provided powerful descriptions of many social correlations, but its relevance to individual responsibility remains highly contested. That is, there are inevitable gaps between a large-scale population description and the specific characteristics or agency of the individuals who make up that population. Biostatisticians are able to describe many large-scale patterns of illness, causes of death, or anomalous births quite accurately without clear causal explanations of the role that individual attributes or behavior plays in producing these configurations. Hence, the idea of "risk" individualizes these patterns by placing particular people into categories in relation to relevant social groups or factors with which the patterns are correlated. This evolving worldview is at once highly social—statistics powerfully describe patterns we as a culture find relevant—and problematically individual, suggesting modes of behavior for which individuals may take responsibility in the effort to reduce their risks. Thus taking prenatal vitamins and not smoking are risk-reducing strategies which pregnant women overwhelmingly recognize as potentially beneficial to their fetuses; many submit to their discipline. But other risk-reducing strategies are not available at the individual level (e.g., the measurement and monitoring of sufficient folic acid intake during the period directly before and in the earliest weeks of pregnancy, recently found to be associated with reduction in a population's incidence of spina bifida). Whether unambiguously individual (e.g., cessation of smoking) or ambiguously social (e.g., exposure to secondhand smoke), a recognition of risk and consequent steps to contain it entails a kind of scientific literacy.

Scientific literacy has been much discussed in recent years, in sources ranging from Nobel laureate speeches to journalistic accounts of international comparisons of successes and failures in education. Public understandings of science, including acquiescence or resistance to scientific authority, the domestication of scientific controversy through science journalism, and "the public's" ability to use scientific paradigms effectively have all been much debated (see Gieryn 1995; Law 1988; Nelkin 1995). This literature presents a rich range of analyses of how scientific findings and controversies enter public arenas, and the many interested groups who hold stakes in their promulgation and popularization. What does "the public" need to know, and how shall it best know it, if the democratic uses of scientific knowledge are to be expanded? Recently, anthropologists have engaged this problem of scientific literacy by studying its practices in grounded action: homemakers demonstrating abstract mathematical concepts in supermarkets (Lave 1996); community members drawing images of immune systems (Claeson, Martin et al. 1996; Martin 1994); visitors interpreting science museums (MacDonald 1995). In such studies, anthropologists self-consciously move beyond the authoritative frame which technoscientific and mathematical experts provide to describe their own endeavors, analyzing the natural history of popular practices relevant to those experts' social terrain. Such studies have a salutary effect in providing new and expanded empirical grids for the observation of science as a set of cultural practices; they also run the risk of romanticizing popular knowledge at the expense of recognizing both the practical rigor and hegemonic claims that technoscientific practices assert.

This study of the social impact and cultural meaning of prenatal diagnosis joins anthropological perspectives on popular scientific literacy, while attempting to keep the powerful claims, benefits, and burdens of expert knowledge and practical interventions in mind. It is a conclusion of this study that scientific literacy is formulated in many venues not conventionally included in its journalistic, educational, and sociological description: The women among whom I worked learned about heredity, genetics, and disabilities in many places, which included, but were not limited to, those provided by biomedicine. While clinics and genetic counseling addressed issues of prenatal testing, they were not the only places where such discussions occurred. During the course of my fieldwork, *Oprah,* the Tuesday *Science* section and the Sunday *Magazine* of the *New York Times,* and a slew of popular magazines like *Glamour, McCall's, Omni, Parents, Self, Life, Working Woman,* all ran stories about prenatal diagnosis and its intersection with disability consciousness. The very American theme of "choice" figured large in such popular coverage. Such stories are, of course, highly mediated: Exquisitely stratified by consumer markets, the TV and radio talk shows speak to audiences different from that of PBS's *Nova* series; a story on the development of prenatal genetic testing kits in the *Wall Street Journal* targets enlightened investors while the subway ads for city-provided prenatal care and abortion services are aimed at "straphangers anonymous." My clipping files are bursting with such popular representations; they float through the waiting rooms at prenatal clinics, hospital radiology suites, and private obstetrical offices, as well as the grocery store magazine racks and junk mail advertising that pregnant women regularly encounter. A long-standing popular interest in utopian and dystopian visions of transforming heredity informs novels as classic as *Brave New World,* as recent as *The Hand Maid's Tale,* as cinematic as *Gattaca.* The anthropological predilection to query "What the Natives Know" here shifts our attention toward the continually escalating representations of heredity, fetuses, chromosomes, and childhood heritable disorders, and their uptake by pregnant women and their supporters. Increasingly, such highly mediated facts and images lay claim to reaching "everybody."

But not "everybody" encounters nor interprets such popularized and mediated versions of biomedical claims in the same social space. As I have tried to show throughout this book, the technoscientific interventions of prenatal diagnosis share a densely populated terrain that is always already structured by prior social and cultural commitments. This was dramatically clear in those 25 percent of home visits in which I arrived to speak about amniocentesis, only to discover that a pregnant woman (and her supporters) wanted to testify to the Lord's miracles. More mundanely, middle-class respondents were most likely to work with comfort in the segregated and highly specialized categories provided by biomedicine: They were fluent in the etiquette of health interviews, and not made uncomfortable by scientific language. Less privileged women were more likely to mix their opinions and experiences of biomedicine into a landscape with fewer specialized boundaries, where religion, community histories, and folk beliefs bled together as they described their assessment of the value of testing.

On this terrain, ideas about disability, and collective care for disabled members, may develop in relative autonomy from medical interventions. As Alecia Williams, an African-American public relations consultant, noted in speaking about rural, poor members of the family from which she had come, "They live in a landscape that's more populated. They'd take in a baby with Down's without much worry." And in speaking with California-based genetic counselors about the complex folk beliefs of their recent immigrant clients from China and Cambodia, I was struck by the many dietary and household rituals which women from these groups use to affect family health. These rich repertoires of health-seeking behavior and alternatives to biomedical explanation reflect both the burdens and benefits of relatively unprivileged social location. Excluded from the advantages of scientific education, the bearers of such repertoires may also garner alternative resources for accepting both difference and misfortune. And, paradoxically, those with access to biomedical worldviews and interventions may also lose a sense of "nature" as an essentially benign ally in pregnancy outcomes. As a white schoolteacher who had given birth once without amniocentesis, and the second time with it, said,

Once the information has been processed, it's here to stay. It took away my arrogance, my naiveté that having a healthy baby was a natural event. The technology is there, it offers a certain kind of control. But I feel ripped off of my earlier experience of pregnancy, I've lost my confidence. (Carola Mirsky, 37)

Here, my assessment of the power of scientific worldviews intersects the anthropological romance with cultural difference: Living inside of "fate" or "nature" preserves multiple interpretive strategies within which a tolerance of difference may dwell. Yet at the same time, it reproduces the exclusions from biomedical interventions which less privileged groups too often experience. It is on this contradictory social structure that the conundrum of popular scientific literacy is erected: The knowledge of heritable disorders which amniocentesis brings assumes a worldview which is resolutely scientific, modernist, and rationalist. While firmly located on that ground myself, I encountered many women and their supporters in researching this book whose alternative views and values prepared them to accept life's vicissitudes with more equanimity than mine did. Anthropological (and other empirically grounded) contributions to a national concern with scientific literacy surely must take this dilemma seriously: We as a science-seeking nation have much to learn, in all our diversity, from emergent epidemiologies which stress the social, not only the more narrowly biomedical, when thinking about health, illness, and effective interventions. At the same time, an acknowledgment that "diversity" problematically masks exclusion from, and even ignorance of, the benefits of biomedical intervention must surely enter into the ledger of health care accountability and its associated scientific literacy.

In this unstable amalgam of scientific literacy, cultural resources, and fetal health aspirations, reproductive technology occupies a privileged location for analysis. Reproduction lies at the heart of a culture's representations of itself; it is in large measure through imagining reproduction that individuals, families, and social groups conceive of the future toward which they aspire for themselves and the next generation (Ginsburg and Rapp 1995). In contemporary North America, the dominant representations of reproduction are biomedical, epidemiological, and increasingly risk-analytic at the individual level. They are also unmistakably American: The quest for "perfect" babies, the threat of litigation, are densely deployed in popular media accounts. In thinking about individual and collective aspirations for future children, as filtered through the grid of a routinizing and quality-controlling reproductive technology, the contradictory social locations and funds of knowledge which both unite and divide women in all our diversity appear in high relief. Women are both constrained and empowered through technologies like amniocentesis to serve as our contemporary moral pioneers. At once held accountable at the individual level for a cascade of broadly social factors which shape the health outcome of each pregnancy, and individually empowered to decide whether and when there are limits on voluntary parenthood, women offered an amniocentesis are also philosophers and gate-keepers of the limits of who may join our current communities.

Endings Are Really Beginnings

Mike named the fetus XYLO, X-or-Y for its unknown sex, LO for the love we were pouring into it. Together, we watched XYLO grow; together we chose to end his life after a prenatal diagnosis of Down's. My personal pain and confusion as a failed mother led me to investigate the social construction and cultural meaning of amniocentesis. Building outward from the category of "pregnant women," I learned to recognize the diversity of interests, aspi-rations, and experiences which characterize the development, diffusion, and impact of this biomedical technology in contemporary America. Along the way, the intersection of diverse women's reproductive aspirations and their consciousness of disabilities has become a central motif of my research and writing. In mapping this intersection, I am not alone; a growing discourse—biomedical, legal, political, sociocultural—interrogating the connections and separations of practical knowledge about both reproductive interventions and disability integration is rapidly emerging in many locations. XYLO's short life pointed me toward these vital concerns; his ending marked the beginning of my search for contextualized knowledge. If the work accom-plished in this book helps others to think about these evolving issues, his short life will have been a great gift.

Notes

1. When I began this study, the waiting period for results was between three and four weeks. Over the following decade, improvements in growth media, banding reagents, computerization of chromosome sorting, and the very hard work of technicians have all contributed to a dramatic reduction in the time it takes to culture and analyze chromosomes. Average waiting time is now one week to ten days.

2. Autosomal recessive conditions are transmitted when each of two apparently healthy carriers passes on a copy of a gene causing a serious disorder to a child. While autosomal conditions may be relatively rare (e.g., galactosemia) or relatively more fequent (e.g., cystic fibrosis) in any population, two carriers always have a one-in-four chance of passing on the condition with each pregnancy they create together.

3. Bruno Latour's concept of "enrolment" (1987) includes a much heavier load of agonistic, competitive politics enacted by individual scientists and their allies than does the notion of "enrollment" of congeries of disparate actors, interests, and goals implied here. My indebtedness to Latour's work should be obvious.

4. For a historical and sociological account of contemporary biomedical experimentation and therapeutic interventions on fetuses, see Casper 1994a, 1994b, 1998.

5. While early experiments with amniocentesis produced relatively high miscarriage rates—perhaps as high as 2 percent—by the time of the NIH consensus study (1976), the U.S. rate was calculated to be .3 percent. That is, a population of pregnant women using amniocentesis experiences one-third of 1 percent more miscarriages after testing than a matched sample not using this technology does. This number is considered statistically insignificant, although, as genetic counselors quickly point out when discussing miscarriage rates, no number is perceived as insignificant if it adds to your own risk. Canadian and British studies also calculate the miscarriage rate as somewhat higher—about 1 percent—but international disagreement remains about the contributions of both amniocentesis methods and biostatistical calculation to this difference (see Amniocentesis 1978; Development 1976; Kaback et al. 1979).

6. The Polymerase Chain Reaction, for which "invention" Kary Mullis won the Nobel Prize in 1993, enables replication and augmentation of the amount of DNA via laboratory manipulation. By rapidly and dramatically increasing the amount of any specific bit of DNA available, PCR has become a central enabling technology for mapping genomes, and constructing DNA-based genetic diagnoses.

7. Parenthetically and as an illustration of the complexity of enrollment, Jerome Lejeune, the internationally acclaimed "discoverer" of the extra chromosome which

causes Down syndrome, renamed the U.S. National Institutes of Health, "The National Institutes of Death" in protest against their approval of amniocentesis to detect (and presumably abort) this condition. His protest was widely quoted in the popular press, and Lejeune became something of a hero and activist for the then-nascent right-to-life movement. But his resistance to having his work enrolled in the relentless expansion of biomedical science was, of course, futile.

8. Excellent summaries of wrongful-birth and wrongful-life cases are provided in Clayton 1993.

9. An insightful history of the ELSI Working Group is provided in Juengst 1996. Founded under the inspiration of James Watson's desire to "troubleshoot" public concerns about potential eugenic aspects of emergent genetic knowledge, ELSI has funded subsantial social research into the impact of genetic mapping; it has also established procedures and guidelines for monitoring institutional sites where the consequences of new genetic knowledge are being felt. I served briefly as a member of the Working Group, 1995–1997, during the period in which it was externally reviewed and its functions dispersed among three government agencies. In this period, the National Center for Human Genome Research became the National Human Genome Research Institute, a renaming which carried with it a quantum leap of budgetary stability and scientific/governmental prestige.

10. I thank Donna Haraway for making this point in personal communication.

11. Once again, Donna Haraway should be credited for her insistence on this point in personal communication, as well as throughout her work.

12. A translocation occurs during cell division when segments of two chromosomes break off and exchange places. If all the genetic material is rearranged but completely transmitted through duplication and division (meiosis/mitosis), the translocation is balanced. But, if in cell division the exchanged pieces are not transmitted in their entirety, an unbalanced translocation occurs, with some chromosomes having too much material, and others having too little. In this case, spontaneous abortion of a fertilized ovum is a likely outcome.

13. Twenty-four programs now train genetic counselors in the United States and Canada. Counselors are certified through completion of the coursework and clinical field placement requirements at a program affiliated with the American Board of Genetic Counselors, which also offers the mandatory certification examination to qualified graduates.

14. I thank Esther Chin, genetic assistant at Beth Israel Medical Center, for sharing her counseling knowledge with me. From her I learned about the norms of decision-making among Chinese-speaking women.

15. When this study began, virtually all amnioceteses in the state of New York took place through academic medical centers and their affiliates; counseling was a standard part of the practice. As amniocentesis moves into private obstetrical offices

where busy physicians often utilize commercial labs, counseling is becoming more haphazard: Many commercial labs employ genetic counselors on a consultancy basis, making counseling an optional rather than a required part of the process. The impact of this change is fundamentally unknown, although many counselors worry about patient education and, of course, access to more protracted help should the diagnosis of an arcane or ambiguous condition arise.

16. Although my use of code switching employs a framework drawn from sociolinguistics, the relevance of a Bakhtinian orientation, in which language is always already dialogic and interactive even as a speaker initiates an utterance, should also be obvious.

17. Problematic aspects of the test include the following, ranked from least to most significant: Less than one percent of amniocenteses have to be postponed because of fetal dating, fetal position, placental position, or the position of a uterine fibroid. All of these will move or advance within a week or two, so tests are usually rescheduled. Uterine contractions or tenting (a tough spot in the uterus impeding entry of the needle) may also postpone the test for anywhere from a few minutes to a few days. One in fifty amniocenteses has to be repeated because insufficient cell growth or cell contamination of the amniotic fluid make a diagnosis impossible. One in two hundred women who have amniocentesis suffers a complication, of which the most common are: heavy cramping, vaginal bleeding, vaginal leakage of fluid, and/or fever. Of these, one-half (that is, one in four hundred) go on to miscarry. The added one-quarter to one-third of 1 percent additional miscarriages rate is considered "statistically insignificant," but all counselors are careful to point it out, for it is the only serious complication of the test that pregnant women routinely ask about and fear.

18. Of course, guidelines on smoking and alcohol consumption during pregnancy add surveillance as well as reassurance, and are potentially woman-blaming, as recent debates on public warnings to pregnant women indicate (Altfeld, Handler et al. 1997; Paltow 1990). And there may well be contributions to chromosome damage which can be socially influenced, but of which we are currently unaware. Factors such as environmental radiation exposure and diet have been suggested as responsible for reports of "outbreaks" of Down syndrome, but have never been confirmed using epidemiological research methods. While there are no obvious, known environmental causes of this chromosome problem (or any other), we cannot entirely rule out such a possibility. The search for environmental influences of neural tube defects, for example, also used reported "outbreaks." It took several decades of research to eventually link vitamin B/folic acid deficiencies (Koren 1993; Pietrzik et al. 1997; Steegers-Theurrissen 1995) as a contributing cause. Unlike most occurrences of Down syndrome, however, neural tube defects tend to cluster ethnogeographically, suggesting the possibility of a dietary link.

19. In the mid-1970s, demographers, ethicists, and geneticists expressed consid-

erable anxiety about the potentially abusive use of expanding amniocentesis services for sex selection. While in principle, sex selection might affect either females or males, most U.S. researchers worried about sex imbalances brought on by general preferences for male fetuses, especially as first children (see Fraser and Pressor 1977). Historian Ruth Cowan's interviews with doctors involved in the early delivery of prenatal diagnostic services suggest that they used an ad hoc rather than a universal ethic to refuse amniocentesis exclusively for sex selection: Their laboratory facilities were too crowded to take any but "serious" cases (Cowan 1992 and personal communication).

Routinization does not seem to have led to widespread, abusive use in the United States. But over the last twenty years, geneticists in America (and, increasingly, around the world) seem to have become more comfortable with the idea of sex selection. Despite personal opposition to this practice, the majority in recent international surveys said they would perform prenatal diagnosis for sex selection, if the patient had "good" reasons (Wertz and Fletcher 1989c; cf. the widespread use of amniocentesis and ultrasound for sex selection in India, where feminists and their allies have mounted effective national campaigns to contain the technology, e.g. Dasgupta 1994; Dubey 1983; Kumar 1983; Patel 1987; Sharma 1995; and the work of the Forum Against Sex Determination and Sex Pre-Selection, which publishes its own working papers and reports). But geneticists' responses to hypothetical ethical surveys indicate attitudes, not behavior. The problem of sex selection is hard to evaluate empirically in the United States, where statistics on prenatal diagnosis are woefully thin, a problem I discuss in chapter 8. In evaluating all "positive diagnosis" follow-ups at the Prenatal Diagnosis Laboratory in 1987, I tracked miscarriages and abortions following amniocentesis in more than thirteen thousand cases, the entire caseload at that time since the inception of the lab. In principle, the public health facilities of New York City should exhibit the highest use of amniocentesis for sex selection in the country, both because the service is the most widespread, and most widespread among those ethnic groups (primarily, South Asians and Chinese) alleged to be willing to abort female fetuses. Among those, I would estimate that four abortions of healthy female fetuses occurred for reasons of sex selection, two of which proclaimed their reasoning, two of which did not. In all four cases, the patients had Asian surnames. Thus my evaluation teeters between an insistence on cultural specificity and a risk of cultural stereotyping. While I obviously stand with other feminist witnesses in opposition to female feticide, I should also point out that my discovery of four cases I would class as "sex selection" in thirteen thousand does not suggest widespread use of the technology for sex selection.

The abuse of prenatal diagnosis explicitly for sex selection in the United States becomes much more likely with the expansion of chorionic villus sampling, which produces a diagnosis in the first trimester. Earlier diagnosis enables earlier and less traumatic abortions, thus it is at least possible that sex selection will be more wide-spread. Several counselors at Elite Hospitals spoke to me about their anger and despair when clients of many ethnic backgrounds, but primarily Indian, Chinese, and Jewish, used the new technology to abort healthy fetuses.

In California, some health professionals are alleged to have organized against sex selection after CVS because they are experiencing "job burnout" when their work is wrongfully used. They have agreed to return diagnoses relating to health after CVS promptly, but to delay telling patients the sex of their fetuses until after the twenty-sixth week, when abortion is no longer legal. Here, the primacy of their concerns as workers whose product is being perversely appropriated supersedes the ideology of free choice in their evolving practice.

20. Like an anthropologist, she found it easier to begin from difference than to analyze what was all too easily classified as sameness.

21. The waiting period for amniocentesis results dropped dramatically during the span of my research. When I first began interviewing, the waiting period was three to four weeks. It became two weeks at the time that interviews were concluded. As of the time of writing, the waiting period is closer to one week. These reductions are attributable to a number of factors, most notably an improvement in the efficiency of chromosomal banding reagents enabling a denser, earlier harvest of cells which can be characterized, and the computerization of the karyotyping, or arranging a picture of the chromosomes by numerical order.

22. Janelle Taylor (Department of Anthropology, University of Chicago and Grinnell College), is currently conducting dissertation research on the cultural construction of sonograms. The role of paternal "bonding," and the creation of ties of kinship through imaging are among the many questions she is investigating (Taylor 1993; 1997).

23. As all genetic counselors are quick to point out, one never knows what one will do until confronted with the reality of a positive diagnosis. While very high percentages of those receiving the diagnosis of Down syndrome do go on to abortion, every counselor can offer anecdotes of surprising decisions which went against the grain of the attitudes women expressed during counseling, before receiving the actual diagnosis. Moreover, diagnoses which may seem quite clear-cut to geneticists and genetic counselors may feel ambiguous to pregnant women. Indeed, Barbara Katz Rothman argues forcefully that all diagnoses feel ambiguous when pregnant, because the commitment to the pregnancy is real, and because almost no diagnosis can predict the severity or mildness that the condition will have (Rothman 1986). Such stories appear in chapters 7 and 8.

24. The moral status of late abortion is ambiguous in the United States, especially when contrasted with countries where late abortion virtually never happens (Western Europe), or happens without moral distress (e.g., India, Japan) (Glendon

1987; Hardacre 1997). At the present time, abortions at or after twenty weeks of pregnancy are performed 86 percent by dilation and evacuation, and 14 percent by labor induction. During the years in which my interviews were conducted, labor induction methods were far more common, affecting more than 75 percent of my sample. It should be underlined that dilation and evacuation abortions at twenty or more weeks are not "partial birth" abortions, which, although almost never performed, have been used to demonize all second trimester abortions by the antiabortion movement.

25. In a balanced translocation, pieces of two chromosomes break off and exchange places during the earliest cell division of what will become the embryo. The person who grows from that embryo has the correct complement of genetic material, but it is differently placed than in those of his germ cells. When this person contributes gametes to reproduction, there is a 50 percent risk that the two balanced chromosomes which exchanged pieces will not travel together. In that case, too much or too little genetic material may be present, leading to a range of consequences, including miscarriage or mental retardation.

26. An oomphalocele is a developmental midline (gut) defect affecting internal organ formation. Embryologically, it is the ventral equivalent of a neural tube defect (which is dorsal). Satellites consist of extra genetic material attached to the end of chromosomes. The range of problems caused by either is great; hence, both are considered serious but inherently ambiguous diagnoses and further tests and counseling are medically indicated.

27. I thank Lavanya Marfatia Misra, Department of Medical Genetics, University of Dentistry and Medicine of New Jersey, for sending this document to me.

28. In 1988, the Office of Technological Assessment published a "consensus document" on technological treatments for infertility. Appended was a fascinating summary of eighteen religious groups' theological positions on interventions into human reproduction. These included not only the range of Protestant, Catholic, and Jewish opinion, popular sects like the Jehovah's Witnesses, Seventh-day Adventists, and Mormons, but several variants of Islam and Buddhism. Governmental pronouncements on the science of human reproduction can ill afford to exclude or offend anybody (Herdman and Kolsrud 1988).

29. In the state of New York, a combination of private insurance and public funding at the state and municipal levels guarantees access to prenatal diagnosis and selective abortion for those deemed to be medically appropriate candidates; no pregnant woman is in principle denied access for lack of coverage. Nationally, the situation is far more complicated. At the present time, virtually all states underwrite prenatal diagnosis for those without other forms of insurance, but the number guaranteeing funds to cover selective abortion for those who receive a positive diagnosis and want to terminate their pregnancies is much smaller: Eighteen states cover abor-

tion, the rest, adhering to Hyde Amendment restrictions on federal funding, only finance abortions after documented proof that the pregnancy resulted from incest or rape. Few states publicize the availability of these services to their poorer residents as thoroughly as New York does.

30. Satmar Hasids, in particular, are extremely sophisticated about medical technology and services. During the period of my second pregnancy in 1991–92, my obstetrician also served members of the Hasidic community; intrigued by my never-ending research qustions, he told me many stories as a "provider informant" about Hasidic prenatal care practices. Although known carriers try not to become pregnant after having lost children to Tay-Sachs disease, Halasik law can be interpreted to permit testing and even abortion under certain circumstances. But both must be accomplished before the pregnancy is forty days old, the last moment at which the life of a male fetus may be ended. U.S. medical protocols offered chorionic villus sampling at nine to eleven weeks, too late in the pregnancy to accommodate religious teachings. The obstetrician thus told of sending Hasidic "accidental" pregnancies to England, where a cutting-edge experimental program was using CVS for prenatal diagnosis far earlier than it was available here. When I retold this story to a representative from *Dor Yeshurim* in 1994 he laughed and said, "That was yesterday's news. Today, we send them to Philadelphia, where there's a terrific doctor who will do it for us even earlier." In his estimation, the newest of reproductive technologies could be successfully used to sustain religious practice. To accomplish this goal, his organization was highly networked into the interstices of medical experimentation.

31. In following literally hundreds of women through testing, it took me more than three years of fieldwork on this issue to find two women whose miscarriages rapidly followed amniocentesis and appeared to be caused by it.

32. Since the late 1980s, many health facilities have offered early amniocentesis (at ten to twelve weeks gestational age) on an experimental basis. While no national or international concensus studies of this earlier intervention are yet available, miscarriage rates seem to be about the same as with chorionic villus sampling. At 1.5 percent, these two early interventional technologies produce about three times the miscarriage rate of later amniocentesis (.5 percent). Also worrisome, in a Danish national study comparing the two early procedures, 6.45 percent of the newborns suffered talipes equinovarus, congenital malformations of the fingers and toes. While these studies require extensive verification before a judgment on early amniocentesis can be made, there are currently reasons to consider it a riskier procedure (Sundberg, Bang et al. 1997).

33. The point is made throughout Rothman 1986. It was also pointed out to me separately by Shirley Lindenbaum and Emily Martin.

34. Michael Flower and Deborah Heath describe the current work of creating a "consensus object" called the Human Genome (Flower and Heath 1993); I have

borrowed the concept from them. It is easy to spot the development of the chromosome as a consensus object in the history of genetics (Bowler 1989; Sandler and Sandler 1985), but much harder to argue for consensus in the present status of the gene (Kitcher 1992; Portin 1993).

35. This technique separates DNA fragments by size, based on the precise speed with which molecules of specific weights respond to an electric current (Judson 1992). Thus the relative amount of alpha-fetoprotein present in an amniotic fluid sample can be assessed. If the amount is high for gestational age, it strongly suggests a leakage in the developing spine and may lead to a diagnosis of spina bifida. If low, AFP level may indicate a Down syndrome fetus or less specific complications of pregnancy. In either case, an abnormal AFP reading is likely to lead to further testing (including high-resolution sonography) before a diagnosis is established or ruled out.

36. ELSI/NIH (Ethical, Legal, Social Implications of mapping the human genome) has sponsored more than $25 million of research since the inception of its program in 1990. ELSI's grant-making mission is intended to map the arenas in which new knowledge is needed to assess the impact of genomic mapping. Its portfolio includes a grant awarded for 1997–2000 to anthropologists Deborah Heath, Karen Sue Taussig, and me for investigating the production and circulation of new knowledge among geneticists, physician clinicians and patient support groups: It is the interdisciplinarity and interexperiential combinations which we seek to track in the construction of what counts as new genetic knowledge.

37. For years after this case was completed, I carried with me the image of a Jewish geneticist and her Jewish anthropological interrogator along with an Asian geneticist conversing with a Haitian patient, speaking among them at least six languages, asking for and receiving the foreskin. The reduction of multiple cultural differences through the sieve of scientific practices provided a very powerful and humorous lens with which to view the exchange of material (tissue) culture.

38. I here use the concept of "enrollment" in a commonsensical manner, suggesting the coalitions of people and other entities that combine in scientific investigations and interventions. In the technoscience literature, "enrolment" connotes the specificity of actant networks that can be traced through power points and their blockages (e.g., Callon 1986; Latour 1987).

39. I thank Jonas Frichtman and his colleagues in the "Time of the Body" seminar, Lund University, Sweden, August 1995, for a stimulating discussion of the role of bioethics in contemporary Western cultures.

40. At the time of this writing, screening for BRCA1 and BRCA2, two genes associated with heightened risks for breast cancer, is spreading rapidly, but its use is controversial in the general population. While high-risk families in which "everyone" gets breast (and/or ovarian) cancer across several generations may benefit from both the increased surveillance and potential prophylactic surgeries that carriers of these

genes are offered, it remains unclear whether environmental and/or lifestyle factors also trigger disease onset for those from less dramatically affected pedigrees. Baseline longitudinal population statistics concerning the relation between known genetic carriers from families with "sporadic" diagnoses of breast cancer (where one or a very small number of relatives contract the disease) and lifetime rates of disease have not yet been studied, given the recency of both the test and screening experiments. In other words, it is too early to know whether women at "average" risk will benefit from breast cancer genetic screening, or simply have their anxiety levels augmented without increased viable interventions beyond the current nongenetic repertoire: self-examination; mammograms; dietary and other "lifestyle" regimes; regular physician-assisted checkups.

41. The diagnosis of a dead fetus by ultrasound is relatively common in early testing (e.g., CVS), where about 10 percent of pregnancies scheduled for testing turn out to be "nonviable." Before the advent of early technological interventions, such pregnancies woud have ended in early miscarriages. Now, they are visually inscribed before they produce the embodied experience of pregnancy loss. Counselors, radiologists, and obstetricians have a pressing need to develop compassionate protocols for dealing with this technologically produced, dramatic experience, a point made to me by sociologist Aliza Kolker (personal communication, 1994).

42. Some pro-choice medical professionals object to this description of the D&E as physically or emotionally problematic for health care workers; they consider this discourse to represent an antiabortion stance, for it separates out a specific procedure when many surgical interventions are no less difficult. Their criticism should be weighed against a national shorage of doctors trained to perform abortions, a procedure which is rarely or insufficiently taught in medical schools. In response, the Board of the National Planned Parenthood Federation has begun an abortion training project to increase the number of competent abortion providers (Hitt 1998).

43. "Viability" is itself a highly contested concept, the term covers a medically "grey area" and is more beholden to legal struggles concerning abortion rights than to medical precision (Epner 1998). On the one hand, neonatal medicine has had increasing success in rescuing extremely premature babies; on the other hand, such babies are hardly "viable" in any straightforward way. They are cyborg-figures, highly dependent on technical intervention and life support for critical and lengthy periods of time, and some remain highly dependent on life-sustaining technology indefinitely. Thus, the concept of "viability" masks the social world in which concrete adults (including, of course, the mother and her supporters) and their technologies must devote their efforts to ensure even the slimmest hope of the baby's survival.

44. Medical memoirs which chart the psychosocial and ethical terrain of coming to grips with illness, suffering, and death, and the limits of medical efficacy have become a popular and compelling genre. But this literary genre is perceived as

"apart from" rather than "inside of" medical research and clinical protocols. Examples include: Baxter 1997; Hilton 1991; Klass 1992; Konner 1988; Vergehese 1995.

45. In the decade-plus during which my research and writing have been conducted, this situation has changed. There is a feminist-inspired health and social work literature emerging on the psychosocial effects of positive diagnosis (e.g., Black 1993, 1994; Kolker and Burke 1994), and several women have chosen to speak out about their own experiences in the hopes of encouraging public discussion (e.g., Green 1992; Rapp 1984).

46. Yiddish: "expert."

47. I should point out that I have never heard this discourse of displacement/relocation of Down syndrome children in African-American or Hispanic families (cf. MacDonald and Oden 1978), only in white ones.

48. Young adults with Down syndrome are either infertile (males) or have a reduced fertility (females). If impregnated by a man without this chromosome condition, a woman with Down syndrome has a 50 percent chance of passing the condition on to her offspring. But the fear of sexual relations and reproduction among the mentally retarded runs deeper than such statistical information suggests: Sterilization laws and policies have been developed most explicitly since the late Nineteenth century with regard to mentally retarded people, and documented abuse, especially sexual abuse, of mentally retarded inmates influenced campaigns for deinstitutionalization.

49. These autosomal recessive conditions can be produced only when two carriers mate. Perhaps parents who discover themselves to be carriers have a very different perception of connection to their affected children (to whom they have transmitted a "hidden" familial trait) than do parents of children with trisomic chromosomal conditions which occur de novo almost every time. And when a condition runs at relatively high rates within an ethnically or racially marked population, complex notions of membership and belonging are probably invoked. By contrast, chromosomal syndromes almost always arise de novo and therefore do not express hidden continuities in a lineage. Such a difference makes acute anthropological sense, but has yet to be tested in research practice. I owe this speculation to many conversations with anthropologist Faye Ginsburg.

50. The influence of Williams (1977) in thinking about the language-borne traditions of political and cultural agency deserves grateful acknowledgment.

51. A conversation with Susan Gal and Brackette Williams in 1991 suggested the importance of unraveling the racialized term "mongoloid." I thank them both for their recommendation.

52. The disability rights movement has often modeled its activist/policy interventions on the successes of the civil rights movement. In constructing their ethical

claims, disability rights activists have pointed to the stigma and bias with which many disabled persons are viewed, linking it to the fear that we all may be or become disabled. They have also noted, however, that disabled people represent a "hidden majority," as virtually all able-bodied people have friends, relatives, or colleagues with disabled members in their families. Their hopes for mass mobilization are thus expansive. For a history and sociology of this movement, see Finger 1990; Gliedman and Roth 1980; Hahn 1988; Miringoff 1991; Scotch 1984; Shapiro 1993.

53. Since the 1970s when early-intervention/infant-stimulation protocols were pioneered by Alice Hayden and her colleagues, programs for stimulating and integrating developmentally delayed babies, toddlers, and preschoolers have become widespread. Among the services offered are physical/occupational therapy, speech and language development, and social skills training directed at family members as well as affected children. (See Bailey, McWilliam et al. 1992; Jeppson and Thomas 1994; McWilliam, Winton et al. 1996.)

54. M. Susan Lindee, professor of the history of science, University of Pennsylvania, is currently writing a history of modern medical genetics in the United States. She suggests that the "emotional knowledge" produced in families with genetically disabled children subtly enters professional "technical knowledge" of diagnosed conditions (personal communication, 1997–1998).

References

Agar, Michael (1980). *The Professional Stranger.* New York, Academic Press.

Alberman, E., D. Mutton et al. (1995). "Down's Syndrome Births and Pregnancy Terminations in 1989 to 1993: Preliminary Findings." *British Journal of Obstetrics and Gynaecology* 102 (6): 445–447.

Allen, Garland E. (1989). "Eugenics and American Social History." *Genome* 31 (2): 885–889.

Altfeld, Susan, Arden Handler et al. (1997). "Wantedness of Pregnancy and Prenatal Health Behavior." *Women & Health* 26 (4): 29–43.

American Academy of Pediatrics, and American College of Obstetricians and Gynecologists (1983). Guidelines for Perinatal Care. Washington, DC.

Amniocentesis, Report to the M.R.C. by Their Working Party on (1978). "An Assessment of the Hazards of Amniocentesis." *British Journal of Obstetrics and Gynaecology* 85 (suppl. 2): 1–41.

Angrosino, Michael V. (1986). "The Self Behind the Stigma: Life Histories of Mentally Retarded Adults." Southern Anthropological Society, Wrightsville Beach, NC.

_____(1994). "On the Bus with Vonnie Lee: Explorations in Life History and Metaphor." *Journal of Contemporary Ethnography* 23: 14–28.

_____(1997). *Opportunity House.* Walnut Creek, CA, AltaMira Press.

Angrosino, Michael V., and Lucinda J. Zagnoli (1992). "Gender Constructs and Social Identity: Implications for Community-Based Care of Retarded Adults." *Gender Constructs and Social Issues.* T. L. Whitehead and B. V. Reid., eds. Urbana, University of Illinois Press: 40–69.

Annas, George, and Sherman Elias, eds. (1992). *Gene Mapping: Using Law and Ethics as Guides.* New York, Oxford.

Appadurai, Arjun (1996). *Modernity at Large: Cultural Dimensions of Globalization.* Minneapolis, University of Minnesota Press.

Arditti, Rita, Renate Duelli-Klein et al., eds. (1984). *Test-Tube Woman.* Boston, Routledge and Kegan Paul.

Arms, Suzanne (1975). *Immaculate Deception.* Boston, Houghton Mifflin.

Asad, Talal (1994). "Ethnographic Representation, Statistics and Modern Power." *Social Research* 61 (1): 55–88.

Asch, Adrienne (1989). "Reproductive Technology and Disability." *Reproductive Laws for the 1990s.* S. Cohen and N. Taub. Clifton, NJ, Humana Press: 69–124.

Asch, Adrienne, and Michelle Fine (1984). "Shared Dreams: A Left Perspective on Disability Rights and Reproductive Rights." *Radical America* 18: 51–58.

_____eds. (1988). *Women with Disabilities: Essays on Psychology, Culture, and Politics.* Philadelphia, PA, Temple University Press.

Association, American Anthropological (1996). "The New Code of Ethics." *Anthropology Newsletter* 37 (4): 13–17.

Axelrod, Toby (1990). "Kol Ishan: Finding Homes for Jewish Babies." *Lillith: The Magazine for Jewish Women* 15 (3): 4–5.

Bailey, D. B., P. J. McWilliam et al. (1992). *Implementing Family-Centered Services in Early Intervention: A Team-Based Model for Change.* Brookline, MA, Brookline Books.

Battaglia, Debbora (1985). "'We Feed Our Father': Paternal Nurture Among the Sabarl of Papua New Guinea." *American Ethnologist* 12 (3): 427–441.

Baxter, Daniel (1997). *Least of My Brethren: A Doctor's Story of Hope and Miracles on an Inner City AIDS Ward.* New York, Random House.

Beale, Frances (1970). "Double Jeopardy: To Be Black and Female." *The Black Woman: An Anthology.* T. Cade, ed. New York, New American Library: 90–100.

Beckwith, Jon (1993). "A Historical View of Social Responsibility in Genetics." *BioScience* 43 (5): 327–333.

Behar, Ruth (1993). *Translated Woman: Crossing the Border with Esperanza's Story.* Boston, Beacon.

Berg, Marc, and Monica J. Casper (1995). "Special Issue: Constructivist Perspectives on Medical Work." *Science, Technology, and Human Values* 20 (4).

Berger, Roy E., with Linda Mittiga (1994). *Common Bonds: Reflections of a Cancer Doctor.* Westbury, NY: Health Education Literary Publishers.

Bernal, John Desmond (1965). *Science in History.* New York, Hawthorn Books.

Bernard, Jessie (1972). *The Future of Marriage.* New York, World.

Berube, Michael (1996). *Life As We Know It: A Father, a Family, and an Exceptional Child.* New York, Pantheon.

Bettelheim, Bruno (1954). *Symbolic Wounds: Puberty Rites and the Envious Male.* Glencoe, IL: The Free Press.

Biesecker, Barbara, Patricia Magyari et al. (1987). "Strategies in Genetic Counseling II: Religious, Cultural and Ethnic Influences on the Counseling Process." *Birth Defects* 23 (6).

Bijker, Wiebe E. (1995). "Sociohistorical Technology Studies." *Handbook of Science and Technology Studies.* S. Jasanoff, G. E. Markle, J. C. Petersen, and T. Pinch, eds. Thousand Oaks, CA, Sage: 229–256.

Bijker, Wiebe E., Thomas P. Hughes et al., eds. (1989). *The Social Construction of Technological Systems.* Cambridge, MIT Press.

Billings, Paul, M. Kohn et al. (1992). "Discrimination as a Consequence of Genetic Testing." *American Journal of Human Genetics* 50 (3): 476–482.

Birke, Lynda, Susan Himmelweit et al. (1990). *Tomorrow's Child: Reproductive Technologies in the '90s.* London, Virago.

Bishop, Jerry E., and Michael Waldholz (1990). *Genome.* New York, Simon and Schuster.

Black, Rita Beck (1984). "Prenatal Diagnosis: The Experience in Families Who Have Children." *American Journal of Medical Genetics* 19 (1): 729–739.

_____(1993). "Psychosocial Issues in Reproductive Genetic Testing and Pregnancy Loss." *Fetal Diagnosis and Therapy* 8 (suppl. 1): 164–173.

_____(1994). "Reproductive Genetic Testing and Pregnancy Loss: The Experience of Women." *Women and Prenatal Testing: Facing the Challenges of Genetic Technology.* K. H. Rothenberg and E. J. Thomson. Columbus, Ohio State University Press.

Black, Rita Beck, and Joan O. Weiss (1990). "Genetic Support Groups and Social Workers as Partners." *Health and Social Work* 15 (2): 91–99.

Bluebond-Langner, Myra (1991). "Living With Cystic Fibrosis." *Medical Anthropology Quarterly* 5 (2): 99–122.

Blumberg, Bruce D., Mitchell S. Golbus et al. (1975). "The Psychological Sequelae of Abortion Performed for a Genetic Indication." *American Journal of Obstetrics and Gynecology* 122 (7): 799–808.

Bonavoglia, Angela, Ed. (1991). *The Choices We Made: Twenty-Five Women and Men Speak Out About Abortion*. New York, Random House.

Bowler, Peter J. (1989). *The Mendelian Revolution*. Baltimore, MD, Johns Hopkins University Press.

Brain, Lord (1967). "Chairman's Opening Remarks: Historical Introduction." *Mongolism (C.I.B.A. Foundation Study Group #25)*. G. E. W. Wolstenholme and R. Porter. Boston, Little, Brown and Company: 1–5.

Brewster, Arlene (1984). "After Hours: A Patient's Reaction to Amniocentesis." *Obstetrics and Gynecology* 64 (3): 443–444.

Brown, JoAnne (1986). "Professional Language: Words That Succeed." *Radical History Review* 34: 33–52.

Burke, Chris, and Jo Beth McDaniel (1991). *A Special Kind of Hero*. New York, Doubleday.

Bynum, Caroline (1989). "The Female Body and Religious Practice in the Later Middle Ages." *Fragments for a History of the Body, Part I*. M. Feher, R. Naddaff, and N. Tazi, eds. New York, Zone.

_____(1992). *Fragmentation and Redemption: Essays on Gender and the Human Body in Medieval Religion*. New York, Zone.

Callon, Michael (1986). "Some Elements of a Sociology of Translation: Domestication of the Scallops and the Fishermen of the St. Brieuc Bay." *Power, Action, and Belief: A New Sociology of Knowledge?* J. Law, ed. London, Routledge and Kegan Paul: 196–233.

Cantor, Charles (1992). "The Challenge of Technology and Informatics." *The Code of Codes: Scientific and Social Issues in the Human Genome Project*. D. Kevles and L. Hood, eds. Cambridge, MA, Harvard University Press: 98–111.

Casper, Monica (1994a). "At the Margins of Humanity: Fetal Positions in Science and Medicine." *Science, Technology, and Human Values* 19 (3): 307–323.

_____(1994b). "Reframing and Grounding Nonhuman Agency: What Makes a Fetus an Agent?" *American Behavioral Scientist* 37 (6): 839–856.

_____(1998). *The Making of the Unborn Patient: A Social Anatomy of Fetal Surgery*. New Brunswick, NJ: Rutgers University Press.

Chalmers, Irwin (1987). "Evaluation of the Long-Term Consequences of Chorion Villus Sampling." *Chorionic Villus Sampling*. E. M. Symonds and M. S. Golbus. London, Chapman and Hall: 187–201.

Chang, Grace (1994). "Undocumented Latinas: The New 'Employable Mothers.'" *Mothering: Ideology, Experience, and Agency*. E. N. Glenn, G. Chang, and L. R. Forcey. New York, Routledge: 259–285.

Chavkin, Wendy (1990). "Drug Addiction and Pregnancy: Policy Crossroads." *American Journal of Public Health* 8 (2): 483–487.

Christmas, June Jackson (n.d.). Growing Up Against the Odds: The Health of Black Children and Adolescents in New York City. New York, Urban Issues Group.

Claeson, Bjorn, Emily Martin et al. (1996). "Scientific Literacy, What It Is, Why It's Important, and Why Scientists Don't Think We Have It: The Case of Immunology and the Immune System." *Naked Science: Anthropological Inquiry into Boundaries, Power, and Knowledge*. L. Nader, ed. New York, Routledge: 101–118.

Clarke, Adele (1998). *Disciplining Reproduction: Modernity, American Life Sciences, and "the Problems of Sex."* Berkeley, University of California Press.

Clarke, Adele, and Joan Fujimura, eds. (1992). *The Right Tools for the Job: At Work in Twentieth-Century Life Sciences*. Princeton, NJ, Princeton University Press.

Clayton, Ellen Wright (1993). "Reproductive Genetic Testing: Regulatory and Liability Issues." *Fetal Diagnosis and Therapy* 8 (supp. 1): 39–59.

Clifford, James (1988). *The Predicament of Culture*. Cambridge, MA, Harvard University Press.

Colen, Shellee (1986). "'With Respect and Feelings': Voices of West Indian Child Care and Domestic Workers in New York City." *All American Women: Lines That Divide, Ties That Bind*. J. B. Cole, ed. New York, Free Press.

———(1990). "'Housekeeping' for the Green Card: West Indian Household Workers, the State, and Stratified Reproduction in New York." *At Work in Homes: Household Workers in World Perspective*. Roger C. Sanjek and Shellee Colen, eds. Washington, DC, American Anthropological Association. AES Monograph #3: 89–118.

———(1995). "'Like a Mother to Them': Stratified Reproduction and West Indian Childcare Workers and Employers in New York." *Conceiving the New World Order: The Global Politics of Reproduction*. F. D. Ginsburg and Rayna Rapp, eds. Berkeley, University of California Press: 78–102.

Collective, Boston Women's Health (1978). *Our Bodies, Ourselves*. New York, Simon and Schuster.

Collins, Francis S. (1996). "BRCA1—Lots of Mutations, Lots of Dilemmas." *New England Journal of Medicine* 334 (3): 186–188.

Collins, Patricia Hill (1994). "Shifting the Center: Race, Class, and Feminist Theorizing About Motherhood." *Mothering: Ideology, Experience, and Agency*. E. N. Glenn, Grace Chang et al., eds. New York, Routledge: 45–66.

Corcoran, J. (1998). "What Are the Molecular Mechanisms of Neural Tube Defects?" *Bioassays* 20 (1): 6–8.

Corea, Gena (1985). *The Mother Machine: Reproductive Technologies from Artificial Insemination to the Artificial Womb*. New York, Harper and Row.

Corea, Gena, Renate Duelli-Klein et al., eds. (1987). *Man-Made Women: How New Reproductive Technologies Affect Women*. Bloomington, Indiana University Press.

Cornell, Drucilla (1993). *Transformations*. New York, Routledge.

Cornwell, John, ed. (1995). *Nature's Imagination: The Frontiers of Scientific Vision*. Oxford, Oxford University Press.

Correa, Sonia (1994). *Population and Reproductive Rights: Feminist Perspectives from the South*. London and New York, Zed Books.

Correa, Sonia, and Rosalind Petchesky (1994). "Reproductive and Sexual Rights: A Feminist Perpsective." *Population Policies Reconsidered: Health, Empowerment, and Rights*. G. Sen, A. Germain, and L. Chen, eds. Cambridge, MA, Harvard University Press: 107–123.

Council on Scientific Affairs, American Medical Association (1992). "Induced Termination of Pregnancy Before and After Roe v. Wade." *Journal of the American Medical Association* 268: 3231–3239.

Cowan, Ruth Schwartz (1992). "Genetic Technology and Reproductive Choice: An Ethics for Autonomy." *The Code of Codes: Scientific and Social Issues in the Human Genome Project*. D. Kevles and L. Hood, eds. Cambridge, MA, Harvard University Press: 244–263.

_____(1993). "Aspects of the History of Prenatal Diagnosis." *Fetal Diagnosis and Therapy* 8 (supp. 1): 10–17.

Crane, Diana (1972). *Invisible Colleges: Diffusion of Knowledge in Scientific Communities*. Chicago, University of Chicago Press.

Cunningham, George (1998). "An Evaluation of California's Public-Private Material Serum Screening Program." Ninth International Conference on Prenatal Diagnosis and Therapy. Los Angeles, CA. June 11.

Dasgupta, Rajashri (1994). "Is It 'Freedom of Choice' or Female Foeticide?" *The Telegraph*, 27 October. Calcutta.

Daston, Lorraine (1987). "Rational Individuals versus Laws of Society: From Probability to Statistics." *The Probabilistic Revolution Volume 1*. L. D. Kruger, L. J. Daston, Michael Heidelberger, eds. Cambridge, MA: MIT Press.: 295–304.

Davis, Angela (1981). *Women, Race and Class*. New York, Random House.

Davis, Jessica (1993). "Reproductive Technologies for Prenatal Diagnosis." *Fetal Diagnosis and Therapy* 8 (supp. 1): 28–38.

Davis-Floyd, Robbie (1992). *Birth as an American Rite of Passage*. Berkeley, University of California Press.

Davis-Floyd, Robbie, and Caroline Sargent, eds. (1997). *Childbirth and Authoritative Knowledge*. Berkeley, CA, University of California Press.

Delaney, Carol (1986). "The Meaning of Paternity and the Virgin Birth Debate." *Man* 21 (3): 494–513.

DeLeon, Judy, and Judy Westerberg (1980). Who Adopts Retarded Children? Westfield, NJ, Spaulding for Children.

Development, National Institute of Child Health and (1976). "Midtrimester Amniocentesis for Prenatal Diagnosis." *Journal of the American Medical Association* 236: 1471–1476.

Dicker, M., and L. Dicker (1978). "Genetic Counseling as an Occupational Specialty: A Sociological Perspective." *Social Biology* 25 (4): 272–278.

Down, John Langdon (1866). Observations on an Ethnic Classification of Idiots. London, London Hospital Reports.

_____(1877). *Mental Affections of Childhood and Youth*. London, J & A Churchill.

Doyle, Debra Lochner (1996). "The 1996 Professional Status Survey." *Perspectives in Genetic Counseling* 18 (3): 1–8.

Draper, Elaine (1992). *Risky Business.* New York, Cambridge University Press.

Dreifus, Claudia T. (1996). "Who Gets the Liver Transplant? Which One's the Mother? When Do You Lie? (And These Are the Easy Ones)." *New York Times Sunday Magazine,* 15 December.

Drugan, Arie, Anne Greb et al. (1990). "Determinants of Parental Decisions to Abort for Chromosome Abnormalities." *Prenatal Diagnosis* 10 (8): 483–490.

Dubey, Leela (1983). "Misadventures in Amniocentesis." *Economic and Political Weekly,* 19 February. Calcutta.

Duden, Barbara (1993). *Disembodying Women: Perspectives on Pregnancy and the Unborn.* Cambridge, MA, Harvard University Press.

Duster, Troy (1990). *Backdoor to Eugenics.* New York, Routledge.

Edgerton, Robert B. (1993 [1967]). *The Cloak of Competence.* Berkeley, University of California Press.

Ehrenreich, Barbara, and Deidre English (1978). *For Her Own Good: 150 Years of Experts' Advice to Women.* Garden City, NY, Doubleday.

Epner, Janet Gans, Harry S. Jonas, et al. (1988). "Late Abortion." *Journal of the American Medical Association* 280 (8): 727–729.

Farrant, Wendy (1985). "Who's for Amniocentesis? The Politics of Prenatal Testing." *The Sexual Politics of Reproduction.* H. Homans. London, Gower: 96–122.

Featherstone, Helen (1980). *A Difference in the Family.* New York, Free Press.

Feenberg, Andrew, and Alastair Hannay, eds. (1995). *Technology and the Politics of Knowledge.* Bloomington, Indiana University Press.

Feminist Studies (1997). "Special Issue: Feminists and Fetuses." *Feminist Studies* 23 (2).

Ferguson, Tom (1996). *Health Online: How to Find Health Information, Support Groups, and More in Cyberspace.* Reading, MA, Addison-Wesley.

Fertel, Patricia, Suzanne Holowinsky et al. (1988). *Difficult Decisions: For Families Whose Unborn Baby Has a Serious Problem.* Omaha, NE, Centering Corporation.

Finger, Anne (1984). "Claiming All of Our Bodies: Reproductive Rights and Disabilities." *Test-Tube Woman.* R. Arditti, R. Duelli-Klein, and S. Minden, eds. Boston, Routledge and Kegan Paul: 281–297.

———(1990). *Past Due: A Story of Disability, Pregnancy, and Birth.* Seattle, Seal Press.

Firth, H. V. (1991). "Severe Limb Abnormalities After Chorionic Villus Sampling." *Lancet* 337: 762–763.

Fisher, Ian (1998). "Families Provide Medical Care, Tubes and All." *New York Times,* 1, 30. 7 June.

Fleising, Usher, and Alan Smart (1993). "The Development of Property Rights in Biotechnology." *Culture, Medicine, and Psychiatry* 17 (4): 43–58.

Flower, Michael J., and Deborah Heath (1993). "Micro-Anatomo Politics: Mapping the Human Genome Project." *Culture, Medicine, and Psychiatry* 17: 27–41.

Forum Against Sex Determination and Sex Pre-Selection (1994). "Using Technology, Choosing Sex: The Campaign Against Sex Determination and the Question of Choice." *Close to Home: Women Reconnect Ecology, Health and Development Worldwide.* V. Shiva, ed. New Delhi, New Society Publishers, Kali for Women: 527–534.

Fox, Renee C. (1990). "The Evolution of Social Science Perspectives." *Social Science Perspectives on Medical Ethics.* G. Weisz. Philadelphia, PA, Temple University Press.

Fox, Richard, Ed. (1991). *Recapturing Anthropology: Working in the Present.* St. Louis, WA, SAR Press/Washington University Press.

France, David (1998). "Challenging the Conventional Stance on AIDS." *New York Times,* 22 December, F6.

Franklin, Sarah (1995). "Science as Culture, Cultures of Science." *Annual Review of Anthropology* 24: 163–184.

Fraser, F. Clarke, and Charles Pressor (1977). "Attitudes of Counselors in Relation to Prenatal Sex Selection Simply for Choice of Sex." *Genetic Counseling.* H. A. Lubs and F. de la Cruz. New York, Raven Press.

Fujimura, Joan (1992). "Crafting Science: Standardized Packages, Boundary Objects, and 'Translation.'" *Science as Culture and Practice.* A. Pickering, ed. Chicago, University of Chicago Press.

———(1996). *Crafting Science: A Sociohistory of the Quest for the Genetics of Cancer.* Cambridge, MA, Harvard University Press.

Furlong, Regina M., and Rita Beck Black (1984). "Pregnancy Termination for Genetic Indications: The Impact on Families." *Social Work in Health Care* 10 (1): 17–34.

Fyfe, Gordon, and John Law (1988). "On the Invisibility of the Visual: Editors' Introduction." *Picturing Power: Visual Depictions and Social Relations.* G. Fyfe and J. Law, eds. London, Routledge: 1–14.

Garrow, David J. (1994). *Liberty and Sexuality: The Right to Privacy and the Making of Roe v. Wade.* New York, MacMillan.

Geertz, Clifford (1967). "'From the Native's Point of View': On the Nature of Anthropological Understanding." *Meaning in Anthropology.* K. H. Basso and H. A. Selby, eds. Albuquerque, School of American Research Press/University of New Mexico: 221–238.

Gieryn, Thomas F. (1995). "Boundaries of Science." *Handbook of Science and Technology Studies.* S. Jasanoff, G. E. Markle, J. C. Petersen, and T. Pinch, eds. Thousand Oaks, CA, Sage: 393–443.

Gilbert, Walter (1992). "A Vision of the Grail." *The Code of Codes: Scientific and Social Issues in the Human Genome Project.* D. Kevles and L. Hood, eds. Cambridge, MA, Harvard University Press: 83–97.

Ginsburg, Faye (1989a). *Contested Lives: The Abortion Debate in an American Community.* Berkeley, CA, University of California Press.

———(1989b). "Dissonance and Harmony: The Symbolic Function of Abortion in Activists' Life Stories." *Interpreting Women's Lives: Feminist Theory and Personal Narratives.* T. P. N. Group. Bloomington, Indiana University Press: 59–84.

———(1993). "Saving America's Souls: Operation Rescue's Crusade Against Abortion." *Fun-

damentalisms and the State: Remaking Polities, Economies, and Militance. M. Marty and R. S. Appleby, eds. Chicago, University of Chicago Press: 567–588.

Ginsburg, Faye, and Rayna Rapp (1991). "The Politics of Reproduction." *Annual Review of Anthropology* 20: 311–344.

_____(1995). "Introduction: Conceiving the New World Order." *Conceiving the New World Order.* F. Ginsburg and R. Rapp, eds. Berkeley, University of California Press: 1–17.

_____(1999). "Fetal Reflections: Confessions of Two Feminist Anthropologists as Mutual Informants." *The Fetal Imperative.* M. Michaels and L. Morgan, eds. Philadelphia, University of Pennsylvania Press.

Glendon, Mary (1987). *Abortion and Divorce in Western Law: American Failures, European Challenges.* Cambridge, MA, Harvard University Press.

Glenn, Evelyn Nakano (1992). "From Servitude to Service Work: Historical Continuities in the Racial Division of Paid Reproductive Labor." *Signs* 18 (1): 1–43.

Glenn, Evelyn Nakano, Grace Chang et al., eds. (1994). *Mothering: Ideology, Experience, and Agency.* New York, Routledge.

Gliedman, John, and William Roth (1980). *The Unexpected Minority: Handicapped Children in America.* New York, Harcourt Brace Jovanovich.

Gluck, Sherna, and Daphne Patai, eds. (1991). *Women's Words: The Practice of Feminist Oral History.* Bloomington, Indiana University Press.

Goldberg, Carey, and Janet Elder (1998). "Public Still Backs Abortion, But Wants Limits, Polls Say." *New York Times,* January 16, A1, A16.

Gordon, Linda (1976). *Women's Body, Women's Right.* New York, Penguin.

Gorney, Cynthia (1998). *Articles of Faith: A Frontline History of the Abortion Wars.* New York, Simon and Schuster.

Gould, Stephen Jay (1980). "Dr. Down's Syndrome." *The Panda's Thumb: More Reflections in Natural History.* S. J. Gould. New York, W. W. Norton: 160–168.

Greely, Henry T. (1992). "Health Insurance, Employment Discrimination, and the Genetics Revolution." *The Code of Codes: Scientific and Social Issues in the Human Genome Project.* D. J. Kevles and L. Hood, eds. Cambridge, MA, Harvard University Press: 264–280.

Green, Jeremy (1985). "Media Sensationalism and Science: The Case of the Criminal Chromosome." *Expository Science.* T. Shinn and R. Whitley, eds. Sociology of the Sciences Yearbook 9: 139–161.

Green, Rose (pseudonym) (1992). "Letter to a Genetic Counselor." *Journal of Genetic Counseling* 1 (1): 55–70.

Gunther, John (1949). *Death Be Not Proud: A Memoir.* New York, Harper.

Gupta, Akhil, and James Ferguson, eds. (1997a). *Culture, Power, Place: Explorations in Critical Anthropology.* Durham, NC, Duke University Press.

_____(1997b). *Anthropological Locations: Boundaries and Grounds of a Field Science.* Berkeley, University of California Press.

Hacking, Ian (1983). *Representing and Intervening: Introductory Topics in the Philosophy of Natural Science.* Cambridge, UK, Cambridge University Press.

_____(1990). *The Taming of Chance.* Cambridge, UK, Cambridge University Press.

_____(1992). "Statistical Language, Statistical Truth, and Statistical Reason: The Self-Authentication of a Style of Scientific Reasoning." *The Social Dimensions of Science.* E. McMullin, ed. Notre Dame, IN, University of Notre Dame Press: 130–157.

Hahn, Harlan (1988). "The Politics of Human Difference." *Journal of Social Issues* 44 (1): 39–47.

Hanmer, Jalna (1981). "Sex Predetermination, Artificial Insemination, and the Maintenance of Male-Dominated Culture." *Women, Health and Reproduction.* H. Roberts, ed. London, Routledge and Kegan Paul: 163–190.

Haraway, Donna (1979). "The Biological Enterprise: Sex, Mind and Profit from Human Engineering to Sociobiology." *Radical History Review* (20): 206–237.

_____(1981–82). "The High Cost of Information in Post–World War II Evolutionary Biology: Ergonomics, Semiotics, and the Sociobiology of Comunications Systems." *Philosophical Forum* 13 (2–3): 244–278.

_____(1983). "Signs of Dominance: From a Physiology to a Cybernetics of Primate Society, C. R. Carpenter, 1930–70." *Studies in the History of Biology* 6: 129–219.

_____(1988a). "Remodeling the Human Way of Life: Sherwood Washurn and the New Physical Anthropology, 1950–1980." *Bones, Bodies, Behaviors: Essays on Biological Anthropology.* G. Stocking, ed. Madison, University of Wisconsin Press.

_____(1988b). "Situated Knowledge: The Science Question in Feminism and the Privilege of Partial Perspective." *Feminist Studies* 14 (3): 575–600.

_____(1989a). "The Biopolitics of Postmodern Bodies: Determinations of Self in Immune System Discourse." *Differences* 1 (1): 3–43.

_____(1989b). *Primate Visions: Gender, Race and Nation in the World of Modern Science.* New York, Routledge.

_____(1991). *Simians, Cyborgs, and Women: The Reinvention of Nature.* New York, Routledge.

_____(1997). *Modest Witness@Second Millennium.FemaleMan Meets OncoMouse^{tm}*. New York, Routledge.

Hardacre, Helen (1997). *Marketing the Menacing Fetus in Japan.* Berkeley, CA, University of California Press.

Harding, Sandra (1991). *Whose Science? Whose Knowledge?* Ithaca, NY, Cornell University Press.

Harding, Susan (1994). "Further Reflections." *Cultural Anthropology* 9 (3): 276–278.

Hartouni, Valerie (1992). "Fetal Exposures: Abortion Politics and the Optics of Allusion." *Camera Obscura* 29: 130–149.

Heath, Deborah (1994). "Recombinant Fieldsites: Chimeric Ethnography and the Co-Production of Technoscientific Research." Annual Meeting of the American Anthropological Association, Atlanta, GA.

_____(1998). "Locating Genetic Knowledge: Picturing Marfan Syndrome and Its Traveling Constituencies." *Science, Technology, and Human Values* 23 (1): 71–97.

Heath, Deborah, and Paul Rabinow (1993). "The Anthropology of the New Genetics and Immunology." *Culture, Medicine, and Psychiatry* 17 (4): 1–3.

Henshaw, Stanley K., and Kathryn Kost (1996). "Abortion Patients in 1994–95: Characteristics and Contraceptive Use." *Family Planning Perspectives* 28 (4): 140–147, 158.

Herdman, Roger C., and Gretchen S. Kolsrud (1988). *Infertility: Medical and Social Choices.* Washington, DC, Office of Technology Assessment.

Hess, David (1995). *Science and Technology in a Multicultural World.* New York, Columbia University Press.

_____(1997). *Can Bacteria Cause Cancer?* New York, New York University Press.

_____(1998). "If You're Thinking of Living in STS." *Cyborgs and Citadels: Anthropological Interventions in Emerging Sciences and Technologies.* G. L. Downey and J. Dumit, eds. Santa Fe, NM, School of American Research Press: 143–164.

Hewlett, Barry (1991). *Intimate Fathers: The Nature and Context of Aka Pygmy Paternal Infant Care.* Ann Arbor, University of Michigan Press.

Hilton, Bruce (1991). *First Do No Harm: Wrestling with New Medical Life and Death Dilemmas,* Nashville, TN: Abingdon Books.

Hilton, Bruce, Daniel Callahan et al., eds. (1973). *Ethical Issues in Human Genetics.* New York, Plenum.

Hitt, Jack (1998). "Who Will Do Abortions Here?" *New York Times Sunday Magazine:* 19-27, 42, 45, 54–55, 56. 18 January.

Holtzman, Neil (1989). *Proceed With Caution: Predicting Genetic Risks in the Recombinant DNA Era.* Baltimore, MD, Johns Hopkins University Press.

Hook, Ernest B. (1973). "Behavioral Implications of the Human XYY Genotype." *Science* 179 (4069): 139–150.

_____(1978). "Differences Between Rates of Trisomy 21 (Down syndrome) and Other Chromosomal Abnormalities Diagnosed in Livebirths and in Cells Cultured After Second Trimester Amniocentesis: Suggested Explanations and Implications for Genetic Counseling and Program Planning." *Birth Defects* 14 (6C): 249–267.

_____(1989). Personal communication.

Hook, Ernest B., Philip K. Cross et al. (1983). "Chromosomal Abnormality Rates at Amniocentesis and in Live-Born Infants." *Journal of the American Medical Association* 249 (15): 2034–2038.

hooks, bell (1982). *Ain't I a Woman?* Boston, South End Press.

Horgan, John (1996). *The End of Science: Facing the Limits of Knowledge in the Twilight of the Scientific Age.* Reading, MA, Addison-Wesley.

Hsu, Lillian (1989). Portrait of the Prenatal Diagnosis Laboratory, a Tenth Anniversary Report. New York University Medical School, 10 June.

Hsu, Lillian, and Kurt Hirschhorn (1977). "Numerical and Structural Chromosome Abnormalities." *Handbook of Teratology.* J. G. Wilson and F. Clarke Fraser, eds. New York, Plenum: 41–79.

Hubbard, Ruth (1990). *The Politics of Women's Biology.* New Brunswick, NJ, Rutgers University Press.

Hubbard, Ruth, and Richard Lewontin (1996). "Sounding Board." *New England Journal of Medicine* 334 (18): 1193–1194.

Hull, Gloria, Patricia Bell Scott et al., eds. (1982). *All the Women Are White, All the Blacks Are Men, But Some of Us Are Brave.* Old Westbury, NY, Feminist Press.

Ilse, Sherokee (1993). *Precious Lives, Painful Choices: A Prenatal Decision-Making Guide.* Long Lake, MN, Wintergreen Press.

Ingstad, Benedicte, and Susan R. White, eds. (1995). *Disability and Culture.* Berkeley, University of California Press.

Institute, Alan Guttmacher (1987). Blessed Events and the Bottom Line. New York, Alan Guttmacher Institute.

Jasanoff, Sheila, Gerald E. Markle et al., eds. (1995). *Handbook of Science and Technology Studies.* Thousand Oaks, CA, Sage.

Jeppson, E., and J. Thomas (1994). *Essential Allies: Families and Advisors.* Bethesda, MD, Institute for Family-Centered Care.

Joffe, Carole (1995). *Doctors of Conscience: The Struggle to Provide Abortions Before and After Roe v. Wade.* Boston, Beacon.

Jordanova, Ludmilla (1989). *Sexual Visions: Images of Gender in Science and Medicine Between the Eighteenth and Twentieth Centuries.* Madison, University of Wisconsin Press.

_____(1995). "Interrogating the Concept of Reproduction in the Eighteenth Century." In Faye D. Ginsburg and Rayna Rapp, eds. *Conceiving the New World Order: The Global Politics of Reproduction.* Berkeley, University of California Press: 369–386.

Judson, Horace Freeland (1992). "A History of the Science and Technology Behind Gene Mapping and Sequencing." *The Code of Codes: Scientific and Social Issues in the Human Genome Project.* D. J. Kevles and L. Hood, eds. Cambridge, MA, Harvard University Press: 37–80.

Juengst, Eric T. (1996). "Self-Critical Federal Science? The Ethics Experiments Within the U.S. Human Genome Project." *Social Philosophy and Policy* 13 (2): 63–95.

Julian-Reynier, C., Y. Aurran et al. (1995). "Attitudes Toward Down's Syndrome: Follow-Up of a Cohort of 280 Cases." *Journal of Medical Genetics* 32 (8): 597–599.

Juma, Calestous (1989). *The Gene Hunters: Biotechnology and the Scramble for Seeds.* Princeton, NJ, Princeton University Press.

Kaback, Michael M., et al. (1979). Antenatal Diagnosis: Report of a Consensus Development Conference. Bethesda, MD, National Institutes of Health.

Kaplan, Deborah (1993). "Prenatal Screening and Its Impact on Persons with Disabilities." *Fetal Diagnosis and Therapy* 8 (supp. 1): 64–69.

Kaplan, Laura (1996). *The Story of Jane: The Legendary Underground Feminist Abortion Service.* New York, Pantheon.

Keller, Evelyn Fox (1983). *A Feeling for the Organism: The Life and Work of Barbara McClintock.* San Francisco, Freeman.

_____(1992a). "Nature, Nurture, and the Human Genome Project." *The Code of Codes: Scientific and Social Issues in the Human Genome Project.* D. J. Kevles and L. Hood, eds. Cambridge, MA, Harvard University Press: 281–299.

_____(1992b). *Secrets of Life, Secrets of Death: Essays on Language, Gender and Science.* New York, Routledge.

_____(1995). "Genetics, Embryology and the Discourse of Gene Action." In EF Keller, *Refiguring Life: Metaphors of Twentieth Century Biology.* New York: Columbia University Press.

_____(1996). "Drosophila Embryos as Transitional Objects: The Work of Donald Poulson and Christiane Nusslein-Volhard." *Historical Studies in the Physical and Biological Sciences* 26 (2): 313–346.

_____(nd). "Decoding the Genetic Program."

Kenen, Regina (1984). "Genetic Counseling: The Development of a New Interdisciplinary Occupational Field." *Social Science and Medicine* 18 (7): 541–549.

_____(1986). "Growing Pains of a New Health Care Field: Genetic Counseling in Australia and the United States." *Australian Journal of Social Issues* 21: 172–182.

Kenyon, S. L., G. A. Hackett et al. (1988). "Termination of Pregnancy Following Diagnosis of Fetal Malformation: The Need for Improved Follow-Up Services." *Clinical Obstetrics and Gynecology* 31: 97–100.

Kessler, Seymour (1979). *Genetic Counseling: Psychological Dimensions.* New York, Academic Press.

_____(1989). "Psychological Aspects of Genetic Counseling VI: A Critical Review of the Literature Dealing with Education and Reproduction." *American Journal of Medical Genetics* 34: 340–353.

Kevles, Daniel (1985). *In the Name of Eugenics: Genetics and the Uses of Human Heredity.* New York, Knopf.

_____(1992). "Out of Eugenics: The Historical Politics of the Human Genome." *The Code of Codes: Scientific and Social Issues in the Human Genome Project.* D. Kevles and L. Hood. eds. Cambridge, MA, Harvard University Press: 3–36.

King, Patricia A. (1992). "The Past as Prologue: Race, Class and Gene Discrimination." *Gene Mapping: Using Law and Ethics as Guides.* G. J. Annas and S. Elias, eds. New York, Oxford University Press: 94–111.

Kingsley, Mitchell, and Mitchell Levitz (1994). *Count Us In: Growing Up with Down Syndrome.* New York, Harcourt Brace.

Kitcher, Philip (1992). "Gene." *Keywords in Evolutionary Biology.* E. F. Keller and E. A. Lloyd, eds. Cambridge, MA, Harvard University Press: 125–128.

_____(1996). *The Lives to Come: The Genetic Revolution and Human Possibilities.* New York, Simon and Schuster.

Kittay, Eva (1997). "On the Expressivity and Ethics of Selective Abortion for Disability: Conversations with My Son." Briarcliff Manor, NY, Hastings Center.

Klass, Perri (1992). *Other Women's Children.* New York, Ivy Books.

Knorr-Cetina (1995). "Laboratory Studies: The Cultural Approach to the Study of Science." *Handbook of Science and Technology Studies.* S. Jasanoff, G. E. Markle, J. C. Petersen, and T. Pinch, eds. Thousand Oaks, CA, Sage: 140–166.

Kobrin, Frances (1966). "The American Midwife Controversy: A Crisis of Professionalization." *Bulletin of the History of Medicine* 40: 350–363.

Kochanek, Kenneth, Jeffrey Maurer, and Harry Rosenberg (1994). "Why Did Black Life Expectancy Decline from 1984 to1989 in the US?" *American Journal of Public Health* 84 (6): 938–944.

Koenig, Barbara (1996). "Gene Tests: What You Know Can Hurt You." *New York Times,* 6 April, op-ed.

Koenig, Barbara, and Monica J. Casper, eds. (1996). "Special Issue: Biomedical Technologies:

Reconfiguring Nature and Culture." *Medical Anthropology Quarterly* 10 (4).

Kohn, Ingrid, and Perry Moffit (1993). *Silent Sorrow: Pregnancy Loss, Guidance and Support*. New York, Dell.

Kolata, Gina (1996). "Breaking Ranks, Lab Offers Test to Assess Risk of Breast Cancer." *New York Times*. New York: A1, A15. 1 April.

Kolker, Aliza, and Meredith Burke (1993). "Grieving the Wanted Child." *Health Care for Women International* 14 (6): 513–526.

———(1994). *Prenatal Testing: A Sociological Perspective*. Westport, CN, Bergin & Garvey (Greenwood Publishing Groups).

Konner, Melvin (1988). *Becoming a Doctor: A Journey of Initiation in Medical School*. NY, Penguin.

Koonin, Lisa, J. C. Smith et al. (1996). "Abortion Surveillance in the U.S.A., 1992." *Morbidity Mortality Weelky Review* 45 (SS-9): 1–36.

Koren, G. (1993). "Preconceptual Folate and Neural Tube Defects: Time for Rethinking." *Canadian Journal of Public Health* 84 (3): 207–208.

Kornberg (1995). *The Golden Helix: Inside Biotech Ventures*. Sausalito, CA, University Science Books.

Kumar, Dharma (1983). "Amniocentesis Again." *Economic and Political Weekly*. Calcutta. June 11. (Bombay) 10,85.

Lakoff, George, and Mark Johnson (1980). *Metaphors We Live By*. Chicago, University of Chicago Press.

Lather, Patti (1999). Naked Methodology: Researching the Lives of Women with HIV/AIDS. *Revisioning Women, Health, and Healing: Feminist, Cultural, and Technoscience Studies Perspectives*. A. Clarke and V. Olesen, eds. New York, Routledg: 136–154.

Latour, Bruno (1986). "Visualization and Cognition: Thinking with Eyes and Hands." *Knowledge and Society: Studies in the Sociology of Culture Past and Present* 6: 1–40.

———(1987). *Science in Action: How to Follow Scientists and Engineers Through Society*. Cambridge, MA, Harvard University Press.

———(1990). "Drawing Things Together." *Representation in Scientific Practice*. M. Lynch and S. Woolgar. Cambridge, MA, MIT Press: 19–68.

———(1994). "Pragmatogonies: A Mythical Account of How Humans and Nonhumans Swap Together." *American Behavioral Scientist* 37 (6): 791–808.

Latour, Bruno, and Steve Woolgar (1979). *Laboratory Life: The Construction of Scientific Facts*. Beverly Hills, CA, Sage.

Lave, Jean (1996). "The Savagery of the Domestic Mind." *Naked Science: Anthropological Inquiry into Boundaries, Power, and Knowledge*. L. Nader, ed. New York, Routledge: 87–100.

Law, John, and John Whittaker (1988). "On the Art of Representation; Notes on the Politics of Representation." *Picturing Power: Visual Depictions and Social Relations*. G. Fyfe and J. Law, eds. London and New York, Routledge: 160–183.

Layne, Linda (1990). "Motherhood Lost: Cultural Dimensions of Miscarriage and Stillbirth in America." *Women and Health* 16 (3): 75–104.

———(1992). "Of Fetuses and Angels: Fragmentation and Integration in Narratives of Pregnancy Loss." *Knowledge and Society* 9: 29–58.

_____(1997). "Breaking the Silence: An Agenda for Feminist Discourse on Pregnancy Loss." *Feminist Studies* 23 (2): 289–316.

_____(1998a). "Introduction: Technoscience Studies and Anthropology." *Science, Technology, and Human Values* 23 (1): 4–23.

_____ed. (1998b). "Special Issue: Anthropological Approaches in Science and Technology Studies." *Science, Technology, and Human Values* 23 (1).

Leavitt, Judith Walzer (1986). "Under the Shadow of Maternity: American Women's Responses to Death and Debility Fears in Nineteenth Century Childbirth." *Feminist Studies* 12 (1): 129–154.

Levins, Richard, and Richard Lewontin (1985). *The Dialectical Biologist.* Cambridge, Harvard University Press.

Lewenstein, Bruce (1995). "Science and the Media." *Handbook of Science and Technology Studies.* S. Jasanoff, G. E. Markle, J. C. Petersen, and T. Pinch, eds. Thousand Oaks, CA, Sage: 343–360.

Lewontin, Richard (1991). *Biology as Ideology: The Doctrine of DNA.* New York, Harper Collins.

Lindenbaum, Shirley, and Margaret Lock, eds. (1993). *Knowledge, Power and Practice: The Anthropology of Medicine and Everyday Life.* Berkeley, University of California Press.

Linton, Simi, Ed. (1998). *Claiming Disability: Knowledge and Identity.* New York, New York University Press.

Lipkin, Mack, and Peter Rowley (1974). *Genetic Responsibility.* New York, Plenum.

Lippman, Abby (1989). "Prenatal Diagnosis: Reproductive Choice? Reproductive Control?" *The Future of Human Reproduction.* C. Overall, ed. Toronto, Women's Press.

_____(1991). "Prenatal Genetic Testing and Screening: Constructing Needs and Reinforcing Inequities." *American Journal of Law and Medicine* 17 (1–2): 15–50.

_____(1993). "Prenatal Genetic Testing and Geneticization: Mother Matters for All." *Fetal Diagnosis and Therapy* 8 (supp. 1): 175–188.

Lippman, Abby, and F. Brunger (1991). "Constructing Down syndrome: Texts as Informants." *Santé Culture Health* 8 (1–2): 109–131.

Lippman-Hand, Abby, and F. Clarke Fraser (1979a). "Genetic Counseling: Parents' Responses to Uncertainty." *Birth Defects* 15 (5C): 325–339.

_____(1979b). "Genetic Counseling, The Postcounseling Period: Parents' Perceptions of Uncertainty." *American Journal of Medical Genetics* 4: 51–71.

Loma Linda University School of Medicine (1984). "Support for Prenatal Decision." Redlands, CA.

Lubinsky, Mark S. (1993). "Scientific Aspects of Early Eugenics." *Journal of Genetic Counseling* 2 (2): 77–92.

Lubs, Herbert A., and Felix de la Cruz, eds. (1977). *Genetic Counseling.* New York, Raven Press.

Lustig, L., and L. Poskanzer (1976). "Genetic Associates." *New England Journal of Medicine* 295 (25): 1436.

Lynch, Michael (1985). "Discipline and the Material Form of Images: An Analysis of Scientific Visibility." *Social Studies of Science* 15 (1): 37–66.

Lynch, Michael, and Steven Woolgar (1990). "Introduction: Sociological Orientations to Representational Practice in Science." *Representation in Scientific Practice*. M. Lynch and S. Woolgar, eds. Cambridge, MA, MIT Press: 1–18.

MacDonald, Sharon, ed. (1995). "Science on Display." *Science as Culture* 5 (1).

MacDonald, Scott, and Chester Oden (1978). *Moose: The Story of a Very Special Person*. Brookline, MA, Brookline Books.

Mairs, Nancy (1997). *Waist-High in the World: A Life Among the Non-Disabled*. Boston, Beacon.

Marcus, George (1995). "Ethnography in/of the World System: The Emergence of Multi-Sited Ethnography." *Annual Review of Anthropology* 24: 95–117.

Marks, Jonathan (1996a). "The Anthropology of Science, Part I: Science as a Humanities." *Evolutionary Anthropology* 5 (1): 6–10.

_____(1996b). "Racism, Eugenics, and the Burdens of History." *Yale Journal of Ethics* 5: 12–15; 40–42.

_____(1997). "The Anthropology of Science, Part II: Scientific Norms and Behaviors." *Evolutionary Anthropology* 5 (3): 75–80.

Marshall, Eliot (1995). "Gene Therapy's Growing Pains." *Science* 269 (25 August): 1050–1055.

Marshall, Patricia (1992). "Anthropology and Bioethics." *Medical Anthropology Quarterly* 6 (1): 49–73.

Martin, Emily (1991). "The Drama of the Egg and the Sperm: How Science Has Constructed a Romance Based on Stereotypical Male-Female Roles." *Signs* 16 (3): 485–501.

_____(1992). "The End of the Body?" *American Ethnologist* 19 (1): 121–149.

_____(1994). *Flexible Bodies: From the Age of Polio to the Age of AIDS*. Boston, Beacon.

_____(1998). "Anthropology and the Cultural Study of Science." *Science, Technology, and Human Values* 23 (1): 24–44.

McCorvey, Norma, with Andy Meisler (1994). *I Am Roe: My Life, Roe v. Wade, and Freedom of Choice*. New York, HarperCollins.

McDermott, Ray P., and Hervé Varenne (1995). "Culture as Disability." *Anthropology and Education Quarterly* 26: 324–348.

_____(1996). "Culture, Development, Disability." *Ethnography and Human Development*. R. Jessor, A. Colby, and R. Schweder, eds. Chicago, University of Chicago Press: 101–126.

McDonough, Peggy (1990). "Congenital Disability and Medical Research." *Women and Health* 16 (3/4): 137–153.

McNeil, Maureen, Ian Varcoe et al., eds. (1990). *The New Reproductive Technologies*. New York, St. Martin's Press.

McWilliam, P. J., P. J. Winton et al. (1996). *Practical Strategies for Family Centered Early Intervention*. San Diego, CA, Singular Publishing Group.

Meaney, F. John (1992). "The Future of Genetics in Public Health." *Journal of Genetic Counseling* 1 (1): 71–80.

Meaney, F. John, and S. P. Chang (1991). "Survey of State Genetic Services Programs in the United States." *American Journal of Human Genetics Supplement* 49 (4): 322.

Meaney, F. John, Susan M. Riggle et al. (1993). "Providers and Consumers of Prenatal Genetic Testing Services: What Do the National Data Tell Us?" *Fetal Diagnosis and Therapy* 8 (supp.1): 18–27.

Michaels, Meredith, and Lynn Morgan, eds. (1999). *The Fetal Imperative*. Philadelphia, University of Pennsylvania Press.

Milkman, Ruth (1986). "Women's History and the Sears Case." *Feminist Studies* 12 (2): 375–400.

Milunsky, Aubrey (1993). "Commercialization of Clinical Genetic Laboratory Services: In Whose Best Interest?" *Obstetrics and Gynecology* 81 (4): 627–629.

Minnick, Molly A., Kathleen J. Delp et al., eds. (1990). *A Time to Decide, a Time to Heal*. East Lansing, MI, Pineapple Press.

Minow, Martha (1990). *Making All the Difference: Inclusion, Exclusion, and American Law*. Ithaca, NY, Cornell University Press.

Miringoff, Marque-Luisa (1991). *The Social Costs of Genetic Welfare*. New Brunswick, NJ, Rutgers University Press.

Mitchell, Lisa (1993). "Making Babies: Routine Ultrasound Imaging and the Cultural Construction of the Fetus in Montreal, Canada." Anthropology Department. Cleveland, OH, Case Western Reserve University, doctoral dissertation.

_____(1994). "The Routinization of the Other: Ultrasound, Women and the Fetus." *Misconceptions: The Social Construction of Choice and the New Reproductive Technologies*. G. Basen, M. Eichler, and A. Lippman, eds. Quebec, Voyageur.

Mohanty, Chandra Talpade (1991). "Cartographies of Struggle: Third World Women and the Politics of Feminism." *Third World Women and the Politics of Feminism*. C. T. Mohanty, A. Russo and L. Torres, eds. Bloomington, Indiana University Press: 1–47.

Morrow, J. D. (1988). "Folic Acid for Prevention of Neural Tube Defects: Pediatric Anticipatory Guidance." *Journal of Pediatric Health Care* 12 (2): 55–59.

Muller-Hill, Benno (1994). "Lessons From a Dark and Distant Past." *Genetic Counseling: Practice and Principles*. A. Clarke, ed. London, Routledge: 133–141.

Nader, Laura, Ed. (1996). *Naked Science: Anthropological Inquiry into Boundaries, Power, and Knowledge*. New York, Routledge.

National Institutes of Health–Department of Education Working Group on Ethical, Legal and Social Implications of Human Genome Research (1993). Genetic Information and Health Insurance. Bethesda, MD, U.S. Department of Health and Human Services.

Natowicz, Marvin R., and Joseph S. Alper (1991). "Genetic Sceening: Triumphs, Problems, Controversies." *Journal of Public Health Policy* 12 (4): 475–491.

_____(1992). "Genetic Discrimination and the Law." *American Journal of Human Genetics* 50 (3): 464–475.

Natowicz, Marvin R., and Catherine Ard (1997). "The Commercialization of Clinical Genetics: An Analysis of Interrelations Between Academic Centers and For-Profit Clinical Genetics Diagnostics Companies." *Journal of Genetic Counseling* 6 (3): 337–355.

Nelkin, Dorothy (1995). "Science Controversies, the Dynamics of Public Disputes in the United States." *Handbook of Science and Technology Studies*. S. Jasanoff, G. E. Markle, J. C. Petersen, and T. Pinch, eds. Thousand Oaks, CA, Sage: 444–457.

Nelkin, Dorothy, and M. Susan Lindee (1995). *The DNA Mystique: The Gene as Cultural Icon*. New York, W. W. Freeman.

Nelkin, Dorothy, and Laurence Tancredi (1989). *Dangerous Diagnostics: The Social Power of Biological Information*. New York, Basic Books.

Nelson, Margaret K. (1994). "Family Daycare Providers: Dilemmas of Daily Practice." *Mothering: Ideology, Experience, and Agency*. E. N. Glenn, G. Chang, and L. R. Forcey, eds. New York, Routledge: 181–209.

New York Times (1993). "Sex Adds to Fears of Parents of the Retarded." *New York Times*. New York: A1, B4. 26 January.

Nsiah-Jefferson, Laurie (1989). "Reproductive Laws, Women of Color, and Low-Income Women." *Reproductive Laws for the 1990s*. S. Cohen and N. Taub, eds. Clifton, NJ, Humana Press: 23–68.

Oakley, Ann (1984). *The Captured Womb: A History of the Medical Care of Pregnant Women*. London, Blackwell.

———(1993). *Essays on Women, Medicine and Health*. Edinburgh, Edinburgh University Press.

Olby, Robert (1990a). "The Emergence of Genetics." In *Companion to the History of Modern Science*. R. C. Olby, G. N. Canton, J. R. R. Christie, and M. J. S. Hodge. eds. London, Routledge: 521–536.

———(1990b). "The Molecular Revolution in Biology." *Companion to the History of Modern Science*. R. C. Olby, G. N. Canton, J. R. R. Christie, and M. J. S. Hodge. eds. London, Routledge: 503–520.

Oudshoorn, Nelly (1994). *Beyond the Natural Body: An Archaeology of Sex Hormones*. London, Routledge.

Palmer, Shane, Joanne Spencer et al. (1993). "Follow-Up Survey of Pregnancies with Diagnoses of Chromosome Abnormality." *Journal of Genetic Counseling* 2 (3): 139–152.

Paltrow, Lynn M. (1990). "When Becoming Pregnant Is a Crime." *Criminal Justice Ethics* (winter/spring): 41–47.

Patel, Vibhuti (1989). "Sex Determination and Sex Pre-Selection Tests in India: Recent Techniques in Femicide." *Journal of Reproductive and Genetic Engineering* 2 (2): 111–119.

Paul, Diane (1984). "Eugenics and the Left." *Journal of the History of Ideas* 45 (4): 567–590.

———(1986). "A History of the Eugenics Movement and of Its Multiple Effects on Public Policy." *Scientific American* (January): 27–31.

———(1995). *Controlling Human Heredity, 1865 to the Present*. Atlantic Highlands, NJ, Humanities Press.

———(1998). *The Politics of Heredity: Essays on Eugenics, Biomedicine, and the Nature-Nurture Debate*. Albany, SUNY Press.

Paul, Diane, and Hamish G. Spencer (1995). "The Hidden Science of Eugenics." *Nature* 374: 302–304.

Pessar, Patricia (1996). *A Visa for a Dream: New Dominican Immigration*. Boston: Allyn and Bacon.

Petchesky, Rosalind (1984). *Abortion and Women's Choice*. Boston, Longman's (Northeastern University Press).

———(1987). "Fetal Images: The Power of Visual Culture in the Politics of Reproduction." *Feminist Studies* 2 (2): 263–293.

———(1995). "The Body as Property: A Feminist Re-Vision." *Conceiving the New World Order:*

The Global Politics of Reproduction. F. Ginsburg and R. Rapp, eds. Berkeley, University of California Press: 387–406.

Petrucelli, Nancie, Martha Walker et al. (1998). "Continuation of Pregnancy Following the Diagnosis of a Fetal Sex Chromosome Abnormality: A Study of Parents' Counseling Needs and Experiences." *Journal of Genetic Counseling* 7 (5): 401–416.

Pickering, Andrew (1995). *The Mangle of Practice.* Chicago, University of Chicago Press.

———ed. (1992). *Science as Practice and Culture.* Chicago, University of Chicago Press.

Pietrzik, K. F., et al., (1997). "Folate Economy in Pregnancy." *Nutrition* 13 (11/12): 975–977.

Porter, Theodore (1995). *Trust in Numbers: The Pursuit of Objectivity in Science and Public Life.* Princeton, NJ, Princeton University Press.

Portin, P. (1993). "The Concept of the Gene: Short History and Present Status." *Review of Biology* 68: 172–222.

Powledge, Tabitha (1979). "Genetic Counselors Without Doctorates." *Birth Defects* 15, 9 (3): 105–112.

Powledge, Tabitha, and John Fletcher (1979). "Guidelines for the Ethical, Social, Legal Issues in Prenatal Diagnosis." *New England Journal of Medicine* 300 (4): 168–172.

Press, Nancy Anne, and Carole Browner (1993). "'Collective Fictions': Similarities in Reasons for Accepting Maternal Serum Alpha-Fetoprotein Screening Among Women of Diverse Ethnic and Social Class Backgrounds." *Fetal Diagnosis and Therapy* 8 (supp. 1): 97–106.

———(1994). "Policy Issues in Maternal Serum Alpha-Fetoprotein Screening: The View from California." Proceedings, Washington, DC, National Academy of Sciences Institute of Medicine.

———(1995). "Risk, Autonomy and Responsibility: Informed Consent for Prenatal Testing." *Hastings Center Report* 25 (3): 9–12.

Proctor, Robert N. (1992). "Genomics and Eugenics: How Fair Is the Comparison?" *Gene Mapping: Using Law and Ethics as Guides.* G. J. Annas and S. Elias, eds. New York, Oxford University Press: 57–93.

Punales-Morejon, Diana, and Rayna Rapp (1991). "Training Genetic Counselors for Ethnocultural Sensitivities." Washington, DC, International Congress of Human Genetics.

———(1993). "Ethnocultural Diversity and Genetic Counseling Training: The Challenge for a Twenty-First Century." *Journal of Genetic Counseling* 2 (3): 155–158.

Purdy, Laura (1996). *Reproducing Persons: Issues in Feminist Bioethics.* Ithaca, NY, Cornell University Press.

Queen et al. (1994). "The Widening Gap Between Socioeconomic Status and Mortality." *Statistical Bulletin* 75 (2): 31–34.

Rabinow, Paul (1992). "Artificiality and Enlightenment: From Sociobiology to Biosociality." *Incorporations.* J. Crary and S. Kwinter. New York, Zone: 234–252.

———(1996). *Making PCR: A Story of Biotechnology.* Chicago, University of Chicago Press.

Rapp, Rayna (1984). "The Ethics of Choice." *Ms. Magazine:* 97–100. April.

———(1993). "Amniocentesis in Sociocultural Perspective." *Journal of Genetic Counseling* 2 (3): 183–196.

———(1998). "Real-Time Fetus: The Role of the Sonogram in the Age of Monitored Reproduction." *Cyborgs and Citadels: Anthropological Interventions in Emerging Sciences and Technologies.* G. L. Downey and J. Dumit, eds. Santa Fe, NM, School of American Research Press: 31–48.

Reed, Sheldon (1974). "A Short History of Genetic Counseling." *Social Biology* 21: 332–339.

Reilly, Philip (1977). *Genetics, the Law and Social Policy.* Cambridge, MA, Harvard University Press.

———(1979). "Professional Identification: Issues in Licensing and Certification." *Genetic Counseling: Facts, Values, and Norms.* A. Capron, ed. New York, Alan R. Liss.

Resta, Robert (1992). "The Twisted Helix: An Essay on Genetic Counselors, Eugenics, and Social Responsibility." *Journal of Genetic Counseling* 1 (3): 227–244.

Risen, James, and Judy L. Thomas (1998). *Wrath of Angels: The American Abortion Wars.* New York, Basic.

Robinson, Arthur, Bruce G. Bender et al. (1989). "Decisions Following the Intrauterine Diagnosis of Sex Chromosome Aneuploidy." *American Journal of Medical Genetics* 34 (4): 552–554.

Rogers, Dale Evans (1956, republished 1984). *Angel Unaware.* Old Tappan, NJ, F. H. Revell Co.

Rollnick, Betty (1984). "The National Society of Genetic Counselors: An Historical Perspective." *Birth Defects* 20: 3–7.

Rose, Hilary (1983). "Hand, Brain and Heart: Toward a Feminist Epistemology for the Natural Sciences." *Signs* 9 (1): 73–96.

Roseberry, William (1989). *Anthropologies and Histories.* New Brunswick, NJ, Rutgers University Press.

Rothman, Barbara Katz (1982). *In Labor: Women and Power in the Birthplace.* New York, W. W. Norton.

———(1986). *The Tentative Pregnancy, Prenatal Diagnosis and the Future of Motherhood.* New York, W. W. Norton.

———(1989). *Recreating Motherhood: Ideology and Technology in a Patriarchal Society.* New York, W. W. Norton.

Rothman, Barbara Katz, and Melinda Detlefs (1988). "Women Talking to Women: Abortion Counselors and Genetic Counselors." *The Worth of Women's Work: A Qualitative Synthesis.* A. Stratham, E. M. Miller, and H. O. Mauksch, eds. Albany, State University of New York Press: 151–165.

Rubin, Alissa (1992). "Project Rachel: Regretting Abortions." *The AFP Reporter* 15 (2): 40–47.

Ruddick, Sara (1989). *Maternal Thinking: Toward a Politics of Peace.* Boston, Beacon.

Ruiz, Vicki L., and Ellen C. DuBois (1994). "Introduction to the Second Edition." *Unequal Sisters: A Multicultural Reader in U.S. Women's History.* V. L. Ruiz and E. C. DuBois, eds. New York, Routledge: xi–xvi.

Sandler, I., and L. Sandler (1985). "A Conceptual Ambiguity That Contributed to the Neglect of Mendel's Paper." *History and Philosophy of the Life Sciences* 7: 3–70.

Saxton, Marsha (1984). "Born and Unborn: The Implications of Reproductive Technologies for People with Disabilities." *Test-Tube Woman.* R. Arditti, R. Duelli-Klein, and S. Minden, eds. Boston, Routledge and Kegan Paul: 298–312.

———(1987). "'I'm on a Lot of Committees': An Interview with Frances Deloatch." *With*

Wings. M. Saxton. New York, Feminist Press: 76–80.

Schneider, David M. (1980 [1968]). *American Kinship, a Cultural Account.* Chicago, University of Chicago Press.

Schrimshaw, Susan, and D. M. March (1984). "I Had a Baby Sister But She Only Lasted One Day." *Journal of the American Medical Association* 251 (6): 732–733.

Scotch, R. K. (1984). *From Good Will to Civil Rights: Transforming Federal Disability Policy.* Philadelphia, PA, Temple University Press.

Scott, J. A., Ann P. Walker et al. (1987). "Genetic Counselor Training: A Review and Considerations for the Future." *American Journal of Human Genetics* 43 (1): 191–199.

Scott, Joan W. (1988). "Deconstructing Equality-versus-Difference: Or, the Uses of Post-Structuralist Theory for Feminism." *Feminist Studies* 14 (1): 33–50.

———(1992). "Experience." *Feminists Theorize the Political.* J. Butler and J. W. Scott, eds. New York, Routledge: 22–40.

Seachrist, L. (1995). "Testing Genes: Physicians Wrestle with the Information that Genetic Tests Provide." *Science News* 148: 394–395.

Seagoe, Mary V. (1964). *Yesterday Was Tuesday All Day and All Night: The Story of a Unique Education.* Boston, Little, Brown.

Segura, Denise A. (1994). "Working at Motherhood: Chicana and Mexican Immigrant Mothers and Employment." *Mothering: Ideology, Experience, and Agency.* E. N. Glenn, G. Chang, and L. R. Forcey, eds. New York, Routledge: 211–233.

Seligman, Milton, and Rosalyn Benjamin Darling (1989). *Ordinary Families, Special Chidren.* New York, Guilford Press.

Seller, M. J. (1987). "Unanswered Questions on Neural Tube Defects." *British Medical Journal* 294 (Jan. 3 [6563]): 1–2.

Shapiro, Joseph (1993). *No Pity: How the Disability Rights Movement Is Changing America.* New York, Times Books.

Sharma, Geeta (1995). "Loopholes in Act to Ban Sex Determination of Foetus." *The Telegraph,* 11 January. Calcutta.

Shaw, Nancy Stoller (1974). *Forced Labor: Maternity Care in the United States.* Oxford and New York, Pergamon.

Smith, Stephanie, Nancy Steinberg Warren et al. (1993). "Minority Recruitment into the Genetic Counselng Profession." *Journal of Genetic Counseling* 2 (2): 171–182.

Solinger, Rickie (1993). "'A Complete Disaster': Abortion and the Politics of Hospital Abortion Committees, 1950–1970." *Feminist Studies* 19 (2): 241–268.

———ed. (1998). *The Abortion Wars: A Half-Century of Abortion Politics.* Berkeley, University of California Press.

Spallone, Patricia, and Deborah Lynn Steinberg, eds. (1987). *Made to Order: The Myth of Reproductive and Genetic Progress.* Elmsford, NY, Pergamon.

Spanier, Bonnie (1995). *Im/partial Science: Gender Ideology in Molecular Biology.* Bloomington, Indiana University Press.

Stabile, Carol (1992). "Shooting the Mother: Fetal Photography and the Politics of Disappearance." *Camera Obscura* 28: 179–206.

Stacey, Judith (1988). "Can There Be a Feminist Ethnography?" *Women's Studies International Forum* 11 (1): 21–27.

_____(1990). *Brave New Families*. New York, Basic Books.

Stafford, Barbara Maria (1991). *Body Criticism: Imaging the Unseen in Enlightenment Art and Medicine*. Cambridge, MIT Press.

Stanworth, Michelle, Ed. (1987). *Reproductive Technologies: Gender, Motherhood and Medicine*. Minneapolis, University of Minnesota Press.

Starr, Susan Leigh, Ed. (1995). *Ecologies of Knowledge: Work and Politics in Science and Technology*. Albany, SUNY Press.

Steegers-Theurrissen, R. P. (1995). "Folate Metabolism and Neural Tube Defects: A Review." *European Journal of Obstetrical Gynecology and Reproductive Biology* 61 (1): 39–48.

Stewart, Nancy (1986). "Women's Views of Ultrasonography in Obstetrics." *Birth* 13 (1): 39–43.

Stolcke, Verena (1986). "New Reproductive Technologies: Same Old Fatherhood." *Critique of Anthropology* 6 (3): 5–31.

Strathern, Marilyn (1992). *Reproducing the Future: Anthropology, Kinship, and the New Reproductive Technologies*. Manchester, UK, Manchester University Press.

Sundberg, K., K. Bang et al. (1997). "Randomised Study of Risk of Fetal Loss Related to Early Amniocentesis versus Chorionic Villus Sampling." *Lancet* 350 (9079): 697–703.

Sutherland, G. A. (1900). "The Differential Diagnosis of Mongolism and Cretinism in Infancy." *The Lancet*: 6 January, 23–24.

Suzuki, David, and Peter Knudtson (1989). *Genethics*. Cambridge, MA, Harvard University Press.

Tatsugawa, Zina H., Michelle A. Fox et al. (1994). "Education and Testing Strategy for Large-Scale Cystic Fibrosis Carrier Screening." *Journal of Genetic Counseling* 3 (4): 279–289.

Taylor, Janelle (1992). "The Public Fetus and the Family Car: From Abortion Politics in a Volvo Advertisement." *Public Culture* 4 (2): 67–80.

_____(1993). "Envisioning Kinship: Fetal Imagery and Relatedness." American Anthropological Association, Washington, DC.

_____(1997). "Image of Contradiction: Obstetrical Ultrasound in American Culture." *Reproducing Reproduction: Kinship, Power and Technological Innovation*. S. Franklin and H. Ragone, eds. Philadelphia, University of Pennsylvania Press: 15–45.

Thompson, Edward P. (1963). *The Making of the English Working Class*. Harmondsworth, Middlesex, Penguin.

Touchette, Nancy, Neil A. Holtzman et al. (1997). *Toward the 21ˢᵗ Century: Incorporating Genetics into Primary Health Care*. Plainview, NY, Cold Spring Harbor Laboratory Press.

Trainer, Marilyn (1991). *Differences in Common: Straight Talk on Mental Retardation, Down Syndrome, and Life*. Rockville, MD, Woodbine House.

Trautman, Mary Winfrey (1984). *The Absence of the Dead Is Their Way of Appearing*. Pittsburgh, PA, Cleis Press.

Traweek, Sharon (1992). "Border Crossings: Narrative Strategies in Science Studies and Among Physicists in Tsukuba Science City, Japan." *Science as Practice and Culture*. A. Pickering, ed. Chicago, University of Chicago Press: 429–466.

———(1993). "An Introduction to Cultural and Social Studies of Sciences and Technologies." *Culture, Medicine and Psychiatry* 17 (1): 3–25.

Trouillot, Michel-Rolph (1991). "Anthropology and the Savage Slot: The Poetics and Politics of Otherness." *Recapturing Anthropology: Working in the Present.* R. Fox, ed. Santa Fe, School of American Research Press: 17–44.

Ubell, Robert (1997a). "Desktop Libraries." *biomednet.com/hmsbeagle/1997/01*(1).

———(1997b). "Lively Links: Ramping Journals onto the Highway." *biomednet/hmsbeagle/1997/15*(2).

Visweswaran, Kamala (1994). *Fictions of Feminist Ethnography.* Minneapolis, University of Minnesota Press.

Vogel, Lise (1990). "Debating Difference: Feminism, Pregnancy, and the Workplace." *Feminist Studies* 16 (1): 9–32.

Walker, Ann P., Joan A. Scott et al. (1990). "Report of the 1989 Asilomar Meeting on Education in Genetic Counseling." *American Journal of Human Genetics* 46 (6): 1223–1230.

Warner, Marina (1976). *Alone of All Her Sex: The Myth and the Cult of the Virgin Mary.* New York, Knopf.

Weil, Jon, and Ilana Mittman (1993). "A Teaching Framework for Cross-Cultural Genetic Counseling." *Journal of Genetic Counseling* 2 (3): 159–170.

Weiss, Joan O., and Jane Mackta (1996). *How to Start and Sustain Genetic Support Groups.* Baltimore, MD, Johns Hopkins University Press.

Wertz, Dorothy C., and John Fletcher (1987). "Communicating Genetic Risks." *Science, Technology, and Human Values* 12 (3/4): 60–66.

———(1989a). "Ethical Decision Making in Medical Genetics: Women as Patients and Practitioners in Eighteen Nations." *Healing Technologies: Feminist Perspectives.* K. S. Ratcliff, M. M. Ferree, G. O. Mellow et al., eds. Ann Arbor, University of Michigan Press: 221–241.

———(1989b). *Ethics and Human Genetics: Cross-Cultural Perspectives.* Heidelberg and New York, Springer-Verlag.

———(1989c). "Fatal Knowledge? Prenatal Diagnosis and Sex Selection." *Hastings Center Report* 19 (3) May: 21–27.

Wertz, Dorothy, and James R. Sorenson (1986). "Client Reactions to Genetic Counseling: Self-Reports of Influence." *Clinical Genetics* 30 (6): 494–502.

Wertz, Dorothy C., James R. Sorenson et al. (1986). "Clients' Interpretation of Risks Provided in Genetic Counseling." *American Journal of Human Genetics* 39 (2): 253–264.

Wertz, Dorothy, and Richard Wertz (1977). *Lying In: A History of Childbirth in America.* New York, Free Press.

Wexler, Alice (1995). *Mapping Fate: A Memoir of Family, Risk, and Genetic Research.* New York, Random House.

Wexler, Nancy (1992). Personal communication.

Williams, Patricia J. (1991). *The Alchemy of Race and Rights: Diary of a Law Professor.* Cambridge, MA, Harvard University Press.

Williams, Raymond (1977). *Marxism and Literature.* Oxford, UK, Oxford University Press.

Wolf, Marjorie (1992). *A Thrice Told Tale.* Stanford, CA, Stanford University Press.

Yearley, Steven (1995). "The Environmental Challenge to Science Studies." *Handbook of Science and Technology Studies,* S. Jasanoff, G. E. Markle, J. C. Petersen, and T. Pinch, eds. Thousand Oaks, CA, Sage: 457–479.

Young, Allan (1996). *The Harmony of Illusions.* Princeton, NJ, Princeton University Press.

Yoxen, Edward (1989). "Seeing with Sound: A Study of the Development of Medical Images." *The Social Construction of Technological Systems.* W. E. Bijker, T. P. Hughes, and T. Pinch, eds. Cambridge, MIT Press: 281–301.

Zare, Nancy, James R. Sorenson et al. (1984). "Sex of Provider as a Variable in Effective Genetic Counseling." *Social Science and Medicine* 19 (7): 671–675.

Permissions

Index